THE SUMMER GAME

THE SUMMER GAME

Australian Test Cricket

1949-71

GIDEON HAIGH

t

TEXT PUBLISHING
MELBOURNE AUSTRALIA

The Text Publishing Company
171 La Trobe Street
Melbourne Victoria 3000
Australia

First published 1997

Printed and bound by Griffin Paperbacks, Adelaide
Designed by Chong Weng-Ho
Typeset in Bembo 11.5/14 by J&M Typesetting

National Library of Australia

Cataloguing-in-Publication data:

Haigh, Gideon.
The summer game: Australia in test cricket 1949–71.

Bibliography.
Includes index.
ISBN 1 875847 44 8.

1. Test matches (Cricket) – Australia – History – 20th century. I. Title.
796.358650994

This project has been assisted by the Commonwealth Government through the Australia Council, its arts funding and advisory body.

Photographs are reproduced courtesy of AP/AAP, *Adelaide Advertiser*, *Age*, *Argus* Collection, Central Press, *Herald & Weekly Times*, the Melbourne Cricket Club Museum, Reuters, *Sentinel*, Sport & General, and Alan Walker.

Every effort has been made to trace the original source material contained in this book. Where the attempt has been unsuccessful, the publishers would be pleased to hear from the author/publisher to rectify any omission.

FOR MY MOTHER, ISABEL

Acknowledgments

This book could not have been completed without the kind and generous assistance of many people.

In particular, there were the cricketers, cricket personalities and others with whom I talked and/or corresponded while researching: Ken Archer, Ron Archer, Percy Beames, Richie Benaud, Brian Booth, Bill Brown, Peter Burge, Jack Cameron, Ian Chappell, Michael Charlton, Tony Charlton, Alan Connolly, Dr Brian Corrigan, Hazel Craig, Ian Craig, Pat Crawford, Shirley Crouch, Alan Davidson, Eric Freeman, Barry Gibbs, Clive Harburg, Neil Harvey, Neil Hawke, Col Hoy, Jim Hubble, Bill Jacobs, Barry Jarman, Ian Johnson, Bill Johnston, Ray Jordon, Lindsay Kline, Bill Lawry, Jack Ledward, Sam Loxton, Colin McDonald, Dr Ian McDonald, the Hon. Ian McLachlan, Jack McLaughlin, Ashley Mallett, Ian Meckiff, Frank Misson, Jack Moroney, Arthur Morris, Jack Neary, Geff Noblet, Norm O'Neill, Peter Philpott, Ian Quick, Ian Redpath, Phil Ridings, Doug Ring, Gordon Rorke, John Rutherford, Rex Sellers, Paul Sheahan, Bob Simpson, David Sincock, Keith Stackpole, Alf Stafford, Gavin Stevens, Brian Taber, Grahame Thomas, George Thoms, Ernie Toovey, Phil Tresidder, Tom Veivers and Alan Walker.

Sometimes, this was as quick as a phone call. Usually, it meant them putting up with a very long and detailed interview. Many went to extraordinary lengths to assist me. Thanks to them all, and also to Warwick Franks, Robert Coleman and Pat Mullins who helped me locate my subjects.

A special thanks is also due to Heather Henderson, who could not have been more obliging when I sought her permission to use material from the private papers of her father, the late Sir Robert Menzies, at the National Library of Australia. These papers were a joy to read, and are a pleasure to introduce to a wider public.

The Summer Game was rendered viable by financial assistance from the Literature Board. As it is, I finished it with $12.16 in the bank. Thanks to those who stretched my resources by providing lodgings when I visited Sydney, Brisbane and Adelaide: Louise Nemeth de Bikal, John Harms and Michael Bollen. All I can do is hope to return their hospitality one day.

My great friends at the Melbourne Cricket Club Library have seen me so often that I must look like part of the furniture. David Studham, Ross Peacock, Alf Batchelard, Ray Webster and Jenna Pulman were unfailingly helpful as I availed myself of their wonderful resources. For most of the lovely pictures in this book, you can thank Paul Revere of the *Age* newspaper. As I wasted hours of his time with strange requests, he was exceptionally patient and accommodating.

Many people allowed me to talk this project over with them, enabling me to clarify it in my own mind even as I probably bored them senseless. I am indebted to Bob Stewart of Victoria University, who discussed with me his splendid PhD thesis on 'The Commercial and Cultural Development of Australian First-Class Cricket 1946–1985' at great length. When undergoing one of my regular crises of confidence, Michelle Fincke, Angela Martinkus, Richard Sproull, Karen Cooke and Philippa Hawker also offered their ears for bending, and conned me into believing I could do it. Thanks to them all.

Had it not been for the past kindnesses of David Frith, Mal Schmidtke, Jim Schembri, Wendy Tuohy and Tony Nagy, I wouldn't have had the bottle to begin this project. Had it not been for the support of Michael Heyward, Emma Gordon Williams, Melanie Ostell, Di Gribble and Patty Brown of Text Publishing, I would never have finished it. There has also been the reassurance of knowing that I have the unique talents of George Thomas, proofreader extraordinaire.

My partner, Caroline Wilson, has been unstinting in her love and support throughout the last year or so, tolerant of my frequent cat-kicking crankiness and periods of disillusionment. It can't be easy to share someone with his computer and library, but she has done so. Bless her.

Contents

Preface

They say the past is another country. The way that academics, historians and the media treat it, the 1950s and 1960s in Australia might have taken place on another planet.

From time to time, you'll see a publication or program ostensibly devoted to the period. The same stock images will be trotted out: men in suits and hats, women in twin-sets, crackly recordings of 'Blue Hills' and 'The Argonauts', battalions of Hills Hoists, and perhaps a glimpse of Sir Robert Menzies, usually depicted as a craven Anglophile. Ho-hum. Nostalgia, as they say, isn't what it used to be.

So it is with cricket. Compared with the epoch where Bradman ruled the earth, and the boisterous nationalism that Chappell XIs brought to the 1970s, the 1950s and 1960s are considered poor copy. Revisiting the Tied Test may buy a few minutes of air time or consume a few column inches, but even larger chronological histories dispose of the decades perfunctorily.

Yet the period rewards curiosity. While it would be improper to argue the decades' status as a Golden Age, they represent at least a silver lining to the game in this country. They were enriched by some of Australian cricket's most prodigious talents: Lindsay Hassett, Keith Miller, Ray Lindwall, Richie Benaud, Neil Harvey, Alan Davidson, Bob Simpson, Bill Lawry, Wally Grout, Ian Chappell. They involved some of our most undersung cricketers: Bill Johnston, Graham McKenzie, Brian Booth, Peter Burge, Colin McDonald, Norman O'Neill. And they offered a pageant of characters and controversies: from Jack Iverson and Ken Mackay to Sid Barnes and Ian Meckiff.

While the long-distance view is of an orderly procession of Tests and tours, the 1950s and 1960s were also a period of convulsive change for Australian cricket. There were heady successes and disconcerting failures. The game faced the first palpable threat to its popularity from rival sports and attractions, then began grappling uneasily with the demons of commercialisation.

The choice of the start and end points for *The Summer Game* is deliberate. Australia's 1949–50 tour of South Africa was our first after the retirement of Sir Donald Bradman. It continued a cycle of unequalled success and prestige for Australian cricket. The cricketers on it regarded the game as their passion, not their profession. Cricket itself still revolved on its Anglo-Australian axis—for there was still a British Empire—and was seen by the new prime minister Robert Menzies as a 'powerful diplomatic contributor to international understanding and a widening tolerance'.

By the time Australia toured India and South Africa twenty years later, however, much of that had changed. The tour began in considerable hardship and ended with overwhelming defeat. The cricketers were still classed as 'semi-amateurs', but they began on this trip to writhe under the thumb of their administrative elite. Cricket had become the international pursuit we recognise today—no longer the preserve of a contracted Commonwealth—and been pockmarked by politics in the process.

The Summer Game begins with the departure of one epoch-making Australian captain, Bradman, and ends with the appointment of another, Ian Chappell. It commences when the Test match was undisputed as the game's summit. It concludes with the traditions of Test cricket faltering, and just before the limited-overs international began its astonishing growth and popularity.

The emphasis of *The Summer Game* is people and period rather than games and scores. Certain tours and Tests are followed in detail, but there is as much attention devoted to areas previously glossed over: how cricketers lived and worked in a semi-amateur economy, how the game was run, how tours were organised, and generally the place of cricket in Australia. A considerable superintending presence is Sir Robert Menzies, patron of cricket and friend of cricketers throughout his premiership from December 1949 to January 1966. It has always surprised me that those who purport to analyse Australia's longest-serving prime minister are so incurious about his fascination for cricket: devotions and hobbies are so often an index of personality.

As I've said, something that has struck me throughout this project is the dearth of genuinely insightful writing on the 1950s and 1960s in Australia. For it was a period of great social change here, one where we achieved the levels of prosperity to which we are today accustomed, one in which we discovered and began to deal with a wider world. I hope this book will provoke others to reconsider these decades as an area for historical inquiry.

Gideon Haigh
Melbourne 1997

'Life Was for Living, Cricket Was for Fun'

AUSTRALIA V SOUTH AFRICA
1949-50

In Australia in 1949, cricket was king of games. Sir Donald Bradman's scarcely human genius had seen to that, captivating an empire in the process. The country's cricket team had not been defeated for more than a decade. Two million had attended first-class matches since World War II. About 200,000 males played cricket competitively. It dominated the summer scene.

Yet, in 1949, cricket was also fording a new frontier. After Bradman's valediction, knighthood and apotheosis in March, the game's foremost personality had become a non-player, an administrator, a selector. Cricket without him seemed unthinkable, in writer Ray Robinson's phrase, 'like a room with the light switched off'. And, certainly, in the week after Bradman's final bow at the SCG, cricket would seem like a man bumping round a darkened chamber.

'THE MILLER BLOW'

On Wednesday, 2 March 1949—the day selectors Bradman, 'Chappie' Dwyer and Jack Ryder were due to announce Australia's team to tour South Africa—Keith Miller was at the New South Wales Cricketers' Club at Cricket House, 254 George Street. He was the most clubbable of men, almost Bradman's magnetic equal as a player, a fairytale figure who'd sprung from nowhere to colour postwar cricket.

I

The defining experience of Miller's life had been duty with the RAAF from January 1942, flying Bristol Beauforts and de Havilland Mosquitos on cross-channel raids with a pronounced degree of flair and a huge ration of fortune. One day, at Bournemouth, his favourite bar was bombed and its occupants killed; but Miller had been playing cricket at Dulwich. Another day, near Kiel Canal, one of his Mosquito's incendiary tanks had failed to release; but, as he approached Bournemouth to land, the unexploded capsule fell away. From such scrapes arose the legend of 'Miller's Luck'.

Miller tackled cricket with the same flair and disregard for danger. Playing for the Services XI in the 1945 Victory Tests and in Australia's first three postwar Test series, he'd emerged as a batsman of nonchalant panache, and a medium-pacer who could bowl at life-threatening speed when so moved. Englishman Len Hutton recalled facing Miller at Trent Bridge in 1948 and making the mistake of poaching two boundaries: 'I knew what to expect, and in eight balls I had five bouncers, one of which left the manufacturer's imprint on my left shoulder. Two others leapt at my throat from just short of a length as if they had been bowled from no more than ten yards away with a tennis ball.'

Above all, Miller was a communicative cricketer: a batsman whose dander was raised by the best bowling, a bowler who followed a boun- cer with a smiling toss of his black mane, a slipsman who lounged deceptively until required. The aura extended beyond his cricket: high- brows relished his Edwardian manner and taste for classical music; ordinary fans appreciated his common touch and love of the turf. When he moved to NSW in October 1947 and became an habitué of Randwick racecourse, bookmakers would lengthen odds whenever he approached: 'Six-to-four now that so-and-so Miller's here.'

This day at the Cricketers' Club, though, was different. By Miller's standards, 1948–49 had been nondescript. Troubled by conjunctivitis, he had scored just 400 runs at 33. Still sore after a heavy bowling regimen in England with Bradman's 1948 side, he had taken only 11 wickets at 24. Miller's career first-class figures still beggared belief: 6140 runs at 50 piled on 167 wickets at 22. But he had known differences with Bradman—their cricketing creeds were oil and water—and now the Don held Miller's destiny in his selectorial hands.

As Miller entertained, Dwyer came in. An able, affable fifty-four-year- old who had been picking Australian players since 1931, Dwyer would normally have greeted Miller expansively. But today he averted his gaze and sought a corner for a quiet drink with Lindsay Hassett. Miller sensed something amiss. When NSW Cricket Association secretary Alan Barnes pinned up a list of the touring party, Miller was unsurprised to find his name missing.

Others felt surprised for him. Arthur Mailey wrote in the *Argus* that the omission had 'hit cricket supporters like a thunderbolt'. Bill O'Reilly of the *Sydney Morning Herald* opined: 'To say that Keith Miller's omission from the tour of South Africa was a complete surprise would be a cowardly way of understating a botch which the selectors have made of a responsible job.' Jack Fingleton told *Sydney Sun* readers: 'Australian cricket is reeling today under the Miller blow...On playing ability I would unhesitatingly place him today in the top six cricketers in the world.'

The team still bore a strong look. Ten were alumni of the 1948 Australian side who'd toured England without defeat: Hassett, Bill Johnston, Ian Johnson, Neil Harvey and Sam Loxton of Victoria; Arthur Morris, Ray Lindwall and Ron Saggers of New South Wales, plus Queenslanders Don Tallon and Colin McCool.* They were augmented by the uncapped openers Ken Archer and Jack Moroney, and well-performed pacemen Alan Walker and Geff Noblet.

But no Miller. Private and public arguments continued for weeks afterward: two citizens of Sydney were fined for settling theirs with punches. As Stalin had just replaced his foreign minister Vyacheslav Molotov with Andrei Gromyko in a Politburo power struggle, the possibilities for punning commentary were ample. A cartoon in Sydney's *Sunday Sun* depicted two blimpish cricket lovers ruminating: 'Fancy! Miller and Molotov in one week.'

A CLOSE-RUN THING

It was still undecided who would lead Australia into the post-Bradman age. A telegraphic vote on the captaincy by the thirteen delegates of the Australian Board of Control at the weekend of 5–6 March divided over the relative merits of the thirty-five-year-old Hassett and twenty-seven-year-old Morris.

A tiny figure of five feet six inches who cast a shadow only slightly longer than his bat, the Victorian Hassett had first toured England with Bradman's 1938 side. His dainty footwork had there won a Test at Headingley, and Hassett a reputation for aplomb in adversity.

---

* Tallon subsequently declared himself unavailable, citing pressures of work, and was replaced by South Australian Gil Langley.

Like Miller, Hassett had found war service a defining experience: in the trying conditions of the Western Desert and Lae with anti-aircraft units, his blithe spirit had made him a popular companion. Once, at Haifa, Hassett was confronted by a commander whose fondness for belittling subordinates was matched only by his misplaced confidence in his capacities as a cricketer. Snatching Hassett's firearm, he advised: 'If you took the trouble to clean your rifle, Gunner Hassett, you might manage to become a good soldier in a long war.'

Poker-faced, Hassett replied: 'If you cleaned and oiled your bat for twenty years, sir, you'd never score a run.'

In the Services XI in which Miller first proclaimed his talents, Warrant Officer II Hassett was a universally popular captain for sixty-four matches in nine months through England, India, Ceylon and Australia. And while Bradman had been Australia's centre of gravity for three series since the war, his vice-captain Hassett had been the centre of levity. Anecdotes clung to him: how he introduced a toy duck to Australia's Trent Bridge dressing-room in 1948 to the grave discomfiture of superstitious teammates; how he hid the ball from a bowler in a saw-dust pile against Nottinghamshire; how a parrot at his South Melbourne club was trained to squawk: 'Hassett's a bastard! Hassett's a bastard!'

NSW captain Morris, however, had abruptly emerged as a rival. Denied prime run-getting years by the war after scoring twin centuries on his first-class debut in December 1941, the left-hander had arrived in Test cricket the finished article five years later. Three consecutive hundreds in his first Ashes series had heralded greater glories in his second: 700 runs in five 1948 Tests establishing him as the world's foremost opening batsman.

A mild, modest man, Morris could look indolent at the crease. It was deceptive. Ken Archer recalls Morris confiding on the morning of a Brisbane Sheffield Shield match: 'Not feeling too well, dear boy. Don't think I'll want to bat too long today.' But when a couple of wickets fell early, the New South Welshman flashed Archer a long-suffering look, and buckled down to 253 out of 400, the last 50 in seventeen minutes.

Hassett had come this way before. Despite his canny captaincy of the Services XI, he had been passed over in Bradman's absence to lead the national side on its first postwar tour to New Zealand, receiving only one vote in thirteen as the Board plumped for Queenslander Bill Brown. Some suspected that this was because, war-weary after two years away, he had skipped one of the Services XI's final matches against Victoria in order to spend four days with his wife Tess and two-year-old daughter: a decision that incensed the Victorian Cricket Association. Others ascribed it to vestiges of sectarianism: Hassett was Catholic, and Australia had not been led by a Catholic since Percy McDonnell in 1888.

The vote orchestrated in Adelaide by the board's secretary Bill Jeanes was not decided until the final two telegrams arrived on the Monday. It was Hassett, by the slimmest majority, who became Australia's twenty-third captain, and first of the post-Bradman age.

THE GOOD SHIP *NESTOR*

Australia's 1949–50 tour of South Africa was a model of its epoch. It was long: more than six months away from home and hearth. And it was poorly paid: the tour fee was £450. But, even for a senior player like off-spinner Ian Johnson, the excitement was infectious. Driving with his wife Lal to Essendon Airport on 2 March for a cricket trip to Adelaide, Johnson stopped at the air depot on the off-chance that someone there knew the side. As it happened, VCA secretary Harry Brereton was able to confirm his inclusion. Johnson prattled for the rest of the journey about the team's composition, and of distant and exotic South Africa, pausing only to wonder why Lal seemed so uninterested. It wasn't until he returned that he realised why: 2 March was her birthday.

Thirty-three-year-old Geff Noblet had special reason to see the tour as the summit of his ambition. In May 1939, an Adelaide doctor had diagnosed him as suffering from a pulled back muscle. But when weeks of gymwork did no good and he sought a second opinion, it turned out to be pleurisy. Doctors at Hutt Street Private Hospital, in fact, gave him days to live.

It took four months to fight off the disease, and seven years would elapse before he opened South Australia's bowling. But finally the moment had come. 'I was in Sydney the day the team was picked and my wife and I were walking to the railway station,' he says. 'We bought the paper and read I was in the team. I don't think my feet touched the ground for the rest of the journey.'

The *Nestor*, in which the team departed with manager 'Chappie' Dwyer on Wednesday, 21 September, was a small, elderly liner that had served as a troopship in both wars, and would take sixteen days crossing the Indian Ocean. Shipboard entertainments kept players amused: Harvey won the deck tennis, Hassett and Walker the deck quoits. A fancy dress ball saw Dwyer and Hassett appearing as mother and son, Noblet and Archer as Arabs, Johnson as Nero. Walker and Lindwall celebrated birthdays, while Hassett led communal singing: 'The Bridle Hanging on the Wall' and 'The Blackbird Song', with a few South African tunes he'd learned including 'Sarie Marais' and 'Izigi Zumba'. 'The sea voyage was a very good way for us to get accustomed to each other,' Noblet says. 'We'd played against each other a lot but we didn't know one another all that well. By the time we got off the ship we were all friends.'

The *Nestor* arrived in Durban in mist and drizzle at dawn on Friday, 7 October 1949. South African dignitaries and pressmen thronged the foredeck, and the players were introduced to Australia's high commissioner Alfred Stirling and the Springboks' thirty-eight-year-old captain and master batsman Dudley Nourse. 'How are you Dudley?' Hassett inquired. 'I hope you're not feeling too well.'

Tours of the time were intensely ceremonial, and the opening function was a City Hall civic reception. 'We have come to you with greetings from the Australian government, from the Australian Board of Control and the cricket lovers of our country,' said Dwyer. 'We have brought a good side. They will, I am sure, play good cricket. If we are defeated we will make no excuses and if we are victorious we will be modest. We will try to play the game in every sense.' Durban's mayor Leo Boyd replied in similar Empire-building terms, saying that Australians and South Africans had much in common, having chosen to stand together 'in common friendship in the free association of people called the Commonwealth'.

Standing for his address, the elfin Hassett cut an unlikely figure of authority. But, after some innocuous comment about playing attractive cricket, he brought the house down with a cautionary tale of his maiden Test century in Brisbane:

> It fell on the day that one of my brothers got married. I was at 92 and he was due at the church for the ceremony, but thought he would wait a minute or two for the other eight runs. After ten minutes I got four runs, so he rushed away and duly got married. When he arrived home he turned on the wireless and heard I was at 97. I can assure you, gentlemen, that I got my century before he went on his honeymoon.

Hassett was on his way to becoming one of the most popular captains Australia had sent abroad.

TOURING LIFE

Where teams today step straight from their airliners into a one-day international, seventy-six days would elapse before Hassett's Australians played their First Test. After a week practising at the Old Fort nets, they left Durban for Hluhluwe Game Reserve. Cars took them to Richards Bay for a two-day match, which the Australians won by an innings and 280 runs. On the coach trip back to Durban, Hassett laid a wreath on the grave of J. J. Ferris, the brilliant Sydney medium-pacer and Boer War casualty.

The South Africa they saw seemed very like their own country, and local whites professed a strong affinity for things Australian. A popular South African book of the time on Australia by Colin Dighton expressed the bond in its title, *Sisters of the South*. Cricket, too, was belatedly ceasing to be the preserve of the local English, with Afrikaner communities in Transvaal and Orange Free State belatedly taking up the game, and Afrikaner periodicals covering the tour in depth. Hassett could find himself profiled as a *beskik oor skitterende speelhoue* (brilliant stroke maker), Colin McCool as a *baul bykantrdraaibaale, ook briljante veldwerker in die glippe* (leg-spin bowler, also brilliant slip fielder).

The Australians, however, found South Africa in transition. Daniel Malan's newly elected Nationalists had laid the first legislative plank of apartheid by proclaiming the *Prohibition on Mixed Marriages Act* in June. Subjugation of the 'non-white' populations was taking on sinister new force. 'Coming from a monoculture like Australia, the situation in South Africa was a bit of shock to all of us,' Ken Archer recalls. 'You saw it as soon as you arrived: on the docks there were hundreds of coloureds working effectively in a chain gang, as slaves. Being a good little Australian boy, I'd never seen people treated like that before.'

The Union had a vibrant coloured cricket scene, African, Coloured and Indian competitions having amalgamated under the auspices of the South African Cricket Board of Control in July 1947. But the Australians saw none of this: a tour of South Africa then meant a tour of white South Africa, and native Africans and Indians were encountered mainly as caddies, waiters and bell-boys. All the tourists could do was treat them courteously: they tipped extravagantly, and spoke to them with a civility the local whites did not.

Hassett still had plenty to do, and handled his public appearances with wry humour. On the rest day of Australia's first game against Natal, players were entertained by a native dance troupe at Durban's Dunlop factory and presented with shields, assegais and knobkberries. Hassett promptly co-opted nine teammates in a chant of 'Izigi Zumba' and 'Jiyolili Mama'. There was delighted applause from the 300 spectators. He and Johnson then visited a Durban preparatory school, encouraging students to attend the tour matches. 'You can learn more from watching good cricketers play than you can from the average coach or from reading books,' Hassett advised. 'When I come to the wicket, then you can have a snooze.'

'I HEARD YOU WERE DEAD'

Without high-speed transport and instant communication, a touring cricket team of the era was very much a self-contained unit. When disasters occurred, home seemed very distant. And on the eve of that Natal match, calamity struck: Bill Johnston, left-arm lynchpin of Australia's attack, was badly injured in a car accident.

Setting out for Pinetown to date a girl he'd met at the local netball association, Johnston missed a turn on a poorly lit stretch of road near Rossburgh, skidded on gravel and concertinaed his car near a railway underpass. He recalls: 'The steering wheel was the shape of my chest, I seemed to have a nine-iron divot out of my skull from the rear-view mirror, and I realised that I must have been injured internally, because I was spitting out blood.'

A signalman called the police, but Johnston explained his identity and implored them not to publicise the crash. It seemed hours before an ambulance arrived, and Johnston was cold and sore by the time it came to take him to Addington Hospital. A doctor there applied Friar's Balsam to his head and lip, but Johnston was still in agony. 'Jeez, Doc, do ya reckon you could give me a couple of aspros?' he asked.

Just then, Dwyer arrived with local liaison officer Sid Pegler. 'Thank God you're alive,' Dwyer blurted. 'I heard you were dead.' The manager dodged the press to keep the incident quiet, but news that Johnston had 'suffered severe head injuries in a car accident' somehow made an ABC radio morning news bulletin. Johnston's mother heard the news in Colac and fainted.

It was at such times that the Australians realised how far away they really were. Booked into a Durban nursing home, Johnston spent three days trying to telephone home. But the cable, which then ran through London to Sydney, was always busy. It wasn't until the following Wednesday that he was able to assure his mother—a widow who'd already seen one son killed during the war—that she wasn't alone in the world.

The converse befell Ian Johnson. A couple of days after leaving Melbourne, his fifteen-month-old son Bob had badly scalded his arm. Now his sixty-six-year-old widowed mother was gravely ill in a St Kilda private hospital. He learned of her condition by radiophone on 4 November, and she died a couple of days later.

Johnston's teammates explained his mishap superstitiously: he and Lindwall had been sharing hotel room number 87. No-one would accept a room with that number for the rest of the trip. But as the Australians headed for Benoni in the Transvaal, Dwyer, Hassett and Morris had to consider their options. Not only was Johnston unlikely to play before New Year, but Lindwall was troubled by fibrositis of the shoulder. They wired for a replacement player: Keith Miller.

THE COMING OF MILLER

Miller had wintered quietly in Sydney, declining four offers to play professional cricket in England, and to discuss his omission from the Australian team. Having accepted the NSW captaincy, he had led them to consecutive victories.

The invitation to tour, nonetheless, was not opportune. Miller's wife Peg was seven months pregnant, and the £400 he was offered would see him out-of-pocket on the venture. But he accepted, saying: 'My wife agrees with me that it is my duty to go to South Africa. Actually it would suit me better to stay in Sydney, but if the boys think I can help, I'll be with them.' He and masseur Charlie O'Brien were booked passages on the *Dominion Monarch* leaving Fremantle on 21 November 1949.

Things would actually get worse before they got better. Bill Johnston was anxious to rejoin teammates in Rhodesia—his late brother David had been stationed there as part of the Empire Air Scheme—and spent a day and a half flying from Durban to Bulawayo via Johannesburg and Salisbury. But, after sight-seeing at Victoria Falls and Kruger National Park, his chest began aching badly. Dwyer took him to a doctor in White River who X-rayed him and discovered two broken ribs. 'Thank God you came now,' the doctor advised. 'Another few days and you'd have been a helluva mess.'

Fortunately, Hassett's team always had plenty to spare. The captain, Harvey, Morris and Moroney were gushing runs, while Johnson, Noblet and McCool had found their bowling form. For twenty-one-year-old Ken Archer, it was an education. 'I'd come out of a Queensland side just after the war that always knew it would be beaten,' he remembers. 'And I was now playing in a team that simply didn't know how to lose and couldn't conceive of it happening. When circumstances conspired against us, it was fascinating to watch these great players find another gear.'

Never was that other gear better seen than against Transvaal at Ellis Park on 10 December. The tourists were routed in a couple of hours on a rain-affected pitch for 84 and, after Transvaal had made heavy weather of 9–125, bundled out again for 108. On the eve of the opening of the Voortrekker Monument at Pretoria—commemorating the Afrikaners' defeat of the Zulus at Blood River in 1838—locals anticipated a double celebration. Yet the Australians cruelled it by bowling the home side out 16 runs short of victory, Johnson taking 9–38.

The Australians' spirits had by now been lifted by the arrival in Cape Town of Keith Miller. Typically, he made a beeline for the Kenilworth races with Johnston and local racehorse owner Freddy Burmeister, backing four winners and two seconds.

Dwyer, part of the selection panel that had omitted Miller, had kept his own counsel about the voting underlying that decision. But, according to Miller, the manager was not amused when the topic was broached with him:

> After the team had gone, Johnnie Moyes, one of Australia's leading critics and a friend of Bradman, showed me a letter he had received from Bradman. A postscript to it said, 'I hope Keith doesn't think I had anything to do with his omission from the team to South Africa.' When 'Chappie' Dwyer in South Africa got to hear of this he was livid. Apparently he had nothing to do with it either. So Ryder must have left me out—he must have had three votes!

NINNA AND BIG BILL

The Australians swept commandingly through the first two Tests, Hassett and Sam Loxton making centuries at Ellis Park, Neil Harvey 178 at Newlands so casually that he appeared to be playing a game of street cricket. That, indeed, had been Harvey's first cricket school: the laneway behind the two-storey, single-fronted family home at 198 Argyle Street, Fitzroy, where he and his brothers Mervyn, Mick, Harold, Ray and Brian had played games with a tennis ball, homemade bat and kerosene tin.

'Ninna' Harvey had burst into cricket as a fresh-faced teenager, with 153 in his second Test at home and 112 in his first abroad, at Headingley in 1948. His confidence at the crease was boundless. He invariably greeted incoming batsmen, regardless of score or conditions, with: 'These blokes are easy. Let's get into them.' And he scored so breezily that he was inclined to leave a slipstream. Sam Loxton recalls of that 178: 'It's the only occasion I ever got out through lack of practice. Never mind singles, he was taking three off the last ball of every over. When I finally got to face the bowling, I hadn't seen one for ages, and got out.'

Star turn with the ball, apparently from beyond the grave, was Harvey's Victorian teammate Johnston. He looked amiable, with his prominent pate and ambling gait, but he was deceptively quick and owned a mean bouncer. 'Bill used to get away with bouncers because he was such a good bloke,' says Alan Walker. 'He'd dig one in, then he'd turn around and smile, and people would say: "What a lovely cheerful fella that Johnston is. Wouldn't hurt a fly." But he bowled just as many bouncers as the rest of us, probably more.'

Johnston's nativity as a fast bowler had been a remarkable one. Not three years earlier, he had been on the fringe of the Victorian team, bowling left-arm spin with occasional quicker deliveries, and receiving conflicting advice. Test selector Jack Ryder wanted him to bowl quick. Richmond captain Jack Ledward wanted him to bowl slow. Then Bradman himself had called Johnston aside for a heart-to-heart during an Adelaide Oval Shield match.

Bradman told him straight: 'If you're interested in furthering your cricket, you'd do better as a fast bowler. There's a few spinners round at the moment, but we've only got Keith and Ray bowling fast, and Keith's back is a bit suspect. You've got a bit of zip when you bend your back, Bill, and if you concentrate on your speed you'll be closer to getting picked.' Throttling up to take the new ball, Johnston had not looked back.

GENTLEMEN OF THE PRESS

The only man not among the wickets was Ray Lindwall. He had arrived with 65 Test wickets at 19 and a scarifying reputation, but now there were some scathing remarks aimed at his accuracy and avoirdupois. When his sisters loyally wired him at Cape Town's Langham Hotel with coverage of his wicketless First Test, he read that the *Sydney Sun's* Dick Whitington had labelled him 'the portly ghost of a once great fast bowler'.

The visiting press contingent on the tour numbered five, including three past players: Whitington, a former South Australian opening batsman who had played in the Services XI with Hassett and Miller; Arthur Mailey of Sydney's *Daily Telegraph*, a much loved figure who'd bowled leg-spin for Warwick Armstrong and Herbie Collins in the 1920s, then become famous as a cartoonist and raconteur; and, on his first tour, Percy Beames, Victoria's captain in its successful 1945–46 Sheffield Shield campaign, who'd succeeded Frank Mauger as cricket correspondent for the *Age*.

Though a good cricketer and a fine Melbourne footballer, Beames was far from sure of his journalistic credentials: in fourteen years of clerical work at Vacuum Oil Company (later Mobil), he'd written little beyond ledgers and memoranda. And in his early days, there wasn't much for him to do: the *Age*, because of paper rationing, ran to only four pages.

So, to educate himself, Beames had spent idle afternoons reading old newspapers in the State Library, fastidiously gleaning the wisdom of past correspondents. He'd declined the opportunity to cover the 1948 Ashes tour—'I thought it was beyond me,' he says—but finally accepted this South African sojourn and was acquitting himself well.

Percy Millard was covering the tour for Australian Associated Press, while Frank Rostron of London's *Daily Express* had come south to report for Sydney's *Daily Mirror*. They huddled in press boxes round Bill Ferguson: the much travelled Australian baggage man and scorer who had accompanied thirty-six international touring teams since 1905, and who was as proud of his record of never mislaying a bag as he was of having shaken hands with four English sovereigns.

The close proximity of the players could lead to some sensitive situations. When Mailey criticised Transvaal's Eric Rowan in a Johannesburg paper, Australian players mischievously rearranged platform sleeper cards to suggest that the pair were sharing the same train compartment. They then watched as Mailey and Rowan spent the evening deferring their bedtimes before discovering the ruse and laughingly settling their differences.

Lindwall's response, in due course, was even drier. Shortly after reading Whitington's unflattering remarks, the Australians attended a dinner dance at the Cape Town Rotunda. When the fast bowler spied Whitington engaged in a smooth 'excuse-me' foxtrot with a pretty partner, he tapped the critic on the shoulder and enquired politely: 'May I have the rest of this dance? Don't mind me. I'm only a ghost.'

NOURSE'S DILEMMA

Rain snapped at the Australians' heels throughout the tour. Early in the New Year, the team's luggage van was marooned by floodwaters between Uniondale Road and Willowmere, en route from Cape Town to Port Elizabeth, compelling Bill Ferguson to hire a railway bus for the 200-mile rescue mission. And rain on the evening of 20 January 1950 would create one of history's most astonishing Test matches at Kingsmead.

South Africa was 2–240 at the time of the furious downpour, and Nourse and Hassett agreed to postpone play next morning for forty-five minutes. But the last ball of Johnston's first over made it clear that the pitch was stirring from its previous day's slumber: Nourse, evading hastily, edged to Saggers.

Hassett had a curly problem. He needed to dismiss South Africa, but not so quickly that Australia was exposed to the problematic pitch. The same dilemma had beset him against Hampshire eighteen months earlier, and he'd resolved it by instructing Johnston and Miller to bowl as full a length as possible with the old ball. The breathing space had secured an unlikely victory. So Johnston and Miller came on again, bowling ramrod-straight to a deep-set field. The new ball was shunned in favour of the older, softer article.

The Springboks were slow to penetrate Hassett's stratagem. They added only 14 in the morning session, as the tourists contrived to prolong the innings by spilling a few none-too-difficult catches. But the pitch was producing chances more quickly than the Australians could spoil them, and seven wickets slid for 57 between lunch and tea.

Hassett's plans had saved the Australians a little time, and Morris and Moroney stemmed the Spingboks for the first hour of their innings. But, at 4.20pm, the latter played on to the young off-spinner Hugh Tayfield, and a subsidence began that had the 16,000 Durban fans hurling hats and cushions into the air. In sixty-eight minutes by the City Hall clock, 10 Australian wickets fell for 44.

Kingsmead had not witnessed such South African sporting ascendancy since 1928, when their rugby team had overrun the All-Blacks 17–0. Local newspapers pulled out all tabloid stops. The *Natal Sunday Post's* four-deck headline read: 'They Longed For It—They Didn't Think It Would Happen—It Did—PHEW HUGH! 7 FOR 23.' The *Sunday Express* chimed in with: 'JOYBELLS RING FOR SPRINGBOKS AT KINGSMEAD.'

On the stoep of the Edward Hotel in Marine Parade that evening, however, Whitington encountered a cheerful, chatty Keith Miller. 'I hope you haven't been stupid enough to write off our chances in your story to Australia?' the all-rounder grinned.

When Whitington said that he hadn't yet filed, Miller mused: 'I'm sorry for Dudley Nourse. He's going to have the whole nation down on him like a ton of bricks when South Africa lose.'

Whitington was dumbfounded: 'When they lose? If they lose, you mean. You're still 236 behind.'

'We're going to win and you'd better say so,' Miller replied. 'You'll probably be the only pressman who does. Just think of the feather that will be in your cap.' He offered £5 on an Australian win. Whitington declined: 'Miller's luck' was too well known.

Hassett's conundrums of Saturday were Nourse's on Sunday, the rest day. Should he enforce the follow-on, risking a last-day chase, or should he set an unattainable fourth-innings target? A visit with teammate John Watkins to the local Bureau of Meteorology decided him: its Monday forecast was for 'a possibility of thunderstorm conditions developing late in the afternoon'. After twenty-five minutes pondering the pitch's mysteries on Monday morning, Nourse informed Hassett that South Africa would bat again, requesting the heavy roller in the hope it would offer his batsmen some respite. At lunch they were 3–85, a lead of 321. Wind which had fanned the ground now dropped, leaving Kingsmead clammy and hot.

The roller's stabilising effects, however, were wearing off, and Johnston and Johnson were undeniable thereafter, sweeping up 7–14. By 2.40pm, Hassett was himself demanding the heavy roller to placate the pitch. Bradman's Australians had famously overhauled 404 in the fourth innings to beat England not eighteen months earlier. But they'd not done so on a pitch where, since the rain, 28 wickets had mustered 245 runs. Asked his opinion, Beames said: 'I wouldn't back them with bad money.'

The hosts struck thrice before the close: Moroney, Hassett and Miller all lbw playing back. But the Australians found stumps in fair shape at 3–80, Morris uncannily fluent, and Harvey playing a few signature square cuts before the close, suggesting that surrender was far from his thoughts.

THE GREAT ESCAPE

As crowds streamed onto the banks of Kingsmead from early on the Tuesday to watch Australia's last seven tackle 256, Bill Ferguson took up his usual position in the press enclosure announcing: 'You're going to see some real Australian batting today.' But after half an hour, Morris heard keeper Bill Wade appeal as he trotted a leg-side single and turned to see that his back foot had dislodged a bail. Sympathetic applause gave way to horrified gasps as Tayfield's first ball to Sam Loxton squirmed past his forward prod.

With his score on 40, Harvey then went agonisingly close to being bowled by the bespectacled left-arm spinner Tufty Mann. He remembers:

> I can still see it. To me it was the perfect delivery. It pitched outside off and spun in towards me, I pushed forward and it beat me. I thought: 'Oh God, that's gone.' I could hear the stumps rattling already, and I was just about to walk. But I heard nothing and, when I turned round, Wade was standing there with his hands above his head: the ball must have just bounced over the stumps and Sam called me for two byes.

So used to dictating terms to bowlers, Harvey found the experience disorienting. It was taking so long. He was actually practising, and counselling, caution.

> The pitch was a shocker, a real sticky. The sun coming out after the storms had baked the top but left the mud underneath, and when the ball hit the hard top it was bouncing almost vertically. The rolling had helped, but there were holes in the surface where balls had dug in. And, when it pitched in those marks, you hadn't a clue what it would do. For the first time in my life, really, I had to pick the ball to hit.

But as the strain of ninety minutes unchanged bowling took its toll, Tayfield and Mann began to stray. Harvey and Loxton pilfered priceless runs. The luck seemed to have changed. Loxton mis-hit Mann to long on ten minutes before lunch, but his grinning walk-off was a charade: he'd heard no-ball called. In the same over, Harvey reached 50 in 137 minutes. As he entered the dressing-room, he heard Miller say: 'We're gonna win this.'

Ken Archer offered Harvey a drink. 'Well played Colt. Great stuff. Keep it going.'

Harvey just chuckled. 'How slow have I been? I've been in for hours and I'm still only 60. Jeez, Merv'll never believe it.'

Hot as it was for Harvey and Loxton, the humidity was doing just as much to sap the South Africans. Chases slackened, returns grew ragged, reflexes slowed. Mann was constantly removing his spectacles to wipe their fog of perspiration. Pressure eased. When Harvey raised the century stand with Loxton, and an Australian pressman asked how long it had taken, a disconsolate South African colleague replied: 'Not long enough.'

Loxton was finally bowled at 3.05pm. But Springbok celebrations were subdued: Harvey was ensconced, and his new partner McCool as unflappable as his name suggested. Harvey neatly pocketed his fifth century in the Union, McCool survived a few alarms against Mann, and the tea score stood at 5–267.

With 69 to win, Harvey was fit to burst with attacking shots. 'Do you think I can have a go now, Col?' he asked as they resumed.

The laconic McCool stressed once more that South Africa was still in the match. 'Take your time,' he replied. 'We've got plenty.'

They closed the gap with singles, twos and the occasional crisp boundary. Finally, as Mann delivered his 52nd over, Harvey slipped the sixth delivery sweetly to the mid-wicket fence to win the match. His unbeaten, chanceless 151 had taken five and half hours. As Harvey, McCool and the South Africans competed to souvenir stumps, Nourse looked reproachfully at the sky: the forecast showers had never come. And Whitington fingered the fiver he had wisely not bet against Australia: Miller had been right again.

FOOL'S PARADISE

With the rubber won, the visitors could return to enjoying themselves. For the life of a touring cricketer in 1950 was a charmed one: few Australians travelled overseas at the time, fewer still to do what they enjoyed. Even for a supernumerary like Ken Archer, twelfth man in all five Tests, the trip was an exciting experience:

> I'm sure it was Australia's happiest tour for years. It was the first without the Don, so that disciplinarian hand was missing, replaced by Hassett, who was a pretty liberal skipper, and 'Chappie', who had the wisdom to allow a bit of levity. And the players—with the exception of myself and Harv— were ex-servicemen, and had the attitude that life was for living and cricket was for fun.

Hassett could, when necessary, exert a quiet discipline. Geff Noblet recalls a provincial match at Ellis Park where Miller accosted his captain late in the day and chirped: 'Reckon I'll slip off now, Lindsay. Wanna play a few holes with Bobby Locke.' (Locke was South Africa's British Open champion.)

'No you won't Keith,' Hassett replied. 'You're in the middle of a cricket match, and you'll stay here.'

Says Noblet: 'It wasn't said in a nasty way. It was just Lindsay reminding Keith of where he was, and what he was there for.'

Usually, though, Hassett was irrepressible. During the match against Griqualand West, the tourists were guests at the estate of local mining magnate Harry Oppenheimer Jnr. Ken Archer recalls:

> I don't know whether Lindsay got a bit bored, but he suddenly decided to hold a bit of a fielding practice. Standing at the front table, he started tossing these priceless brandy balloons over to his ring of catchers, of which I was one. And when he threw one slightly wide and it shattered, he slapped Oppenheimer on the back and said: 'Plenty more where that came from, Harry!' Hassett and Oppenheimer ended up arm-in-arm singing dirty ditties, and Oppenheimer obviously hadn't enjoyed himself so much in years.

Even if they weren't confronted by the full force of South African segregationism, the Australians couldn't help speculating on its implications.

Archer remembers a Johannesburg dinner where he was seated next to a Jewish professor from the University of Witwatersrand:

> Having been brought up as a loyal British subject, I said something to the effect that I felt English whites in Natal treated blacks better than Afrikaners in Transvaal and Orange Free State. The professor said: 'Every colonising nation has treated the indigenous population like animals. You have been misled because the English keep saying how much they love animals.'

Johnson took particular interest in the country's politics. Introduced at Pretoria to the legendary opposition leader, Field-Marshal Jan Smuts, he asked: 'What do you think of this apartheid?'

'I think it is a very good idea in theory,' Smuts replied. 'But I doubt if it will work in practice.'

In a feature series for the *Sunday Express*, Johnson expressed his wariness of future racial disharmony: 'I am certain that your average man-in-the-street avoids the problem too much for, at the moment, you're living in something of a fool's paradise.'

EASY DOES IT

The final two Tests were simple as could be. Morris (111), Harvey (100 not out) and Moroney (118 and 101 not out) made centuries in the Fourth Test. Hassett (167), Morris (157) and Harvey (116) then built a towering 7–549 in the Fifth Test, and the Springboks melted away twice in barely 100 overs.

After playing a baseball game at Johannesburg's Balfour Park for the benefit of Bill Ferguson, the players dispersed for a fortnight's rest and recreation while they waited for their ship to arrive. Hassett and Noblet had their tonsils removed at Port Elizabeth; Johnson, Miller and Morris visited Kruger Park and the resort town of Lourenco Marques in Portuguese East Africa; Archer and Walker hung round Port Elizabeth's King's Beach; Sid Pegler took Hassett, Dwyer and Saggers touring, concluding with a visit to the House of Assemblies at Cape Town. There, rather absent-mindedly, Hassett strolled straight into the middle of a chamber while it was in session. It was the first wrong turn he had taken all tour.

For Hassett had enjoyed a triumph. On the field, he'd been the shrewdest of generals: Australia's tour record was 14 wins, seven draws from 21 games. Off it, he'd spread goodwill everywhere: high commissioner Stirling cabled Canberra that Hassett was the most successful envoy Australia had ever sent to the Union. In a final spontaneous diplomatic act, standing by the rails of the *Athenic* in Table Bay on 1 April 1950, he scattered his remaining rands among excited children on the dock. The post–Bradman age had enjoyed a heady beginning.

'No Way to Live'

AUSTRALIAN CRICKETERS
IN THE
1950S

Australia in 1950 felt like the happiest, healthiest, sunniest and most fortunate country on earth. It was a land of negligible foreign debt, 1 per cent unemployment, spiralling wool prices and booming factory output, a land with both the world's shortest working week *and* 5 per cent annual GDP growth. New Holdens on the road embodied the country's confident embrace of technology, the Snowy Mountains scheme inaugurated in September 1949 its grand plans for industrialisation, while the waves of postwar immigrants surely attested to the blessings of its lifestyle. A quarter of a million dispossessed Europeans couldn't be wrong.

A change of government while Hassett's Australians had been away also seemed to symbolise a national desire to abandon the exigencies of war. On 10 December 1949, restive consumers had left Ben Chifley's Labor Party with just forty-eight of 121 House of Representatives seats, catapulting into power a resurgent Liberal–Country Party coalition led by Robert Menzies.

The new government had at once erased the last vestiges of wartime austerity. Tea, petrol and butter rationing were repealed, child endowment begun, Chifley's plans to nationalise the banks defenestrated. There was free milk in primary schools, free medical care for pensioners. In his inaugural budget address in October 1950, Treasurer Arthur Fadden spoke of 'the faith, held almost universally in Australia and by many people abroad, that this country is capable of immense progress in the coming years'.

One could cavil, of course, with the transparent materialism of the times. Although 95 per cent of Australians still purported to believe in God, the hunger for home comforts often seemed to transcend all spiritual and aesthetic considerations. But by 1950, Australia was enjoying unprecedented international prominence: instrumental in the fertilisation of the United Nations, it had ground troops in Korea fighting the communist threat, aid workers in Asia improving education, health and living standards in the region. And, if the average Australian was uninterested in the minutiae of the Colombo Plan, he could savour the idea that Australian sport had never attained a higher water: it held the Ashes and the Davis Cup, had monopolised the Empire Games in New Zealand and beaten England in rugby league. Australians had ridden the winners in the English, French and Irish Derbies. Cyclists Sid Patterson and Jack Hoobin, swimmer John Marshall and sprinter Marjorie Jackson had broken world records. Jack Young was king of the international speedway.

That mattered. Sport was fundamental to the national self-image. Australians strove to emulate their sporting heroes (four in ten respondents to a 1948 Gallup poll played a sport) and revelled in the pageant of success (a 1953 survey concluded that three-quarters of adult Australians watched at least one of the four leading spectator sports). If occasionally it seemed that the world was less aware of Australia's eight million people than of its 110 million sheep, one was consoled by the thought that Australian athletes enjoyed renown. As Arthur Hodsdon, secretary of the Amateur Athletic Union of Australia, put it in September 1950:

> Sport has become Australia's biggest and best medium of world publicity. I doubt if there is a worthwile newspaper or radio anywhere in the world that has not had to pay some tribute to Australia during the past 12 months...Now no one can deny that our successes this year have been worth a thousand times more than the Government spends yearly on publicity through the Department of Information.

When a key sporting event was staged, distractions were laid aside. The House of Representatives deferred debate for three-quarters of an hour to listen to the 1950 Melbourne Cup and, when new Liberal member Paul Hasluck protested such misuse of parliamentary time, he was overruled by both Menzies and Chifley. Said the prime minister: 'I do not think the four million who listened to the broadcasts will have any complaints.'

If sport in 1950 had become heavily symbolic, so were its rewards more figurative than financial. Work and play had yet to be synthesised by concepts of 'professionalism', and the idea of making a living from sport was fanciful, even contradictory. Selection for one's country at sport was widely considered the greatest honour available to a citizen, and no-one in sports administration was inclined to vitiate that notion with money.

Test cricketers were paid, of course, and in the five years from 1947–48 to 1952–53, the home Test fee grew 40 per cent from £50 to £70: a handy sum, for it was five times weekly earnings. But average weekly salaries grew 55 per cent over the same period, and the differential would worsen: in the four years from 1954–55 to 1958–59, the home Test fee would increase just 6 per cent while average weekly earnings grew 45 per cent.

An irony is that the majority of Australian workers at the time were represented by a union and, in a phase of negligible unemployment, usually successful in bending employers to their will. They had won the forty-hour week at the end of 1947 and, even as Hassett's team was returning from Cape Town, received a 14 per cent increase in the basic wage from the Arbitration Court.

But Australian cricketers were not 'workers'. They were sportsmen. And sporting administrators went to great lengths in the 1950s to keep 'professionalism' at arm's length. Elaborate codes like the Coulter Law in the Victorian Football League set maximum player payments at miserly levels. Australian athletes could have professional coaches, but the likes of Percy Cerutty and Forbes Carlile were persona non grata at Olympic villages and events. Australian tennis stars could receive substantial 'expenses', but nothing from winning or losing. What, after all, was money as a stimulus to competition when compared to honour and national pride?

PAY AND PLAY

Lindsay Hassett had news for Neil Harvey as the *Athenic* steamed home in March 1950. Henceforward, Harvey would bat at number three for Australia. Henceforward, too, he could work in Hassett's sports store. Harvey accepted gladly. His employment history was chequered. A three-year apprenticeship as a fitter in Melbourne City Council's electric supply department had taken six because of his frequent cricketing absences. And working in sporting goods was a premium job: decent money and generous leave allowances.

For cricketers, finding the elusive job that allowed them money for work and time for play was a constant preoccupation. Even Ray Lindwall, the most lauded fast bowler of his generation, was familiar with financial insecurity. He had begun his Test career while working at Sydney's Commercial Steel and Forge but, when his boss carped at the amount of time he spent playing cricket, accepted a public service job arranged for him by 'Doc' Evatt, Australia's deputy prime minister. After a couple of years there, though, the Public Service Board also refused him time off, so he went to work for Stan McCabe's sports emporium, and later with Cobb & Co in Queensland. Lindwall's reckoning was that he returned with money from only one of seven tours: the 1956 Ashes series when, at the recommendation of a doctor who diagnosed him with hepatitis, he abstained from alcohol.

Plenty of cricketers became salesmen, among them Ian Johnson, Keith Miller (cordials and liquor), Bill Johnston (Dunlop sporting goods), Arthur Morris (cars) and Colin McCool (commercial traveller). It was a flexible occupation, one also in which their public prominence could be valuable. There were several teachers, including Ken Archer (Brisbane CEGS), Jack Moroney (Glebe Junior Secondary) and Victorian opener Colin McDonald (Elwood Central School). They could cram cricket into their summer holidays.

Bank telling was also popular, although Sam Loxton at the ES & A, Geff Noblet at the SA State Savings Bank and Alan Walker at the CBC all encountered difficulties in obtaining leave to play. Just before the South African tour, in fact, a CBC manager had tried curtailing Walker's sporting ambitions by transferring him from Manly to Bondi. Walker recalls: 'The bank was saying: "Well, you've had a good sporting career, but we'd now like you to concentrate on banking." I said: "Sorry, but I'm only twenty-three and I don't think I've finished yet." So I quit, and counted on getting another job when I got home.'

As for supplementing income by becoming a celebrity scribe, opportunities were limited by the player–writer rule: an Australian board ordinance forbidding players from describing any match in which they were participating. Neither were there the lucrative endorsement contracts available to players today. Lindwall endorsed equipment made by the British batmaker Shaw and Shrewsbury, but received bats in lieu of royalties (which he then on-sold). Neil Harvey was on a £300 annuity to use Stuart Surridge equipment, but his circumstances didn't change much: he remained at home, sharing a bedroom with brothers Brian and Ray until he was married in 1953, and he continued for many years to wear the cricket trousers he'd worn in England in 1948. Most of the rest forked out for their own equipment, using it until it wore out and beyond. The great gloveman Don Tallon kept in gauntlets that seemed to predate him. Queenslander Peter Burge recalls: 'I had to substitute for Donny one day against South Australia and his gloves were just atrocious. My wife wouldn't have used them for gardening. But Donny couldn't afford a new pair.'

GIVING IT AWAY

In these circumstances, many players retired early. Australia's keeper in South Africa, Ron Saggers, retired immediately after the trip to further his job in insurance. Jack Moroney retired a couple of seasons later. 'I'd been married ten years, had four kids, and half an income,' he says. 'It was no way to live.' South Australian captain Phil Ridings declined the 1953 Ashes tour because he had just helped set up Custom Credit in that state. His handy twenty-four-year-old state colleague Ron Haddrick went to England, but not as a cricketer: having impressed Anthony Quayle as a radio actor, he accepted an invitation to join the Royal Shakespeare Company. And for those in the professions, cricket steadily became an impossibility. Two medicos in the Victorian side of the time—Ian McDonald and George Thoms—were destined for brief cricket careers.

McDonald graduated in 1946, and learned of his state selection during his second year at the Royal Children's Hospital when registrar Dinny Maginn looked up from his newspaper and grunted: 'What's the fucking northern tour?' McDonald persuaded colleagues to cover for him on weekend shifts but, over the three ensuing seasons, they were less and less inclined to do so. Finally, in December 1952, he was called in by the senior anaesthetist, Dr Vern Collins, who asked: 'What chance do you think you have of playing for Australia?'

'I'd like to give it another year,' McDonald said. 'If I'm not picked for England I'll give it away.' He wasn't, and that was it.

Born in Footscray to parents who ran a milk bar, Thoms grew up with few prospects. 'In the western suburbs then,' he says, 'the ambition of every mother and father was for their son to do intermediate [four years of secondary school], then join a bank or the public service.' But, when his elder brother Jim persuaded him to stay and finish his leaving certificate, he completed an engineering diploma at RMIT and decided, rather quixotically, to study medicine.

A scholarship paid Thoms' tuition fees but not his living expenses, and he subsisted on the £10 he received for Sheffield Shield matches, and the odd £5 for umpiring amateur football. Thoms senior was unimpressed. 'My father thought I was mad,' Thoms recalls. 'He just saw it as more expense, and he couldn't really accept what I was doing.'

A sympathetic anatomy professor, Sid Sunderland, allowed Thoms to sit exams privately when they interfered with cricket matches. It was thanks to a rescheduled viva exam that he scored the 150 in Perth that smoothed his path into the Australian side. And, after winning his Test cap, Thoms continued to play club and state cricket with the blessing of Leslie Gleadhill, honorary gynaecologist at Royal Melbourne Hospital. But the work was increasingly onerous, and his cricketing peers were hardly understanding of the situation. One Saturday, Thoms turned up late to resume his innings in a grade game for Essendon after working the clock around, and was chided by Des Fothergill. Thoms retorted: 'I only hope your wife is never on the operating table.'

Matters finally came to a head in November 1954 when Thoms began the grade season in a blaze of runs. He recalls:

> Leslie Gleadhill was a beautiful surgeon with a lovely pair of hands, but he was also the son of a butcher, so he could be pretty gruff. One day he said to me suddenly: 'I suppose you think you've gotta chance of getting back in the Victorian team, George. Well, you've gotta make up your mind: are you going to be a cricketer or a surgeon? I want you to tell me before the operating list on Wednesday.' It hit me right between the eyes…And that was it. I was twenty-six and my cricket was over. And, of course, Leslie was quite right.

AUSSIES ABROAD

The only way a cricketer could earn more than a subsistence income from the game was by playing in England. For most, it was the short-term proposition of a contract in the Lancashire or Central Lancashire Leagues. Every season, a gang of Australian cricketers headed for England to take up contracts.

Established Test players could earn a tidy sum there. Ray Lindwall's 1952 contract with Nelson—£1300 with free accommodation and regular post-match collections—was worth 40 per cent more than he earned as a Test tourist a year later.

But not everyone regarded a visit to England as a busman's holiday. As county cricket promised long-term professional employment, some elected to stay and qualify for the first-class game. The flood of import-ed superstars was still some years off: county cricket's strict qualifying rules at the time virtually disbarred one from playing cricket elsewhere. But once the postwar trail was blazed to Leicestershire by the New South Welshmen Vic Jackson and Jack Walsh in 1946, a powerful expat-riate cricket community began establishing itself in England.

By the 1950s Nottinghamshire was served by the brilliant South Australian leg-spinner Bruce Dooland and whippy left-armer Alan Walker, Lancashire by the ebullient right-hander and unerring slip catch-er Ken Grieves, Warwickshire by Queensland quick Keith Dollery, Kent by the former Services XI all-rounder Jack Pettiford, Somerset by the former Test all-rounder Colin McCool and Surrey by the wry Sydney leg-spinner John McMahon. Northamptonshire had no fewer than three Australians, all left-handers: batsman/keeper Jock Livingston, wrist-spin-ner George Tribe and finger-spinner Jack Manning.

In time, they became county institutions, as revered off the field as on. Walker, who qualified for Notts after seasons with Rawtenstall and Stoke in the East Staffordshire League, says that even being associated with his cobber Dooland was a point in one's favour. He recalls:

> I'd been driving a few years when I got to England and got a visitor's licence. But when I stayed I decided to get a full licence, and I did my first test in Nottingham. Well, the guy failed me. I couldn't believe it, but appar-ently I wasn't paying 'due care and attention'. So I sat it again, more carefully this time, and he failed me again. When I booked for another test, I decided not to take any chances. I got Bruce to come with me, and we had a couple of bats in the back seat and cricket gear strewn everywhere. And I had no trouble. Bruce was a hero in Nottingham.

After five years in England and three seasons at Notts, Walker and his family applied to emigrate back to Australia and returned on the *Iberia*. Thanks to a lump sum on severance and winter work with George Wimpey, he returned with the small fortune of £8000: a sum most Australian cricketers could only dream of.

CEC PEPPER AND BILL ALLEY

Two figures stand out among Australian cricket emigres: Cec Pepper and Bill Alley, feisty all-rounders from NSW, became legends of the leagues, both for their combative cricket and combustible tempers.

Pepper, a key component of Hassett's Services XI, left Australia in 1946, piqued by his omission from the national team touring New

Zealand. He became the first overseas pro to achieve the double of 1000 runs and 100 wickets in the Central Lancashire League, for Rochdale two years later, before moving on to Burnley in the Lancashire League. His self-belief was unrestrained. One day, as he released a leg-spinner to Frank Worrell, he exulted with the ball in flight: 'That's it!' When the West Indian was duly bowled, Pepper explained to his colleagues: 'Soon as I let the ball go, I knew that there wasn't a man alive who could have played it.'

Pepper's move to qualify for Lancashire was thwarted. The county club thought him too hot to handle. So he carried on scoring thousands of full-blooded runs and harvesting hundreds of wickets for Royton, Radcliffe and Oldham in the CLL, before qualifying in 1964 as a first-class umpire notorious for politically impure observations (he was known, for instance, to welcome West Indian fast bowlers by advising batsmen: 'New bowler, same direction, different colour').

Bill Alley could turn his hand to almost anything. He began work on an oyster farm at fifteen, and went on to be a boilermaker's assistant, concrete pourer and nightclub bouncer, while remaining unbeaten in twenty-eight welterweight bouts. And, after quitting Australia in 1948, this belligerent batsman and sapient seamer clubbed almost 6000 runs in five seasons for Colne and 20 centuries in four years for the Northern League club of Blackpool.

When Blackpool declined to offer thirty-eight-year-old Alley any more than a one-year contract for 1957, a lesser man may have beaten his bat into a ploughshare. Instead, Alley accepted an invitation to join Somerset. Notwithstanding that the county had been last in four of the preceding five seasons, Alley led them to third within two years. In one match at Lord's against Middlesex, he opened the batting, the bowling and substituted as wicketkeeper.

With his labourer's physique, boxer's countenance and navvy's repartee, Alley was known as one of the fiercest competitors on the circuit. He even out-talked a player as voluble as Fred Trueman. 'Not a bad feller that Alley,' the Yorkshireman once said. 'Only, he doesn't half swear.' And Alley outlasted almost everyone he played: he was a first-team regular with Somerset into his fiftieth year, then followed Pepper into umpiring.

Alley blended into the English landscape: he married a Lancashire girl and, after a hugely successful 1961 benefit season, bought a two-acre smallholding near Taunton. But he was galled that playing in England made him unwelcome in cricket at home. 'The Australian Board of Control never forgave us for flying off to England,' he wrote. 'The bitterness was so deep that the state selectors wouldn't even entertain the idea of us as guest players.' Australian administrators were resolved that 'professional cricketer' should remain an oxymoron.

AGE SHALL NOT WEARY THEM

A cursory glance at any Australian team photo from the 1950s reveals another salient fact about the period's cricket. There are a great many older faces. The average age of the Australian team in 1952 was thirty-one and, because state associations relied on players for personal details, teams were sometimes older than they read on paper. A year before the 1949–50 tour of South Africa, for example, Ron Saggers told his Marrickville teammate Jack Moroney: 'You should push your age back a bit, Jack. They won't wanna take a thirty-two-year-old to South Africa.' So, as Moroney filled in the annual NSWCA registration form, three years slipped from his shoulders. He made the team.

The orientation towards older cricketers was a function of the times. War had erased seven years of junior cricket. Teenagers who might have been emerging by the late 1940s to challenge their elders were simply not there. Geff Noblet, who bowled into his thirty-sixth year for South Australia, says: 'The war cost me seven years of cricket but it also pro-longed my career. Aside from Neil Harvey and Ken Archer, there were very few good youngsters around pushing for your place.'

There was also national service, which recommenced in November 1950. Within a year, district clubs were complaining about the frequent absences of junior players. The situation grew so dire in Adelaide that SACA secretary Bill Jeanes had to ask the defence minister Philip McBride to release soldier-cricketers early on Saturdays. And a call-up would check the careers of future Test men like Ron Archer, Pat Crawford, Peter Philpott, Ian Craig, Ian Meckiff, Lindsay Kline and Bill Lawry.

Yet, an impression many hold of the 1950s—that sport in general was then played by older athletes, and that the teen champion is a modern phenomenon—is mistaken. Keith Bromage, who first played for Collingwood at fifteen years 287 days in August 1953, was and remains the youngest senior VFL footballer. Top seeds at Wimbledon in 1953, Ken Rosewall and Maureen Connolly, were eighteen, while five of Australia's seven-member 1954 Davis Cup team were teenagers. At the Empire Games that year medallists included cyclist Dick Ploog (seventeen), hurdler David Lean (eighteen), and swimmers Lorraine Crapp (fifteen), Jon

Henricks (nineteen) and Gary Chapman (sixteen). And, notwithstanding the seniority of many cricketers, the 1950s produced two of Australia's youngest: in due course, both Ian Craig (sixteen years 249 days on first-class debut) and Bob Simpson (sixteen years 354 days) would captain their country.

THE SERVICES TRADITION

A strong tradition of ex-servicemen—embodied in Hassett, Miller, Lindwall, Morris and Johnson—continued in state and national teams into the mid-1950s. Alan Davidson remembers the strong sense of ex-military camaraderie he experienced when entering the NSW side in 1949. 'They were mad on mateship, the old blokes,' he says. 'Guys like Sid Carroll and Tom Brooks would get to Adelaide and straight away be off to visit their army buddies. We were all very aware of the sacrifices they'd made. I think their attitude was passed on to the young players who were coming through the side.'

There has been much conjecture about the consequences of that services influence in Australian XIs after the war. Keith Miller often contended that the strong core of servicemen in Test cricket in the 1950s lent the game a friendlier atmosphere. And, though the evidence is anecdotal rather than definitive, the period is illuminated by many instances of cricket chivalry. At Port Elizabeth in January 1950, for instance, Lindwall felled Eastern Province's Ray Connell with a bouncer, the ball glancing from behind his ear onto the stumps. As Connell was escorted from the field, Lindwall glanced meaningfully at Hassett. And—with umpire Peter Prin turning a blind eye—Johnson strolled from slip and replaced the bails so that Connell could resume his innings later.

Needing wickets in the Durban Test a fortnight later, Hassett darted from mid-on and ran out Springbok Jack Nel. Given out, Nel had walked ten metres toward the pavilion when bowler Johnson noticed his captain's serious expression.

'I obstructed him, didn't I? Hassett said.

'I don't know, Lindsay,' Johnson replied. 'I was watching the ball.'

'I think I did,' Hassett commented. 'I'll call him back.'

There are, though, almost as many instances of fierce competition. Alarm over the intensity of short-pitched bowling came to a head, as it were, during January 1952. In the space of a month, umpire Hugh McKinnon warned bowlers on both sides of a Victoria–NSW Shield match for 'intimidatory bowling', umpire Herb Elphinston cautioned

Alan Walker for a fierce spell against South Australia's Bruce Bowley and Phil Ridings, and Ray Lindwall was condemned by the likes of Bill O'Reilly, Johnnie Moyes, Jack Fingleton and Alan McGilvray for five consecutive bouncers at Everton Weekes in the Fifth Test against the West Indies at the SCG. George Thoms remembers Hassett issuing the instructions for the controversial spell: 'Right fellas, we're going to take the new ball. And we're gonna turn the heat on.'

As the 1950s wore on, too, and younger players emerged like batsmen Graeme Hole and Ian Craig, and all-rounders Richie Benaud, Alan Davidson and Ron Archer, some generational tensions also manifested themselves. On Australia's 1953 Ashes tour, the senior half-dozen players, all ex-servicemen, tended to stick together and enjoy a drink; the youngsters, mostly teetotal, were left mainly to their own devices.

Ron Archer remembers the day of the Coronation, which the Australians watched from a bombed-out building in the Haymarket:

> We started at 8am: breakfast was served, lunch was served, the grog was on all day. And the drinkers in the side had a great time. A lot of those guys had seen service during the war and they kind of had the attitude that they were glad to be alive. They'd seen their mates die and they liked a bit of a party.
>
> We were supposed to get on the bus at 6pm, for a two-hour run to Brighton. And of course we did a pub crawl all the way down the road and we didn't get there until 3am. For the non-drinkers it was a pretty long day. Ian Craig said something to Doug Ring, for instance, and Doug growled at him: 'Listen, son, have you ever looked down the barrel of a Nip rifle?'

Craig himself observes:

> There really were two groups in the side and it did cause some friction off the field. We'd go by bus between matches and, because most of the older players on tour were drinkers, we tended to stop every ten miles along the road at a pub. We worked on an average speed on trips of about 10mph: if somewhere was seventy miles away and we left at 5pm, you could be pretty sure we wouldn't get there till midnight. There was a group of us who'd sit in the bus and get very frustrated, Neil (Harvey) being our leader because he didn't drink in those days, and it did occasionally cause a little dissension.

But this pronounced difference of attitude caused less trouble than it might have done. It was not an era in which the young routinely questioned their elders. When there were a few heavy heads in the field against Sussex the day after that bibulous post-Coronation drive, the juniors obediently did the lion's share of fielding. 'As the kids in the side, we knew we'd have to do the running round,' Davidson says. 'You never questioned it.'

Richie Benaud recalls: 'It never worried me that those who had been in the war tended to stick together. Nor did it surprise me in the slightest. They were lucky to be alive and had been, with all the others, responsible for the rest of us being free.'

AMATEUR PROFESSIONALS

It's a common cry today that cricketers of the 1950s did not train as hard as their modern counterparts. That, because cricket was a 'pastime', they did not have the tough-minded 'professionalism' that developed in the late 1970s.

Coaching, it's true, was a less formal, less mechanical affair. Most cricketers of the era were self-taught, and the orientation of coaches like George Lowe in New South Wales and Arthur Liddicut in Victoria was towards supervision rather than instruction. 'I don't remember anyone ever coaching me,' says Ian Craig. 'If you were doing something wrong, then they'd tell you.'

There was, though, a strong spirit of peer review. Lindwall, Miller and Morris were known as fonts of cricket wisdom in the NSW side, and practices were conducted in an atmosphere both willing and competitive. Alan Davidson remembers hitting Miller in the ribs at the SCG nets and receiving the growling response: 'Have you had a bat yet?'

'Yes,' said Davidson. 'Thank goodness.'

And, if the Australian side under Hassett was a relaxed ensemble, senior members could be strict. Ron Archer remembers how, even after taking 11–61 against Surrey in England in 1953, he raised Arthur Morris's ire by getting out carelessly to Tony Lock for 14:

> I guess I thought my job was done, and I got myself out. But before I could even get a pad off back in the dressing-room, Arthur was over and really went through me. It took me a while to work out why he was so angry, but he was right: it was only a couple of overs to the new ball and I'd missed an opportunity to bat against [Alec] Bedser, whom I'd never played before, and was going to be England's most dangerous bowler that summer. He actually said to me: 'This tells me that you're not ready to play Test cricket.'

Archer's punishment was batting at number nine in the next match against Cambridge University, and he atoned with a diligent, undefeated 63. 'That's better,' Morris told him. 'But it's one game too late.'

One must, of course, be wary of romanticising the past. But, according to Bob Simpson and Richie Benaud, whose involvement in the game has stretched from the 1950s into the 1990s, cricket as Australians played it forty years ago was not the gay, carefree pastime it is now painted. 'We had just as many team meetings as they do now,' says Simpson. 'We were just as rigorous in our analysis of the opposition. We spent just as much time on our games as they do now. Nobody talked about team spirit. It just happened.'

In Benaud's words: 'The game and the players were certainly just as professional in the time I played. The only difference was that there was little money round then. These days professionalism sometimes seems to equate merely to more money being earned.'

FIT TO DROP?

As far as fitness is concerned, there was certainly little precept in the 1950s in terms of specialised physical training: the training track was for runners, the gymnasium for boxers, the idea of diet optimising performance was decades away, and there remained an undeviating faith in beer's rehydrating properties. Fast bowler Gordon Rorke remembers Sid Carroll introducing him to ale at the end of one filthy day in Perth: 'We were staying in the Palace Hotel, where there was no air-conditioning and it was stinking hot, and WA made about eight for a million. At stumps Siddy came up with a beer and says: "Here, have this." And when I told him I didn't drink, he said: "If you don't drink this you won't be back tomorrow."'

The surmise that first-class cricketers were unfit by modern standards, though, may be overhasty. With the preponderance of employment still in primary and secondary industries, and almost half Australia's population still outside the capital cities, it is arguable that they brought to the game higher levels of general fitness than today. Certainly, someone brought up on the land like Alan Davidson felt he had a natural advantage. 'Physically I was luckier in my upbringing than players now,' he says. 'I chopped wood as soon as I was big enough to hold an axe. I was naturally pretty fit. I mean, you get a guy in a produce store. One minute he's carrying a bag of chaff, next minute he's carrying a bag of wheat: he's doing weights ten hours a day.'

As cricket had yet to consume the entire calendar, too, cricketers could also play winter sports. Australian teams of the 1950s could boast several fine Australian rules footballers (notably Gil Langley, Keith Slater and Barry Jarman), two outstanding rugby players (Ray Lindwall, Wally Grout, and Alan Walker, a 1948 Wallaby) and a top-class hockey player (Brian Booth, a 1956 Olympian). Continuing the traditions of Victor Trumper and Alan Kippax, moreover, many played baseball to a high standard: notably Neil Harvey, Bill Johnston, Ian Craig and Geff Noblet, and later Norm O'Neill, Bill Lawry, Alan Connolly and Ian Chappell.

Indeed, if one wanted to argue that cricketers of the 1950s and 1960s were fitter than they are today, some useful statistical ammunition exists. Consider that Australian-born cricketers were responsible for almost a hundred double-centuries between 1949 and 1971 and, in the next twenty years, managed fifty. And that they bowled between 14 and 15 eight-ball overs an hour, where modern Test teams struggle to attain an hourly rate of 15 six-ball overs.

That is not, however, the intention here. Put simply, where fitness was concerned, there were advantages and disadvantages to playing in the 1950s. Take Victorian teammates Bill Johnston and Doug Ring. Training, for them, was a light-hearted affair. As Johnston explains: 'I used to go out to Doug's place, bowl a few in his backyard, talk a bit of cricket, run round the block three times and have a big roast dinner and a couple of beers. Good training, eh?'

For both, though, injury was a serious business. Ring, who appeared a world-beater before the war with his leg-break, top-spinner and home-spun flipper, suffered after it from a herniated disc that he had sustained while lifting the carriage on a 25-pounder in Papua New Guinea. 'I had to change my action as a result,' he remembers. 'Couldn't get quite as side-on again so I opened my shoulders a bit, and I'm not sure I ever got back my original spin.'

Doctors were helpless and, some very cold days, Ring felt as stiff as a stump. Once he began a spell against Western Australia with an over of full tosses. Hassett took him aside for a confidential council-of-war, whispering: 'There's a spot I want you to aim for. It's about four feet wide. And twenty-two yards long.'

Johnston, meanwhile, suffered throughout his career from severe shin soreness. When doctors could provide no solution, he followed a Bill O'Reilly recommendation. 'Tiger taught me to get a towel and wrap it long ways, then tie it tight round my shin,' Johnston recalls. 'It cut off the circulation, I think, but it stopped the pain and allowed me to get to sleep.'

Eventually, injuries cruelled the pair's 1953 Ashes tour. Ring aggravated his back complaint and, in the cold weather, nothing seemed to put it right. And Johnston was injured in the first match, labouring on only by remodelling his action and submitting to the removal of the cartilages in his right knee: a speculative operation at best that, while it could free movement in the leg, also severely destabilised it. Two years later, the knee gave way again at Sabina Park, and Johnston exited Test cricket in blinding agony, on a bench that Alan Davidson and Peter Burge had wrenched from the dressing-room wall.

What 'sports medicine' existed at the time was the domain of Arthur James, a Tasmanian masseur who accompanied Australia on its Ashes tours from 1930 to 1968. He was an endearing character, with a deep knowledge of England and a wealth of contacts, one who took care of many sensitive problems (such as obtaining and doling out condoms).

Where injuries required more than a rub, however, it may be that James and his brethren did as much harm as good. For example, the conventional method for treating a muscular injury in the 1950s was to apply heat, either with a hot bath and hot packs, or with a so-called 'ray machine': a treatment quite at odds with the way such injuries would be treated today. One of sports medicine's Australian pioneers, Dr Brian Corrigan, says: 'Artie James was one of the nicest gentlemen you could hope to meet, a lovely man. But Christ! He and his kind were dangerous. Enthusiasts!'

LOTHAR AND TARZAN

The time when cricketers took their physical fitness seriously, however, was approaching. By the end of the 1950s, two NSW pace bowlers were exploring the uncharted terrain of premeditated training.

Gordon Rorke stood six feet five inches, weighed fifteen stone, and touched speeds with the ball reserved for very few. But in his debut season of 1957–58, all he could do *was* touch them:

> In those days, to get on the southern tour was everyone's dream. And the NSW–Victoria game was like a Test match. All the guys who'd played it before said: 'Forget these other games. It's the Vics that matter.' Well, I was naturally highly strung anyway. And, by the time I got there, I was wound up like a clock. It went everywhere. I took three wickets, bowled 12 wides, and after three overs I said to Sid Carroll: 'Sid, I'm exhausted. I just can't go on.'

In the winter of 1958, NSW selector Dudley Seddon sent Rorke to see Brian Corrigan, then just established in practice at Dee Why. Corrigan laid out a fitness regime of weights, eighteen-yard sprints and exercise on a rowing machine, periodically measuring Rorke's recovery rates. A Dr Deakin, for whom Rorke's mother worked as a medical secretary, also prescribed an energy drink: a spoonful of honey, three raw eggs and lemon juice. 'Drink this drink, and you won't have to eat for the day,' he said. Rorke made his Test debut in January 1959, and bowled 52.1 eight-ball overs. Teammates called him 'Lothar'.

Seeing Ray Lindwall in 1950 made Frank Misson want to be a fast bowler, and watching the Olympics in 1956 made him want to be an athlete. The latter instinct seemed to win out for a few years: at nineteen, he trekked to Portsea to train with the legendary Percy Cerutty, paying £2 2s a week for the privilege. And, when he finally played first-class cricket, Misson did so with an acute consciousness of fitness. There were four-mile runs every morning, lots of fruit, nuts and honey, even an experimental vegetarian diet. 'I didn't have the natural ability of other bowlers,' he explains. 'But I thought that it would be in my favour if I was at least standing at the end of the day.' Teammates called Misson 'Tarzan', though some were loath to room with him: the noise of his juice extractor mulching carrots in the early morning could be hard to take after a late night.

Ironically, after five Tests, injuries to the calf and achilles tendon on the 1961 Ashes tour would curtail Misson's career, probably aggravated by the primitive treatment administered by Arthur James.

> Lovely bloke Artie, one of nature's gentlemen, but I remember what happened toward the end of the tour when I pulled that calf muscle. I had to go on and replace someone and did all the things you shouldn't do: jumped out of a chair, didn't warm up, ran on the field and straight away chased a ball to the boundary. Bang! Well, I hobbled off and Artie says: 'Hot bath for you, hot as you can stand it, and stay there for an hour.' Which I now know is the exact opposite of what you should do: for a pulled muscle you need ice and elevation. Not his fault, of course, because we didn't know any better. And I remember a couple of days later the bruise and bleeding came out and it was obvious that I'd had completely the wrong treatment.

Though Misson played on in Sheffield Shield cricket, he never again threatened to gain Australian selection. Cricketers of the 1950s enjoyed their cricket, for sure. Perhaps they had to. One never knew what was round the corner.

'Good God! He's Caught the Bloody Thing!

AUSTRALIA V ENGLAND, WEST INDIES AND SOUTH AFRICA
1950-53

By 1950, Australia had achieved a level of superiority in international cricket of which it is today difficult to conceive. It had not suffered a defeat in 94 Tests and tour matches over a dozen years in England, South Africa, New Zealand and Ceylon. From this zenith, however, the only possible direction was down. In three home series between 1950 and 1953, as its great XI aged and rivals improved, Australia came steadily back to the field. And administrators looked askance, wondering what to do about the first discernible slippage in cricket's popularity since the 1880s.

BROWN AND COMPANY

England's visit in 1950–51 occasioned no great hopes. England had won seven and lost 15 of 35 postwar Tests, and the nation's endlessly forgiving cricket public could not decide if this was a phase, or manifested irreversible decay. As E. W. Swanton of the *Daily Telegraph* observed: 'If the effects of war could still be justly pleaded as the underlying cause of some of the seemingly inescapable limitations of English cricket, that was an excuse which had grown stale and wearisome by repetition.' The sixteen that left Tilbury on 14 September, moreover, was widely reviled as short on experience, the junior half mustering just a score of Tests between them.

35

Yet their sanguine amateur skipper Freddie Brown made a forceful impression on journalists from the moment the SS *Stratheden* moored at Fremantle Gages on 9 October. In contrast to Wally Hammond—who had kept the press at bat's length in Australia four years earlier—Brown invited them to meet his team at the Palace Hotel. 'We hope this will be a happy tour,' he said. 'You have a job of work to do, and so have we.' He then puffed contentedly on his pipe throughout an interrogation by forty Australian and English reporters.

Journalist: 'Mr Brown, do you feel you have a good side?'

Brown: 'I should be a bloody fool if I didn't think I had a good side.'

Journalist: 'Won't you be loath to face Lindwall and Miller's bumpers?'

Brown: 'I should not be loath to face anything.'

Journalist: 'Mr Brown, do you feel any happier now that Bradman has retired?'

Brown: 'How would you feel?'

Australians loved it, for Brown's Churchillian resolve reflected fond beliefs in the virtues of English character. Australia had faithfully assisted Britain's postwar rebuilding, trebling its sterling reserves to defend the currency and donating £20 million to alleviate its people's privations. Australia's immigration programs now centred on Britons, and faith in British institutions remained robust. Churches had been full to overflowing for the recent visit of the Archbishop of Canterbury.

Brown's manager, Brigadier Michael Green, was warmly received at Perth Town Hall, when he told the assembly that coming to Australia fulfilled a thirty-four-year-old wish, formed when he had served alongside members of the First AIF at Pozieres. As Swanton noted: 'This was a reference very much to the liking of a people whose loyalty is so close to the surface that they will not go through an informal cricket luncheon without drinking the health of the King.'

Ultimately the team and Brown would be extremely popular, and receive great sympathy for a succession of bad breaks that cost them in the clinches. Certainly, few teams have been as ill-favoured by fortune as Brown's in the First Test at the Gabba that began on Friday, 1 December.

RAIN AND RUIN

Jack Fingleton described the first day at Brisbane as 'the best Test day English cricket had known since the war'. Alec Bedser, his medium pace hammering at the batsmen like a wrecker's ball, dismissed Australia for 228 in four and a half hours: the smallest home total for more than thirteen years. But the evening ranked as one of English cricket's worst nights. Disturbed by strange noises on the roof of Lennon's Hotel, Brown woke at 3am. 'All windows were closed,' he wrote. 'I thought that someone's bath was over-running and went to sleep again. But when I awoke again I knew the worst.'

The monsoon ruled out play the next day, to the fury of 16,000 confounded Queenslanders who maintained a vigil at the gates, and who pelted turnstile attendants with pies when it was finally cancelled. Then a hot Sunday rest day turned wet in the afternoon, rain so copious that some locals blamed it on the simultaneous H-bomb test at Bikini Atoll. By its end, curator Jack Farquhar's patchwork pitch of Merri Creek and Redbank Plain soil resembled a stretch of the Kokoda Trail.

A weird tactical battle ensued. England's openers eked out 28 runs before lunch on Monday but, when seven wickets then fell for 40, Brown whistled his batsmen in at 3.22pm. Fraternally placing an arm round Hassett, he smiled: 'It's up to you now skipper. The ball's at your feet.'

After twenty minutes of their second dig, the Australians were 3-0. Hassett picked up his bat and said: 'Well I suppose some poor bastard's gotta start this innings.' Only a few blows by Harvey and Miller raised the score to 7–32 before Hassett himself declared at 4.40pm.

'Well, what happens now?' asked England's captain.

'Your move now, my dear Brown,' Hassett replied.

About seventy minutes remained with a full day to follow for England's sally at 193, and Brown called for Dobbin—the horse that Farquhar used to draw his roller—to do its duty. Four return journeys were laboriously completed. But it was to no avail. England were 6–30 at the close, 20 wickets having fallen since lunch in the space of 102 runs, a spectacle so extraordinary that a *Courier-Mail* Test score switchboard had dealt with 900 inquiries an hour.

Brown had one glimmer of hope on the Tuesday: that Len Hutton, kept from harm at heavy cost, could make the most of an improvement in the pitch. As the laws of cricket entitled him to another seven minutes rolling because of the damage to the pitch, Brown prevailed on umpires Herb Elphinston and Andy Barlow to help supervise the 8am operation with a stop watch to ensure the surface received the full seven minutes. Brown recorded:

The horse had four leather pads on its hooves, with a sack slung behind it in an appropriate position in the event of any natural emergency. The sack was by no means a sure safeguard, for the groundsman always carried out a pan and a brush with which to sweep up anything that might escape the sacking. Horse and roller would complete one journey down the wicket; then the horse would be taken out of the shafts; the shafts turned over; the horse backed in again and hitched up; and the return journey would then be made. A fantastic arrangement it was.

Slow, too. It took thirty-two minutes of hitching and unhitching to administer the treatment.

Hutton *did* play an imperishable innings of 62 not out, including 43 of a thirty-eight-minute 45-run last-wicket stand. But England were 71 shy of victory when Doug Wright was bowled and the crowd encircled the pitch like visitors to Vesuvius pondering its primeval force. A couple used pennies to gouge out pieces of turf as mementoes of what Fingleton called 'surely the craziest and maddest Test match of all time'.

'A GREAT FIGHTING CAPTAIN'

So it went for the Test series: English pluck, Australian luck. Indifferent umpiring cost the tourists a close-run Second Test at the MCG, injuries to two key bowlers undermined them in the Third Test at the SCG, and the shallowness of their attack was exposed in the Fourth Test at Adelaide Oval. Locals were deeply sympathetic, regarding Brown as an English avatar. He was animated on the field: a mixture of John Bull and Farmer Giles, with kerchief and sunhat framing his rubicund features. He was ambassadorial off it: declaring at every stop that he was 'glad to be back in my favourite Australian city' (with no national newspaper, nobody quibbled). Even Brown's failures with the toss attracted condolences. Letters from various two-up magnates advised him that one should always call heads with a florin and tails with a penny. An Empire Society meeting presented him with a double-headed penny. 'It's no good,' Brown replied. 'I always call tails.'

Brown was actually a gruff, fierce man who could be a bully. Ian Johnson recalls walking into England's dressing-room on the second day in Melbourne to invite Brown to lunch, and finding teenage all-rounder Brian Close in tears over a poor shot he had just played. 'You should have a bit of a word to Brian,' Johnson told Brown. 'I think he's a little upset.'

Brown exploded. 'Serves him bloody well right. He shouldn't have gone out that way and I told him so.'

But Australians found Brown's obvious determination endearing. And when England finally won the Fifth Test at the MCG at the end of February, the reception was rapturous. Asked to wire a tribute to Brown at a celebratory dinner staged for him by Claude Harper at the Savoy on

17 July 1951, prime minister Robert Menzies waxed lyrical: 'In Australia we thought him a great fighting captain and all-round cricketer. Add to this that you have never sent a more popular representative. Give him my affectionate greetings.'

THE RISE OF JACK IVERSON

The Australians did light upon one extraordinary talent during the season, all 195 centimetres and 95 kilograms of him: John Brian Iverson. Thirty-five-year-old Iverson had been a nondescript school cricketer at Geelong College in Lindsay Hassett's heyday there, and renounced the game altogether to work in the family real estate business until the war took him to Port Moresby. There during periods of inactivity he'd turned his mind to the art of spin, and perfected on a ping-pong ball a grip that rotated it by extending his huge and prehensile middle finger.

After the war, Iverson was inspired to perfect his method in subdistrict cricket for Brighton. His impact was immediate. In the 1949–50 summer, Iverson reaped 142 wickets: 21 at 11 for Melbourne, 46 at 16 for Victoria, and 75 at seven for an auxiliary Australian team that toured New Zealand in February 1950. Newspaper and magazine columnists quickly baptised him 'Wrong Grip Jake'.

Iverson had two shining virtues. His accuracy was astounding, almost robotic. And unlike other spinners, Iverson could not be read from the hand: his off-spinner, top-spinner and occasional leg-break were bowled with an identical action. Victorian keeper Dr Ian McDonald insisted that he signal his intentions by turning different ways at the end of his mark.

Against this, he seldom seemed to have what others called a 'cricket brain'. State teammate George Thoms recalls:

> Jake was a very mechanical bowler. Once, when my club Essendon were playing Melbourne, Ken Meuleman started taking a few runs off him. Jake didn't know what was happening. Eventually our captain Clive Fairbairn went up and said that Meuleman was batting two feet in front of his crease. So Jake started bowling two feet behind the bowling crease to shorten his length.

Beyond his specialist task, Iverson seldom had a clue. Fellow Victorians sheltered him at mid-on, but perversely looked forward to watching him field. Doug Ring recalls: 'One day against NSW this batsman hit the ball an enormous distance into the sky and there was no-one but Jake around. We watched in awe as the ball began its descent. Jake sized it up, circled underneath it, moved back then forward, put his hands up into the correct position. The ball fell six feet behind him.'

Iverson was also something of a loner, prone to taking offence where none was intended. One day in New Zealand, he confronted captain Bill Brown with a face like thunder demanding explanation for his omission from a particular game. 'We're just giving you a bit of a rest, Jake,' Brown said mildly. 'You've played all the games so far, and a few boys haven't had a lot of cricket.'

'Well, as far as I'm concerned, you've dropped me,' Iverson said, spun on his heel and walked away.

But Iverson quickly became a sporting celebrity. *Sporting Life* profiled him at enormous depth, publishing 'magic eye' photos of his fingers doing their deadly work, and he was the subject of a Cinesound newsreel. Queenslander Ken Mackay recalled becoming an Iverson victim in Melbourne: 'I played confidently for a leg-break, but it zipped the other way and I was stranded down the wicket. How the Melbourne crowd loved it. Cushions and hats went flying in the air…Iverson was a wizard.' And when Iverson claimed 21 wickets at 15 against Brown's team, he seemed on the brink of a great career.

THE FALL OF JACK IVERSON

Success, however, made Iverson a marked man. When Morris and Miller punished him for the first time in the Sheffield Shield that season, he very quickly lost heart. Addicted to success, Iverson appeared constitutionally incapable of absorbing failure.

Pleading pressure of work the following season, Iverson played only one abortive match in December 1951, and visited Adelaide with Victoria eleven months later in two minds about continuing. Though he took 4–65, he was evidently far from his peak, and took umbrage at the laughter that followed one characteristic fielding effort of allowing five at deep fine leg.

Thoms remembers coming home: 'I was sharing a sleeper with Jake, and he didn't say a word the whole trip. Next day I opened the paper and there was Jake saying that he wasn't available to play against NSW in Melbourne, and for the rest of the season, because of his work.' Thoms also had an indication of the pressure under which Iverson now found himself when he had a pre-match drink with the combative New South Welshmen Sid Barnes. 'I see Iverson pulled out,' Barnes said. 'We were going to fix him right up.'

It was not quite the end for the ephemeral Iverson. In January 1954, he joined a Commonwealth XI in India, taking 27 wickets in six matches. Fellow tourist Sam Loxton recalls his last spell against a Prime Minister's XI at Eden Gardens:

> I was standing at silly mid-on. I saw this fella miss the first six from Jake, then the second six, and Jake says: 'Mr Umpire, I propose to bowl the ball underarm.' Oh, the umpire's face was a sight to behold. I thought: 'This I gotta see.' Anyway, it floats down and the guy's mesmerised. He pushes forward, straight into my hands, and I caught it and put it in my pocket.

It was Iverson's last act on a first-class field, a suitable coda for one of cricket's craziest melodies.

THE FRIENDLY SERIES

Hassett's Australians succeeded in one respect during the 1950–51 rubber. It was an enormously congenial series, devoid of controversy and characterised by fair play on both sides.

This had not of recent years consistently been the case. Bradman's tough-minded captaincy on the 1948 tour had come in for criticism, BBC broadcaster John Arlott causing a minor storm in 1950 by contending in his *Concerning Cricket* that the Australian cricket method involved 'a single-minded determination to win the game—to win within laws, but if necessary, to the last limit within them'.

Jack Ryder, Bill Ponsford and Doug Ring were moved to defend Australian honour; Hassett's players provided an eloquent response. During the Adelaide Test, for instance, Ian Johnson walked for a catch at the wicket in order to grant England's John Warr at least one wicket for the series:

> I got the faintest of faint touches and Godfrey [Evans] went up, half-heartedly. John followed him, but the umpire said not out. Well, I saw John's shoulders sag, and he looked so crestfallen that on the spur of the moment I nodded to the umpire and walked. It's the only time I ever did it, I can tell you, but it seemed in keeping with the spirit of the game.

In an article at summer's end under the title 'Test Cricket Is Becoming Friendlier', Keith Miller bordered on *lèse majesté*: 'Do we want another Bradman era in cricket? Certainly that cricket did produce record gates and dazzling batting from one or two individuals. But it almost brought the cessation of Anglo-Australian Tests when Bodyline was introduced to combat one man's undoubted genius. Then cricket lost its real value as a sport. It became a war.'

There was, however, a caveat. The 1950–51 series, closely contested and often entertaining as it was, had not seduced the crowds: where almost 850,000 had watched the first postwar Ashes series paying £116,000, only 600,000 had paid £80,000 to watch Brown's men pit themselves against Hassett's. The tour consequently made only a small surplus for England's counties: £5000 against £17,800 four years earlier. Post-Bradman cricket was proving friendlier, but not nearly so lucrative.

PANIC ATTACKS

With an eye on their ledgers in March 1951, the Australian Board of Control ambivalently accepted a visit from the West Indies. The West Indies' only previous tour, two decades earlier, had lost £2500, and the financial terms to which the board would consent left their much poorer cousin bearing the bulk of costs: £12,000 for player fees, £7000 for passage money, £4000 for internal travel, £2000 for selection and assembly, £5000 in coach hire, laundry, medical fees and insurance.

Even worse, the board offered the visitors an economy itinerary with just one first-class match before the First Test. Criticism was widespread, for the recent record of John Goddard's team merited respect. Eighteen months before, they had trounced England in England 3–1, coalescing into a talented unit revolving round the batting of the 'Three Ws', Everton Weekes, Frank Worrell and Clyde Walcott, and the bowling of spin prodigies Sonny Ramadhin and Alf Valentine.

Yet, the board was right. The West Indies performed only spasmodically, and were inclined to panic once Hassett and Miller had deciphered the encryptions of Ramadhin and Valentine. Fewer than 400,000 attended the series. The tourists lost four Tests, and won one on a damp and damaged Adelaide Oval surface.

The worst instance of the West Indies' weakness came on the last day of the Fourth Test in Melbourne, 3 January 1952. The visitors did everything right for four days and, when the Australians resumed on the final morning at 2–68 needing a further 192, bespectacled left-armer Valentine baffled the middle order. A poised Hassett century prolonged the chase, but by 5pm Australia was 38 adrift of its target with its last pair at the wicket: Richmond's Doug Ring and Bill Johnston. Cries of 'Carn the Tigers! The Tigers can do it!' echoed from the bowels of the grandstand, but they sounded superfluous. Sight of the gangling Johnston was usually a cue for the constabulary to begin encircling the MCG perimeter.

In fact, Johnston was surprisingly confident:

When I went out I had nothing to lose. Nobody expected me to do anything. But I'd learned over a period of years not to throw my wicket away. Bradman in 1948 had been very insistent that tailenders should bat properly and play straight because the time might come when we did have to stick around. And this was the sort of time he'd had in mind.

For his part, Ring believed that they should die game. 'We'll never get these in singles,' he advised Johnston. 'I'm gonna have a go.'

'In that case, I'll stick around,' Johnston replied.

When Ring did hit out, Johnston was as good as his word. The crowd cheered Johnston's forward prods as wildly as they did Ring's offensive strokes, and teammates laughed and yelled unheard advice. As Hassett emerged from the shower to watch the final rites of the match, his towel slid to the floor. He stood in their midst naked, transfixed.

Goddard, meanwhile, was being exposed as a very limited leader. He unaccountably failed to crowd the pair. Heads dropped when Ring poached 13 from an over by Valentine. 'Their field was very badly set,' Johnston says. 'They had guys out halfway to the boundary rather than on it or in close enough to stop the single, so I was able to take a few short ones and Ringy could play a few shots.'

'When we needed about a dozen, I thought for the first time we had a real chance,' Ring remembers. 'Suddenly all the West Indies players seemed to be pointing and changing the field, and Goddard took Valentine off, then Ramadhin. So I told Bill we'd try to get the rest in singles.'

Which they did. At 5.35pm, Johnston turned the last ball of Worrell's ninth over for the winning single behind square leg. The pair ran through waving their bats and whooping with joy, their priceless partnership having won the series.

BLACK FACES

Despite the results, it was not an unhappy tour, and the West Indies were well liked. Australians might have barely acknowledged their own black population, denied them the vote and broken up their families, but they saw nothing incongruous about applauding a coloured cricket team.

Authority in the islands' cricket still wore a fair skin. Thirty-two-year-old Goddard was a white Barbadian whose family controlled one of the island's major trading houses. Thirty-year-old vice-captain Jeffrey

Stollmeyer was born in Santa Cruz of German and English extraction, and his ancestral home Stollmeyer's Castle was one of Trinidad's landmarks. Leading all-rounder Gerry Gomez was of Portuguese stock, while batsman Robert Christiani had Scottish blood in his veins.

But most of the side was dark, and often of humble origin. Valentine was a machinist, fast bowler Prior Jones and leggie Wilfred Ferguson customs guards. And Ramadhin had enjoyed the steepest rise of all: an orphan who played for the Trinidad Leaseholds Oil Company, he had been selected at the age of twenty to tour England on the basis of two first-class games.

Black players in the side left for the trip with many misgivings: the White Australia policy still flourished and they had heard many stories about the country's maltreatment of people with coloured skin. But fears were allayed by the friendliness of Australian passengers aboard the *Strathmore* returning from 1951's Festival of Britain.

This probably had more to do with an instinctive respect for sportsmen than any enlightened indifference to pigmentation. Walcott overheard one old man asking a fellow passenger: 'Why is it that these coloured boys mix so well with you people? I suppose it must be because they are cricketers...' But the journey prefigured a happy trip. Hassett's players made a point of befriending the visitors. Miller went to greet them at their first net session, while Johnson and keeper Gil Langley opened their homes to the tourists. They appreciated especially the droll humour of Worrell, who grew so accustomed to descriptions of his suicidal strokeplay that he dangled a razor blade from the SCG dressing-room door. The only obstacle to communication proved to be accent: when Valentine told Johnson that he enjoyed records by 'Sirravon', the Victorian traipsed vainly round Melbourne searching for this artist's work. It transpired that Valentine's preference was for Sarah Vaughan.

The one embarrassing incident of the tour came in Melbourne over the new year, when there were newspaper reports that 'white girls had been evicted' from the West Indian digs. But this, it seems, was puritanism rather than racism at work: Clyde Walcott explained in his autobiography that the girls were evicted because of a hotel rule that guests of the opposite sex were not allowed in residents' rooms.

Wrote Walcott: 'The rumour-mongers, in their own clever way, managed to suggest a terrifying combination of immorality and colour prejudice—where nothing of the kind existed. Otherwise, there were no "incidents", real or imaginary, and everything went very smoothly.'

Only the Australian Board of Control could not join in this atmosphere of good fellowship. Disappointing Test attendances meant lacklustre distributions to the state associations, and the VCA and NSWCA both ran red ink for the season. The prospect of a 1952–53 visit from South Africa hardly reassured them: the Springboks had won one of 33 preceding Tests and hardly represented the greatest of drawcards. The board imposed financial conditions even more stringent than a year earlier, leaving the South African Cricket Association to cover the tour's expenses in their entirety.

In thirty-two-year-old Jack Cheetham, however, South Africa chanced upon a remarkable captain. A former army officer and engineer, Cheetham was a meticulous student of the game with an advanced notion that fitness and fielding were necessary for rather than ancillary to successful cricket. As soon as his squad left Cape Town aboard the *Dominion Monarch* on 3 October 1952, Cheetham and manager Ken Viljoen set the tone of their trip. There were daily team meetings at 7.45am, and compulsory PT classes incorporating exercises designed by Springbok rugby coach Danie Craven at 11.45am. The day after their arrival in Fremantle on 14 October, Cheetham ran his team through the first of many rigorous fielding drills at the WACA Ground.

Cheetham regulated the tour at every level. He instituted a light-hearted 'bounce committee', which levied fines for stipulated misdemeanours: lateness at any shipboard function was worth 2/6, being unshaven 1/-, missing church 1/6, moving in on a colleague's girlfriend 2/6. He imposed an 11pm curfew, and even banned players from golf before the First Test, on grounds that whacking a stationary ball might upset their preparation for meeting a moving one.

By night, Cheetham and Viljoen pored over scoring graphics prepared by the long-serving retainer Bill Ferguson, while Viljoen doubled as a masseur, rubbing the captain's troublesome legs in order to see him through another day in the field. By day, Cheetham radiated confidence and remarkable omnicompetence. At Lennon's Hotel before the First Test, he even acted as an interpreter for the Italian Davis Cup side, using Italian he had learned from POWs in the Western Desert.

HONOURS UNEVEN

When the hosts won a poorly attended First Test at the Gabba, the board fretted about the rest of the summer. Queensland umpire Col Hoy was told by NSWCA delegate Dudley Seddon during the tour match that he'd been selected to umpire the Second Test. But afterwards he heard nothing, and Victorians Ron Wright and Herb Elphinston were appointed instead. A few weeks later, Hoy's telephone rang. 'I'm sorry Col,' said Seddon. 'The gates have been so bad, the board didn't think they could afford to bring you down.'

But, so far as South African cricket was concerned, the series would turn out a triumph. Victory in Melbourne vindicated Cheetham's unswerving faith in constant fielding rehearsal, the sine qua non Russell Endean's miraculous catch of Miller. The all-rounder drove straight over bowler Hugh Tayfield's head, and almost into the clutches of spectators. But the boundary-riding Endean, in only his third Test, stepped calmly into the line of flight, sized up the approaching ball, leapt feet in the air and caught it in his extended right hand. 'Good God!' Miller blurted. 'He's caught the bloody thing!' ABC commentator Johnnie Moyes believed it the best catch he had seen in forty years watching, and invoked Macaulay's *Lays of Ancient Rome* to describe it: 'Miller, like the ranks of Tuscany, could scarce forbear to cheer.'

Australia retaliated in Sydney, but the tourists stampeded home again at the MCG to win the Fifth Test and tie up the series, the electric zeal of their fielding highlighting the age and deteriorating mobility of the home side. Australia had been matched for the first time since the war.

THE IAN CRAIG STORY

Local writers took the reverse in good part. 'The South African team did good for our cricket,' wrote Jack Fingleton. 'It showed, in the first instance, that nothing is beyond the capabilities of youth; that the game is never won until it is lost; and that some day…South Africa may become cock of the world's cricketing walk. Their spirit is destined to win fame.' The series, too, had not been without redemption in Australian eyes. In particular, a seventeen-year-old called Ian Craig consoled locals that the Springboks did not have a monopoly on youth by making 53 and 47 in the Fifth Test.

Craig was a classic Australian autodidact. His bank manager father quipped after his birth: 'Australia's next Bradman has arrived.' But because banks then opened on Saturdays, John Rochford Craig did not see evidence of his prophecy until, sneaking out of his office and peering from behind a tree at Trumper Park, he watched his fourteen-year-old son playing for Mosman fourths. He was staggered. So were many others.

John Craig's career advanced smartly. He became chief manager of the Wales's Sydney office, and briefed lawyers in the banks' High Court challenge to nationalisation. But his son's moved even more quickly: vice-captain of the First XI at North Sydney Boy's High, he joined Mosman's first-grade side in November 1951, and made 91 in four hours on his first-class debut four months later at sixteen years 249 days.

Where cricket prodigies are often underpinned by unusually advanced physical development, Craig assuredly looked a boy, weighing less than 63kg and standing 170cm. As he came out to bat with NSW 3–80 against South Africa on 2 January 1953, he looked like a PMG bicyclist carrying a telegram.

The impression did not last. Craig recalls:

> I was terribly embarrassed in the first hour. Michael Melle was swinging the ball away late, and I followed so many it was like I was trying to get out. Fortunately, the inswingers from Anton Murray at the other end didn't give me as much trouble, so I was able to get him away for a few. And once I'd got to 50, runs came pretty easily.

With 105 not out on the board, Craig headed to work in the evening at Eric Crane's Mosman pharmacy, where he'd just begun an apprenticeship. But, as they resumed next morning, Sid Barnes grabbed Craig's attention. 'Listen son,' he said. 'You've gotta stick around today. Make 100 and you're just another player. Make 200 and people remember you. In fact, tell you what: get 200 today and I'll give you a new bat.'

It was a good offer. Craig buckled down and, just before tea, became Australia's youngest first-class double-centurion, and owner of a new Gunn and Moore. He also discovered that Barnes was right: people did remember 200s. Phil Tresidder's comment in the *Daily Telegraph* was typical: 'There was a grim purposefulness about his batting as he moved towards his 200 that was reminiscent of Bradman.' The newspaper's front page proclaimed: 'A New "Don".'

AUSTRALIA V AUSTRALIA

Unhappy the land that needs heroes, however. And the haste with which Craig and the Don were bracketed revealed anxieties about cricket in the post-Bradman period. Australia still had many great players: Hassett, Harvey, Lindwall, Miller, Johnston. But notable in accounts of all three series against England, West Indies and South Africa are the references to strong local support for the touring teams.

English followers found the favour Brown's team enjoyed almost mortifying. Swanton wrote of the Second Test in Melbourne that popular sympathy for the Englishmen was 'always strongly and often embarrassingly in evidence'. His account concluded: 'Indeed I never expect to see again such a reaction to the ending of a Test match, least of all one that has been fought through with such tenseness, to so close a conclusion. When the last English wicket fell the crowd just melted silently and sadly away, while the victors [Australia]...stole quietly back to their dressing-room.'

When Reg Simpson completed a match-winning 156 not out in the Fifth Test in the company of last man Roy Tattersall, the manic activity captivated the MCG. 'They cheered every scoring shot and went into ecstasy over Tattersall's efforts,' wrote Bill O'Reilly. 'It was quite obvious they had decided to fight the battle out for England and were plainly partisan.'

There were several explosions of popular support for the West Indies a year later. Hassett and Johnston were mercilessly barracked in the Fourth Test by their own Melbourne crowd for a belated and successful caught-behind appeal against Ramadhin. But the most sustained hostility that Australia encountered from its own fans was that lasting almost the entirety of the First Test at Brisbane against South Africa in December 1952. Enraged by the selectors' failure to pick any Queenslanders, spectators roasted the home side from the moment that openers Morris and Colin McDonald appeared. Cheetham wrote: 'At once, the hostility of the crowd toward this Australian side became apparent. Insults, taunts and advice were hurled at both batsmen, and our bowlers and fielders were spurred to greater efforts by the applause and cheers meted out.'

When the Australians fielded, Brisbanites roared for every Springbok run. One startling display of parochialism occurred when Johnson was bowling to John Watkins. 'I stranded him by about two yards, so he just kept walking, tucking the bat under his arm,' Johnson recalls. 'But Gil [Langley] was fumbling the ball and trying to recover it, and Watkins— he must have been four yards down—looked round, saw what was happening and hurried back.' The crowd's joy was unconfined: not only had Johnson, Colin McCool's replacement, lost a wicket, but Langley, Don Tallon's successor, had missed a stumping. Cheetham commented: 'It was a most unpleasant performance.'

Listening to the Victorians beef about the crowd that evening, in fact, their friend Dr Bluey Stewart proposed a solution: 'Tell you what. I'll see if I can't round up a few Vics for Monday to give you a bit of support.' He was as good as his word. As Lindwall bowled Australia to victory from Monday, Stewart and his pals could be heard through the general tirade shouting: 'Come on, you Aussies! Up there, the Swans!' (Hassett and Johnson both came from South Melbourne).

The worst aspect of the spectators, however, was their number. Daily Test attendances of 15,500 for the series against South Africa were the lowest since the war. The VCA, QCA and NSWCA lost money again. Was something the matter with cricket?

'Very Difficult People'

AUSTRALIAN CRICKET ADMINISTRATORS IN THE 1950S

Responsibility for answering this question fell on a cricket government little altered in structure, policy and personnel for fifty years. Administrators at state associations and on the Australian Board of Control for international cricket were almost exclusively from the professional classes, predominantly lawyers, doctors, accountants, public servants and businessmen.

Sydney's ruling presences were career public servant Syd Smith, a member of the association executive since 1907 and president from 1935 to 1966, and lawyer Aubrey Oxlade, a member since 1910 and four times chairman of the national board. South of the border were Collins Street surgeon Allen Robertson, thrice board chairman, and hotel broker Bill Dowling, a VCA delegate for twenty-one years and board chairman between 1957 and 1960. Tasmanian Harold Bushby and the Queenslanders Jack Hutcheon and Roger Hartigan were lawyers, South Australian Roy Middleton a former manager at Trustees & Agency Co. Many were Masons, with an especially strong NSWCA clique including Smith, Oxlade, Syd Webb, Ewart Macmillan and Harry Heydon.

Some, notably Dowling, were personable and fair. Others were not. Smith, a short, officious man who abstained from tobacco and alcohol, and Oxlade, a cooler figure with a taste for whisky and cigarettes, were both renowed for their intransigence. Reminiscing about his time as a

Sydney Cricket Ground trustee, former governor-general Sir William McKell said: 'Oxlade wasn't a bad sort of fellow, but he was an impossible man to deal with. He was always with (Syd) Smith and Smith was a difficult man, very difficult—one-eyed and very hard. Oxlade and Smith—they were very difficult people.'

Nowhere was the distinction between high-caste administrators and members and the lower ranks of players and public better seen than in Brisbane. The Gabba Members' Stand was separated from the hoi polloi by a concrete wall topped with broken bottles, from the tin-roofed public grandstand by barbed wire, and was ruled by Hutcheon and secretary Ted Williams with patrician authority. As Jack Fingleton noted: 'One quickly senses with all the social flapdoodle in the local newspapers that a Test here is regarded by many as a grand social occasion. On all sides are cocktail parties. In no other cricketing city I know does "society" attach itself so closely to cricket as in Brisbane.' It was a 'society' that took itself seriously. Brisbane's standard middle-class summer rig of collar, tie, shorts and long socks did not pass muster in the Gabba Members', and dress-code infringements were punishable by expulsion.

Beyond the members' precincts, the ground was spartan. Provisions for player comfort were rudimentary: dressing-room furniture consisted of a trestle table for kits and a dozen six-inch nails in the walls for clothing. Sam Loxton recalls the preparation of player luncheons: 'Just before we went out, this little chap'd come in and sweep everything off the table, unroll a big sheet of butcher's paper—which I guess was a table cloth—and put down twelve plates. On each plate he'd stand a leaf of lettuce and lay a piece of corned beef, then throw a mosquito net over the top of it all.'

Hutcheon–Williams etiquette was strict. In his early Sheffield Shield days, for example, Ken Mackay was reproached for the vigour of his chewing whilst batting. He recalled:

> Some august officials in the Members' Stand at the Gabba had noticed my chewing—they could hardly fail to—and so the tip was passed to me privately to make my—I believe the word used was masticating—less obvious. This was apparently such a delicate subject that a high official had been told to take me aside and administer the rebuke. After all the other cricket controls in force at the time, to be ordered to control one's chewing was just about the end.

There's little doubting the diligence and devotion to cricket that these elderly, amateur administrators brought to their roles. Oxlade was a diabetic, and arrived early for all meetings to self-administer insulin. Dowling had an enlarged heart, which often debilitated him. Especially hard-working were the board's secretaries, on whom executive duties devolved almost entirely: SACA's Bill Jeanes, former town clerk of Woodville and Glenelg, who served from 1927 to 1954, followed by former bank officers Jack Ledward of Victoria and Alan Barnes of New South Wales.

But there's equally little doubt that many administrators viewed cricket as an avenue to social advancement, and held onto their posts too long. Many actually died in office or shortly after it: SACA president Harry Blinman in July 1950, VCA secretary Harry Brereton in December 1950, Oxlade in September 1955, Jeanes three years later. Smith was eighty-six by the time he reluctantly retired.

That they were able to hold power so long was a function of their electoral systems. Administrators were elected first by their district or grade clubs. Once delegates to their state association, they might then be nominated to represent it on the board or the Interstate Conference (which ran the Sheffield Shield).

Superficially, this was a fair system, encouraging government by the game's grass roots. In reality, it had grave problems. As clubs invariably promoted hard-working clubmen, authorities seldom heard from anyone with recent practical experience of Test and first-class cricket. A classic case was Lindsay Hassett, who nominated for election as South Melbourne delegate to the VCA, but was defeated in the ballot on 23 December 1953 by a man called Tom Pye. Though Hassett became a much loved commentator instead, his canny cricket brain might have been even better employed in the management of the game.

The myriad interests represented also meant that change was glacial. Barry Gibbs, one of very few young administrators when he became QCA secretary at twenty-seven in January 1961, vividly recalls its byzantine structure: 'There were twenty members of the executive committee, eighty-four delegates and three full-time staff. It was basically unworkable. And because you had to get a majority of 75 per cent of the delegates on all matters of constitution, it was a nightmare getting anything done.'

THE DON

The exception to the rule, of course, was Sir Donald Bradman, who'd been elected a South Australian delegate to the board just after the war.

Stockbroker and Mason, Bradman was cut from the same social cloth as his administrative fellows. But in the shrewdness and acuity with which he approached his task, Bradman was in a class of his own. He quickly turned the SACA from one of the more backward state associations into one of the best, continued to wield a persuasive pen in Australian and English newspapers, and from 1954 to 1967 formed with Jack Ryder and Dudley Seddon a national selection triumvirate rarely equalled in wisdom. ABC radio commentator Michael Charlton recalls:

> Commentating at the SCG always used to be a very intimidating experience because the box used to be directly behind the bowler's arm, and Bradman, Seddon and Ryder would come and sit just in front of us and watch the course of play. And if you said anything out of place or debatable, you'd see Bradman's head toss slightly. It was very exacting to commentate on cricket from the same perspective as Donald Bradman, I can tell you.

Bradman in the 1950s was not quite the object of reverence he later became. Englishman Alan Ross observed in 1955 that Bradman was 'still an equivocal object of love-hate to many Australians' and 'regarded by his own contemporaries with something less than idolatry'. On a personal level, the Don also remained a man apart, occasionally insensitive in dealings with others. Ken Archer recalls feeling quite pleased with himself after battling through the first session of his Test debut in December 1950 until Bradman buttonholed him. 'What are you saying to yourself as they come in to bowl?' Bradman asked.

'I suppose I'm saying: "You're not going to get me out,"' Archer replied.

'Wrong wrong wrong,' Bradman stated. 'Alec [Bedser] gave you two half volleys that session and you pushed them both back. You know what I used to say as the bowler came in? No matter who it was, I'd tell myself: "Where can I best hit this for four?"'

Archer responded meekly: 'Well Don, I don't think I'm as good as you.' And after lunch he was out essaying an extravagant drive. 'I suppose I was still thinking about what Don had said,' he recalls.

Nor did Bradman develop a sense of humour about himself. Archer also recalls, as captain of Queensland, lunching next to Bradman during an Adelaide Oval Shield match. After listening as the Don explained how he'd lost his local golf club championship by three-putting the 17th, Archer said jovially: 'That's always been your problem, Don. No big match temperament!' Bradman sat in silence for the rest of the lunch and didn't speak to Archer for the rest of the match.

But Bradman enjoyed greater respect and faith than all his fellow administrators put together, and his questing intelligence was widely admired, even by the prime minister. Menzies said:

> He happens to have been a highly intelligent man in anybody's language. He seldom ever discussed cricket with me. Why should he? You know you don't discuss cricket with the incompetent. But he used to discuss with me international finance, the economic movements in the country, and I used to say to myself: 'If I was satisfied that I knew more about these things than Don I would be rather proud. In fact, I might almost be kept as Prime Minister.'

THE BOARD V SID BARNES

Bradman, however, was but one man in thirteen board members. For the most part, it carried out its duties with chill formality. At one of his first meetings as secretary, Jack Ledward was asked a question. When he began his reply with 'I think…', another member retorted caustically: 'You are not here to tell us what you think, Mr Secretary, but to give us facts.' Embarrassed silence was finally broken by Syd Webb of NSW, who said: 'Mr Chairman, I move that the secretary be heard.'

The board certainly took little interest in the welfare of players at their beck. Many stories from the period tell the same tale. When West Australian John Rutherford became the first born-and-bred West Australian selected for his country in 1956, for instance, he not surprisingly expected to join the Ashes team for its preliminary matches in Hobart.

When Rutherford arrived at the team hotel in Launceston, however, board chairman Frank Cush took one look at him and said: 'You're not meant to be here, Rutherford. We're picking you up in Perth. Can you go back?'

Rutherford stood his ground. 'I'm part of the Australian XI,' he replied. 'And I'm staying.'

'But you can't,' Cush said. 'The hotel is booked out.'

Fortunately for Rutherford, Neil Harvey overheard the conversation. 'It's OK John,' he said. 'You can come in with me and [Len] Maddocks. We'll order another bed.'

Nowadays, such strained relations between players and administrators would be recognised as a tinder-box. And there *was* one celebrated insurrection that caused the board acute embarrassment: the case of Sid Barnes.

Next to the Don, Barnes was Australia's most destructive postwar batsman. Having appeared in Test cricket in 1938 as a stylist, he had re-emerged in 1946 as a scientist, bent on banishing risk from batting. Though he had mastery of every stroke, he observed maxims of self-preservation like: 'No runs in front of the wicket until 40.' It worked: since the war, he'd collected 1000 runs in a dozen Tests.

Barnes was also, however, a wilful character who chased a pound as hard as he chased runs. On the 1948 tour, he carried on a flourishing business selling hard-to-get luxuries to war-starved Britons. When there was talk of Bradman scoring 1000 runs in May, he complained: 'They never mention me and I've made 1000 quid in May.' And, on returning from that trip, Barnes stood out of Test cricket on the grounds that he could not afford it. He declined to tour South Africa in order to run his fleet of cabs and start a building business, and chose to write about the 1950–51 Ashes series rather than participate. His outspoken *Daily Telegraph* column was called 'Like It Or Lump It'. It might have been Barnes' motto.

Colleagues were divided in their opinions of him. Jack Moroney remembers:

> On my first state trip, we'd hardly got to Strathfield when Sid opens his bag and pulls out all these Viyella shirts and offers them round all the new-comers in the side. They were 25s, which was pretty expensive, but they all looked brand new, so I bought one. Anyway, the second time my wife washed it, the collar came off. Old Sid, he'd put one of his old shirts in the box and sold it as new.

When a rugby colleague, Ray Stehr, arranged for Alan Walker to play with Rawtenstall in the Lancashire League, Walker decided to run the contract past Barnes. When Walker arrived in England, he found that Barnes had unsuccessfully offered his own services to the club for less.

Barnes could also, however, be kind and generous. When Bill Alley suffered a terrible series of misfortunes in 1945—his wife, mother and mother-in-law died within six months—Barnes helped cover the funeral expenses. And as Barnes returned to NSW colours in October 1951, he was patently a class above his competitors.

When selectors Bradman, Dwyer and Ryder chose Barnes for the Third Test against West Indies at an Adelaide meeting on 11 December 1951, however, the board for the first time in its history exercised its prerogative to veto a selection. While chairman Oxlade, Cush and Bradman opposed the motion, the ten other delegates voted against Barnes' inclusion. They even prevented the discussion being minuted, Queenslanders Hartigan and Hutcheon successfully moving that 'approval of selections of Australian teams shall be dealt with upon a confidential basis'.

Pressmen awaiting the team's announcement had instead another story: selection of an unnamed player had been annulled for 'reasons other than cricket ability', and that anonymous figure was almost certainly Barnes. As the *Sydney Morning Herald* editorialised: 'If the board thinks its decisions are beyond question it is due for disillusionment. This secretive and even furtive method of damning a player deserves strong censure. A very serious reproach has been laid upon Barnes. He has been condemned not only unheard but without knowledge of the complaint against him.'

Oxlade saw Barnes a few days later in Stan McCabe's sports store at Cricket House and, having commended him for a century against Victoria, apologised for 'this nasty business' and the 'scandalous thing that has occurred'. But when Barnes sought further information from the NSWCA, a three-hour meeting in committee on 21 January 1952 did nothing. Though vice-presidents Ted Adams and 'Doc' Evatt moved that the association 'reaffirm its confidence in him as a fit and proper person to represent NSW and Australia', Oxlade persuaded other delegates that Barnes' queries should really be directed to the board.

'I was,' wrote Barnes, 'apparently banned for life—with no hope of being told what crime if any I had committed.'

Barnes v the Board

Barnes passed the summer in purdah, writing fruitlessly to each board member, and eventually retaining the noted silk Jack Shand to compose a 21 February press release that pleaded with administrators to clear his name. 'I fear that unless the position is immediately cleared up it may affect myself and also the future of my children,' Barnes said.

Just as his resolve was failing, however, Barnes was unexpectedly offered an opportunity to retaliate. A letter appeared in Sydney's *Daily Mirror* on 24 April signed by a Jacob Raith of Stanmore, a master baker and past president of Petersham Cricket Club. It stated inter alia:

> The board is an impartial body of cricket administrators made up of men who have given outstanding service to the game. It must be abundantly clear to all that they would not have excluded Mr Barnes from an Australian XI capriciously and only for some matter of a sufficiently serious nature. In declining to meet his request to publish reasons, the board may well be acting kindly toward him.

Barnes sued Raith for libel. But, when the case began in Sydney District Court on 21 August 1952, it was effectively the board in the dock. Shand successfully characterised board members as a cloistered and unaccountable elite. Keith Johnson, manager of the 1948 tour and a NSW delegate to the board who had vetoed Barnes' selection, was forced to concede that he had given that team, without exception, a glowing report for its behaviour in England. The few objections he could now cite seemed pettifogging, even vindictive. Justice Alan Lloyd nodded appreciatively when 'Chappie' Dwyer testified: 'I have a high opinion of him [Barnes] as a cricketer and no objection to him as a man.'

Raith's counsel John Smyth, QC, apologised abjectly: 'By the plea of truth and public benefit it was my duty to indicate that Barnes had not been excluded capriciously. Seldom in the history of libel actions has such a plea failed so completely and utterly.' The case was settled out of court by Raith's apology. 'VINDICATED,' thundered the *Daily Mirror* poster of Friday, 22 August 1952.

THE BOARD V ITSELF

Recriminations followed. At the board's meeting on 18 September, Oxlade was told that he would not be supported for re-election. SACA president Roy Middleton replaced him. When votes were then cast for the national selection panel, 'Chappie' Dwyer was unexpectedly defeated by QCA nominee Bill Brown. The NSWCA was infuriated by the inference that it was being punished for supporting Barnes and, after its own 30 September meeting, came out swinging. 'We want no more stiletto in the back,' said Syd Webb. 'Australian cricket needs a Board of Control, but not this Board of Control. It is diseased.'

Against the will of Syd Smith—who proclaimed himself 'constitutional to the backbone'—Webb and Frank Cush pushed for a 'reform' of the board that concentrated power in NSW and Victoria. Pointing out that seven in ten Australian Test players had come from those states, they proposed a plan under which other states should be prohibited from nominating chairmen and from outvoting NSW and Victoria when those states' delegates were unanimous. The word 'secession' was used freely, if not wildly.

Not surprisingly, the VCA disagreed. After its 13 October meeting, VCA president Arnold Seitz informed the NSWCA by letter that 'any change to the set-up of the Board should be along constitutional lines'. The NSWCA had to take its setbacks on the chin.

Sid Barnes doubtless enjoyed the spectacle. But, within six weeks, he had squandered much of the goodwill he'd accumulated. A week after scoring 152 for NSW against Victoria but failing to make the Test team, he volunteered to act as twelfth man at Adelaide Oval. Act he did, to the extent of emerging at 5pm on 29 November in a double-breasted suit accompanied by a steward with two jugs of squash, a box of cigars, a wireless, clothes brush, comb and mirror.

The 9155 spectators initially thought the gesture uproarious. But, when Barnes' impedimenta prolonged the break to eight minutes, the atmosphere soured. Specially unimpressed was South Australia's captain, Phil Ridings, one of the selectors who'd just overlooked Barnes, and who suspected the prank was for his benefit. 'It was a boiling hot day and I was dying of thirst,' he recalls. 'But I wasn't going to accept a drink from him.' Barnes exited, booing in his wake.

The SACA's Middleton wrote tersely to the NSWCA that 'in compliance with its duty to the game' it had no alternative but to 'ask that all possible steps be taken to guard against a recurrence of such embarrassing behaviour on the field of first-class cricket'. The NSWCA met three weeks later, questioning captain Keith Miller about the incident, and asking Barnes to express regret.

Barnes was evasive, declining to make a written statement until the NSWCA did so, and forcing the association to despatch its own letter of apology to the SACA. But Barnes knew that his card was marked. A few months later he turned up on the doorstep of young NSW all-rounder Alan Davidson, just selected for the forthcoming Ashes tour, to offer his cricket trunk. Barnes didn't feel he'd need it any more.

And far from saving cricket, as he put it, 'from the hands of the autocratic few, drunk with power and self-importance', the Barnes case left few ripples. Barnes was simply too singular a character for his battle with the board to become a watershed in player–administrator relations. As Richie Benaud observed: 'Those were the days when you spoke with a touch of reverence and a certain amount of humility to cricket officials in their navy blue suits, white shirts and strong leather shoes. Jack might have been as good as his mate in the outback of Australia in the 1800s but it took a while for the idea to permeate through to the various state associations and the Australian Cricket Board.'

Stagnating cricket crowds in the early 1950s caught administrators unprepared. Essentially, the finances of Australian cricket depended on big Ashes summers to subsidise tours by other countries and the Sheffield Shield. So when the 1950–51 summer was only a qualified success, there was little left to underwrite the visits by the West Indies and South Africa, and a domestic cricket scene whose support seemed to be atrophying (178,000 attended Shield matches in 1951–52, compared to almost 300,000 in 1949–50 and the Shield's 1927–28 peak of 430,000). Bottom line impact was immediately measurable: from 1951 to 1953, the VCA and NSWCA aggregated losses of £12,543.

Administrators accustomed to the Bradman boom had seen nothing like this. Various theories were advanced for cricket's decline, the most popular being Australia's Davis Cup successes. Contrasts were drawn between the robust organisational skills of the Lawn Tennis Association of Australia, and cricket's administrative adhocracy. Jack Fingleton complained: 'Tennis in postwar years has cut the ground from beneath cricket, and that is mainly because of its vigorous organisation. It is fostered in every nook and corner in Australia and is geared so that lads while still in their teens can rise to the very top.' And certainly, while Australian cricket was losing money in the early 1950s, tennis was prospering. In four Davis Cup finals from 1951 to 1954, the LTAA made profits of almost £100,000.

It wasn't a problem Australia faced alone. Having aggregated attendances in excess of 2.1 million immediately after the war, English cricket crowds were in unremitting decline. *Wisden* editor Norman Preston summarised in 1952: 'Cricket, and not just English cricket, needs an injection of culture and enterprise.' The cause would be taken up in both countries under the banner of 'brighter cricket'.

Though 'brighter cricket' was earnestly debated from England's *Cricketer* magazine to ABC Radio's *National Forum of the Air*, definition was elusive. Minutes of the Board of Control's March 1952 meeting refer to a need to 'combat negative cricket', those of the Interstate Conference's September 1952 meeting to the necessity to 'brighten the game', but little more. Bradman proposed one practical measure—that of discouraging padplay by altering the lbw rule to allow for dismissal to a ball turning either way—but it was kiboshed by the NSWCA, the VCA and the QCA.

In England, there were innovations like the *News Chronicle* 'Brighter Cricket Table' which from 1952 tabulated such figures as scoring rates and sixes hit in county cricket. In Australia, though, 'brighter cricket' remained largely talk. The SACA convened a seminar in August 1952 with speakers including Victor Richardson, Clarrie Grimmett and Len Darling. The QCA commissioned 'Negative Cricket Reports' from five past and present players including Ray Lindwall. The NSWCA institut-ed a plan conceived by Frank Cush aimed at improving school and country cricket and effecting 'closer cooperation with representatives of the press'. But the only tangible outcomes at first-class level were econ-omy measures, like the halving of the 1954–55 Sheffield Shield season.* As Bill O'Reilly put it in the *Sydney Morning Herald*: 'Perhaps they [administrators] have realised at last that they have done as much damage as the game can stand [and] have asked their manual labourers to "use their own initiative and clean up the mess".'

In some respects, alarm was well-founded. Some turgid, attritional cricket was being played with over rates to match. In 1936–37, Gubby Allen's Englishmen had scampered through 73 eight-ball overs a day. Three Australian tours later, Len Hutton condoned a daily rate of about 55 overs, sedulously husbanding the energies of his pace attack.

Essentially, however, all moves missed the point: the Australian game had been spoiled by bumper profits in the Bradman years, achieved first in a time of economic hardship, then in one of ravenous postwar hunger for sporting triumph. Now there was no Bradman, a general satiety with success reflected in the support for Australia's opponents, and the fact that people had far more on which to spend their rising wages.

For suddenly there were alternatives to the Australian sporting staples of cricket, racing, golf, and the various football codes. Tennis, always extremely popular as a social sport, had suddenly boomed: thousands flocked to see the Davis Cup when it was displayed after Australia's October 1950 victory. Sydney had no squash courts in 1951: ten years later, there were ninety. Interest in motor sports surged after the first Redex Reliability Trial in August 1953 and Jack Brabham's victory in the 1955 Australian Grand Prix at Southport. The late 1950s saw a boom in skiing, resulting in the opening of what was the world's longest chairlift at Mt Kosciusko. In January 1961, Ampol offered a record £30,000 prize

---

* The 1954–55 program, with just nine matches, was a disastrous experiment. Because of rain, Perth saw just two days of first-class cricket for the summer. The trial was never repeated. Future truncations of the Shield schedule, like the NSWCA's September 1957 suggestion that matches be shortened to three days, were resisted.

money for a fishing contest at Tuggerah Lakes, NSW, and flushed out more than 9000 competitors.

Other forms of entertainment were also launched into a more affluent age. The Union Theatre Repertory Company (forerunner to the Melbourne Theatre Company) staged its first production in August 1953. The Australian Elizabethan Theatre Trust was endowed after the royal visit the following year. 1956 brought drive-ins, poker machines and, of course, television. Ice-skating rinks popped up, ten-pin bowling alleys, then in October 1960 the prototype of the modern shopping centre: the £6 million Myer Chadstone, with its 860-foot mall. Citizens, too, were suddenly mobile enough to enjoy these new attractions. In the decade after the war, the number of cars on Australian roads more than doubled to 1.7 million. As intra-Australian tourism burgeoned, domestic air passenger volumes quadrupled between 1950 and 1970. In retrospect, it's a wonder cricket held its appeal so well.

Indeed, the 'brighter cricket' movement now seems a thinly veiled attempt to shift the blame onto players for the effects of quite explicable social changes. For players did cop it. Although NSW won the 1951–52 Sheffield Shield, for instance, Arthur Morris was replaced as captain on 13 October 1952 by Keith Miller, ostensibly because of the latter's more vibrant image.

In keeping with the times, Morris heard of his replacement second-hand: in Hong Kong, where he was engaged in a twelve-day preseason tour organised by Jack Chegwyn to mark the centenary of the local cricket league. 'Of all people, it was a Chinese journalist who told me,' he recalls. 'I guess they wanted someone more flamboyant, but it wasn't very pleasant at the time. Administrators didn't tell you anything in those days.'

TAKING OFF

If 1950s cricket may by now seem like a century ago in the amateur outlook of players and the conservative gerontocracy of its management, it couldn't resist progress altogether. The 1950–51 summer, for instance, was the first in which all internal travel by the touring team was undertaken by air, shortening the visit by about a fortnight.

The development was not universally welcomed. England's Freddie Brown expressed reservations: 'I have nothing against flying. But a team might suffer from strain if it has to do too much. Many people take forty-eight hours to get over the effects of a long flight.'

Brown was understanding when leg-spinner Eric Hollies decided that he did not wish to fly at all, allowing him to travel terrestrially with scorer Bill Ferguson, and rejected such helter-skelter on his own homeward journey to England. While his team returned to London from the New Zealand epilogue of their tour by Pan Am and BOAC, Brown returned independently through Melbourne, staying with Victoria's gubernatorial couple Sir Dallas and Lady Brooks. He then flew to Perth to pick up the *Orontes* bound for Marseilles, and toured Europe overland before arriving in London in May.

The ocean liner remained as yet unchallenged for global travel. An Australian cricket team would not fly to and from a tour until 1959, and not to and from an Ashes tour for a further nine years. But authorities had been awakened to the potential of air transport: where Hammond's 1946–47 team had taken 163 days to traverse Australia, Brown's took 142, with commensurate reduction in cost.

The postwar years also saw a vast increase in the print media's coverage of cricket, especially Ashes tours. Where prewar cricket trips had been covered by no more than a handful of visiting reporters, there were abruptly scores of pressmen demanding good seats, press conferences and decent facilities.

Some newspapers fielded whole gangs. Frank Packer's *Daily Telegraph* threw no fewer than seven writers at the 1954–55 Ashes series: Dick Whitington, Arthur Mailey, Sid Barnes, Freddie Brown, Lindsay Hassett, Phil Tresidder and Englishwoman Margaret Hughes. 'Sir Frank loved hiring writers,' says Tresidder. 'He always wanted the best. I'm not sure we needed all of them, but he liked getting the better of the *Sydney Morning Herald*.'

In press boxes of prewar specifications, tempers could fray. There were frequent accusations that journalists were cribbing neighbours' copy and, with such volatile characters as Lyn Wellings of London's *Evening News* and Jim Mathers of Sydney's *Mirror*, the odd punch was thrown.

The surge caught administrators largely unawares. In February 1955, the SACA informed brother associations of a staggering statistic: no fewer than sixty-two journalists had partaken of a free lunch offered during the first MCC tour match there, and 120 had done the same during the Test. The other associations replied gloomily that the SACA had escaped lightly.

The summer of 1950–51 also set a vital principle in the broadcasting of Australian sport. A quarter-century after cricket had first been carried on radio, the transmitter paid for the privilege.

Cricket had been integral to radio's development in Australia, and a strong symbiosis had developed. Radio used cricket to broaden its spread (by 1949, nine in ten Australian households owned a wireless); cricket exploited radio for free publicity.

Cricket had a particular hold on the Australian Broadcasting Commission. Its managing director Sir Charles Moses had conceived the original synthetic Test broadcasts from England in the 1930s, and on-air personalities like Victor Richardson, Arthur Gilligan, Alan McGilvray and Michael Charlton were as popular as the characters of 'Dad and Dave' and 'Blue Hills'.

During summer, up to thirty hours of ABC weekly programming was devoted to cricket. Even when the commission decided in 1948 that it carried too much sport, cricket was never threatened. Most savings over the next few years came at the expense of horse-racing: a pursuit which chairman Sir Richard Boyer, a former Methodist minister, disliked. In appreciation of such unswerving support, the ABC was never charged more than a nominal seasonal fee by state cricket associations. And this figure—usually a few hundred pounds—was invariably defined as payment for ground facilities rather than for the right to broadcast.

While the NSWCA was content with this arrangement, the VCA decided in 1949–50 to demand the payment of a rights fee. The staunchest advocate was delegate Ernest Yeomans, who contended that sporting fixtures were akin to theatrical or musical events, and that artists in the latter were always paid for their services. When the ABC refused, there were no broadcasts of Sheffield Shield matches from the MCG for the season. In its 1949–50 annual report, the VCA commented: 'The Association will…not allow itself to be robbed of one of its legitimate forms of revenue—payment for the use of its fixtures for the benefit of the listening public.'

In March 1950, VCA delegates took the crusade to the board. And when the national broadcaster opened annual discussions with the Interstate Conference on behalf of all sportscasting stations five months later, it was alarmed by the administrators' intransigence.

An impasse developed. The VCA held its ground on the basis that pay-ment was 'necessary to compensate for decreased attendances, as listeners do not contribute to cricket's finances'. The ABC protested that their broadcasts had developed great goodwill for Australian cricket, and that the 'cost per day was far greater than broadcasting any other sport'. Moses himself wrote bitterly to prime minister Menzies:

> The thing is this: We feel, and the broadcasting stations feel, that it is quite wrong to be asked to publicise a sport; it has been shown that the broadcasting has had quite a pronounced effect and has actually helped increase the number of supporters. We actually publicise the game and it seems wrong that we should have to PAY TO PUBLICISE IT. This is recognised by the NSWCA and also by the WA group. The rest are just ganging up on us.

Menzies' minister for posts and telegraphs, Hubert Anthony, finally ended the stand-off by convening a meeting of disputants on 25 September 1950. It was deemed that standard fees would be payable to the association hosting each fixture: £450 for Tests, £125 for tour matches, £100 for Sheffield Shield matches.

The ABC was peeved: the payments more than doubled its annual expenditure on cricket broadcasting. It was further displeased that the commercial stations had decided amongst themselves to pay no more than 45 per cent of the fees. But the broadcasts again attracted huge audiences. The Gabba Test of December 1950 was even carried over the public address system at Brisbane Gaol, the prisons comptroller evidently believing in cricket's efficacy as a means of reform.

The VCA crowed about the victory in its 1950–51 annual report: 'It is very pleasing to report that in the "Battle of Broadcasting", common-sense and fair play eventually prevailed.' It had, in fact, established a fundamental tenet of sport: that events were a valuable broadcasting commodity. When Kerry Packer called on the board twenty-five years later, of course, administrators discovered that this was a double-edged sword.

PRIME MINISTER AND PATRON

If administrators were anxious about an apparent ebb tide in their game, there was one source on whom they could rely for constant support and considerable prestige. If communism was prime minister Robert Menzies' greatest public concern, cricket was seldom far from his private thoughts.

Menzies' lifetime of cricket patronage began as soon as he entered public life. He joined the Melbourne Cricket Club on 25 October 1919, a year after being called as a barrister. And upon joining Victoria's

Legislative Council in 1928, Menzies KC became a regular turn at its Test match dinners, addressing farewell banquets for the 1930, 1934 and 1938 Ashes touring parties.

Why was Menzies so besotted with cricket? Certainly, with his unflinching faith in British institutions, he enjoyed the game's pageantry and tradition. While addressing Westminster Hall with Stanley Baldwin was the highlight of Menzies' first visit to the United Kingdom in 1935, forming the same double act for the touring Australians at Lord's three years later felt almost as exhilarating. He told his brother Frank that: 'I have now completed an admirable double, speaking with Baldwin on high matters of state in Westminster Hall, and speaking with him on cricket in the almost equally sacred precincts of Lord's.'

At Lord's he struck up life-long friendships with those dual pillars of the Marylebone Cricket Club, the former captains of England Sir Pelham Warner and Gubby Allen. Indeed, it was in Allen in 1936 that Joseph Lyons confided his percipient forecast of Menzies' political future: 'He has the best brain in Australia and I am determined he shall succeed me. But he has got a dangerous tongue and the first time he won't last long. I believe he'll come back and become one of Australia's greatest prime ministers.'

But Menzies' affection for cricket was not simply an avenue to hob-nobbing with the game's grandees. The game's aesthetics absorbed him. Alongside a Tom Roberts painting in his office at Parliament House hung a famous photograph of Keith Miller, in appreciation of which he wrote: 'Cricket has this command over people like me, not because it produces statistics (heaven knows I see enough of those everyday) but because it produces a million things of beauty for the eye.'* Menzies' driver Alf Stafford recalls acting as a messenger for scores during Cabinet meetings, and driving Menzies to Manuka Oval to watch weekend club games where they would sit quietly swapping reminiscences.

The prime minister also relished the society of cricketers: 'They are, in Dr Johnson's words, the most clubbable of people, full of anecdote and, almost always, of genial goodwill…they have no snobbery.' Menzies succeeded the late Lord Somers as VCA patron in 1944, holding the first of many celebratory dinners at Melbourne's Australia Hotel for the team which won the 1945–46 Sheffield Shield. He entertained Walter

---

* The photograph of Keith Miller square-cutting—one of cricket's most enduring images—was taken in November 1950 by Ross Freeman of Sydney's *Daily Telegraph*.

Hammond's touring Englishmen the following season, greeting the guests with place cards personalised by apposite lines of Shakespeare. Hammond found in his seat the words from *Hamlet* ('We go to gain a little patch of ground/That hath in it no profit but the name'), the umpires a citation from *Julius Caesar* ('With an angry wafture of your hand/Give sign for me to leave you').

MENZIES AND 'THE DOC'

Menzies was by no means alone in his fondness for cricket at Parliament House. In his Cabinet, social services minister Athol Townley could handle a bat, immigration minister Harold Holt bowled passable leg spin, and deputy clerk of the Senate Ian Emerton was president of the Australian Capital Territory Cricket Association.

Opposition leader Ben Chifley played in his boyhood at Bathurst and prevailed on siblings to sleep in a tent in the backyard so that they could convert their room into a gallery of sporting illustrations from the *Referee*. Former immigration minister Arthur Calwell—trustee of the Melbourne Cricket Ground from 1931 and chairman of trustees from 1953—never missed a Test summer. And Chifley's successor 'Doc' Evatt was an encyclopedia of cricket facts who served from 1929 to 1951 as patron and vice-patron of the Balmain club, and vice-president of the NSWCA from 1935 to 1955.

Evatt as cricket lover affords an interesting contrast to Menzies. Like Menzies, he was seriously infatuated with the game. As a boy, according to biographer Kylie Tennant, he slept with a bat given him by his father, and carried a small scar on his cheek from a rising delivery that had broken his spectacles. Like Menzies, he was a generous patron to players like Archie Jackson, Bill Hunt and Arthur Morris.

Each, though, was dismissive of the other's critical pretensions. Jack Fingleton, Test cricketer turned gallery correspondent, remembered: 'I had to be diplomatic to steer my course between him [Menzies] and the Doc on cricket. Each was jealous of the other and would say to me: "Of course, he doesn't know anything about the game. All theory."'

And where Menzies was content with his lot as a connoisseur, Evatt's lack of cricketing ability appeared to rankle with him. Captain of Fort Street Boys' High School but captain only of its Second XI, Evatt once exerted his authority by overthrowing the First XI's skipper and leading the side himself. He was duly criticised by an anonymous contributor to the *Fortian* for ignorance of his players' abilities and unwarranted assumption of leadership. He subsequently gave many cricketers the impression that he would have loved above all to play the game well. A witness at Lord's in 1926 to Warren Bardsley's unbeaten 193, the young lawyer Evatt went to congratulate the player.

'I'd swap it for one of your degrees,' said Bardsley.

'Well, give me the 93,' said Evatt. 'You keep the 100 and the not out and you can have any of the degrees I've got.'

Biographer Peter Crockett also believes that Evatt was drawn to cricketers because he admired in them 'an ease and naturalness...which he lacked'. Evatt, for instance, esteemed Bill O'Reilly's ability to engage an audience, and sought unsuccessfully to coax him into politics.

Menzies, by contrast, took lack of ability in his stride. His long-time private secretary John Bunting wrote: 'For Menzies, cricket was holiday. It was equally a holiday to be with him. Any match at all would do.' And, as the political fortunes of Menzies and Evatt diverged throughout the 1950s, the ways they expressed their affection for cricket seemed increasingly to reflect their characters.

The PM's XI

As his premiership unfolded, Menzies became Australian cricket's leading benefactor and a semi-official patron of the Australian team. Hassett was a special favourite, and the correspondence between national leader and national cricket captain shows an obvious mutual regard. When Menzies' first grandson was born in October 1951, for instance, the prime minister was moved to receive an autographed bat. He wrote back: 'I shall guard it jealously until Alexander Robert is a bit older. Perhaps you will see through this flimsy excuse of mine and realise that I just don't want to give it up!'

Menzies even tore himself away from the hugely popular royal tour on 28 February 1954—interrupting a day at the races with the Duke of Edinburgh and Sir Dallas Brooks—to present Hassett with a testimonial cheque for £5503 during the tea interval of a district match. 'Today is a remarkable day for me,' he said. 'Not only have I come to South Melbourne without being counted out, rather I am welcomed.'

Hassett replied: 'For me too this has been a remarkable day. Three extraordinary things have happened. I have been given £5000, the prime minister has been to the races, and a few moments ago I clean-bowled a batsman. It must be fifteen or sixteen years since I last did that, and I sincerely congratulate the batsman on his feat.'

Menzies' most visible contribution to Australian cricket, however, was the prime minister's match which he inaugurated after his successful April 1951 re-election campaign. It resulted from a chance meeting in the parliamentary library with Ian Emerton, who expressed disappointment that the board had overlooked Canberra as a venue for the forthcoming West Indies tour. Menzies wondered aloud about a match organised under his aegis and, having assured Oxlade that he would personally guarantee all expenses and donate any profits to Legacy, selected a choice XI composed of six current or former internationals (captain Fingleton, Hassett, Johnson, Loxton, Bill O'Reilly and New Zealander Martin Donnelly), three locals and two politicians (Athol Townley and Tasmanian Bill Falkinder).

A crowd of 2300 attended, including 600 children and NSW governor Sir John Northcott. In a dinner at the Lodge the prime minister extemporised for a full hour on cricket and cricketers, concluding: 'The world is for the people who play cricket and those who laugh. Perhaps the future of the world will depend on whether these people are in the majority.'

And, while the game had originally been conceived as a one-off, Menzies wrote to Fingleton on 27 October 1951: 'The more I think of the game we had at Canberra with the West Indies last week the more I am convinced we should repeat such actions. I do think the social side helps to keep the spirit of friendship alive and acts as a good counter to the serious business of Test matches.' So it proved. A further five were staged, Legacy receiving profits of $11,000.

Menzies was in his element on such occasions. He was a generous host: when England's Bob Appleyard mentioned casually in December 1954 how much he liked the local Rheingold, for instance, the prime minister shipped a case to his home in Bradford. Occasionally, he also dispensed a little fatherly advice. NSW batsman Brian Booth recalls Menzies advising him at the February 1961 match that he should ignore journalists and all such kibitzers: 'If I took notice of all the things that were shouted at me, I'd be in a mental hospital. You know what it takes to play at your level better than anyone. If the people shouting knew as much as you did, they'd be out there themselves.'

Those who played the games, Menzies regarded as 'his boys'. Some years after playing for the last PM's XI in December 1965, in fact, Victorian medium-pacer Alan Connolly visited Mercy Hospital to wish Menzies speedy convalescence from illness. He recalls: 'It wasn't easy getting in to see the former prime minister of Australia, I can tell you.

So I said to the nursing sister: "Tell him that one of his boys is here to see him." And I gave her the PM's XI tie. When she got back, she said: "Mr Menzies will see you now.'"

MENZIES AS ADMINISTRATOR

When Menzies entertained cricketers or staged a match, however, there was more to it than a politician indulging in a favoured pastime. Within a few years of his election, the prime minister was playing a part in Australian cricket's organisation, applying his belief that cricket was a 'powerful diplomatic contributor to international understanding and a widening tolerance'.

In January 1952, for instance, Menzies wrote to Bill Jeanes proposing a fixture against the Netherlands on Australia's next tour of England. He'd heard of the keen Dutch cricket scene from ambassador Alf Stirling and, as Canberra and the Hague had been at loggerheads over the status of Indonesia, advised: 'I believe that it would be a splendid thing for cricket in Holland and therefore a most useful gesture to a country that has occasionally in recent years had some reason to misunderstand us, if the Australian Board of Control would arrange for the next Australian team to England to go across to Holland to play a match or so.' A match was scheduled. Australia won by 157 runs.

In November 1952, in the unlikely setting of a Commonwealth Economic Conference dinner at London's Gray's Inn, Menzies was accosted by Jamaica's governor Sir Hugh Foot. Foot told him of the island's desperate keenness for a cricket visit in 1955—the 300th anniversary of British settlement—and that the West Indies Cricket Board of Control's representations to the Australian board had so far fallen on deaf ears. Menzies was receptive and, when Foot reiterated his plea by letter in February 1953, replied:

> At the outset I might say that in principle the proposal has my whole-hearted support. It is a move which could not do otherwise than advance the game in both our countries and I can see that there are obvious advantages from the West Indian point of view for having the tour in that particular year. I intend to discuss the proposal with the controlling cricket interests in Australia and I shall write to you again as soon as possible.

He forwarded a copy of Foot's letter to Jeanes, annotated: 'From the point of view of British–Commonwealth relations I think it would be a very sound move.'

Outside its time-honoured Ashes cycle, the board was loath to accept touring invitations. In addition to its filibustering of the WICBC, it had recently declined invitations to visit South Africa and New Zealand, and withheld blessing from a Commonwealth XI trip to India. But, faced with an informal prime ministerial fiat, it was ill-placed to refuse. It consented to tour in March–May 1955.

As the time for team selection neared, Menzies again took a hand, writing to Harold Holt requesting prompt processing of visas and passports; to Amos J. Peaslee of the US Pacific Fleet at Pearl Harbour seeking an expeditious passage through customs, as 'the lads will have very little time for sight-seeing'; and to his high commissioner in Canada, Sir Douglas Copland. 'I have had quite a hand in this tour taking place and so I want the boys to enjoy your section of the trip,' Menzies advised.

As the tour was in progress in May 1955, the prime minister received another courteous cricketing caller. India's high commissioner General Kodendra Cariappa brought with him a letter from the Board of Cricket Control in India soliciting an Australian tour while the team was in transit to England for the Ashes in 1956.

Menzies, this time, was more guarded. He wrote to Jeanes' successor Jack Ledward:

> You will at once see the international political advantages for Australia in building up goodwill in India; but you will also, of course, be familiar with other problems with which I am only dimly acquainted…Do make it clear to your Board that I am not seeking to make an impertinent intrusion on matters which are their affair and which they are much better qualified to deal with than I am. But the reasons I have indicated earlier, plus my own enthusiasm about the game, will, I hope, constitute a respectable excuse.

Menzies' external affairs minister, Richard Casey, also strongly advocated a tour, noting cricket's 'cult' status in India and the public relations success enjoyed in the country by Soviet hockey teams. And, in September 1955, although it had previously declined all Indian invitations, the board sanctioned a brief tour. It occurred a year later, as Menzies had recommended, after the Ashes expedition.

CRICKET AND DEMOCRACY

The idea of a sort of Pax Cricketana may now seem a quaint Menzian conceit. But, in the 1950s at least, he was by no means alone in his view. Even his nemesis Evatt shared it. In the last of three contributions to *Wisden Cricketers' Almanack* in 1949, Evatt wrote:

Looking back over the vista of 40 years of Test cricket, one is deeply impressed with the fact that cricket has no equal in its sustained contribution not only to the dignified leisure but to the happiness of our countrymen…It remains a perpetual source of deep enjoyment, of good fellowship and of sincere comradeship. It helps to strengthen the ties which bind all the people in the British Commonwealth of Nations.

In his 1951 autobiography *Three Straight Sticks*, former English captain Bob Wyatt extended the idea by positing that cricket and democracy were somehow of a kind: 'Both require patience, tolerance and understanding. Both are not as spectacular as many other forms of government or forms of games, and are only appreciated when their finer points are grasped.'

Menzies did not hold his view of cricket's diplomatic properties uncritically. He recollected vividly the way the 1932–33 Bodyline tour had strained Anglo-Australian relations and, in a letter to Bradman before the 1948 tour, opined that international sporting contests could do as much harm as good:

If they are to be seized upon as a vehicle for distortion, for stirring up sensation, for looking for trouble, and if necessary creating it, they can do almost as much to create international bitterness as any political factor. Indeed, they may do more, because far more people in Great Britain, for example, are interested in Anglo-Australian cricket than in the constitutional relations between the United Kingdom and Australia.

Where cricket and Commonwealth interests converged, however, Menzies was quick to recognise it.

'Homeward Bound'

AUSTRALIA V ENGLAND

1953

Welcome home, good captain Hassett!
Rich in runs, you'll give us pain
But we have one ancient asset
English grass—and English rain.

The speaker was former independent MP and *Punch* columnist Sir Alan Herbert, the occasion the British Sportsmen's Club luncheon of 14 April 1953 chaired by Lord Aberdare and the Earl of Athlone. Australia's twenty-first tour of England was under way.

'The pain is coming now,' responded Hassett, rising to his feet. 'The runs may follow later on.' Then, in typical fashion: 'It is the practice to introduce to the Club the members of the Australian team. I will do this and, as they stand and acknowledge the introduction, you will notice how closely their features follow the rather classical lines of their skipper's.' Laughter and applause filled the Pinafore Room of the Savoy Hotel.

'Welcome home, good captain Hassett'? The notion that an Australian arriving in England was 'going home' required no explanation in 1953. The emotional kinship between the two countries was still acute. Jack Fingleton, similarly, saw nothing contradictory about entitling the first chapter of his book on the tour 'Homeward Bound'.

Cricket tours reasserted such notions of interdependence. With Britain still in the grip of wartime privations, Don Bradman's 1948 tourists had brought with them 200 cases of victuals for presentation to the minister of food. And, for Hassett's 1953 band, the sense of pilgrimage was heightened by touring in the year of the Coronation of Queen Elizabeth II. The *Orcades* ferrying them from Sydney on 4 March had been crammed with hundreds more Australians heading north for the 2 June ceremony at Westminster Abbey. As Sir Alan Herbert put it: 'Here and there I hear a scoffer/But we know, Sweet Seventeen/You'll be eager, too, to offer/Something special for the Queen.'

Arriving at Tilbury on 13 April, the touring cricketers were quickly taken up in the march of pomp and circumstance. Training before BBC cameras at Alexandra Palace, they were introduced to Britons for the first time via television: unknown in Australia, but already reaching a British audience of eight million. A camera behind the net intimated the menace of Lindwall and Miller, England's bogeys five years earlier.

After the British Sportsmen's Club luncheon, there followed one with the Institute of Journalists at the Dorchester, the opening of Lord's Imperial Cricket Memorial Gallery orchestrated by the Duke of Edinburgh, cocktails with the Royal Empire Society at Hampton Court with guests including opposition leader Clement Attlee, golf at Burnham, visits to Wembley on successive Saturdays for the England–Scotland soccer international and the Huddersfield–St Helens rugby league final and the England–Scotland soccer international, an Anzac Day pilgrimage to the cenotaph.

Nets in the Nursery at Lord's on 20 April were followed by the pukka Cricket Writers' Dinner at the Skinner's Hall, addressed by Lord Birkett, senior presiding judge at Nuremberg. He singled out Ian Craig, still seven weeks short of his eighteenth birthday: 'If I know the English as I think I do, every Mother in the land will pray for him: "The Lord bless thy going out—and thy coming in."' Society chairman Charles Bray of the *Daily Herald* then asked Craig to share a drink with the mighty Sydney Barnes (eighty) and Jack Hobbs (seventy). The teenager sipped lemonade while his elders drank wine.

For the first time since the war, Britain was feeling cheerful: rationing was about to end, people were once again dressing for dinner and for Ascot, London's crime rate had fallen to its lowest level since the war.

Fingleton noted that conditions had improved vastly in the five years since Australia's last tour: 'In 1948 the city was low-spirited, people were poorly dressed and the food was in keeping. Now London is brightly painted and...the Londoner is a much happier person...I am going to enjoy England this time for many reasons. The Old Country is herself again.'

73

As the Coronation went ahead, Fingleton had the benefit of a seat in the nave of Westminster Abbey—courtesy of his friend, prime minister Menzies—and reported with appropriately unalloyed sentiment:

> As I saw the Queen enter…this day I felt centuries of English tradition and history and suffering following in her train. As she left to the ringing peals of the Anthem, I thought of England's future unfolding in front of her and in her presence of youthful beauty and majestic bearing all doubts and tribulations of the future seemed to fade away. And so may it be. God Save and aid Queen Elizabeth!

JOHNSTON IN TROUBLE

For the Australians, it would be a tour full of frustrations. And there was a foretaste of hindrances ahead in the very first match: a social affair by the Thames against East Molesey Cricket Club. The Australians treated it as such: Morris made 103 in eighty minutes out of 314 in 43 overs, and Miller just missed a £600 incentive for the first man to hit a six 140 yards onto Tagg's Island. But Hassett would rue the event, for Bill Johnston, pivot of his bowling attack, pulled up at the end of his fourth over.

Johnston recalls it with hurt clarity:

> Just before the tour I'd been down to see [the bootmaker] Hope Sweeney in Little Bourke Street to get some handmade boots, light leather, but they weren't ready when I left so he said: "Oh no worries, I'll send them to you in Perth." When I got them I found that the spikes were a bit long and were sticking in the ground, and if I'd been at home I would have been to see him and had them ground down a bit, but I thought I'd just keep going in them. For some reason Artie [James] didn't strap my ankle that day, I guess because it was only a sort of social game, but I let one go, had my head up watching it go past off stump and all of a sudden my leg just went from under me. There was no pain, but the leg just wouldn't support me.

After another abortive delivery, manager George Davies rushed Johnston to a Queen's Gate clinic. Orthopaedic surgeon Dr Bill Tucker kept them waiting, and arrived full of apologies: 'Sorry I'm late. I was playing golf and my Rolls broke down.' He fussed over the knee, rubbed it and tapped it inquisitively, then prescribed a month's rest and pumped Johnston full of pentathol for an X-ray at Oxford Hospital: a primitive process that involved filling the joint with air so that the cartilages were discernable. 'Done a few cricketers, actually,' Tucker advised. 'Denis Compton. Heard of him? That man shouldn't be walking down the

74

street, let alone playing cricket.' Johnston shrank a little, wondering whether he, too, would fall into that category.

Not that it seemed to matter at first. The Australians were in thumping form. Miller paraded his batting spurs at Worcester with an unbeaten 220, and his teenage understudy Ron Archer became the youngest Australian to score a hundred at first blush on English soil: 108 in eighty-six minutes at nineteen years and 188 days.

Like his elder brother Ken, Ron had been a formidable all-round sportsman at Brisbane Church of England Grammar, and brimmed with youthful confidence. Where the Queensland team of his day was an apologetic lot, Archer junior was an upstart and proud of it. 'I was an aggressive young bugger,' he says. 'I'd always been a winner in sport and I just believed I could do it.'

Harvey matched Miller's double-century at Leicester, Miller retorted with an unbeaten 159 at Bradford, then Harvey reeled off hundreds at Stoke-on-Trent, Hove and Southampton. If Craig and opener Colin McDonald could find little form, the apprentice batsmen Graeme Hole and Jimmy de Courcy and all-rounders Richie Benaud and Alan Davidson pitched in well.

Above all, there was Lindwall. The home summer before had been his best and he hit the ground running in England. Though age had worn the keen edge off his pace, the tantalising arc of his outswing kept Australia's chevron of slips constantly busy. Australia won six of its first eight matches by an innings.

When Menzies threw a grand cricket dinner in the River Room of the Savoy for fifty guests on 27 June, Hassett's team was in high humour. No expense was spared—Menzies had shipped steaks from home for the occasion—but the tone was distinctly informal. The prime minister recited a poem he had penned whose twenty-three verses devoted themselves individually to the virtues of the Australian players, and Hassett replied in kind.*

Of all the guests, none held so much fascination for the Australians as Douglas Jardine, the last English captain to reclaim the Ashes in an acrimonious atmosphere. They were surprised. 'Being from Australia I'd been brought up on stories about what a bastard Jardine was,' recalls Ron Archer. 'But now I was across the table from him, he was just this charming, interesting, aristocratic Englishman.'

At one stage Menzies began a story: 'As you all know, I am the man in Australia who has most often had the legitimacy of his birth queried...'

* see 'He's Merely Our Worthy Prime Minister', page 321

'Surely, sir,' came the voice of Jardine, 'I still hold that honour.'

Menzies complimented the players on their deportment: 'I have never known better ambassadors than this current Australian team.' All that remained, of course, was for them to ratify Australia's tenure of the Ashes. But that would not be easy.

HASSETT V HUTTON

Seldom in a series can two captains have afforded such a contrast. Lindsay Hassett remained a leader well loved for his informality and insouciance. On one occasion after a rain break in a county match, pressmen watched Hassett probing the pitch dubiously with his thumb. 'Any chance of play?' a reporter wondered.

'I dunno,' Hassett replied sardonically. 'I only do that to look intelligent in front of the crowd.'

England's Len Hutton would never have allowed himself such a quip. Like his Yorkshire mentor Herbert Sutcliffe, Hutton was the master builder of English batsmanship. Geff Noblet remembers bowling against the MCC for South Australia in 1950, and coyly launching a leg-cutter that he had spent years rehearsing in the nets. Hutton, at the non-striker's end, remarked: 'You didn't bowl that four years ago, Geff.' When Noblet bowled to him, Hutton pushed the leg-cutter back, grinning broadly.

From the local perspective, the most important aspect of Hutton's ascension was that he was a professional: the first to lead his country in an era in which English cricket still distinguished between gentlemen (amateurs) and players (professionals), still allocated them different changing-rooms and entry gates.

The Australians knew, however, that Hutton's leadership would make England that much more formidable. He was well versed in Australian methods, citing as his captaincy primer *The Game's the Thing* (the autobiography of the former Australian captain Monty Noble) and admired them. 'They have the utmost ability for producing that little extra,' he said, 'or instilling into opposition an inferiority complex that can have, and has had, a crushing effect. Australians have no inhibitions.'

The 150 journalists covering the series, accordingly, foresaw a tight contest. Hassett could still call on Lindwall, Miller and Arthur Morris. But Hutton had Alec Bedser, Denis Compton and Godfrey Evans. On the evidence of its drawn rubber with South Africa, Australia appeared in cyclical decline. A cadre of young players round Hutton implied an

England on the cusp of a new age. Even Sir Donald Bradman—who arrived in London on 5 June with his wife to become the £10,000 guest columnist of the *Daily Mail*—wrote in his first despatch: 'On paper England must be conceded at least a 50–50 chance this time against Australia. This is something no unbiased prophet has been able to forecast for 20 years.'

HELD OUT

By the Monday evening of the Second Test at Lord's, Australia seemed about to confound their doubters. Thanks to authoritative hundreds from Hassett and Miller, England faced an almost unassailable 343 in the fourth innings. And England's chase began badly, Lindwall reducing them to 3–12. In Fingleton's words, the great fast bowler 'plunged a double-edged dagger deep into English cricket'.

In the day's last over, however, Lindwall missed the chance to twist that dagger. Left-handed Yorkshireman Willy Watson turned Ring low but straight to Lindwall at backward short leg. 'Straight in, straight out,' the bowler recalls. 'He should've got it. Of course, we didn't realise the significance at the time.'

The significance was that Watson—a cool customer who'd played football for England in the 1950 World Cup—stubbornly refused to budge on Tuesday. Greeted pessimistically by a crowd of only 5000 at 11.30am, he and Compton saw off the new ball, and settled solidly against the leg-spin of Ring and Benaud.

There were alarms. Bowling from the Pavilion end, Ring spun one into Watson that squeezed between bat and pad and rolled purposefully towards off-stump. A soccer player's kick deflected it. And Compton, after seventy minutes, was lbw to a ball from Johnston that stayed low. But he was replaced by the obdurate Essex all-rounder Trevor Bailey, whose native stubbornness had been stiffened by perusing the gloomy newspaper prognostications of English defeat on the morning train from Westcliff-on-Sea.

The pair bridged the remaining fifty minutes to lunch, Watson essaying some attractive shots, Bailey wedging his bat incorruptibly next to his front pad and apparently enjoying every second. While Watson drank milk during the adjournment, Bailey ate his normal hearty repast, cleaning several teammates' plates for them.

Hassett had some problems. Johnston, scarcely recovered from his knee strain, had felt the injury give again while fielding on the boundary, while Ring and Benaud were proving ineffectual. But Australia's captain did not take the obvious option of uncorking Lindwall and Miller until the new ball fell due at 2.55pm. And, by that time, Watson and Bailey were well entrenched: although Lindwall twice hit Bailey across the knuckles, and only six runs accrued in half an hour, the pair survived.

The ground was filling as news of the resistance spread. 'I cannot remember when a crowd so revelled in defence for defence's sake,' reported E. W. Swanton. 'As Bailey got right behind the ball immediately following those that hit him, the crowd applauded with a fervour that in different circumstances might have greeted a six.' The audience beyond the ground hung on proceedings with equal enthusiasm: newspapers reported that John Christie, the Rillington Place murderer just sentenced to hang, had asked for updates from his cell.

Miller and Davidson bowled at a clip after tea, Bailey weaving from one fierce Miller full toss, but every over's passing was now greeted with rapture. Not until Ring was employed at the Nursery end from 5.20pm, so that his leg break could turn down the Lord's slope, were the batsmen incommoded. Watson raised his six-hour hundred by swinging Ring just wide of Benaud at square leg. And, twenty minutes later, a Ring leg-break infiltrated Watson's defence and squirted low to Hole at slip. But only forty minutes remained and—though two further wickets fell—the match had been saved.

The local press rejoiced. John Arlott wrote: 'I have seen Test teams with fewer obvious weaknesses, but I have never seen a game more epically, more evenly or more fluctuatingly fought out, nor one which so held the attention and the imagination and the heroic vein.' Neville Cardus' *Manchester Guardian* report was headlined: 'Miracle of Faith at Lord's.' The Australians lamented a lost opportunity, and wondered at its cost.

BAILEY AGAIN

Their frustrations had hardly begun. The Australian again won the toss and led on the first innings in the Third Test at Old Trafford, but rain enveloped the match. And, as often happened on a long tour, injuries were taking their toll: Johnston's knee, Colin McDonald's knees, Ring's bad back (actually a herniated disc), Don Tallon's stomach ulcers.

At the Nursery at Lord's, too, onlookers regularly observed the odd couple of Johnston and Craig trying to redeem their star-crossed tours. Johnston was methodically remodelling his action, pointing his front foot down the pitch rather than parallel to the crease in order to ease the strain on his leg. Craig, who'd not passed fifty on tour and lost his Test berth, batted to him for hours, striving to play straighter.

Not that Craig was necessarily having a bad time on the trip. For an eighteen-year-old, the attention was quite enjoyable. He'd been interviewed on TV at Trent Bridge, and presented with a cake for his birthday. Nor was the financial strain so great for him as for his married peers: he was planning to buy an Austin A30 with his £938 tour fee. But Craig desperately wanted some runs and, failing again in the Australians' twentieth match, against Middlesex at Lord's, was rueful. The Queen expressed sympathy when the Australians were presented to her during the tea interval on the second day, saying: 'I understand this is your first trip to England.'

Craig replied: 'Yes, Your Majesty. And, unless my batting improves, it will be my last.'

The Fourth Test at Headingley, five days later, began propitiously. After Hutton had entered to a hometown salute, Lindwall's second delivery, a full, fast inswinger, bisected middle and off stumps: with no sightscreen behind the bowler's arm, Hutton had lost the ball in his own adulatory crowd. Anxious batting and electric fast bowling, with the well-kept outfield preserving the ball's shine, reduced England to 7–142 from ninety-six overs at stumps: the poorest total for a Test day's play in England. And, by stumps on the second day, Australia led by almost a hundred.

Then came the rain, however, prolonging the home side's 275 until tea on the last day. Australia needed 177 in the final two hours. Morris, Hole and Harvey combined so forcefully that 66 were wanted in the last forty-five minutes, but Bailey again rescued England. Spearing the ball wide of leg-stump for six overs from the Kirkstall Lane end, he slowed the game to a dawdle.

Harvey was scandalised:

Trevor Bailey's bowling was absolutely disgusting. He bowled round the wicket to me and speared them diagonally yards down leg side. Godfrey Evans was standing eight feet wide of leg stump taking the ball. If one-day rules had been in force they would have been wides. I made 34 in about even time and, if they'd've bowled properly, we'd have got them. But they got away with it.

Though Hassett's team joined the Englishmen for a post-match drink, they were far from happy. Evans wrote: 'The Australians, every single one of them, were absolutely livid and I think rightly so. They had been cheated of victory, they said, by the worst kind of negative cricket. They were right.'

A NATION WAITS

The disgruntled Australians left Leeds on a 10.30pm train. Even worse, someone had blundered: sleepers had not been booked, and the players were forced to sit up all night on the trip to London.

On the sleepless journey south, Johnston had further bad news: having not bowled since pulling up lame in the Second Test, he learned that he had been overlooked again for the Australians' return match against Surrey later that morning.

Johnston's hackles were not easily raised, but now he was genuinely aggrieved. When the team arrived in London at 5am, he sought an audience with his skipper. No good: Hassett had told reception that he wanted some sleep.

Finally, Johnston found Morris. 'It's not going to prove anything, me being twelfth man,' the Victorian said. 'I should either play or not be in the twelve. This is bloody silly. I'm getting tired of doing nothing when I think I'm fit to play.'

Morris consented, delegating Davidson the drinks instead, and Johnston took 4–51, followed by 6–63 against Glamorgan and 6–39 against Essex. It was a tonic for the Australians approaching the decisive Fifth Test.

Seldom, however, can two teams have prepared as differently for a Test. England's team announced on 9 August included Surrey's spin pair, off-spinner Jim Laker and left-armer Tony Lock. Hassett and Morris subscribed to the view that Bert Lock's Oval pitch would favour pace, as it had during both Australia's tour matches there. Hassett even sent Lindwall and Miller to the RAC Club in Epsom for four days before the game, to relax and have a few early nights.

The atmosphere nearing the ground on the first morning, Saturday, 15 August, was decidedly grave, and complemented by overcast weather. Approaching Oval station on the Underground, Fingleton noted: 'This appears to be a serious day for England—the last time I saw looks like this on the gentry in London was in the middle of the 1938 crisis.' Local despondency deepened when Hassett won his fifth consecutive toss.

It wasn't long, however, before Hassett began having second thoughts about his selections. Hitting the pitch just short of a good length, Bedser's first ball left a dark, powdery indentation. Australia's captain turned to Evans and observed: 'I can see who this wicket's been made for.'

THE DECIDER

Before a partisan crowd and in indifferent light, it became a trying day for the tourists. Bedser removed Morris for the eighteenth time in twenty Tests, and Bailey claimed Miller lbw padding up. Hassett and Harvey rallied, but the captain edged behind, and Hutton anxiously backpedalled to accept Harvey's top edge at square leg. Only Lindwall retrieved the situation, contributing 62 of Australia's 275 with some uncomplicated driving.

With a rest day to recover from his batting exertions, Lindwall opened searchingly to Hutton. It was a crucial juncture: if pace could be handled, Hassett had little else to call on. There were moral victories for the bowler: a ball edged at catchable height through the short legs, a French-cut boundary. But Hutton was as attentive as a man handling hot liquid.

The one definitive chance was a run-out, Hassett returning smartly to the bowler's end from an aborted single. But with Hutton well short, Archer dropped the ball. 'Lindsay threw it a lot harder than I thought he would,' he says. 'And, because I was trying to sweep the bails off like Don Tallon, I fumbled it. I never did it again because he never let me forget. For the next month, he'd greet me by saying: "How's my favourite wicketkeeper today?"'

Finally, after lunch, Johnston came into his own. He had the twenty-three-year-old Surrey prodigy Peter May caught at short leg, and hurried Hutton into playing on, before Lindwall contained the English lead to 31. But, in turning several slower deliveries sharply, Johnston had also revealed to Hutton that his slow bowlers would prosper. They were deployed after ten overs of Australia's second innings.

Laker, a tall Yorkshireman who bowled his off-spin with a quizzical air, came on at the Vauxhall end, and at once trapped Hassett, then Hole. At the Pavilion end came Lock, a brawny, balding, demonstrative Londoner, to bowl Harvey and trap Morris. When Laker had Miller pocketed at short leg, four wickets had fallen for two runs in 19 deliveries, and the Oval crowd was rocking deliriously. Fingleton recorded:

Members stood and cheered themselves hoarse; the whole outer stood, roaring and laughing; I saw the passengers from the top level of the buses waving newspapers and umbrellas; I saw the occupants of flat windows rocking in ecstasy...What had happened to traditional English reserve, you ask? On this bright Oval day of August 18 it had gone, unreservedly, and like Australia's prospects of winning, completely up the spout.

With Archer joining de Courcy, the last of the accredited batsman, Australia was just 30 runs to the good and utterly deserted by luck. Archer pushed Lock to mid-wicket and advanced a few paces with the shot, drawing de Courcy on. But the ball had travelled straight to Bailey. 'No!' Archer cried. Too late: de Courcy was almost upon him, and was easily run out.

Archer showed composure beyond his years by on-driving the next ball for six. And for an hour he and Davidson reanimated Australia's innings with strokes that drove the spinners from the attack.

But the pitch would have the last word. Lock's first ball after tea leapt from a length, rebounding from Davidson's hip into his face, the next whistled through him. Lock also ended Archer's spirited 49 with one that spun across him. Three-quarters of an hour after tea, England was savouring a target of just 132. By the close they needed 94 and, as Archer discovered, celebrations were starting early: 'Jack Hilton had left me some tickets for the theatre that night. But it turned out to be a bit embarrassing. One of the fellas on stage decided to get the audience to cheer for the fact that England was about to win the Ashes, and to boo this fella called Ron Archer who was in the audience that night.'

The Ashes Lost

England acquired the winning runs methodically the next day, the venerable Middlesex pair of Bill Edrich and Denis Compton proving inseparable. Doug Ring looked on regretfully as Australia's pace trio tried to wring life from the pitch:

> It was frustrating. We had a pitch spinning like a top and all our spinners sitting in the pavilion. Keith [Miller] tried bowling off-breaks but he wasn't accurate enough and Bill Johnston, though he would have bowled very well on such a pitch in 1948, hadn't been the same since his injury because he couldn't follow through.

Johnston bowled probingly, his 23 overs on the last day costing just 36 runs, but could not take a trick:

> Edrich and Compton were a great pair for England to have at that time. Because they didn't take a single bloody risk. You couldn't even buy a wicket. With someone else less experienced we might have broken

through but they shut us right out. I tried everything I knew: I bowled fast, I bowled slow, I went round the wicket, I went over the wicket. But it wasn't any good.

When the battle was lost, Hassett bowled an over, then had Morris do the same. And at 2.55pm, Compton tugged Morris through square leg for the climactic boundary, then scampered off through the encroaching floodtide of well-wishers. Hutton, in collar and tie and smoking a sly victory cigarette, accepted the encomiums of the 25,000 from the pavilion balcony.

Introduced as the 'happy warrior', Hassett was generous. 'I would just like to offer my congratulations to Len and the English team,' he said. 'They have earned this victory from the very first ball—to the second last over anyway.' But, away from the pandemonium, the Australians were not so happy. It was a lousy way to lose the Ashes: the first match of any kind that Australia had lost in England since the war had been the only one it could not afford to. They were also suspicious of the cock to Lock's left elbow when he released his quicker ball. 'We all reckoned he threw his express delivery,' says Harvey. 'It was like a 90mph yorker and he used to knock the county blokes over left, right and centre.' A dressing-room clock was smashed. So was Ron Archer:

> There was just an extraordinary amount of champagne coming up to the rooms. And the boys decided they'd get me drunk for the first time. I didn't realise how quickly you could get drunk on the stuff. I got back to the hotel and I was violently ill, the first time I ever threw up because of alcohol. I had a friend from Queensland coming to me that night and we'd been planning to go to the Palladium. When he got to my room I was on my hands and knees trying to clean the vomit off the floor. Ever since, I've hardly touched champagne.

In many respects, the 1953 team had been one of Australia's most successful. Lindwall had swept away 85 wickets on the tour for 16 apiece with the finest sustained form of his career, and six other bowlers had exceeded 50 wickets. Harvey had belted 2040 runs and ten centuries, and another five batsmen had achieved four-figure tallies. They had played attractively in the Tests, scoring 48 runs an hour to England's 37, bowled 18 overs an hour to England's 17.3, and the Oval Test represented their only defeat among sixteen wins and sixteen draws. The £100,000 profit with which the team returned, moreover, represented Australian cricket's biggest pay day. After the financial worries of the preceding couple of seasons, all state associations returned handsome surpluses in the ensuing financial year.

But the Ashes were gone, and Australia's dominance of postwar cricket had run its course. The tour still produces ambivalent reactions among those Australians who played in it. 'We were a good side in 1953, and we played the better cricket,' says Harvey. 'But we lost.'

Blithe Spirit: Fleet of foot, quick of wit, Lindsay Hassett was the perfect emissary as Australia's captain in South Africa in 1949–50. His prime minister, Robert Menzies, declared: 'I can say that Australia has never had a better representative abroad.'

On Location: 'Touring' in 1949–50 meant just that. In the eleven weeks between Australia's arrival and the First Test there was ample time to sample the sights of Africa. One interlude was at Victoria Falls (above), another at a Dunlop factory in Durban (below), where Hassett led members of his team in an impromptu imitation of a native dance troupe.

The Enigma: Congratulated here by his parents and wife on being selected for the First Test of the 1950–51 Ashes series, prehensile spinner Jack Iverson was for one crowded hour the talk of the cricket world. But he played little thereafter. A man of brittle confidence, he took his own life in October 1973.

The Pro: The only places where an Australian cricketer could earn more than a subsistence income from the game in the 1950s and 1960s were the leagues in Lancashire. Here, receiving best wishes from Bill Johnston (right), Ray and Peg Lindwall are about to leave for England on the *Stratheden* in February 1952. Ray took 96 wickets for Nelson, and Peg bore their first son.

The Sid Barnes Affair: The mysterious omission of enfant terrible Sid Barnes from the Australian team in December 1951 rocked cricket to its foundations. Respondent Jacob Raith and plaintiff Barnes shake hands at the end of the defamation dispute which mortified the Australian Board of Control in August 1952 (left); but, ten weeks later, Barnes is back in the dog house after carrying his twelfth man duties a little far for NSW at Adelaide Oval (right).

Dressed to Kill: You'd scarcely pick this dapper sextet in London in 1953 as Australian cricketers. Upholding sartorial standards are (front) Graeme Hole, Lindsay Hassett, Neil Harvey, Arthur Morris and (rear) Ron Archer and masseur Artie James.

On the Attack: Searching for a breakthrough in the decisive Fifth Test at the Oval in August 1953, Ray Lindwall bowls to England's captain Len Hutton with an attacking formation in support. Lindwall's 26 series wickets cost fewer than 19 runs each, but Hutton's 443 runs and Alec Bedser's 39 wickets tilted the series the way of the hosts.

On the Job: After cricket, it was back to work. Young all-rounder Alan Davidson remained in England after the 1953 tour where he was employed in the London branch of the Commonwealth Bank.

Two Aces, One King: Keith Miller and Ray Lindwall (above) excelled in the West Indies in February–May 1955: in the five Tests, they took 40 wickets and scored more than 600 runs between them. For captain Ian Johnson (right), the 3–0 victory was a triumph of tact and diplomacy. He was honoured with an MBE for his efforts. But his reign would end in disappointment.

Sand and Grit: 'Let's have it straight,' reported Bill O'Reilly during the Fourth Test of the 1956 Ashes series. 'This pitch is a complete disgrace.' The image of groundsmen tending the Old Trafford surface amid an apparent sandstorm (above) summed up its character. For Johnson's Australians, incredulous at Jim Laker's 19–90, the only consolation was the solitary defiance of opener Colin McDonald (below). He top-scored in both innings with 33 out of 84 and 89 out of 205.

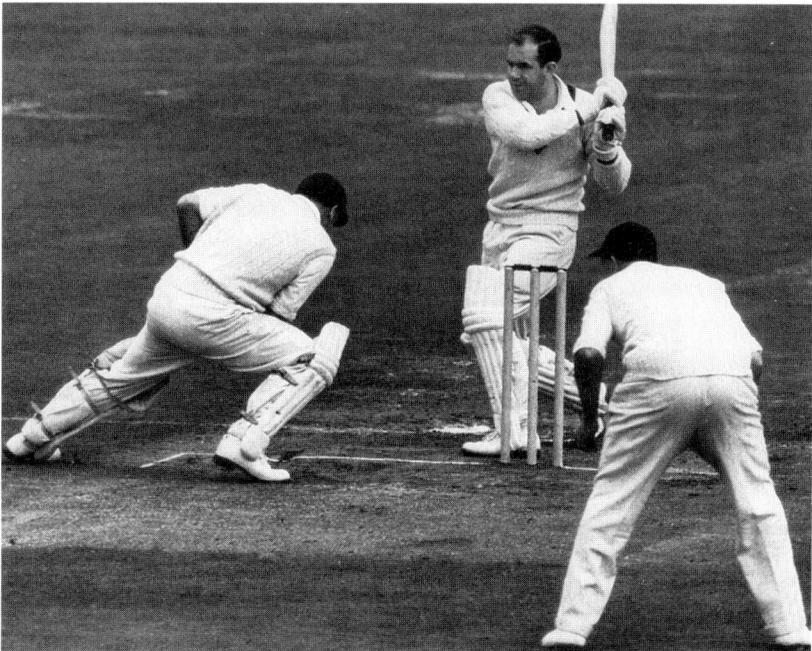

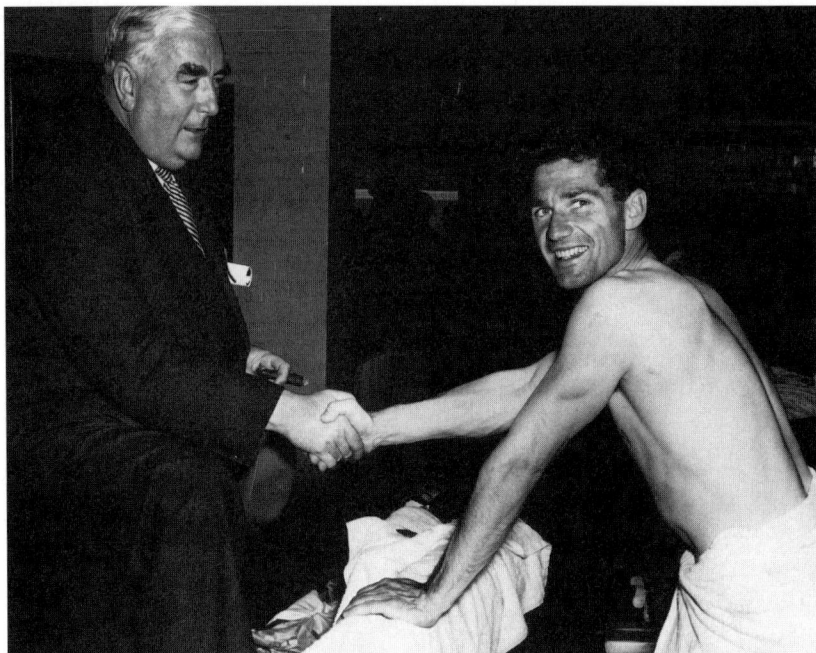

New Order: Foremost Australian batsman of the 1950s was the daring Victorian left-hander Neil Harvey, congratulated (above) by prime minister Robert Menzies after his undefeated 92 against England at the SCG in December 1954. Ian Johnson's successor as Australia's captain in South Africa in 1957–58 was, however, twenty-one-year-old New South Welshman Ian Craig (below left) who set off from Tilbury on the *Capetown Castle* in September 1957 to join his team. And Australia's 3–0 victory unearthed a host of outstanding new players, including the indestructible Queenslander Wally Grout (below right).

'People Only Remember Your Last Game'

AUSTRALIA V ENGLAND AND
WEST INDIES
1954-56

Despite succeeding the retired Hassett as Victoria's captain for the 1953–54 season, Ian Johnson couldn't help feeling listless. Cricket had been his life since he could remember, yet he sensed that some of his zeal for the game was missing. Though sorry to miss the 1953 Ashes tour, he hadn't had a bad winter, calling football on 3AW with Norman Banks, writing sports columns for the *Argus*. Perhaps, at thirty-five, it was time to start building a life for his wife Lal and two boys.

With that at the back of his mind, on 31 December, he drove to the home of his friend Cecil Kellett, a popular local cricket supporter who always hosted a New Year bash. But, though 1953 passed into 1954 uneventfully, Johnson found himself cornered at 3am by none other than Hassett. 'Now, you listen to me, Johnno,' Hassett began. 'You've had a bad season and I reckon you know why.'

Johnson was surprised by Hassett's sudden seriousness. 'Oh yeah, Lindsay,' he said. 'Why do you reckon I'm not getting wickets?'

'The problem is that you're not getting stuck in,' Hassett said pointedly. 'You're not trying.'

Johnson scoffed. 'Waddya talking about Lindsay? Course I'm trying.'

'No you're not,' Hassett continued. 'You're just mucking round. If you've got any brains at all, you'll start taking this game seriously. Because if you do, you'll end up captaining Australia next year.'

Johnson left the party angry. Not because Hassett was wrong, but because he might be right. It was time Johnson demonstrated that at least a few of his best days lay ahead. In the match against South Australia beginning that day, the tall off-spinner took 8–80. In four further matches, he harvested 28 wickets at 14.5. But the last laugh was Hassett's. By summer's end, Johnson *was* being mentioned in Test captaincy despatches.

MILLER MISSES OUT

Johnson's clearest rival—and unbackable favourite north of the Murray—was Keith Miller. He, too, excelled in 1953–54, with 510 runs at 64, 14 wickets at 27 and twin centuries in Hassett's testimonial match for good measure. He led his state to the Sheffield Shield, moreover, with captaincy of rare intuition. On the first morning of the season, for instance, he pressed the ball on an unwilling Richie Benaud after five overs, dismissing protestations that it was still new. 'Don't worry about that,' Miller replied. 'Just think about what field you want. And don't worry. It'll spin like a top for an hour and we've got a great chance to bowl them out.' Benaud had 5–17 before lunch.

Newspaper front pages of 1954 busily chronicled the Petrov defection, Menzies' canny campaign for re-election on 29 May, and the ensuing Labor fratricide. But the back pages were consumed with debate over who should lead Australia in its forthcoming home Ashes rubber. On cricketing merits, Miller was vastly Johnson's superior. One Sydney newspaper held that 'to choose Johnson in preference to Keith Miller would be tantamount to choosing Edmund Gwenn for the role of Robin Hood when you had Errol Flynn under contract'. But argument did not stop there. Johnson had by far the better establishment credentials: he was son of a former national selector, an alumnus of Wesley College, and had the poise and eloquence of one at home with high office. Miller, meanwhile, was a Melbourne High School boy who enjoyed good company, a drink and the turf.

Miller was also handicapped by the residual ill-feeling of the Barnes affair. For one, board delegates from Victoria and South Australia retained a dim view of NSW support for Barnes at their infamous December 1951 vote. For another, Barnes' drinks indiscretion at Adelaide Oval a year later was taken as evidence that Miller was a poor disciplinarian.

The way the thirteen votes fell on 18 November 1954 will never be known, although Dick Whitington speculated that the six Victorians and South Australians voted for Johnson, the three NSW delegates for Miller, and Queensland's two representatives for the compromise candidate of Morris. Johnson, therefore, needed only a vote from either Western Australia and Tasmania for an absolute majority.

South of the Murray, the decision was hailed. Without disclosing his vested interest, Hassett wrote: 'Johnson's determination together with his profound cricket knowledge and the respect in which he is held by the men whom he will lead makes him a wise choice for the position.' Those to the north saw Miller as capriciously disinherited. The *Daily Telegraph* editorialised: 'There is strong feeling among cricket enthusiasts that horse trading on a state basis rather than objective valuation of cricket skills has dominated selectors' discussions. The operating principle seems to have been: "You look after my man and we'll look after yours."' The Johnson years had made a shaky start.

GABBA GAMBIT

Eight days after his appointment, Johnson was walking out to toss with Len Hutton at the Gabba in the First Test. And walking was all: Hutton offered not a word as they completed a final examination of Jack McAndrew's pitch.

Johnson could sense Hutton's thinking. England's XI was loaded to the gunwales with fast bowling: three old boys of 1950–51 in Bedser, Bailey and Brian Statham, plus a twenty-four-year-old called Frank Tyson with receding hair, shoulders like a nightclub bouncer, and a nickname 'Typhoon' that reflected both searing speed and inconstant accuracy. Clearly, Hutton was thinking of sending Australia in. But surely not on this pitch. Johnson studied it and saw only runs.

Hutton called correctly, then fell silent. Johnson waited as his rival peered at the pitch a second time, then began to walk off. They were almost off the arena when Hutton finally said: 'Ian?'

Johnson: 'Yes Len.'

Hutton: 'I think you can have strike.'

Johnson: 'Thanks Len.'

Johnson managed to contain his joy until Hutton was out of sight. It wasn't until he reached the Australian dressing-room that Johnson broke into a seraphic smile. 'Fellas, he's put us in,' he announced. 'But it's a beauty and I think he's made a blue.'

It was. Hutton had. Australia was 2–208 at the close, and pressed on to 6–503 by Saturday evening with Morris (153) and Harvey (162) lording it over Hutton's much vaunted attack. The declaration came at lunch on Monday and, by 4.15pm on Wednesday, Johnson had won his first Test by an innings and 154 runs: a stunning reversal. Even a week later at the Lodge, where the Englishmen were entertained during their Prime Minister's XI match, Hutton's face had not lost its doleful expression. 'Ian tells me I look glum,' he explained. 'Well, people in England are going through snow and ice at the moment. There's little comfort or happiness for them there, and any they get will only come from our victories over here.'

GOVER STEPS IN

The match at Manuka was a good-natured romp, featuring 525 runs in five and a half hours. The 4500 spectators included governor-general Sir William Slim, who fielded one of Richie Benaud's sixes in the official enclosure, and Jack Fingleton, who umpired in a pith helmet. Over dinner, Hassett irrepressibly lectured the four current Testmen in his side on how they should hook Tyson. When a rumble of thunder outside momentarily silenced him, the prime minister interjected: 'There you are. The Typhoon has started his run-up already.'

But the 'Typhoon'—who'd conceded 160 runs for a solitary wicket at the Gabba—was actually Hutton's deepest concern. The captain knew that Tyson was fit: he'd spent the previous winter tree-felling, and the journey to Australia pounding the decks of the *Orsova* even in the heat of the Red Sea. Yet in Brisbane, his marathon run-up had exhausted him quickly.

After two days of that Test, however, Hutton had had a fortuitous meeting with Alf Gover, a former Surrey fast bowler turned professional coach who was covering the tour for London's *Sunday Mirror*. Gover told Hutton that the young paceman was wasting his time running so far: truncating his approach would improve his stamina and rhythm.

Tyson was amenable, and began experimenting. Two days after the MCC's Canberra jaunt, he bowled five Victorian batsmen from the shortened approach, split Colin McDonald's right thumb, and hit Harvey's front pad at such velocity that the batsman had to remove it in order to restore sensation. Hutton was impressed. When he revealed his team for the Second Test at Sydney on 17 December, there was no place for Alec Bedser, England's most admired bowler for a decade. Australians were stupefied. A woman accosted Hutton at a tour function a few days later and complained: 'Who are the awful people who dropped poor Alec?'

'Well, you know,' Hutton mumbled, 'a good young 'un is always better than a good old 'un.'

Though unrecognised as such at the time, the series' pivotal point came a quarter-hour from lunch on the Tuesday of the Second Test. England led by 150, thanks to a sterling second-innings stand by vice-captain Peter May and twenty-one-year-old Colin Cowdrey, and Lindwall was striving in spite of liver trouble to mop up the tail. He dropped short, Tyson turned his head and was knocked senseless. Manager Geoffrey Howard spirited him to a Macquarie Street radiologist for X-rays on the outsized lump.

It was hardly an act of premeditated violence, for Lindwall had a puritan streak when bowling to lower-order batsmen. When Alan Davidson bounced a tailender in one of their first Shield matches together, Lindwall sternly admonished him: 'You've just insulted all fast bowlers. You've admitted that number seven can bat better than you can bowl.' And, in truth, Tyson had made a hash of it, ducking into one not all that quick. 'Ray just couldn't put anything into his bowling that day,' Morris recalls. 'The one that hit Frank was the slowest bouncer you've ever seen. He played about three shots before it hit him.'

But Hutton considered the ball directly responsible for Tyson emerging as probably England's fastest postwar bowler: 'When he came out of his concussed state, I swear there was a new light in his eyes, as if a spark had been kindled deep down inside him.' As Australia began its victory chase for 223 just before tea, Tyson was perceptibly quicker: Godfrey Evans encouraged his cordon to retreat further.

When Australia set off after 151 with eight wickets preserved on the final morning, Tyson promptly made inroads. He bowled Jim Burke in his second over, Hole four deliveries later, caught Benaud at square leg, then bowled Archer off an edge after lunch. A piquant contest was promised when Lindwall faced the man he'd decked not twenty-four hours earlier. But Tyson was too shrewd: cringing from a retaliatory bouncer, Lindwall was yorked.

Neil Harvey held fearlessly firm, cutting cleverly, reproving anything on his pads, but barely able to acquaint himself with partners before they vanished. When last man Bill Johnston entered at 2.30pm with 78 needed, Harvey finally seized the match, commandeering the strike where possible and backing his judgment. At one stage, Tyson motioned his fine leg finer and dropped short, but Harvey hooked anyway, over Bailey's head and the fence on the first bounce.

As Johnston trusted in his homespun technique, the target was halved in 40 minutes. Harvey was in sight of his century and, after a dozen devastating overs, Tyson nearly spent. 'I hadn't thought at the start that we could get 70,' says Harvey. 'But, after Bill stuck round for a while, I started having a few ideas. Tyson was just about rooted by that time and I didn't consider Bailey a problem. They'd have brought Statham back but Bill could have handled him, because he played pretty straight.' As Tyson took the ball for his 19th over, Johnston said: 'I'll try to hang round at least for your hundred, because I think Frank's had it.'

But there was no fairytale Australian victory, nor the century Harvey merited. After three deliveries, Statham advised Tyson: 'Try one a little closer to his body and a little shorter.' Johnston's self-protective one-handed glide ended in Evans' gloves. Tyson's 10th wicket of the match for 130 runs at 3.11pm brought victory by 38 runs. Without conscious irony, *Wisden* reported that Tyson had 'won the match for England because he kept his head'.

THE MYSTERY PITCH

1955 would be a vintage year for intrigue: the Petrov Royal Commission, B. A. Santamaria and 'The Movement', the fall of Joe McCarthy, the further fall of Guy Burgess and Donald Maclean. Yet the Third Test at the MCG over the New Year threw up a mystery that, at least for a time, was just as confounding.

The Melbourne Cricket Club's preparations had been fraught. Demolition of the old Public Stand ahead of the 1956 Olympics had torn a huge hole in its flank, while pitches had been so mediocre that secretary Vernon Ransford asked Albert Ground curator Jack House to assist groundsman Bill Vanthoff in preparing the square.

When the pitch for the traditional Boxing Day encounter between Victoria and NSW proved sound, Ransford expressed optimism about the Test. But House told Dick Whitington the day before the match: 'There should be a packet of runs in it on Friday and Saturday but I wouldn't go further than that. If conditions are cool over the weekend it may last until Monday. But if they are hot it will crack badly.' And, when Hutton won the toss on Friday, it *was* stiflingly hot.

Argument about the pitch was temporarily eclipsed by the drama of the play, dominated first by Keith Miller then by Colin Cowdrey. Having missed the previous Test with a sore knee, Miller had not been expected to bowl. Yet on the first morning he told Johnson excitedly: 'I tried the knee in the bedroom this morning. It might be OK.' Finishing his first over and savouring the strong breeze for his outswinger, he was even more excited: 'It's better than I expected. Gimme another go.' Bowling unchanged until lunch, he extracted Edrich, Hutton and Compton and allowed just two scoring strokes.

When Miller was spelled, though, Cowdrey made a poised hundred. And, happy as they were at rolling England for 191, the Australians were staring daggers at the pitch. The little moisture binding it had disappeared and, without a covering of couch, it was threatening to disintegrate. Harvey muttered to Benaud as they walked off: 'I don't reckon we'll be able to play on this on Monday.'

The chances faded further when record temperatures and an infernal northern wind on New Year's Day baked the pitch to a crumbling crust. Though Victorians Johnson and keeper Len Maddocks saw Australia to within four runs of the lead, the captain grew more anxious by the over. 'We went in on Saturday and the wicket was doing all sorts of things,' says Johnson. 'When I was in with Len toward the end of the day, you could see the ball starting to fly off the cracks.'

A Tip-off

Melbourne's hottest night-time temperature of 96 degrees fahrenheit was recorded that evening, and players dispersed on the rest day: Harvey had Benaud, Davidson and MCC player Jim McConnon to his home in Heidelberg; Miller and Lindwall played golf with Ossie Pickworth; Johnson spent a fretful day in Middle Park: 'I was thinking: "God! What's this wicket going to look like on Monday?"'

At the Collins Street offices of the *Age*, Percy Beames was filing for Monday's edition when his telephone rang. It was Bill Vanthoff: an old friend, with whom he'd played VFL football for Melbourne twenty years earlier. He sounded distraught. 'Percy, something terrible's happened,' the MCG curator said. 'Jack House's flooded the square. He's put too much water on.' Beames was stunned. Such a watering was completely at odds with Law 10 of MCC's 1947 Code: 'Under no circumstances shall the pitch be watered during a match.' He went at once to his editor, Harold Austin.

The story was sensational. But Austin did not want to be the cause of controversy jeopardising Anglo-Australian cricketing relations. 'Do you think it will affect the game?' he asked.

'It might,' Beames replied.

'Do you think there was any evil intent involved?' Austin asked.

Beames said honestly: 'No I don't.'

Austin thought a moment, then proposed: 'Then we won't run the story. What we'll do is black [print in bold] a paragraph saying that watering a pitch during a match is illegal.' Beames was full of admiration: 'I thought to myself that it showed what a great editor Harold Austin was. He was more interested in the game than in a scoop for his newspaper.'

'SAY NOTHING TO ANYBODY'

Johnson arrived early on Monday to inspect the wicket. It looked surprisingly firm, and the cracks seemed to have closed. He ran his spikes along it. It was moist. He fetched his deputy Morris. 'This has been watered,' Johnson said.

'Crikey,' Morris said. 'So it has.'

As Johnson and Morris went to notify VCA secretary Jack Ledward, umpires Col Hoy and Mel McInnes arrived from their digs at the Commercial Travellers' Club in Flinders Street. Hoy blanched, and McInnes advised from the corner of his mouth: 'Say nothing to anybody.'

The secret was out, and the press-box in pandemonium. Englishwoman Margaret Hughes, writing for Sydney's *Daily Telegraph,* recalled: 'Pressmen could be seen rushing here and there, chatting together in groups, snatching phones—the inexplicable feather-bed state of the wicket had been explained—"it had been watered".' Beames knew that there was no holding his story.

With the pitch momentarily tamed, Hutton and Edrich mopped up England's arrears themselves. The tourists led by 119 at the close with seven wickets remaining, and all talk centred on what had changed the wicket's spots. And next morning, Melburnians awoke to the bold *Age* headline: 'Test pitch watered during game.'

'AFTER A SEARCHING INQUIRY...'

Tuesday's play furnished further evidence of the pitch's placation. Though Johnston winkled out five in 25 overs of probing left-arm spin, May's elegant blade and Bailey's dead one prolonged the English innings. Johnson felt thwarted, especially when tailender Johnny Wardle came in waving his bat like a banner and hit 38 in even time. 'There was nothing we could do,' he says. 'It was like losing the toss twice.'

The MCC was in uproar. Secretary Ransford and president William McClelland spent the day collecting statutory declarations from Vanthoff, House and the nightwatchmen denying all knowledge of watering. At the close, Ransford's assistant entered the press-box in the manner of a town crier to proclaim: 'After a searching inquiry, it is emphatically denied that the pitch or any part of the cricket ground has been watered since the commencement of the Third Test match on Friday, 31 December.'

But no effort was made to force the *Age* to withdraw its story. When the newspaper printed the MCC's self-exculpation, it was with the addendum that Beames still believed his information correct. And, without admitting it, VCA president Arnold Seitz dined Beames at the Amateur Sport Club in Little Collins Street in an effort to learn the reporter's sources. 'I wouldn't bite,' says Beames.

Off-field dramas were temporarily suspended when England's last four tumbled in fifty minutes, suggesting that the watering's effect was wearing off. There was, after all, a Test match in session and the Ashes at stake. Johnson requested the heavy roller before Australia began its chase for 240, and it seemed to bind the surface for the balance of the day as Benaud and Harvey saw out proceedings. Australia needed 165 and England eight wickets on the Wednesday for a 2–1 series lead. The *Age* headline forecast: 'Stage is set for great Test finish.'

ROUTED

It was, but hardly one to Australians' liking. When Evans darted to leg to accept Harvey's glance from the day's seventh delivery, it was the first of eight wickets to fall in an hour and a quarter for 34 runs. Statham enlisted Evans in Hole's dismissal and bowled Archer with a full toss, but the rest bowed before Tyson.

The pitch played its part. Inconsistent bounce perplexed all the batsmen. 'It was fast bouncers one minute, fast grubbers the next,' says Harvey. 'One'd go past your ear off a good length, another'd go along the deck.' But Tyson would have been fast on mud and, when he ended play on the stroke of lunch, many of the 20,000 who'd attended the last day in good faith remained afterwards to hail him outside the players' enclosure. Hutton accepted Menzies' congratulations, then confided wrily in Tyson's mentor Alf Gover: 'Alfred, there is one thing I'm worried about. The poor caterers now have 20,000 pies and sausage rolls on their hands.'

The only favourable aspect of Australia's defeat was that it appeased many in the public mortified by what Whitington dubbed 'The Great MCG Mirage'. There had been recommendations that the Test be either voided or replayed if Australia won. But the heat remained on the Melbourne Cricket Club. The *Sydney Morning Herald* published a waspish editorial asking why so many officials continued to deny what they knew to be true. No-one was convinced when the club produced two experts—senior CSIRO research officer G. D. Aitchison and Melbourne University civil engineering lecturer D. H. Trollope—to explain that the combination of the hot weather and the tarpaulins could have drawn water from an underground stream. Secretary Ransford took several weeks leave later in the season to recover from the strain of public odium.

Though the watering's precise nature remains a mystery, Ian Johnson heard some years later a convincing version of events from a ground staff member. Examining the pitch on the Sunday, House had apparently been appalled. 'Someone's going to be killed on this wicket,' he told Vanthoff. 'We can't leave it like this.'

'What are you gonna do?' Vanthoff asked.

House told him: 'Think I'll give it a bit of a fizz.'

Vanthoff baulked. 'I'm not in it,' he replied. 'I'm going home.' In leaving, however, Vanthoff would have realised that the operation could not be clandestine: because of the Olympic refurbishments at the MCG, the centre was visible to passers-by in Jolimont Park. Which may be why he contacted Beames: in the hope that, if details did emerge, at least a responsible journalist would have full possession of the facts.

CALYPSO CAPTAIN

England's 3–1 series victory was an unpleasant comeuppance for the hosts. So accustomed to holding sway with speed, they now discovered the bowling boot on the other foot. Tyson was simply too fast. Ron Archer recalls facing him with a second new ball at the SCG. The first delivery passed Archer before he could even conceive of a stroke, the second flew off the full face of the bat to second slip: 'It wasn't an edge. The ball was so fast that the force of it turned the bat in my hand. I can remember being able to watch the ball flying to Hutton at slip: he was so far back it was like being caught in the outfield.'

Statham, a whip-thin Lancastrian who supplanted Bedser, was an ideal foil, pushing up hills and into breezes without complaint. Seeing him in the bar at the Windsor Hotel, Bradman told Hutton: 'I do hope that man gets the credit he deserves.'

Lindwall, by contrast, was in his thirty-fourth year and sapped by what proved to be hepatitis, while Miller seemed unsure whether he wished to be remembered as batsman or bowler. Or captain. But, unfortunately for the Sydney lobby favouring Miller's promotion, Johnson had done little wrong against England and was about to do a great deal right in the West Indies. Few captains have filled their brief more fully than Johnson in the Caribbean, on field and off.

In the two years since Menzies had advocated the trip, diplomatic sensitivities had heightened. Against a backdrop of rising anti-colonial feeling and heated demands for self-government, England's 1953–54 tour had been among the ugliest and most violent cricket tours anywhere. Riots in Georgetown were judged so serious that the local governor offered the services of the First Battalion of the Argyll and Sutherland Highlanders. Coming from a country whose immigration policies were so restrictive, Johnson knew he might be in for an uncomfortable reception.

But Johnson was noted for his public relations skills, his open hand and flair for the *mot juste*. As he strolled across the tarmac of Kingston's Palisados Airport at 3am on 14 March 1955 and observed the discreet contingents of English and West Indian pressmen, Johnson headed for the latter. 'Let's forget these Pommy boys,' he told Miller. 'The West Indies reporters are more important to us.' The welcoming crowd of 3000 were delighted, even more so as Johnson's legendary all-rounder approached with hand outstretched. 'I'm Miller,' he said. 'What's your name and what do you want to know?'

Practice at Sabina Park the next day was attended by 4000, and the team enhanced its popularity during an evening cocktail party at the residence of local cricket lover Vernon Sassoo. Johnson was photographed by Kingston's *Star* improvising a rumba, and captioned the next day as the 'Calypso Captain'. Rustic Melbourne Park overflowed three days later for the tour opener, fans acclaiming Morris's fluency, Lindwall's athleticism and Miller's extroversion, whether he was donning a Jamaican cap, taking guard with the handle of his bat, sipping Coca-Cola with the crowd or hitting the ball into the surrounding mango trees.

The biggest hit, though, was Johnson. As the Australians left the field through a wave of adoring children, Johnson picked up a little boy, exchanged a few laughing words and set him down again. A spontaneous stroke of diplomatic genius. 'There were people who thought I'd done it deliberately, but it was quite an unselfconscious thing to do,' Johnson says. 'And it went down a storm.' Comparisons were immediately drawn with Hutton's stand-offish Englishmen. A Jamaican magistrate observed: 'Whereas the MCC as a whole gave us the impression that they felt they were stepping down, the Australians seem to have come on a level.'

The home side had a phalanx of fine batsmen. Muscle-bound Clyde Walcott, who cut so hard that Richie Benaud wore protective gear in the gully, made a record five centuries in the series. Wristy Everton Weekes struck the ball almost as hard with a fraction of the effort. But, on pitches of shaven perfection, the West Indies had not the bowling to curb Australian batsmen intent on exorcising the demons of Tyson. Harvey harvested 650 runs at 108, while Miller, McDonald and Archer all averaged more than 60. There were 20 wickets each for Lindwall and Miller, 20 dismissals in four Tests for the immensely reliable Gil Langley.

Initially, the tourists were startled by the excited hubbub of the crowds and the pitches' unearthly sheen. 'We were used to playing in Australia and England in relative silence,' says McDonald. 'But I can still remember, first the hush, then the roar as Frank King started his run-up to me for the first ball of the series. It was amazing. After a while I also began to realise I could see his reflection in the pitch. Which was a bit of a shock.' Once that shock dissipated, however, run-getting was relatively straightforward. Groundsmen prided themselves on the flawlessness of their surfaces. When a few Australian bowlers chided Queen's Park's curator for his lifeless turf, he replied: 'Ah have no feelin' for de bowlers. Ah was a batsman.'

Following in the footsteps of Hutton's team was a sensitive business. Locals seized on anything reminiscent of the dissent or umpire intimidation in which the Englishmen had allegedly indulged. Characteristic was what became known as 'The Archer Incident' in the Second Test at Port-of-Spain.

From the third delivery of the last over on the penultimate day, Archer bellowed an lbw appeal against Jackie Holt. Umpire Eric Lee Kow shook his head and, when the ball returned from Benaud, Archer snatched, fumbled and dropped it. 'It looked like I'd thrown the ball down,' says Archer. 'And the crowd erupted.' Jeering had not subsided when Archer hit Holt's pads two balls later and, although the bowler refrained from appealing, Lee Kow agreed with shouts from behind the wicket. 'The ball was missing leg by about six inches but the ump gave Holt out,' Archer recalls. 'And the West Indians—who were very knowledgeable—knew what had happened. It was a square-up.'

Booing trailed Archer and Lee Kow all the way off, and the Australian all-rounder was pilloried. A. G. Alkins of the *Evening News* invoked memories of England's tour: 'Will we get these incidents under control now that we still have our fingers on the pulse of them, or will we wait until they grow into a horrible, vexatious monster and devour us all as they did during the English tour? High Heavens forbid!' But Johnson immediately expressed full confidence in the local umpiring: 'I am very happy with the umpiring. It is up to the usual standard of Test match umpiring.' And at the next stop in Georgetown, he put the Australians through seven cocktail parties in nine evenings, winning friends and influencing people.

Not all the Australians, however, were enamoured of their captain. Some dubbed him 'Mr Kolynos' after the toothpaste, because of the constancy of his smile. Others called him 'Myxomatosis', observing that he always seemed to bowl when the rabbits were in. And Johnson could be insensitive in the way he encouraged his troops. Bill Johnston lost some of his usual good humour after a brush with the captain during the tour's first net session. Johnson upbraided the genial Johnston for going through the motions: 'Just 'cos you're one of the old blokes in the side doesn't mean you don't have to bloody well put in, you know.'

Johnston was hurt. 'I know I'm one of the old blokes,' he replied. 'There's no need to rub it in.'

There was also unspoken tension between Johnson and Miller throughout the trip. Although heated words were exchanged only once, in the Bridgetown dressing-room after the latter objected to being replaced at the bowling crease, many players felt that Miller should have been captain. 'Keith really should have led us on that tour,' says Johnston. 'In the West Indies, he did just as much off-field PR stuff as Johnson, because I think he'd made up his mind to prove he could do it.'

One could hardly cavil, of course, with a captain who won a series 3–0 and made such an overwhelmingly favourable impression. A couple of days before the Australians boarded the SS *Rangitane* for home, Sir Hugh Foot wrote to Menzies:

> I wish I could describe to you adequately the resounding success of the Australian team during their tour of the West Indies. You have seen the scores and the accounts of the great feats which they performed. But you can scarcely imagine the great popularity which the team has achieved. West Indians do not like being soundly beaten any more than anyone else but…we could not withhold our admiration for every member of the Australian team.

Bradman wrote to Menzies recommending an honour for Johnson and, next year, both the captain and Miller received MBEs.

Perhaps the fairest view of Johnson, however, comes from Alan Davidson:

Ian did the best PR job of any captain I've ever seen on that tour. The locals were looking for anything that happened on the field to prove that we were having a go at their umpires, but really nothing happened. Unfortunately, though, Ian was starting to wane as a player. He was always confident in his own ability, but things were getting hard for him. And I do think players have to realise when they are playing that season too many. It's sad that people only ever remember your last game, but they do.

SOMETHING HAPPENED

1956 is remembered as one of Australian sport's *anni mirabiles*. Golfer Peter Thomson won his third consecutive British Open. Lew Hoad and Ken Rosewall dominated Wimbledon and the Davis Cup. And it was, of course, Melbourne's Olympiad, with a succession of triumphs in the pool and on the track. Yet the Ashes tour of 1956 ranks as a nadir for the country's cricket: the high summer of Surrey's peerless off-spinner Jim Laker, a winter of discontent for Johnson's Australians.

It did not seem a bad touring team. Although Morris and Johnston had retired, Johnson, Miller, Lindwall and Harvey remained from that benchmark 1948 side. The apprentice all-rounders of 1953—Archer, Benaud and Davidson—were three years older and wiser. Ian Craig was back, having missed the two preceding series with national service and pharmacy exams, while there was ample promise in opener Jim Burke and paceman Pat Crawford.

The tour started indifferently. Australia unambitiously drew seven of its first ten matches and succumbed to Surrey at The Oval, where Laker bagged 10–88 in their first innings. But, after surviving the First Test with the help of rain, Australia won a fluctuating Second Test at Lord's before 135,000 spectators. Miller (10–152) and Archer (6–118) bowled through injuries to clinch the match by 185 runs.

Then something happened. Harvey remembers talking after the Lord's Test to Peter May, the thoroughbred amateur batsman who'd succeeded to England's captaincy on Hutton's retirement. 'Well Neil,' May remarked, 'that's the last pitch you'll see like that.' Northamptonshire's Australian pair, Jock Livingston and George Tribe, told Johnson that May had advised the injured Frank Tyson: 'We won't be wanting you from here on, Frank. From now on, they'll all be spinners.'

Whatever the explanation, the pitches turned poisonous. The surface at Headingley for the Third Test on 12 July was the worst Johnson had seen. He recalls: 'It played all right until tea on the first day, then it started to go. Richie bowled a ball late on the first day that gripped and spun over Peter May's right shoulder. And I thought: "My God! This will be a shocker." Then it rained and got wet, so I don't think anyone really appreciated how bad it was.' It was bad enough for Laker to bag a match-winning 11–113.

The pitch for the Fourth Test at Old Trafford a fortnight later lasted longer but, even as England completed its first innings of 459 on the second day, Johnson's men were gazing darkly at its thick coating of marl. Once the 48-run opening alliance of McDonald and Burke had been broken, Laker gnawed through an acquiescent middle order, his 9–37 routing the tourists for 84. 'Jim bowled well, and we batted very badly,' says Ian Craig. 'We were all pissed off, felt we'd been dudded, and we dropped our bundle a bit.'

Harvey's 'pair' to Laker within the day was a microcosm of Australia's ordeal. First innings he fetched an impossible delivery: 'The only ball I've seen similar was the ball that Warne got Gatting with: exactly the same the other way round. It pitched outside leg and I did everything right, I thought, covered the ball, bat and pad close together. But I must've missed it by a fraction, 'cos it hit the top of off stump. Too good.' Second innings he fluffed a knee-high full-toss to short mid-on: 'I should have hit it into the Members'. But I was so surprised that, by the time I'd made up my mind, I miscued completely, straight up in the air. I laughed, actually, threw my bat up in the air. When I got back inside it wasn't too funny, though.'

Cables to Australia hummed with scorn for the pitch. Fingleton despatched: 'If a team is invited to a series of five-day Tests then the pitches should be prepared accordingly.' Bill O'Reilly agreed: 'Let's have it straight. This pitch is a complete disgrace. What lies in store for Test cricket if the groundsmen are allowed to play the fool like this again?' A famous photo of groundsmen sweeping the surface in the middle of an apparent dust storm flashed round the world, and Johnson overheard curator Bert Flack blessing the deepening Suez crisis and Arthur Miller's marriage to Marilyn Monroe: 'If it wasn't for Nasser and Monroe, I'd be on the front pages every day.'

There was more flint to Australia's second effort, and rain on Saturday and Monday permitted just two hours of play and soothed the surface. McDonald and Craig stayed four hours. Then, at lunch on the final day, the pitch's personality changed again. Craig recalls:

> We actually went down that day expecting not to play and were astounded when they said we were starting on time. The pitch was quite easy in the morning, and Col and I got through it without too much trouble.

Then the sun came out at lunchtime, and Tony Lock's second ball bounced and spun past second slip for four byes.

Craig, Ken Mackay, Miller and Archer succumbed in nine Laker overs for three runs, and McDonald was removed by the second ball after tea for 89: a five-and-a-half-hour soliloquy. It was all over by 5.27pm. Laker shouldered his sweater and left the field trying to look as if he took 19–90 every other day.

Laker's unparalleled 46 series wickets cost nine runs each. On pitches tailored for his talents, his subtle variations and relentless accuracy preyed on minds like a dripping tap. By the Fifth Test at The Oval, he was taking wickets almost by rote. Ian Craig, out for 2 and 7, remembers:

> Those innings showed how the frustration was getting to us. In the first innings, I just got sick of the constant defensive play all the time and decided to hit over the top before the ball was bowled. All I did was slice it to cover. In the second innings I thought I batted pretty well. I was there forty-five minutes and didn't really play a false shot. But, when you look at it, it's a disaster: out for seven, caught in the leg-trap.

Only McDonald, who made 89 and 45 against Surrey and 33 and 89 in the Fourth Test, seemed able to make Laker work up a sweat. His views on the series are pungent:

> England cheated: if by cheating you include the practice of preparing wickets to suit your own purposes. I mean, we wouldn't have minded so much if the pitches had played true to character. But we'd played Lancashire at the start of the tour, and it seamed like a normal Manchester wicket. Then the Test pitch was like Bondi Beach when it was dry and a mud-heap when it was wet.
>
> In truth, though, Australians were poor at playing off-spin on slow turning wickets. They tended to thrust at it with firm hands, where the way to do it was play side-on, close to your body, bat inside pad. They bowled well. We batted very badly.

'WE'VE ONLY GOT TO MAKE 500...'

No beaten team is harmonious, and this tour was no exception. While Johnson was applauded for tact and courtesy, he found Test cricket in his thirty-ninth year a struggle. With just six wickets and 61 runs in five Tests, he struggled to gain his players' respect. And the optimism which had served him so well in the Caribbean now seemed artless. Craig says:

I don't think Ian was ever realistic about the situation. You'd have a situation where wickets were falling and we were miles behind on first innings, and Ian would say: 'We've only got to make 500 and we're back in it.' It seemed pretty naive. I suppose he felt obliged to make rallying speeches, but the team knew what was going on.

Most of Craig's NSW teammates believed that Miller should have been in charge. 'Johnson couldn't get anything out the players,' says Pat Crawford. 'Whereas the guys would have busted a gut for Keith. Mainly because they knew that, if he put his mind to it, he could do their job as well as they could.' Davidson felt also that Johnson relied overmuch on older players: 'Ian was still trying to lead from the front, and he wasn't up to it. I guess he was trying to help us, but he should have realised that guys like Richie [Benaud], Ron [Archer], Ian [Craig] and myself had toured in 1953, and weren't as wet behind the ears as he thought.'

Roommates Benaud and Harvey became particularly disillusioned. They resented Johnson's insistence that the whole party attend all matches before the First Test, a decision meaning that no-one had a break from cricket for seven weeks. And Harvey appeared to become demoralised by the first prolonged dry spell in his career. 'I think Neil got a bit depressed on that tour,' says Craig. 'He was somewhere where he'd got 2000 runs before, and suddenly he was struggling. It got to him a bit.'

Press suggestions that Johnson was a *roi fainéant*, however, simply stiffened his resolve. 'I was over the hill, no doubt about it,' he says. 'So were Keith and Ray. But even though I wasn't performing terribly well, I felt I was still important to the side. I remember a journalist asking me: "Will you pick yourself in the next Test?" I replied: "Well, I've got one vote." '

And it's unlikely that dropping the pilot would have made much difference to the outcome of the series. Australia in 1956 was waging an unwinnable war.

'He Has a Few Moody Boys to Lead'

AUSTRALIA V NEW ZEALAND AND SOUTH AFRICA
1957–58

W hen Johnson's Ashes team returned home on 10 November 1956, after a four-week epilogue to their trip on the Indian subcontinent, earnest soul-searching began. Not only had their eight-month journey brought scant reward, but it had witnessed the end of the great ex-services cricketing generation. Following Hassett, Morris and Johnston, Miller, Johnson and Langley announced their retirements. Lindwall, too, appeared a shadow of his former self. The reins of Australian cricket were suddenly slack.

WHO'S IN CHARGE?

Frontrunner for the captaincy was Harvey. A batsman of impudent attacking instincts, a cover fieldsman who dared batsmen to take him on, a cricketer of infectious confidence, he had long been a glass of fashion for younger colleagues. 'Neil had amazing faith in his own abilities,' says Ron Archer. 'When you batted with him, you never called. He'd just take over, and he never misjudged a run.' Some even adopted his sartorial habits, scorning caps because Harvey believed that peaks were distracting.

Two other candidates were also mentioned in despatches. As Miller's NSW understudy, Benaud had impressed with his zest in a handful of matches; as Miller's Australian understudy, Archer himself had begun translating potential into performance. 'Ron in 1956 was a very great cricketer in the making,' says Colin McDonald. 'He could have been anything.'

Neither Harvey nor Benaud, however, stood in good odour with the board. Both heard that they'd been the subject of unflattering 1956 tour reports. And Archer was injured: in the Karachi Test on the homeward leg of Australia's trip, he'd snagged his spikes in the matting surface and wrenched his knee so badly that it cost him the entire domestic season. Then, out of the confusion, a dark horse emerged. On 13 November 1956, NSW installed Ian Craig as skipper.

It was a rude shock. With an average of 23 from six Tests, Craig was hardly the finished cricketing article. And, despite his receding hairline and basso profundo tones, he was still only twenty-one and living at home with his parents in Mosman. Not least surprised was Craig. He'd recently spent more time wondering about his career than his cricket. Having completed a three-year Sydney University pharmacy diploma, he was considering further study at Oxford during 1957. After meeting twenty-one-year-old student nurse Leslie Hornby at a Northampton benefit dance during the Ashes summer, Craig was also engaged. 'Getting the NSW captaincy threw me a bit,' he recalls. 'Like everyone else, I'd assumed that Richie would be the one.' But Craig took stock. Perhaps he might be the man to captain Australia: 'After a while, I reasoned that I was a 50–50 chance. It all depended on how the board judged Neil and Richie's behaviour in England in 1956. I was actually quite relaxed about it. I knew that Neil would be an excellent captain under whom I'd be glad to play. But I also thought I could do it.'

Captains in Collision

Victoria–NSW Sheffield Shield matches, always remorselessly competitive, took on added meaning in 1956–57. The first, over Christmas, could hardly have been more even: a tie, played out on a soft pitch in funereal light at the Junction Oval (the MCG was still off-limits after the Olympics). Harvey made the running, manipulating his bowlers adroitly as NSW chased 161 on the final day. But Craig also emerged well. Hoarse from tonsilitis when he batted, he and Benaud almost wrested the game with a last-day stand of 70.

When the teams arrived at the SCG to practice for the rematch a month later, the team for New Zealand was read out: vice-captain Harvey, captain Craig. Harvey smarted at the rebuke: 'I was pretty pissed-off about it. I reckoned I was entitled. I guess the thinking was that I tended to speak my mind a bit, and I might not be up to the captain's off-field duties. It's one of my failings. A spade's a spade with me, and I've never seen anything wrong with that: the truth never hurt anybody.'

At the toss next morning, Craig was friendly. 'Bad luck, Nin,' he said. 'I thought you might have got it.' Team lists were swapped, Harvey called incorrectly and—to his mild surprise—was invited to bat. But no sooner had Craig made a gesture of conciliation than he indicated he'd be no soft touch. As Harvey returned to the dressing-room to tell his openers to pad up, Jack Edwards told him: 'Bad news, skipper. Col McDonald's had to go to hospital. He was in the nets, and he top-edged a sweep into his nose. They reckon it's busted.'

Harvey rolled his eyes, walked from the room and jogged the length of the Members' Bar to the home dressing-room, looking for Craig. He explained the situation. Could he change his team to include twelfth man Bill Lawry?

In a word, no, said Craig, and the laws of cricket were on his side. 'We'd tossed and exchanged teams,' he says. 'And, well, what are rules for?'

Harvey flushed with anger, spun on his heel and left: 'I was fuming when I got back to our rooms. I'd expected a bit of sportsmanship and I hadn't got it.' He turned to Len Maddocks. 'Come on Maddocko, you and I are going in.'

All Harvey's frustrations now played themselves out through his bat. His 209 took five hours, almost half coming in boundaries. 'I was so furious,' he says. 'They'd just got my back up. But it probably brought out the best in me. First ball with the second new ball was a good length outswinger and I smashed it. It bounced fifteen yards back from the point fence.' None of it,. though, changed the fact that Craig was Australia's captain. All that remained to be settled was who would play under him.

The experimental fourteen that flew from Sydney on 14 February 1957 had an average age of twenty-four, and eight were uncapped in Tests: from Victoria, paceman Ian Meckiff and spinner Lindsay Kline; from South Australia, new-ball bowler John Drennan and keeper Barry Jarman; batsman Norm O'Neill and slow bowler John Martin from NSW; West Australians Bob Simpson and Ron Gaunt.

Although it was a low-key trip, without a full Test match, Craig knew he was on trial and that it wouldn't be easy. Jarman recalls: 'I thought Ian had to do it himself on that tour. Even at my age I wasn't so dumb that I couldn't see the senior players didn't give him much support.' But Craig gradually grew into his role, leading the team to seven victories in ten matches, and earning points when he defied a curfew decreed by manager Jack Norton during the First Unofficial Test.

On the Sunday evening, Norton gathered his charges and issued the instruction that all should return to the hotel by 10pm. 'I'm sorry Jack,' Craig said, in his slow, deliberate rumble. 'But I've arranged to go out to dinner tonight and so have Neil [Harvey] and Peter [Burge] and we're going.' Next morning, Harvey scored 84, Craig an undefeated 123, and there was no further talk of curfews. Craig's appointment was ratified by his nomination to lead Australia in South Africa five months hence.

THE RISE OF RICHIE BENAUD

In hindsight, the 1956–57 season can be seen as the summer in which Australian cricket was revivified. And no-one personifies that regeneration as much as Richie Benaud.

Until 1956, Benaud had the form of a cricket career, but not the substance. His 27 Tests had been full of eye-catching moments, but no more than a handful invited the viewer to linger. Noting the many mannerisms he shared with his former state captain, detractors tagged him 'The Poor Man's Keith Miller'.

Yet Benaud was increasingly his own man. He took a new job. After years itching to be a journalist, he persuaded *Sydney Sun* editor Lindsay Clinch to give him a trial. Clinch threw him onto police rounds under the hard-bitten Noel Bailey, starting first at 5am then later on a midnight beat. Benaud found it exhilarating: chasing round accident scenes and robberies, dictating stories to edition with seconds to spare. 'I was often recognised as the cricketer, and it helped,' he says. 'It was a kind of short-cut where I needed to build up some contacts because I had come in "cold" so to speak as a twenty-six-year-old.'

Benaud's cricket was likewise beginning to click. Two England tours on indifferent pitches had straightened his backlift and improved his defence. And, never forgetting a lesson, he had steadily discovered the secrets of his demanding wrist-spin art. One day on the London–Bristol train in 1953, for instance, Doug Ring had picked an apple from a basket and shown him a grip: a sliding top-spinner. 'It was that ball more than any other which taught me how, on good batting pitches, you did not have to spin a yard,' says Benaud. 'Four inches was enough.' Three years later in the nets at Trent Bridge, Benaud had persuaded the Adelaide expatriate Bruce Dooland to demonstrate a flipper: a ball bowled from beneath the wrist that tended to skid and sometimes come back. He also began to emulate Dooland's tight, truncated run.

Yet variety alone, Benaud knew, was insufficient. He cast his mind back to a dinner at Scarborough in September 1953, where Tom Goodman of the *Sydney Morning Herald* had introduced him to Bill O'Reilly. O'Reilly had been typically direct. Trying for a wicket every delivery was ruining Benaud's control. The whole point of bowling was allowing batsmen nothing to hit.

The solution was practice. A benefit of his new job's antisocial hours was that he could arrive for state training at the SCG No. 2 at 3pm: earlier than anyone bar batsman Bill Watson, who worked a dawn shift at the Flemington markets. Benaud would bowl three hours in the one net: ball after ball, to openers, middle-order batsmen, and tailenders, working out a way to combat each, sometimes forgoing a bat in order to perfect his craft.

For winter, he and Alan Davidson formed a practice pact. Benaud was living at Westmead, Davidson at Epping, and as often as possible after work and at weekends they hefted their gear to the SCG No. 2. 'We'd aim to be there by 3.30pm, bowling by 4pm and finish about 6.30pm,' Davidson recalls. 'And we'd bowl flat out, until we were exhausted: our theory was that anyone can bowl well when they're fresh, but it's when you're tired that it really counts.'

Afterwards there would be a lengthy analysis of where each might be erring. One day, Benaud said suddenly: 'The important thing is rhythm, Davo. Back foot, front arm. Get that right and everything follows. You're very side-on already, but you should be like a windmill, looking inside your arm so you don't fall away.' For his part, Davidson reaffirmed the cardinal virtue of accuracy. 'Look at Laker,' he said. 'He stands on tippie-toe to get the bounce. His arm's always high and he lands it on a threepenny bit. C'mon, where's that spot? You've gotta hit it and hit it and hit it.' Gradually, with increasing frequency, Benaud did so.

While touring New Zealand, Benaud also made a critical discovery in a Timaru chemist. Noticing torn flesh on Benaud's first and third fingers, where incessant bowling had worn away calluses, pharmacist Ivan James gestured to a solution of calomine and boracic acid. Had Benaud tried this? It did wonders for leg ulcers.

Benaud was willing to try anything. And, within a few days, the skin on his fingers turned hard and leathery, but not so dry that the skin peeled again: the perfect texture for imparting spin. Calomine boracic lotion: for the rest of his career, Benaud would never be without it.

While Benaud was experimenting with pharmaceuticals on one side of the world, Ian Craig was selling them on the other. With the board's sanction, Australia's new captain arrived in London on 30 April 1957 to take up a retailing job with pharmaceutical giant Boots Pure Drug Company. Craig lived in a flat in Regent's Park, and worked a stint behind the counter on a dusk-to-dawn shift in Piccadilly Circus.

People, of course, wanted to meet Australia's callow new skipper. Craig was invited to play for Free Foresters and MCC and, when Menzies visited in June, also attended one of the prime minister's grand cricket dinners in the Princess Ida and Pinafore Rooms of the Savoy.*

Craig had half an eye on the South African tour ahead. He had his tonsils out at Guy's Hospital as a precaution against sickness on the trip, and broke off his engagement to Leslie Hornby. 'I realised,' he says, 'that it would have been totally unfair to get married then spend the first few years away, leaving her behind in a strange country.' Then he boarded the *Capetown Castle* on 19 September bound for Cape Town.

Craig's assignment was now personal chemistry, how to get the best from his inchoate team. He walked into a difficult situation. The night before the Australians had boarded their Qantas Super Constellation at Mascot on 5 October, South Australian manager Jack Jantke had suffered a heart attack. Nor had anyone had the foresight to give Jantke's tour documents to stand-in tour leader Harvey.

Craig responded creatively. Instead of assuming all power himself, he spread the wear. He posted a daily roster for collection of gear and laundry from which nobody was exempt. Players were obliged to attend one official function a week, and Craig formed a light-hearted 'amenities committee' that levied fines for misdemeanours like walking away from an earbasher at a reception, telling the same story twice, pinching another player's girlfriend. 'I'd seen the South Africans do it themselves in 1952,' says Craig. 'And it seemed like a good way to break the ice, have a bit of fun, and give the guys something to look out for, rather than being too intense about the cricket all the time.'

Not everyone approved. Writing home about Craig's 'amenities committee', Dick Whitington deplored such 'a penchant for ersatz Anglicised

---

* The Menzies papers at the National Library preserve the drinks bill for the occasion: thirty-six whiskies, two sherries, thirteen lagers, thirty-two cocktails, twenty gins, twenty-seven brandies, three creme de menthes and seven kummels. Craig was not drinking.

fripperies'. Fingleton thought Craig's appointment an affront to Australia's captaincy, and told Menzies: 'I am not at all happy about Craig as leader in South Africa. He has a few moody boys to lead and I think he is much too callow in years and experience to lead a team abroad.'

And there *was* some moodiness. 'Ian was a very nice bloke,' says Colin McDonald. 'But I had the same beef as Benaud and Harvey: I felt he'd jumped the queue.' Peter Burge, an unswerving supporter of Harvey, says: 'Quite simply, Ian should never have been captain of Australia. They said he was an old head on young shoulders, but there's no such thing.'

By the same token, players appreciated that Craig hadn't sought his advancement, and liked his unassuming nature. Unlike Johnson, he willingly accepted advice. Unlike Johnson, he was aware of the players' need to relax and freed those uninvolved in games to do as they pleased. In one match at Benoni, he even acted as a substitute fielder. Davidson recalls: 'I'm sure what happened in the first few weeks of the tour had an effect on the way we blended. Some blokes become captain and don't see anyone anymore. But Craigy never pretended he knew everything. He never overdirected. He never told you how to play. There was no favouritism. He was always completely fair.'

THE UNDERSTUDIES

South African pressmen wasted little time christening Craig's team the weakest Australian side to visit the Union, and it was certainly one of the least performed. Harvey alone had toured South Africa. Lindwall had been left behind, keeper Len Maddocks was unavailable and, just before the tourists' departure, Ron Archer had aggravated his knee injury by jumping off the roof of a tanker at a Shell service station he'd been running in Queensland. It effectively ended his career.

Their understudies, moreover, had little to recommend them. Not two years before, Ian Meckiff had been rolling his left arm over at regulation medium pace. Then, at state practice, teammate Jeff Hallebone had muttered: 'You know, they're desperate for a quick bowler. Mightn't be a bad idea to just bowl flat out, fast as you can, and not care where it goes.' The twenty-two-year-old had followed the advice to the letter: he was intermittently as quick as a bowler could be, and often as inaccurate. There was certainly nothing in him of Lindwall's smooth athleticism and preternatural control.

Lindsay Kline was a wry, self-deprecating twenty-three-year-old, who sold sporting goods at the Myer Emporium and bowled left-arm wrist-spin. His rise had been delayed by a spell of national service at Puckapunyal in 1953, but superiors had been understanding. Kline recalls: 'I tried to get time off for cricket the first time by telling them that my grandmother had died, and that was rejected. Then I told them that my mother was seriously ill and that was rejected. So I told them straight I needed time off to play cricket and they let me. Sometimes it pays to be honest.' Yet his name drew blank looks from South Africans, and his idiosyncratic 'kangaroo hop' was comical rather than threatening.

A boyhood glimpse of Don Tallon had set Queenslander Wally Grout's heart on keeping for his state and country. But Tallon had made him serve a long and dispiriting apprenticeship, and his glovework had seldom impressed southern judges. Whitington called him a long-stop. When the journalist approached him en route for data to include in some pen pix, Grout growled: 'You've left out my team function. I'm long-stop.'

Archer's eleventh-hour replacement, his state teammate Ken Mackay, occasioned even more indignance. 'Slasher' Mackay was one of most distinctive cricketers to don an Australian cap, a teetotal insurance inspector of grim-set features, the build of a pipe-cleaner man, and the bent-kneed stance of a croquet player. Bowling to Mackay on benign Sheffield Shield pitches was one of cricket's most unavailing tasks; it was as if a black-out curtain had been drawn. One of his staunchest fans was the prime minister. At the trial match before the selection of the 1956 Ashes party, Mackay heard Menzies ask selector Jack Ryder: 'When are you going to pick Slasher?'

Ryder replied: 'You pick your Cabinet, I'll help pick the Test team.'

Yet no-one in England in 1956 suffered more mortifyingly. Marooned in the midst of Laker's close catchers, Mackay looked as uncomfortable as an incontinent man on a long train journey. His last four Test innings yielded four runs. Mackay was so sure he had done his dash in Test cricket that, on returning home, he put his Australian cap up for sale.

When Bradman, Seddon and Ryder reopened Mackay's file, the response was scornful. Bill O'Reilly wrote in the *Sydney Morning Herald*: 'Circumspect words fail me now to express adequately my contempt for this howler.' Jim Mathers of the *Daily Mirror* described Mackay's selection as a 'step backwards into the Dark Ages of cricket'.

Nor was the series form guide auspicious. Having bested Australia at home in 1956, England had been held to a draw on South African pitches. No batsman had yet tamed the wily off-spinner Hugh Tayfield, pawky all-rounder Trevor Goddard, and the belligerent pace pair of Peter Heine and Neil Adcock. At a Johannesburg civic reception, the tourists found local journalists offering 4–1 against the visitors maintaining Australia's unbeaten record in South Africa. They took it.

NIGHT RIDE

After three days of the First Test at the Wanderers, Craig's team was in strife: 7–307 chasing the hosts' 470. Nor were they rapt in Jantke's replacement as manager, Jack Norton: as in New Zealand, he'd imposed a 10pm curfew. The South Africans were also under curfew from their manager Ken Viljoen, but it was 11.30pm, and they were enjoying a few laughs at their guests' expense.

That evening, the policy finally got to Alan Davidson. Not that he had any mischief in mind: he just wanted to relax. 'Look,' he told his South Australian roommate Les Favell. 'If I don't get out I'm going to go off my rocker. Let's go out tonight. Bugger the curfew.'

They crossed the road to see a show called *Don't Go Near the Water* and bumped into Springbok Ken Funston as they left. Funston laughed. 'You boys are meant to be tucked up in bed, aren't you? What are you doing here?'

'We just had to get out,' said Davidson. 'We were going crazy.'

Funston gestured at a car. 'That's my Peugeot over there,' he said. 'I can get a lift back to the hotel. Why don't you go for a spin?'

Davidson and Favell took the keys and drove the thirty-five miles to Pretoria for a look-see. The dark streets were uninhabited, so they pulled in at a cafe, ordered some toasted sandwiches and coffee, and talked to a few of the young diners. It was nice to be out after all those early nights, and the pair didn't return from their innocent excursion until 1am. But, when they checked with the concierge to find their room-key, there was only a note: 'Report to me. I've got your keys. Norton.'

After a panicky discussion, the truants headed for the Houghton home of Curt and Natalie Rosenberg: local cricket lovers who'd entertained the Australians for Christmas the previous day. Hearing their explanation, the Rosenbergs offered beds for the night. But, when Davidson and Favell arrived at the Wanderers next morning, teammates filled them with foreboding: 'Cripes, you two are in trouble. You're on the first plane home.'

Davidson was able to seek refuge in the field, and bowled like a man who suddenly wished to be considered indispensable, grabbing three wickets in seven overs before lunch. But, as he re-entered the dressing-room, a wan Favell advised: 'Jack wants to see you.'

Davidson sidled up to Norton, and tried to sound confident: 'I believe you want to see me Jack?'

'Where were you last night?' Norton asked tersely.

'I was at the Rosenbergs,' Davidson replied.

'Hmm,' said Norton. 'That's Favell's story, too.'

Then, through the window, Davidson spied Curt Rosenberg. 'There he is, Jack,' Davidson said, pointing the South African out. 'Why don't you ask him?' Norton did so and, when he returned, said: 'Well, he says so, too. So I suppose I've got to accept it.' Davidson swept on to take 6–34, saving the match, and providing empirical evidence that late nights need not impair performance. The curfew was repealed.

A PAIR OF ACES

Customarily, when a cricketer dominates a summer, it is thanks to a large degree of luck, a fortunate turn of conditions or a prodigious natural flair. And Richie Benaud had all of these as he fashioned Australia's 1957–58 tour of South Africa in his own image. Yet it was mostly old-fashioned graft that gained Benaud his 106 wickets at 19 and 817 runs at 50.

The net practices he had begun in Australia continued in South Africa. When others went golfing or to the races, he would remain, spinning for hour after hour, then balming his corn-embossed fingers with calomine boracic lotion. Ray Robinson estimated that Benaud spun more than 1000 deliveries at practice before his first ball in anger at Kitwe in Northern Rhodesia and wrote home: 'I have never seen a bowler prepare more thoroughly for a Test tour.'

As Benaud's confidence grew, the trip became a pageant. Benaud made two Test centuries at the Wanderers: his 122 with twenty fours retrieved the First Test, his three-hour 100 plus 9–154 ensured a rout in the Fourth. Five wickets for 49 clinched the Second Test at Newlands, 5–82 the Fifth at St George's Park. And when South Africa achieved something approaching supremacy in the Third Test at Kingsmead, Benaud's 50 overs so becalmed the batsmen that they misspent their tactical advantage.

Spectators who'd watched Australia eight years earlier saw vestiges of Miller in Benaud's play. He would nod if a good ball was bowled to him. If near the boundary, he would chat animatedly to the crowd. There were often little touches of the theatrical: when a loud appeal was rejected at Port Elizabeth, for instance, Benaud held his hands to his ears to stifle the crowd's reflex roar. But Benaud, with the responsibilities of being the chief spinner, was finally establishing his own Test identity.

The same was true of Davidson who, after a dozen Tests as an auxil-iary, finally gained unquestioned custody of the new ball. Davidson's broad shoulders suited the responsibility, and his angle of delivery from left-arm over posed constant perplexities: 32 of his 72 wickets were bowled or lbw. When tiring, he would incant the mantra that Benaud had coined: 'Back foot, front arm.'

Davidson was a bowler of varying humours, always in the grip of some malady or strain. So long did he spend in the hands of the Newlands masseur that comrades attached a plaque to the rubbing bench: 'The AK Davidson Autograph Treatment Table.' Yet, as Benaud recalled from that Test, the scent of wickets usually brought him round:

> Alan had been limping back to bowl and then boring in at the batsman and moving the ball late, either into or away from them. Then he would limp back and Craig would ask him if he were all right—he would say 'no' and get a sympathetic pat on the shoulder and then bore in again with yet another magnificent delivery.
>
> The Capetown pitch was very slow and I asked Craig if I could come up three yards at gully for the one that flew off the thick edge and wouldn't normally carry. Davo limped back for the next ball and Waite square-drove it like a bullet. I caught the red blur, body parallel to the ground, and was just rolling over the second time when Davo arrived alongside me saying excitedly: 'It was the old trap, you know, the old trap.' It had taken him just two seconds to get down and the boys thought it was the fastest he'd moved all day.

SLASHER AND THE GRIZ

As the series unfolded, the cricketers who had come to South Africa as unknowns became household names.

Coaxing life from a dead track, Meckiff took 8–177 in the First Test. At the fag end of Australia's Second Test victory, his mate Kline then took a hat-trick with the second, third and fourth deliveries of his second spell. He recalls:

> When Adcock came in to face the third delivery, I thought I was a chance. As I went back, I was thinking I'd give him a leg-break. But as I was run-ning in I decided on a wrong 'un. They said it was hard to pick. It turned

a bit, and he snicked it to slip. I didn't realise what a good catch it was until we went to the pictures a couple of nights later and saw the Movietone News. In Burwood and District it would have been four runs for sure, but Simmo was such a good catcher.

Craig had increasing cause to bless the presence of the vulpine Mackay. He came by runs rather than acquiring them, yet the Springbok bowlers were able to evict him only thrice in the span of 375 runs. By the end of the trip, Springbok Roy McLean was calling him 'Iron Curtain'.

Mackay was a profoundly superstitious man. He used lucky bats until they were black with age, had a dread of the numbers 13 and 87 so absolute that his autobiography proceeds straight from chapter twelve to chapter fourteen, and an allegiance to Wrigley's chewing gum so unstinting that he stockpiled enough to last the tour. But as he masticated his way round the Union, Mackay also chewed away at Hugh Tayfield. In spite of Mackay's sufferings against Laker, Tayfield could find no way past him. Craig recalls: 'Here was someone who'd been ostracised for his technique against off-spin, and Hughie would have been rubbing his hands together. But on the South African wickets where the ball bounced a bit more and maybe didn't turn as much, Slasher had this incredible capacity to leave balls that were inches outside off stump.' Watching the two in opposition at St George's Park, Keith Butler of the *Adelaide Advertiser* quipped: 'You know, Slasher could play this bloke in the middle of the night with a hurricane lamp.'

The other unfancied Queenslander, Grout, also made himself at home. In the six weeks before the First Test, neither he nor his South Australian junior Jarman kept well. Grout was also nursing a finger damaged against Eastern Province but, when an X-ray revealed a break that would require plaster, successfully implored the specialist not to report it to his captain. 'It's only bruised,' Grout told Craig. 'I'll be right for the next match.'

When Craig, Harvey and third selector Peter Burge convened to select the First Test team, the skipper preferred Jarman, his deputy Grout, and the last was undecided. Burge recalls:

I went and thought about it for an hour or two. I reckoned that there wasn't much in it between Barry and Wal standing back. Barry may even have been slightly ahead. But in my final summation—and to this day Barry probably thinks it's because Wally and I were Queenslanders— I thought Wally was better standing up. He'd kept to [Queensland leggies] Wal Walmsley and Brian Flynn and, because I thought Benaud and Kline would do a lot of bowling, I voted for Wal.

Grout never surrendered this initial narrow advantage. After an indifferent first innings at the Wanderers, he scooped a Test record half-dozen catches in the second. 'It was incredible, really,' says Craig. 'From just getting the nod, all of a sudden he was catching them from everywhere. He never looked like putting one down for the rest of the trip.'

As his confidence grew, so Grout became more vocal. Conventional wisdom had it that the best wicketkeepers went unnoticed, but Grout maintained such a constant monologue of encouragement for bowlers and fielders that Harvey baptised him 'Grizzler', shortened to 'Griz'. Wherever he was, one also heard a constant stream of repartee. He told Whitington he'd seen a lion at Kruger National Park. 'A railway lion,' he then muttered to smirking comrades. Or when advised that the protracted stand by Jackie McGlew and John Waite at Durban had reached another record. 'Must be a long-playing record,' Grout groused. Or when a South African asked which public school he'd attended. 'I went to two,' Grout replied. 'Eatin' and drinkin'.'

TEAMING UP

Individual feats piled up. The brilliant twenty-one-year-old slip fielder Bob Simpson claimed 26 catches in 16 matches, his hard-boiled New South Wales teammate Jim Burke took out years of frustration at fickle selection by spending nine hours over 189 at Cape Town. But the prime ministerial telegram that Craig received to mark victory in the series read: 'Congratulations on a remarkable team success.' And above all, the trip had been a triumph of teamwork. Not since the war had an Australian team harmonised so completely. Meckiff explains:

> There's no doubt there was some feeling there about the captaincy. But with Harv and Rich, you'd never have known. The beauty of that tour was that, where previously younger and older players had tended to go their separate ways, Benaud and Harvey made sure that the younger guys were included in everything. If they were playing golf, for instance, you were always asked. That was a huge bonus. Perhaps, they could see the pitfalls of leaving younger players out, because Harv had had it in 1948 and Rich had seen it in '53. They knew the problems and made sure it didn't happen with them round.

Craig himself had a poor batting tour, averaging 15 from seven Test innings. But under the aegis of Harvey and Benaud, Craig had not missed a beat in the field or off it. And the one occasion Craig had equivocated about his form, at Port Elizabeth, Harvey was quick to assuage his concerns. Peter Burge recalls:

> Les Favell was making a lot of runs and Ian wasn't. And Craigy was such an honourable guy that, before practice, he said: 'I'm gonna drop myself. I'm not playing well.' I thought that that was OK, but Harv said no, and we decided to go to practice and have the meeting later. Then, while practice was going, Harv came over and said: 'Peter, I wanna word with you. Now, I've been playing Tests for ten years, and I know that there's never been an Australian captain dropped on tour in cricket history. And as far as I'm concerned, it won't happen this time.'
>
> I stepped back about three paces. Coming from Harvey, whom I respected enormously, that was a big statement. Anyway, we went to our selection meeting and Craigy said: 'I still don't think I should play.' And Neil says: 'Well, I do. Burgey?' And I said: 'As far as I'm concerned Ian, you're in.'

WHO'S IN CHARGE (II)?

Craig *was* in. And, if he had still to persuade some pundits of his captaincy credentials, Bradman left no doubt of his support by meeting the team as it returned on the *Dominion Monarch* in April 1958. Reporters, too, eagerly quizzed Craig about Australia's prospects against the English side that Peter May was expected to bring for the coming summer. After two undefeated tours as Australia's leader, Craig's was the face in the frame.

Another event in the off-season seemed to seal Craig's tenure. Harvey appeared on the Melbourne television program 'Meet the Press' and mentioned that he was unsettled in his employment. He had a wife and two children, but was still living in a small home near Heidelberg Repatriation Hospital. When the show was repeated in Sydney a week later, Harvey was contacted by Joe Ryan, head of a glassware company called John Dynon & Sons, who offered a sales supervisor's job. Ryan was a fanatical sports lover and surrounded himself with athletes: he already employed rugby stars Tiger Black and Keith Holman, as well as Queensland front-rower Brian Davies. And, although Harvey knew that such a move would harm his claims to the Australian captaincy, he felt unable to refuse. He did not have long left in the game and, by the time he transplanted his family in July, a third child was on the way.

A few weeks after Harvey's move, however, the terrain changed again. Craig visited Melbourne to speak to a dinner of pharmaceutical students, and returned home feeling queasy. His parents sent him to bed. He was too weak to play in a baseball semi-final for Mosman at the weekend, and the doctor examining him on Monday could not mistake the symptoms: Craig was suffering hepatitis and prescribed six weeks' bed rest.

The season was under way by the time Craig resumed, and he seemed to find his form with an immediate club hundred. But noughts in his first two first-class innings confirmed Craig's worst fears. In a letter to the Australian board's secretary, Alan Barnes, he declared himself unavailable for the summer's cricket. For the second time in two years, Australian cricket was on the lookout for a leader.

'His Hard Work
Is an Inspiration...'

AUSTRALIA V ENGLAND,
PAKISTAN AND INDIA
1958-60

On 25 November 1958, the telephone rang in Neil Harvey's office at John Dynon & Sons in Kent Street, Sydney. It was Richie Benaud. 'Guess who's captain?' he asked.

'You are,' Harvey replied.

'That's right,' said Benaud. 'I'm sorry. I thought you might have got it.'

Harvey was disappointed, but phlegmatic. 'There was no point moaning about it,' he recalls. 'And Richie and I had been mates for years, so it wasn't so hard missing out to him. I was glad to be his vice-captain.' After a lengthy meal and a few drinks at the Cricketers' Club with his old friend and new skipper, any pangs eased. There was much to be done. Australia had lost three consecutive Ashes series for the first time in the twentieth century, and the band led by Peter May was one of the finest to fill an MCC teamsheet: dependable openers in Arthur Milton and Peter Richardson, the middle order of May, Cowdrey, Tom Graveney and Willy Watson, indestructible gloveman Godfrey Evans, the ornery all-rounder Bailey, the spin of Laker and Lock, the speed of Tyson, Statham, Peter Loader and the garrulous Fred Trueman.

Yet Benaud and Harvey could discern the outline of a serviceable Australian side. McDonald and Burke had knitted into a solid opening partnership. Harvey's batting was buttressed by the all-round skills of the captain, Davidson, Mackay and Grout, and Meckiff's shock potential was unarguable. They were, perhaps, still short a commanding middle-order batsman. But, as it happened, one was ready-made.

THE YOUNG ADONIS

Twenty-one-year-old St George right-hander Norman O'Neill appeared the model of a young Australian sportsman. Tall, bronzed, broad-shouldered, he had it all: a full endowment of strokes, a weight of shot off the back foot that made teammates shy of bowling to him at the nets, and a throwing arm that earned him a place as utility player in the 1957 All-Australian baseball team.

Could this be the charismatic batting talent Australians had pined for since Bradman's retirement? Sydney's popular press had no doubt. They deplored his omission from the 1957–58 tour of South Africa, pilloried the NSWCA when he seemed likely to accept a job with Adelaide grocery magnate Jack Butler in February 1958, breathed a collective sigh of relief a few weeks later when an offer from Rothmans kept him at home. And they followed him en masse to Perth when the MCC played its second match of the tour against a Combined XI, staking out the Palace Hotel in the hope of a few words, filming him at practice, even trying to persuade Bradman to pose with him. The Don declined: 'He hasn't made the grade yet.'

O'Neill felt lost amid it all:

> There were reporters everywhere. I'd never seen anything like it. I spent half an hour, an hour, answering their questions, then they followed me to practice and it kept going. I remember Charles Fortune standing behind the nets with a tape recorder and talking to me while I was batting. Then Phil Tresidder and Percy Beames tapped me on the shoulder and took me to the Tattersall's Club, just to relax me, get me out of the spotlight for a while. We had a few drinks, played a few frames of snooker. It was a very good preparation for the game. As it turned out, I got a few.

Arriving just as Laker was finding his groove, O'Neill endured an anxious few minutes. Then he swept savagely. Laker threw his hand to his head at such irreverence, but the ball skated away for four. By stumps, O'Neill had cruised to 80. By the time he was caught at slip off Laker for 104 on Monday, a new star had been born.

A month later, O'Neill and a friend were driving through Sydney when they saw 'Australian Team Picked' on a *Daily Mirror* poster. 'I guess

I was expecting to make the side,' says O'Neill. 'But I'd already had the experience of missing out on the South African tour, so I pulled up and bought a paper. Seeing my name there was a very nice feeling.'

CAPTAIN'S LOG

O'Neill excelled. So did Harvey. Davidson had the ball on a string. And Benaud emerged as a captain of uncanny resource, gaining momentum at every corner.

Benaud was fortunate to be leading a team whose spirit Craig had brought to the boil, but was careful to consolidate that precious sensation. The night before the series began at the Gabba, Benaud convened the first of many Test match dinners. Everyone from the captain to debutant O'Neill was invited to tender ideas about assailing the Englishmen. Sharp calling and running were recommended, English fielders with poor arms were singled out. Benaud had also noticed in England in 1956 how little players like Cowdrey and Bailey seemed to enjoy proximate catchers: they were to be crowded at every opportunity.

Benaud also impressed all players as a captain with their best interests at heart. In the last over before lunch of the rubber's first day, for instance, Jim Burke asked for a sightscreen to be moved at the Vulture Street end when Peter Loader came round the wicket. It would not budge, having been pegged so as not to impede the view of the QCA official party in the Members'. Burke finally gave up but, after blindly edging the next ball, returned to the dressing-room furious. Benaud took up the fight: 'I went around and had a word with Ted Williams, the QCA secretary, and said I didn't want any more problems with the sightscreen. There were no more problems.'

On the field, the Australians found strength through joy. Unlike his two precursors, Benaud could lift comrades by his own performance. The Englishmen had disparaged his leg spin before the series began, May telling them: 'Play down the line to Benaud. He won't worry you.' But Benaud did: his 31 wickets at 18 in the series confounded all. And, as Hutton had always seemed to stoke the fire in Lindwall, the sight of May seemed to bestir Benaud.

Benaud's spirit was contagious. Where cricketers before him had celebrated a wicket with a pat on the back and a modest hitch of the trousers, he encouraged a more demonstrative manner that he called 'total team spirit'. Some captious critics thought it melodramatic, and even Keith Miller was ambivalent, though ultimately inclined to excuse it:

Benaud's enthusiasm for the game sometimes proves irksome to the onlooker, as, for instance, when he takes a wicket and rushes up to the other end of the pitch to embrace his colleagues. That sort of stuff is best left to soccer players. But it's really only keenness and his hard work is an inspiration to any budding all-rounder, Australian or English.

Benaud also summed up character quickly. Davidson, a regular martyr to injuries real and imagined, needed mothering. Benaud would wring extra overs from him with sympathy and praise. 'Just one more over, Al,' Benaud would say.

'I can't, Richie,' Davidson would reply. 'I'm done.'

'But just try another one, Al. That was a beautiful ball that last over you sent away to Bailey. Come on Al, here's the ball.'

'Where's the ball, Richie? I can't see it.' Then Davidson would bore in again, full of self-sacrificing spirit.

Benaud also developed a priceless reputation as a lucky captain, even when unlucky. He decided to bat at Brisbane but, when he lost the toss and saw England do so instead, discovered first-day conditions ideal for his pacemen. The same happened in Melbourne. He cringed on losing the toss in Adelaide on a bone-jarring flat pitch, and couldn't believe his ears when May elected to bowl. 'Pardon?' asked Benaud. 'You can take strike,' May repeated. Australia made 476.

Benaud was tossing with an 1887 four-shilling piece that Bradman had given him and, at the end of the series, the captain complained to the chairman of selectors: 'This isn't much good—I haven't won a toss with it.'

'No,' Bradman replied. 'And you haven't lost a Test with it either.' Benaud kept the coin.

Young Norm and Old McDonald

O'Neill gratified all his admirers, not so much by the weight of his 282 runs in five completed innings as by the grand manner of their acquisition. Ian Peebles of the *Sunday Times* noted: 'Although O'Neill is in the very early days of his career, it is already something of an occasion when he comes to the wicket, and one can sense the expectancy of the crowd and the heightened tension of the opposition.'

The swiftness of O'Neill's rise also posed him some ticklish questions. During the Fourth Test, US Davis Cup coach Bill Talbert contacted the Australian and invited him to breakfast at his hotel. He was, he explained, representing the New York Yankees: would O'Neill be interested in attending a pre-season camp in California and, perhaps, playing in the National League?

For a cricketer on £75 a Test with £10 expenses, the sign-on fee of £2000 plus fares and accommodation was of more than passing interest. O'Neill consented and received his tickets. But, a couple of days before his departure, he was called to the office of Rothmans' chairman Sir Ronald Irish. 'Norm, I believe you should give this a bit more thought,' Irish said. 'You've just made it as a cricketer and you've got a very promising career ahead of you.'

O'Neill *did* think about. Baseball was in his blood—his uncle had been an interstate baseballer—and it might make him wealthy. But there would be no tang of international competition. And, having come so far, he might regret sacrificing a blossoming cricket career. Irish eventually notified Yankees' manager George Weiss of O'Neill's withdrawal.

For all the tributes showered on O'Neill, however, Australia's batting bulwark was the unfashionable Victorian Colin McDonald. He was a short man, balding, played with too much bottom hand for purists, and tottered round on dicky knees ruined by baseball. But he was tough and enjoyed a contest. Off the field, the son of the first librarian at the Australian National University was known to argue the legs off a chair. On it, he annoyed bowlers like a stone in a shoe.

McDonald had much in common with his captain. Both had served long apprenticeships, and had their appetites for success sharpened by three consecutive Ashes defeats. McDonald had approached the 1958–59 series as he'd approached no other, working out for three months at a gym in Little Collins Street under the guidance of Davis Cup trainer Stan Nicholls to strengthen his troublesome legs.

He had a lot of running to do: 170 in eight hours at Adelaide Oval and 133 in five and a half at the MCG broke English spirit so badly that Fred Trueman was reduced to bartering for wickets. As McDonald and Burke walked out to bat on the last day of the Fifth Test to score the 60 Australia needed for a 4–0 victory, Fred Trueman started chatting: 'Eee, Macca, ah think ah should tell thee ah'm on 99 Test wickets.'

'That's interesting Fred,' said McDonald. 'Are you suggesting that one of us should get out for you?' When Trueman didn't reply, he continued: 'Well Fred, I'm on 490 runs for the series, so I'd like my 500th. And, anyway, you're a good enough bowler to get me out without me having to give it to you. Now piss off.' Trueman took his 100th wicket in New Zealand.

'Your captaincy and play have been outstanding. Congratulations,' read Benaud's telegram from the prime minister. McDonald's said simply: 'I'm proud of you.' The opener wrote in reply: 'Apart from Fred Trueman's language when snicking him for four it was the highlight of my season and I thank you. I might add that it makes the players very happy to know that the result of the series has pleased you as much as it has them.'

'COOLNESS OF ASSOCIATION'

Despite the recapture of the Ashes, victory was not wholly satisfying. With England falling back on old defensive devices, the First Test in particular had been one of the dreariest ever played. Trevor Bailey loitered almost ten hours over 95 runs for the match and Jim Burke almost six for 48. 'It was unbelievable,' remembers O'Neill. 'We knew that they'd probably close up if they got into trouble, but we never thought they'd just stop the way they did. I was just about falling to sleep in the covers. I virtually had nothing to do.'

Spectators had even less to take their minds off the funereal spectacle. Even a sympathetic bystander like Ken Archer could find nothing to redeem the game: 'My entire recollection of that match is of "Slasher" Mackay bowling to Trevor Bailey and Trevor bowling to "Slasher", each as illuminating as the other. And I swore that if Test match cricket was going to be like that, then I wouldn't go again.'

Further stretches of austere cricket followed. England trickled runs at 33 per 100 deliveries, and at Adelaide bowled a miserable 51 eight-ball overs in a day. The younger Australians, too, found a disappointing lack of rapport between the sides. 'Guys like Trueman and Statham and Milton were always friendly,' remembers Meckiff. 'But older guys like Evans and Laker and Watson didn't fraternise, and I don't think there's any doubt they had an internal team problem, a split down the middle. When they got in trouble, there was no way out for them.'

O'Neill comments:

There was a coolness of association that seemed to date back to 1956, where the Australians felt they'd been treated very badly. It annoyed us that a lot of the Englishmen had come over with reputations as walkers, but that they only lived up to them when they were 120 or something. If they got a thin edge early, they'd stay put. I remember batting in Sydney and hitting Tony Lock for a couple of fours before tea, and he hurried after me as we were coming off and gave me a huge serve. You know: 'Have you ever tried walking on water, O'Neill?' That sort of stuff. When I got to the dressing-room I was very upset and Sir Donald came over and asked: 'What was all that about?' When I explained, he said: 'Don't worry about it. They're trying to break your concentration. Just ignore it.'

The atmosphere wasn't aided by a succession of umpiring controversies. Hutton's Englishmen had developed a high regard for Adelaide's tall, bespectacled Mel McInnes, a fair and friendly invigilator, but May's found him dictatorial and worryingly inconsistent. The trouble began in Brisbane in England's second innings. Cowdrey turned Meckiff to short backward square leg and saw Lindsay Kline dive low and come up with the ball. After hesitating momentarily, McInnes raised his finger. Cowdrey left glancing meaningfully over his shoulder.

The Australians themselves were divided about the catch's authenticity. 'Hang on, Kipper,' Burge shouted. 'That's not a catch.'

'Course it's a fucking catch,' Grout retorted. And, when Benaud quizzed Kline, the fielder confirmed that he thought it taken fairly. McInnes stood unruffled at the centre of the gathering storm. As colleague Col Hoy approached, McInnes hissed: 'Piss off. Don't come near me. It makes it look like something's wrong.'

As McInnes had already nettled the Englishmen with a pedantic attitude to no-balls and running on the pitch, May and manager Freddie Brown requested a different official for the Melbourne Test. But amid much rancorous comment from the touring press, who recalled the MCC standing down Frank Chester in 1953 at Lindsay Hassett's request, the protest was rebuffed.

McInnes then had a dire Adelaide Test. He hesitated so long over a caught-behind decision against Mackay that the batsman walked. He ran to the wrong side of the pitch when judging a run-out so that he did not see McDonald's runner Burke a full three metres short of his crease. McDonald remembers:

> I was out by yards. You know, about a third of a pitch. And Mel gave me out, but then he realised that he should have been watching Burkie and changed his decision. I was actually walking past Brian Statham and he said: 'E's given ye not aht.' So I said: 'Well, what do I do now?' And he told me: 'Well, ah suppose ye get back there.'

McDonald, mortified, got himself out a few minutes later. But it could not save McInnes. He announced his 'retirement'…and promptly sold his reminiscences to a newspaper.

FEAR AND LOATHING

Never before, in fact, had the print media exerted such influence on a series. At times, it seemed that Fleet Street was as much a participant as the two sides. Before the MCC had even boarded the *Iberia*, they'd lost one of their number because of a press indiscretion: Johnny Wardle, the tempestuous Yorkshire spinner, had made himself too hot to hold by writing a pungent series of articles in the *Daily Mail* heaping scorn on his county captain and administrators. Once on board, Laker foreshadowed his retirement at the end of the 1959 season to a news agency reporter. Sports editors were unimpressed, sending snarling cables to their men on the *Iberia*: here was the first big story of the tour, and they'd all missed it. The normal competitiveness of the touring pressmen was ratcheted up.

Peter May was one of the first victims. His fiancee Veronica Gilligan had come to Australia chaperoned by her uncle, radio commentator Arthur Gilligan, and rumours that affairs of the heart were consuming too much of May's time climaxed in a concocted story that the couple had secretly married. May was appalled: 'This really was disgraceful and made me very angry. It is all right to look back on it now and have a good laugh. It makes us look rather dashing. But Virginia's parents, Marjorie and Harold Gilligan, were naturally horrified…and it did not increase my respect for certain members of the press.'

Once the Tests commenced, however, the May nuptials took second place to the thorny question of throwing. The English press looked askance at the crooked elbows and open chests of pacemen Ian Meckiff and Gordon Rorke and off-spinners Keith Slater and Jim Burke. Leading the charges at Meckiff was none other than Johnny Wardle, who'd come to Australia to write for Melbourne's *Herald*, ghosted by football scribe Alf Brown.

The attack was inflamed by widespread pre-tour overestimations of the MCC's strength. Many who'd hyped the side now found themselves pressured to explain its failure. Certainly, the vilification gathered pace as Meckiff did. When Col Hoy bumped into Bailey and Cowdrey outside Lennon's Hotel before the First Test, they asked rather tartly where Meckiff had been found.

'I don't really know,' Hoy replied. 'I've not seen him bowl; he's a bit of a newcomer. Why?'

'Because he's the worst bowler ever to represent Australia,' Bailey replied. 'Can't put the ball on the pitch.'

But Meckiff did get the ball on the pitch. In Melbourne, he routed England in just over three hours for 87 with 6–38, including Cowdrey and Bailey. It was a wonderful moment for the genial Meckiff: on his twenty-fourth birthday he'd been urged on by a crowd that sounded like it had been bottled at a VFL Grand Final. Then, an hour after stumps, a player brought in the final edition of the *Herald*: alongside a report of the fourth Russian sputnik, the moon probe Lunik 1, was a furious Wardle *j'accuse*:

> I ACCUSE umpires of not being strong enough to stand by their own convictions, for it's their job to understand the laws of the game and therefore they must know and recognise a throw.
>
> I ACCUSE selectors of all countries of cheating by selecting men who they must be aware have illegal actions.
>
> I ACCUSE captains for not lodging an immediate complaint when they encounter a thrower.

Benaud sprang to Meckiff's defence:

> I have made a very close study of Meckiff's action from every part of the field, and I am absolutely certain that his action conforms entirely with the laws formulated by the MCC. Apparently, so do the umpires in New Zealand, South Africa and Australia where Meckiff has played all his cricket. Consequently, these criticisms would appear in effect to suggest that the umpires in each of these three countries are unfair and incompetent.

The Australian board, similarly, lowered the portcullis at the first mention of throwing. Chairman Bill Dowling said that the problem 'had been magnified out of all proportion'. Most local pressmen wrote in kind. After all, Australia hadn't squealed about the doctored pitches in England thirty months earlier. And, if Meckiff was a mote in Australia's eye, Tony Lock was surely a beam in England's.

Yet there was a problem, and it would not go away. The back-foot no-ball law, too, had never seemed so unsightly as when it allowed the husky twenty-two-year-old Gordon Rorke to issue forth from twenty yards. Fingleton felt that the board, by tacitly condoning so many unorthodox actions, was inviting trouble:

> Never in any summer in any part of the cricketing world have I seen such a crop of dubious bowling actions…It is not a pleasant thing for a former player to deliver an opinion on whether he thinks such-and-such a bowler throws. It could blight a player's career—nobody wants to do that—but the fault is with those officials who have allowed such a position to develop…The full repercussions of this Australian summer have yet to come.

BENAUD'S PLAN

As the Ashes series wound to its conclusion, players could not help thinking of their next international engagement. For those who'd been on the brief stopover three years earlier, eight Tests in Pakistan and India made them uneasy.

Johnson's Australians had arrived in Karachi from Rome in October 1956 after a fortnight break in Europe, and been horror-struck by conditions. Everything was weirdly alien: the heat, the dust, the low-bouncing matting surface on which they lost the Karachi Test, the tendentious umpiring, the untrustworthy food. Everyone had fallen ill, especially Gil Langley (hepatitis) and Benaud (dengue fever) in Madras. Jim Burke was so adamant he'd not return now that he retired, and others thought about absenting themselves. But think about it was all they did after a report from Alan Davidson during the Fourth Test at Adelaide Oval.

Davidson was returning from the nets when he saw Bradman, and thought he'd head over for a chat. After exchanging pleasantries, he popped the question: 'Don, is it compulsory to go to India and Pakistan?'

'You've retired, have you?' Bradman replied, quick as a flash.

Davidson gulped: 'Err, no, Don. I haven't.'

'That's good to hear,' the Don continued genially. 'And, when you get back to the rooms, you might tell them what I've just told you.'

When Benaud's side was named on 10 March 1959, the captain at once set to work. However players regarded it, the journey would be a huge challenge: Pakistan, notably, was unbeaten on home soil.

Benaud was a fastidious planner. In the hiatus between the England and India legs of the 1956 tour, for instance, he'd asked BBC Light Entertainment boss Tom Sloan if he could take a three-week television production course. While teammates cruised the continent, Benaud spent thirteen hours a day observing drama, comedy and sport go to air, culminating in a day at Newbury watching the peerless racecaller Peter O'Sullevan. Not that Benaud intended going into television: it just 'might be handy to know something about it in later years'.

For Pakistan and India, Benaud thought, health would be paramount. He recommended that the Australian board advertise for a medical officer, and Colin McDonald's elder brother Ian was chosen from a short-list. Some political foreknowledge would also be useful, and Benaud wrote to Menzies:

> I have no doubt that, in addition to cricket on this tour there will be a certain amount of diplomatic importance attached to the 14 weeks we are abroad. I know that you are an extremely busy man and the matter probably comes under Mr Casey's department [external affairs] in any case. However, if possible, I would appreciate a few lines of briefing perhaps

from Mr Casey or someone in the department on particular aspects of relations between India, Pakistan and our own country.

Menzies did better: it was arranged for Benaud to talk with senior diplomat Peter Heydon in Canberra four weeks before the team's departure.*

Most critical, however, were the pitches Australia would play on. Three years before at Karachi, the coir mats had nullified Lindwall and Miller, but proved ideal for the brilliant Pakistani medium-pacers Fazal Mahmood and Khan Mohammed. The Pakistan board was now promising turf pitches, but Benaud was wary. As the team gathered in Brisbane on 29 October for a preliminary match marking Queensland cricket's centenary, Benaud ordered four consecutive early morning practices on mats. If his team failed, it wouldn't be for want of preparation.

SLAMMIN' SAM

At the Gabba, Benaud met his manager: erstwhile Test all-rounder and now honourable member for Prahran, Sam Loxton. His had been an unexpected choice: he was the first manager since the war who was not a member of the Australian board. But then, the subcontinent had a reputation among administrators almost as fearful as its reputation amongst players. 'I got the job mainly because I'd been there with the Commonwealth XI in 1953–54,' Loxton recalls. 'And also because, what board member would be silly enough to go there? They called for nominations and I'm not sure they got any apart from me.'

Thoughts of such a gruff, soldierly man acting the diplomat had caused great ribaldry. At the Prime Minister's XI match dinner, Hassett had told the audience: 'I would advise Mr Menzies to have army and navy standing by. A week after Sam gets to India, war is bound to break out between the two countries.' But Loxton had also approached his task methodically. He'd written to Menzies himself, requesting customs clearance for 400 dozen cans of beer: they were forwarded to Ray Gullick, senior trade commissioner in Delhi. And he'd visited Bill Dowling, and digested strict instructions: he should not allow any Test to proceed until presented with a receipt for the telegraphic transfer of £6500.

'No dough, no play?' Loxton asked.

'That's what I'm saying, Sam,' Dowling said. 'You are also under no circumstances to hold out any hope of an invitation to Pakistan from Australia.'

* Heydon, assistant secretary in the Department of External Affairs, had been Australian high commissioner in India from 1955 to 1959.

'What you're saying is that we can't afford to have them here,' replied Loxton. 'Understood.'

VICTORY AT DACCA

The Australians—fifteen cricketers, Loxton, Doc McDonald, masseur Bill Mitchell, ABC commentator Michael Charlton and a solitary journalist in Wally Pugh of Australian Associated Press—left Brisbane on 5 November 1959. After a couple of days at the Raffles Hotel in Singapore, they continued to Dacca in East Pakistan.

It was a steaming city that had literally been carved from the landscape after Partition, and teemed with humanity in a way that left the young players slack-jawed. Norm O'Neill was stunned into silence:

The drive from the airport at Dacca to our hotel was something I'll never forget. There were people everywhere. I have never seen such overcrowding. I was aware of their poverty before I left Australia, but upon seeing them, as they were, I felt bewildered and somewhat depressed. I had no preconceived ideas of their primitiveness and had never imagined them to live as they do, crowded together in shacks and hovels, with none of the usual 'offices' as estate agents back home describe heating, lighting, water, sanitation and so on.

Benaud asked the bus driver to take the team via Dacca Stadium. 'The pitch square was beautifully green and wonderfully grassed,' he remembers. 'Except for the single strip of clay in the middle.' So the Test would be on matting after all. The hotel offered food, but no-one was willing to touch it. On the basis of a refresher course he'd taken in tropical disease, Dr McDonald had issued strict instructions: tap water and salads were out, black coffee and fried fish in. The team retired jesting grimly about the hotel's abundance of spiders and lizards. Everybody felt a long way from home.

The Test began inauspiciously on Friday the 13th, and was a grim business. The incessant din astonished the visitors. 'Crowds are loud in Australia, but at least you get a lull between deliveries,' says Gordon Rorke. 'There the noise was constant, like having a radio on at full blast in your ear all day. Even when you weren't playing in the match, it was exhausting.' Lindsay Kline rose daily at dawn to supervise laying of the mat, but bowling on it was still like pounding the ball into wet cement. 'I should never have played in that match,' Meckiff says. 'The harder you bounced into this mat with its mud base, the slower it came off.'

Having seen his side crawl to 200 in almost a day and a half, Fazal removed Favell, O'Neill and Burge for two runs. But to the rescue came Harvey. Despite a temperature and a bout of dysentery, he played one of his most dazzling innings:

> We'd been at the trade commissioner's the night before, and I hadn't pulled up too well. But as I was putting the pads on, I heard the shout for Les Favell getting out, so I was in straight away. I was feeling so bad when I got out there that I couldn't lift my head up. But because the ball was only bouncing about two feet off the ground, that wasn't so bad: it kept me playing forward, where normally I went back a bit just as the bowler let go, and helped me survive. The crowds were quite amazing, really. They'd been pretty quiet when Ray [Lindwall] had been bowling but, when we batted, the noise was just constant. You could hardly hear the other guy call. It was hard work, grinding cricket.

By the time Harvey was bowled for 96 early on the third day, Michael Charlton was lost in admiration:

> Neil must have been to the toilet about eight times during the innings. I know because the commentary box was directly above the toilet and I'd see him hurrying toward me, disappear into the rooms, hear the chain being pulled. And then this slightly wan figure would totter out again. I asked Richie afterwards: 'Well, what does one say about an innings like that?' He said: 'I'll write it down for you.' I only made one change. He called it 'one of the greatest Test innings of all time' and I crossed out 'of all time'.

The other match-winners were Grout, who extended Australia's lead to 25, and Mackay, who parsimoniously conceded 42 from 45 overs while taking half a dozen wickets. The tourists upended Pakistan for 134 on the fourth day. Almost as satisfying as an eight-wicket victory was discovering some canned meat in the hotel block. Rorke remembers: 'Some guys found a tin of pressed meat, camp pie. And we opened the can like it was the first time any of us had seen food. Then we cut it up into twenty slices. Gee, we were hungry. It was like being prisoners of war.'

WINNING IN LAHORE

Lahore cheered the Australians up a little. It was an attractive city with horse-drawn cabs traversing wide, clean streets, and the bungalows in their Sunnyview Hotel were quite sanitary. They visited the *Civil and Military Gazette* where Rudyard Kipling had written *Kim,* and Akbar's giant fort, then spoke on film at a local studio. 'We were surrounded by these very shy and beautiful creatures,' recalls Charlton. 'All of whom, of course, were cricket fans.'

The Second Test, moreover, was to be the first played on turf in Pakistan, and O'Neill's maiden Test century wrested a first innings lead of 245. But, faced with their first home series defeat, Pakistan rallied: Saeed Ahmed and Hanif Mohammed were entrenched at 3–288 by the close of the fourth day. A Lahore lurgi was also keeping Doc McDonald busy. Kline was running a severe temperature, and sweated so profusely that roommate Meckiff had to change his bed linen five times.

The doctor arrived at Kline's bedside next morning with a remedy: whisky and hot water. The spinner suddenly felt like a new man: 'Actually, I don't think I ever bowled better. Saeed came down the track to a wrong 'un, it beat him and Wally took off the bails. Then Hanif— now he was a hard man to get out at home—he thought I'd given him a wrong 'un but it was the leg-break and he padded up.'

Kline's spirited 7–75 left Australia needing 122 in two hours. But again, the hosts fought tooth and claw. Under instructions issued at tea, captain Imtiaz Ahmed wound down the over rate. As left-handed Harvey and right-handed O'Neill rotated strike during a stand of 62, field changes stopped to a stroll. Says Harvey: 'Overs were starting to take seven minutes instead of three. It reached a stage where they weren't gonna get you out but we weren't gonna win the game.' He took mat- ters into his own hands, throwing his hand away so another right-hander could come in, and told the incoming Benaud: 'You better do something about it, mate, or it'll end up a farce.'

The captain did: 'What I said to Imtiaz as I went past him would these days bring a red card and a letter from the chairman of the board. One thing it did do, though, was have him act like he'd been threatened with summary execution: the over rate came back to normal and we were home safely by ten minutes.' Australia had won its first Test series in Pakistan. It hasn't won there since.

AYUB AND IKE

Quick inspection of the National Stadium square in Karachi on 2 December 1959 told the Australians exactly what they didn't want to know. Once again, despite all pre-tour assurances, the pitch had been excavated to accommodate a mat.

The Australians had taken up the turf cause in Dacca. In speeches at the East Pakistan Sports Federation, Benaud and Loxton had harped on the point that Pakistan would not become full-fledged members of cricket's community until turf wickets were everywhere. The manager then found himself ticklishly placed with Field-Marshal Ayub Khan—Pakistan's Sandhurst-educated military ruler since a coup in October 1958—in the official enclosure at Lahore.

'Now Mr Loxton,' said Ayub. 'When is your board going to invite Pakistan to Australia?'

Mindful of Dowling's advice, Loxton replied: 'Sir, it's going to be quite some time.'

'Why is that?' Ayub asked.

'Firstly, we came here expecting to play all our Tests on turf,' Loxton said. 'We've just come from Dacca where we've played on a mat.'

'This is turf,' Ayub said, gesturing to the Lahore ground.

'Yes, but you had a beautiful turf wicket at Dacca and you dug it up,' countered Loxton. 'You need fast bowlers if you're coming to Australia. And mats'll discourage them. Our man, Lindwall, fast bowler, he was brought up on turf. He saw a result for his efforts. On matting, your quicks'll only hit blokes on the ankle.'

Loxton heard cogs turning in Ayub's mind and, when they met again on the first morning of the Third Test at Karachi, saw dividends for his lobbying. The Field-Marshal summoned the ground manager and asked: 'My man, on what surface is this Test match being played?'

The ground manager replied proudly. 'It is being playing on mats, sir.'

Ayub frowned, then issued a proclamation. 'This is the last Test match played in Pakistan on matting. Otherwise, you will be shot.' Loxton couldn't suppress a smile: cricket administration in Pakistan was so straightforward.

Karachi was readying itself for the visit of US president Dwight Eisenhower, who was on his first significant diplomatic mission, visiting eleven countries in the Mediterranean and Asia. Colin McDonald remembers:

> When he arrived, we all went out to watch his motorcade go from the airport to the US embassy. And we noticed that, every fifty yards or so along the route, there were soldiers with canisters on their backs and holding hand-pumps, and we couldn't work out why. But then, when they saw Ike's car about 100 yards away, these guys'd start pumping furiously and out would come a spray of disinfectant.

One of the entertainments offered Ike was, naturally, a day at the Test: the only time a US president has attended an international cricket match. What he made of the 104 that Pakistan scored he was too polite to say.

The Karachi draw was dreary, but it had been a successful tour on and off the field. The umpiring had been indifferent, but Benaud and his lieutenants Harvey and McDonald had kept complaints private. Forthright Loxton had blasted his way through all bureaucratic barriers, and Doc McDonald had kept everyone upright with Kao Magma and rejuvenating whisky. Michael Charlton and Wally Pugh had proved popular ancillary members of the touring group, while Australia's high commissioner in Karachi Sir Roden Cutler had been generous and accommodating. Peter Burge dubbed him 'Gunga Din' after the water-bearer in his favourite film.

There'd even been the odd chuckle at the local customs. Jarman remembers:

> Richie got me a beauty. When our batsmen came in at a break, he told me to go tell the Paki boys we'd declared. I said: 'Aww, I can't do that Rich.' He says: 'Yes you can. You're a representative of the team.' So I stood up, puffed out my chest, burst down the hallway to their rooms, threw open the door…and they were all sitting on their prayer mats in complete silence.

India, however, would be trying. After Australia won the First Test at Delhi at a canter, the Board of Cricket Control in India became difficult to deal with. When they were late delivering their telegraphic receipt for the Second Test match guarantee at Kanpur on 19 December, Loxton honoured his promise to Dowling and confronted the BCCI's assistant secretary.

The Indian was evasive. 'Do not let us spoil a beautiful friendship over money.'

'Try me,' Loxton barked. 'I want it please. I have instructed Richie that no player is to get togged until I have the money.'

'But what about the game?' queried the official.

'That's not my problem,' Loxton replied. 'You know the rules.'

Loxton's receipt arrived just in time for the match to commence, but most of the Australians wished it hadn't. Davidson (12–124) bowled incisively on a crumbling pitch, but Jasu Patel, a thirty-five-year-old Gujarati off-spinner with a suspiciously cocked elbow, swept India to its first victory against Australia with 14–124.

It was, players agreed, the harshest cricket environment they'd encountered. The umpiring had to be borne philosophically. The heat was stifling. Davidson, bowling 50 overs a Test, was in the process of losing twenty-six pounds: 'At the end of the day I'd be a bloody zombie. I just kept telling myself: "Back foot front arm."' The noise never abated, whether it was explosion of crackers or the clunk of the bottles that flew at the faintest provocation.

The relentless press of the crowds, the spartan accommodation and incipient paranoia about the food gnawed nerves. Christmas was spent pleasantly enough at Kanpur's Kumula Retreat, a rambling estate owned by Sir Parampat Singhania whose precincts were roamed by monkeys, green kingfishers and peacocks, but few fancied the food. 'I had two Jatz crackers with peanut butter and a can of Fosters,' remembers Burge. 'And I didn't normally drink. I'd just got sick of Coca-Cola.'

While the Australians played their next match at Ahmedabad against a Universities XI, their lodgings were a hostelry called the Hotel Ritz: a reconditioned prison whose foyer featured a unlikely endorsement from the Duke of Edinburgh. Says Jarman:

> Gavin Stevens and I were taken to what they called 'the stable wing'. And that's what it was: a stable. There was a dirt floor with a mat on it, no glass on the windows, just bars, two old wooden beds. We said: 'No thanks.' We carried the beds to the foyer, which was this cement floor painted green, and slept there with Wally Pugh and Michael Charlton.

In some degree, it was character-forming. 'You couldn't help but be shaken,' says Meckiff. 'The huge extremes of poverty to wealth, the number of people when you walked down the street. I think I learned more about life in three months on the subcontinent than I have in all the rest of my days.' Rorke says: 'There's no doubt I came back a different person. Living in Australia, we just had no idea. I came back with a huge appreciation of how lucky we were.'

But it could also be deeply unsettling. In Bangalore, Doc McDonald, Gavin Stevens and Charlton visited a birth-control clinic. Stevens recalls: 'The guy who picked us up drove past this body by the side of the road. We all asked whether he shouldn't stop, but he didn't take any notice. When we were coming back, the same body was lying there, and we were a bit more insistent. But he said: "No. He is all right." All right with the Lord, I think.'

Charlton, a perceptive, eloquent man, was intrigued by the cricketers' struggles to assimilate their environment:

> There could have been no greater contrast than that between the Australians with their muscular, rather strident culture, their breadth and uncomplication, and the extraordinarily intricate geology of hierarchies,

huge and minute, in India. The Australians were inclined to do things like put their arm round a bearer and call him mate, then not understand why this was thought unusual.

But Charlton had problems, too. He was striving to arrange an interview with Indian prime minister Jawaharlal Nehru. They'd made provisional arrangements at the Test in Delhi, but finalising matters using Benaud's Bombay room phone proved frustrating. Benaud recalls:

> Michael was as unflappable as they come, but at the end of half an hour explaining that 'no his name was Charlton, not Nehru, and he was in Bombay, not Delhi', he snapped and started shouting and threw the telephone across the room against the concrete wall with a run of expletives I never imagined could come from a true blue ABC and BBC man.

When Charlton finally pinned his subject down, it afforded an insight into cricket's primacy in the subcontinent: 'We went and filmed an interview at his home there on very short magazines of very bad film. To my shame, I'd not realised just how much he loved cricket. On his desk, surrounded by huge piles of paper, was a colour photo of him opening the batting for Harrow.'

In India, all roads led to cricket.

'SPINNER, I'M HUNGRY'

Then came the illness Benaud had always feared. First victim was the tall, raw-boned Rorke, who had found the diet of dry toast, bananas and fried fish especially gruelling. His mother had sent him a Christmas cake at Delhi but, once reclaimed from customs and cut into twenty pieces, it had vanished quickly.

One day at Delhi, Rorke turned to Kline and said miserably: 'Spinner, I'm hungry.'

'Steady on, Gordon,' Kline replied. 'You know what the Doc says. We're not allowed to eat any of the salads.' Kline looked away momentarily and, when he turned back, found Rorke heedlessly tucking in.

The paceman bowled but two overs on the first day of the ensuing Kanpur Test, left the field, and was obviously not up to more. He cabbed to the ground and volunteered to bat when Australia was collapsing in its second innings, but Benaud insisted: 'Don't even think about it.' And that evening, Rorke could think of nothing but the toilet. 'I must have been forty times,' he remembers. 'My roommate Burgey couldn't believe it, and we almost had a fight about it. Not that, at the time, I could have lifted a pin.'

Rorke was admitted to an Ahmedabad military hospital for a blood and stool test which diagnosed hepatitis, then was taken in by a Salvation Army doctor and his pregnant wife. 'I had no idea what was going on,' Rorke recalls. 'Beyond the fact that I felt incredibly weak and my eyes were bright yellow. I moved into this beautiful old Indian house and they put me in a bedroom upstairs.'

It was a remarkable act of kindness, as Rorke discovered when the doctor knocked on the door after a couple of days and asked: 'Gordon, I have to ask you a favour. Can you move downstairs? My wife is about to have a baby.' In ten days' convalescence while the manager organised his home passage Rorke shed three stone.

When Rorke's BOAC Comet landed in Sydney, Mosman cricket official Keith Johnson barely recognised him. He told Rorke's mother and girlfriend: 'Brace yourselves. You'll get a shock when you see him.' Rorke languished six months in bed and the disappointment hit him hard: 'I'd put so much work into that tour. I'd gone to the gym, I'd done miles, I'd built myself right up. And it all disappeared in three days.' He'd played his last Test.

Staying at Brabourne Stadium for the Third Test, Loxton and McDonald had another responsibility foisted on them. It began comically. Loxton recalls:

> I had all the booze and the soft drink in my room in a big tub with ice, and my door was always open. Nothing'd wake me up. The idea was that, if anybody got thirsty during the night, they could come into my room and get what they wanted. This particular night at the end of the day's play, the boys were sitting on my bed having some Foster's, and I said finally: 'Right, that's it. Off my bloody bed! You lot can do what you like, but I'm for sleepy-byes.' Then, about 4am, there was a loud banging on my door, so I jumped out of bed…and I must have knocked over a pyramid of cans three or four feet tall, every single bloody can. The din was incredible: these bloody tin cans banging and rolling round on the concrete floor. That bloody Grout. Anyway, I went and opened the door and who should it be but Arthur Mailey? I'm standing there flabbergasted and all he says is: 'I see now why we lost at Kanpur.'

Seventy-four-year-old Mailey had been despatched by the *Daily Telegraph* to discover how Australia had lost its first Test to India. But Doc McDonald was appalled: 'My heart sank. Arthur was a lovely man, but over seventy, and I thought: "This is no place for him." Sure enough, within a couple of days, he was very ill. I took him to the hospital and we organised a flight home. Poor Arthur. He saw no cricket at all on that trip.'

(ALMOST) THE MOST FAMOUS MAN IN THE HISTORY OF CRICKET

A week later in Madras, the night before the Fourth Test, it was the turn of twenty-seven-year-old South Australian opener Gavin Stevens. He recalls: 'The boys were all going to the cinema that night, but I suddenly felt a bit sick so I said to the Doc: "Look, I'm not too well. I think I'll go home." Pretty soon, I was throwing up, and crawling across the room to the toilet.' Roommate Jarman discovered him and bolted for Doc McDonald, shouting: 'Hurry up, Doc! I think he's gonna die.' Stevens had acute hepatitis. Next morning, Benaud, Harvey and Colin McDonald came to see him. Stevens heard one of them say matter-of-factly: 'Well, he can't play.'

Stevens was confined to bed for ten days. He was too weak to leave for Calcutta with the team, and implored Wally Pugh not to write any-thing home about his condition that might upset his wife. (Pugh refrained.) Eventually, Stevens persuaded reluctant medical staff to book him a flight, and he was the one white face on a Vickers Viscount that left Madras the next day.

By the time he rejoined the team, another player had gone. Kline had been invalided home with hepatitis (to the surprise of his wife Stella, who read of his repatriation in the newspaper and hurried to collect him from Essendon Airport). Indeed, Stevens watched one morning as the Australians took the field with ten men. He hastily called the hotel: Meckiff, who relied on Kline as his alarm clock, had overslept. 'They've just gone out on the field and realised that you weren't there,' Stevens said. 'You better get down here sharpish.' Meckiff recalls: 'Yes, I was a big hit in Calcutta. I think Rich gave me a few extra overs that day to make sure I didn't do it again.'

Stevens' ambition of leaving India with his mates was hard won: 'By the time I got to Sydney I was wrecked, in really bad shape. Les Favell's parents were there, fortunately, so I stayed with them for a while. I can't even remember getting back to Adelaide and seeing my wife again.' Stevens played no further first-class cricket. When he saw Harvey again twenty-five years later, Harvey said: 'You were unlucky, Gav. You could've been the most famous man in the history of cricket.'

'Yeah?' said Stevens. 'How come?'

Harvey answered: 'You could've been the first man to die on tour.'

'A MAGNIFICENT ADVERTISEMENT'

Despite it all, Australia prevailed. O'Neill, Harvey, Favell and Grout guaranteed the better of draws at Brabourne and at Eden Gardens, while Benaud's 8–86 underwrote an innings victory at Corporation Stadium. Benaud also received high marks for diplomacy and sportsmanship. Australia's high commissioner in Delhi, Walter Crocker, informed Menzies that the team had been 'a magnificent advertisement...putting us more firmly on the map than all our other efforts rolled into one'.

It had again been a triumph of team spirit. Friendships formed were lasting. When Favell's first son was born three months after his return, he named it Alan for his roommate Davidson. When Jarman's arrived twelve months later, he named it Gavin after his roommate Stevens. Jarman also sponsored the immigration to Australia of Pakistan's young Anglo-Indian batsman Duncan Sharpe.

Nonetheless, it was probably fortunate that the tour ended when it did. By the Fifth Test in Calcutta on 23 January 1960, the longest fuses had burned short. Harvey recalls:

> Col and Ian McDonald had been giving us lectures all through the tour: 'Come on fellas, be nice to these people. We're all diplomats on this tour.' But even Col got fed up at Calcutta. We had this bloke lbw twice, plumb, and he was given not out. We were all still fuming when Davo bowls him neck and crop, off stump, and Col runs all the way from the fine leg boundary and kicks the remaining stumps over and says: 'That must have been bloody close.'

'The World's Number One Sport'

AUSTRALIA V WEST INDIES
1960–61

As the sixties began, cricket was in a state of unease. Time had marched on and, in the words of MCC President Harry Altham, 'against the increased tempo of modern life, cricket must be regarded as a rather slow-moving activity'.

On the financial face of it, Australian cricket was robust. Attendance figures for the 1958–59 Ashes series had exceeded three-quarters of a million, gate takings reaching a record £185,000. And, from eleven weeks in the subcontinent, Benaud's team had repatriated a striking £40,000 profit.

Yet the game had, irrefutably, lost ground. Thanks to throwing, dragging, tardy over rates and dour play by the tourists, season 1958–59 had generated more heat than light. Domestic cricket in both Australia and England seemed to be slipping into desuetude. After inching up to a daily 5000 in 1955–56, Sheffield Shield attendances had retreated to less than 3000, while county cricket audiences had more than halved since the war. At the extreme of literature bemoaning cricket's decline was 'The Cricket Industry', a rather daring 1956 paper published by England's Political and Economic Planning Group, which described the game as 'fighting a losing battle against shortage of capital, shortage of income and shortage of the highly skilled labour the game requires'.

After a few years' abeyance, the Australian Board of Control's September 1959 meeting again minuted discussion of 'negative play', mooting an addendum to Law 46 (note 4): 'Bowlers taking excessively long time to bowl overs will be disciplined by being taken off.' Further summits at state level were convened to discuss enlivening the game. The QCA's June 1960 meeting featured a long discussion on 'Stimulating the Public Interest in Cricket'. Vice-president Vic Shaefer stirred debate by asserting that cricket was 'not offering the entertainment value it must have to bring people along in numbers to view it'.

'Cricket seems to be in the doldrums all over the world,' said South African Cricket Association secretary Algy Frames in a September 1960 letter to Sir Donald Bradman, the new Australian board chairman. 'Particularly as far as gate receipts are concerned.' Frames wished Australian administrators luck with their summer visit from the 1960–61 West Indian team.

WORRELL'S MEN

The 1960–61 West Indians ran hot and cold as they traversed Australia from west to east. They lost to Western Australia and all but defeated a strong Australian XI in Perth, drew luckily against South Australia, trounced Victoria, were trounced by NSW. Yet, despite their inconsistency, there was a breezy self-possession to them that precursors had lacked.

The most palpable change was in leadership. After years of campaigning, culminating in a deafening series of articles by C. L. R. James in the *Nation* (official organ of Dr Eric Williams' ruling People's National Movement of Trinidad), thirty-six-year-old Frank Worrell had belatedly become the first black man to lead the West Indies on tour.

Worrell was educated, urbane, a model of the respectable Barbadian middle class, a Scout as a young man, a Mason when older, a Manchester University graduate with honours in social sciences. In the dressing-room, he'd long been the coolest head. At Lord's in 1957, Alf Valentine had discovered Worrell bent over a book, reading intently. 'You know you're next man in, Frank,' he said.

'Just studying, Alf,' Worrell replied. 'My finals are coming up.'

The succession had been a model of its kind. Gerry Alexander, West Indies' calm-browed keeper and captain in four series, had quietly and without recrimination accepted the vice-captaincy. James was jubilant: Worrell's ascension was a victory in the struggle for self-determination, an acknowledgment that merit had superseded the ascriptive criteria of race in cricket selection. The team aligned itself strongly with the islands' federalist drive: the pennant of the West Indies Federation, formed in

1958, fluttered over every arena on which the team played, a motivating symbol of political striving.

In the opening weeks of the tour, Worrell instilled a deep discipline on his XVI. When young Garry Sobers visibly rolled his eyes over an lbw decision in Perth, Worrell lectured the team: 'When you are given out you leave the wicket, whether you think you are out or not.' He wanted overs bowled quickly, incoming and outgoing batsmen to cross, and a 10pm curfew during Test matches. 'I don't mind what you do in your room, but don't do it in public,' he said. 'And no cocky nonsense if we win.' He even banned card-playing on tour, explaining:

> The little optics I had studied in 1948 helped me to realise that no player could expect to focus on cards at a distance of eighteen inches in a smoke-filled room, then go onto a cricket field to gaze at infinity without untoward results. Apart from the physical energy expended in those badly lit rooms, there was also the mental condition of the individual who had lost and been ridiculed by other players.

Deputy Alexander, a veterinary surgeon and Cambridge blue in cricket and soccer, lent unstinting support. Managers Gerry Gomez and Max Marshall ran the tour with an invisible hand.

Benaud's Australians were hot favourites for the rubber. After all, the West Indies had beaten Australia just twice in 15 preceding Tests. But Worrell felt a precious and unprecedented unity in the team: 'On previous tours, Barbadians seemed to stick together, and so with players from Trinidad, Jamaica and British Guiana. We cut across all that. We were a team.' As the West Indies arrived at Lennon's Hotel for the First Test at the Gabba, they also discovered a West Indian trio playing there: Jamaican nightclub entertainer Ben Bowers and his Band. It was a reassuring omen.

'THIS COULD BE A WONDERFUL YEAR'

The Australian preparation for the First Test was full of prosaic anxieties. Benaud was taking tablets to fight a throat infection and shaking hands with his left: the legacy of a finger broken on a recent Commonwealth XI tour of South Africa. Colin McDonald was struggling with an injured leg, Ian Meckiff a damaged achilles tendon. And, at practice on 8 December, Davidson broke the little finger of his bowling hand taking a short catch. He bolted off to pack it in ice and, downstairs at Lennon's a few hours later, quietly told his captain: 'I think you broke my finger today, Rich.'

Benaud groaned. 'How bad is it?' he asked.

'Have a look,' replied Davidson. 'I can't bend it.'

'We'll have to see Braddles,' the captain said.

As it happened, Bradman was attending Benaud's Test match dinner that evening. He inspected the finger, and advised: 'Keep it quiet and see how it is in the morning.' Then he asked Benaud: 'Would you mind if I said a few words to the boys tonight?'

The board chairman's speech was *ex tempore* but, Benaud felt, full of forethought:

> His message was not the usual platitudes one might have expected from an administrator of 'Good luck...you're playing for the flag etc etc', but some-thing vastly different. He told us this could be a wonderful year of cricket. He hoped this season that cricket would come back into its own, and some of the play-at-all-costs-for-a-draw attitudes would be forgotten. In partic-ular, he said that this Australian side could lead the way to one of the most attractive cricket series seen in the country for a long time—but that it was up the players themselves.

There was a meaningful pause at its conclusion as the words sank in. Davidson looked at his finger. Suddenly it felt pretty good.

'YOU'LL GET THEM AT THE RIGHT TIME'

On the first morning of the First Test, Richie Benaud read something that made him wince: a journalist asserting confidently that Australia's captain had the measure of the West Indies' twenty-four-year-old Garry Sobers. Benaud detested such articles. Nothing was likelier to arouse a batsman's defiance. Besides, Benaud wasn't sure he did. Granted, he'd dis-missed Sobers a few times. But something about the left-hander defied the natural order.

Sobers had been born in Bridgetown in 1936. Few were as sponta-neously gifted at all sports—he played golf, basketball and soccer for his island before entering first-class cricket at sixteen—and few left first impressions as vivid. Colin McDonald remembers clapping eyes on Sobers at Port-of-Spain in April 1955: 'This kid walked out at Trinidad with what looked like a piece of redgum, which turned out to be a Stuart Surridge two-star, where we were all using four-stars. Ray Lindwall was bowling, but the boy starts blasting and he hit us every-where. He only made 40, but it took him about four overs. You could tell he'd be something amazing.'

The five ensuing years had borne that prophecy out. At Sabina Park in February 1958, Sobers had broken Len Hutton's Test record score with a ten-hour unbeaten 365 against Pakistan, then followed it with a brace of centuries at Bourda. A further half-dozen hundreds had followed, including a double against England before his home crowd in January 1960. Form had eluded him thus far in Australia but, in Bradman, Sobers found a knowledgeable backer. 'Don't worry son,' he told Sobers when the left-hander succumbed cheaply to Benaud against NSW. 'You'll get them at the right time.'

The West Indian batting as the First Test began on 9 December seemed to validate all the stereotypes of brittle Caribbean brilliance. The scoreline after an hour read 3–67. Fingleton recalled Marshal Bosquet's words after Balaclava: '*C'est magnifique, mais ce n'est pas le guerre.*' Sobers began in the same vein, a daring boundary to leg from his first ball, a string of intemperate passes outside off and a square slash that just eluded Benaud at gully.

When Worrell joined him, however, Sobers began blending dash with discretion. Meckiff and Davidson were beaten back, Benaud taken for 53 from 10 overs. As Benaud put it, he knew where every ball would land, but had no idea which stroke Sobers would play. 'Being in the covers was really hard work,' says O'Neill. 'It was very hot and the Gabba was a big ground in those days. Garry'd smash it through the covers, you'd chase it all the way back. And no sooner were you back in position than you'd be off again.' Fielders impeded at their peril. 'I've never seen a ball hit as hard as Garry hit it that day,' says Lindsay Kline. 'I got down behind one at mid on, and I thought it had broken my leg.'

In the commentary box at the Vulture Street end, the ABC's Michael Charlton steadily depleted his superlatives:

> Sobers played one shot through mid-wicket, picking it up and smashing it into the crowd, which can't have risen more than four feet off the ground at any stage. It was literally like a shell. It put me in mind of those early illustrations of exploding cannon balls flattening whole ranks of soldiers. As it flew toward the fence you could see the ranks of Queenslanders falling back and parting.

Sobers and Worrell raised their hundred stand in ninety minutes, the former his hundred in just over two hours, the latter his studious, elegant fifty in just less. It took the day's worst ball to separate them: a jaded Meckiff full-toss wide of leg stump that Sobers pushed imprecisely to mid on. Tom Goodman of the *Sydney Morning Herald*, not prone to hyperbole, judged Sobers' 132 'one of the greatest Test innings of our time'. Bradman, never known to offer a compliment lightly, visited the West Indian dressing-room at stumps to offer his hand: 'Congratulations. You didn't disappoint me.' By then, the tourists were 7–359, and Phil Tresidder of the *Daily Telegraph* contended: 'The Australians, hot favourites in this Test series, are on the run.'

SWINGS AND ROUNDABOUTS

For three further days, the First Test fluctuated. A further 290 were scored on the Saturday, Australia establishing itself through the resolute McDonald and the run-hungry Bob Simpson. The hosts finally wrested a first-innings lead when O'Neill turned a fortunate 28 into a forceful 181 in five hours on Monday. It was the West Indians' turn to pay homage. The Guianese barrister turned BBC cricket correspondent Ernest Eytle commented: 'It was not the first glimpse we had of the tremendous power in his wide shoulders, but this time he seemed to bring to his batting a mixture of brilliance and fortune that always favours the brave.'

When Davidson, who'd taken 5–135 in the West Indies first innings, clawed 6–87 in the second, it seemed that Australia should finally prevail. As the West Indian tail was stubbed out on Wednesday morning, the ABC's Johnnie Moyes forecast a local victory with an hour or two to spare. 'One sensed,' wrote Fingleton, 'that the West Indies realised they were facing defeat.'

They didn't. 'At no stage did we think the match was out of our grasp,' Sobers recalled. 'Frank kept urging us on, convinced we could win.' And the Australian second innings opened explosively. Wes Hall, a muscular twenty-three-year-old Barbadian who seemed to back into Vulture Street to begin his run, swept away a supplicating Simpson in his second over. After another quarter-hour, Harvey was gymnastically caught at second slip by Sobers. Australia at lunch was a woozy 2–28. The probability of a draw was suddenly looming large. So sure of a stalemate was the ABC's Alan McGilvray, in fact, that he informed co-commentator Clive Harburg of his intention to catch the 2.30pm flight to Sydney with Keith Miller.

Harburg, the ABC's Queensland sports editor since 1946, was unimpressed. 'What about it Alan?' Harburg replied. 'I think your job's here. If you want to go back I can't stop you, but I think you have a responsibility to be here.'

'Oh, this match is going to fizzle out into a draw,' McGilvray said. 'You, Michael [Charlton] and Johnnie [Moyes] can handle it.' He headed for Eagle Farm airport.

Over the next two hours, however, the match turned from probable draw into likely West Indies win. Ken Archer, who'd been a QCA luncheon guest, watched the second session with Bradman, waiting for Australian resistance that didn't come:

> First Col [McDonald] got out, then Norm [O'Neill]. I remember Don saying when Les Favell came in: 'This should put a stop to this nonsense.' But Les got out and Slasher [Mackay] came in, so I said: 'Well, looks like you're going to have to depend on a Queenslander to pull us out of it.' Then Slasher got out and, at tea, we both thought it was pretty much over. I said to Don: 'I've got a bit of work to do back at the office so I better go, but it looks like they've got this won. Good luck to 'em. It'll be good for cricket.'

With Australia 6–92 at tea, Davidson 16 and Benaud 6, Ian Meckiff was also accepting defeat. He told the West Indies' deputy keeper Jackie Hendriks: 'Looks like I'll have to congratulate you. The West Indies will have a 1–0 lead.'

Hendriks shook his head. 'Man, I'll accept congratulations only when the game is over.'

In the players' section of the Gabba, Benaud also begged to differ. A target of 123 in even time was steep, but the match that had had everything deserved a suitable finish. 'What are you going for, Richie?' Bradman asked. 'A win or a draw.'

'We're going for a win,' Benaud replied. 'Of course.'

'I'm very pleased to hear it,' said Bradman.

'THIS COULD BE WORTH WATCHING'

There was no prolonged council of war. Benaud simply said to Davidson as they resumed after tea: 'We'll see what we can do. We'll pick up the singles and keep it moving.' It sufficed. The singles came, as did a couple of succulent Davidson hooks from Hall. When Worrell spelled his swiftest bowler to conserve him for the second new ball, Benaud hit firmly down the ground against the spin of Sobers, Valentine and Ramadhin. Only 3000 scattered spectators remained to greet the 50 stand in fifty-five minutes, but some early departures had been enticed back by the drama. 'I'd kept the radio on at my office at 4BC,' recalls Ken Archer. 'And, when they started getting a few after tea, I thought: "Well, if this Benaud's got as much flair as they say, he'll go for a win from here. This could be worth watching."'

Davidson and Benaud gained on the clock in the first hour after tea, so that 60 were needed in the final hour. Davidson reached an intrepid half-century with a fourth four off Ramadhin, celebrated with a fifth and ran for everything. Benaud kept calm by enjoying the crowd's hysterics: 'Spectators hushed to the delivery of every ball and then would come a shaking burst of excitement—or a long sigh if nothing happened.'

Nowhere was more tense than Australia's dressing-room, where next man Grout was steadily smoking his way through a packet of Rothmans and Mackay was refusing to watch. 'It's better that I stay right here,' he explained. 'If I move now, I may bring them bad luck.'

About the only people unconcerned with the target, ironically, were the scorers in front of the press in the new Cricketers' Club: Shirley Crouch, wife of a Sandgate-Redcliffe stalwart Bob Crouch, maintaining the West Indies book, and Vic Fisher, a baker from Marouka, keeping tabs for Australia. 'All we were interested in was the score in the second innings,' says Shirley Crouch. 'We had an arrangement with Col [umpire Hoy] that he'd signal to us when Australia passed the West Indies, but we were concentrating on checking and re-checking at the end of each over to make sure everything tallied.'

By 5.30pm, Davidson and Benaud had changed the Test's complexion. Australia needed 27 in the final half-hour, and all appeared set for a dramatic home victory. The commentators strove to convey the drama of the situation, and Michael Charlton to emulate some of its chivalry. Clive Harburg recalls:

Michael and I were doing the session in thirty minute grabs, so I'd taken over at 5pm and kept going to 5.30pm when I was supposed to finish. I don't know what happened next, but I tried two or three times to hand over to Michael and he wouldn't do it. He was a very fine type of bloke, Michael, and maybe he thought it was such a precious occasion that I should have the honour of calling it.

Hall alone could now win the match for the West Indies but, taking the second new ball at 6–206, conceded eight in his first over. When Sobers allowed nine in the next, including a single that raised Benaud's 50 in two hours, just ten separated Australia from victory. Yet Worrell was still marshalling his men coolly, his deep voice echoing from mid wicket: 'Relax fellas and concentrate...come on now, concentrate.' And Hall bowled an over of searing menace from which Benaud could scratch just a single.

The Australians met in mid-pitch before Sobers began the penultimate over. 'Now, no stupid runs,' Davidson said. 'We've done all the hard work. We don't wanna waste it.' But, after each had taken a short single, Benaud pushed to the right of Joe Solomon at forward square-leg and called: 'One!' A slender East Indian from Berbice, thirty-year-old Solomon was a plucky batsmen with a temperament Worrell felt ideal for Test cricket. It showed. He gathered without fuss, volleyed at the striker's stumps and scattered them. Davidson was run out for 80. 'As I came in,' he says, 'I was as dirty as anyone ever has been.'

The Australians in the dressing-room groaned in unison. Grout hunted for his kit. 'Where's my fucking gloves?' he said. 'Where are they?' He stood up. He'd been sitting on them.

Grout made it six to win with a single from the over's second-last ball, and tension in the middle was spilling over the boundary. Glancing up from her scoresheet, Shirley Crouch noticed that the scoreboard had stopped moving. 'That's Queenslanders for you,' she says. 'I said it, not you. Well, it was exciting wasn't it.'

HALL'S LAST STAND

It was 5.56pm when Hall began the final over, and his first ball skewered Grout, hitting him in the solar plexus. When the keeper looked up, though, he found Benaud almost upon him and stumbled for the safety of the other end. Five needed. Benaud took strike for the second ball, glimpsed the bouncer, swung into a hook…and felt a tell-tale graze on the gloves as it soared through to Alexander. He froze guiltily. Umpire Col Egar's finger rose. 'What now Rich?' Grout asked as Benaud passed.

'All yours Wal,' Benaud replied.

Grout looked straight ahead: 'Thanks very much.'

Grout counselled his new partner Meckiff: if Hall bowled wide of leg stump, they should try for a bye. When Hall did, Grout hollered: 'Come one!' Meckiff recalls: 'It was pure bedlam. Wally was practically on top of me, shouting to run, and I hadn't moved. Wes had got the ball from Alexander: he was in the middle of the pitch and he literally could have strolled to the bowler's end and run me out but he let fly and missed.' Grout, turning at the other end, sniffed overthrows, but Alf Valentine made yards from mid off to back the throw up. Four needed from four balls.

Grout, a forceful hooker, was praying for a bouncer, almost visualising it. But Hall landed his fourth ball on a length and the cramped slog lobbed towards short mid wicket. The ball hung in the air, long enough for Hall to see that Alexander had not moved, so the bowler reversed direction and bounded for the catch. Only at the last instant did he glimpse Rohan Kanhai. Hall's elbow struck the fielder's head, the catch bounced away, and the big paceman sagged inconsolably. 'The good Lord's gone and left us,' he mourned.

Worrell, though, was at his elbow. 'Forget it, Wes,' he said simply.

Three to win, Meckiff on strike. He quite fancied his batting. Like a few golfer-cricketers, he had a handy seven-iron shot. And when Hall's sixth delivery pitched in the slot, Meckiff hit high into the setting sun at deep square-leg. Clive Harburg called it four but, as Benaud had noticed on his arrival in the morning, the outfield had not been mown. The ball pulled up a tantalising yard from the fence. Conrad Hunte's return—flat, fast, accurate and out of the sun—arrived inches over the bails as Grout dived hopelessly for the crease. Groans filled the Australian dressing-room. Lindsay Kline, Australia's last man, heard a voice tell him: 'You're in.'

Kline tried to appear confident as he walked to the centre, but Worrell quickly saw through it. 'You look a little pale, Lindsay,' he said.

'I certainly feel it at the moment,' Kline replied with a wan smile.

In the ABC commentary box, scorer Jim Coates kept his callers up to the minute. 'Australia 9–232, still requiring one run to win,' advised Harburg. 'Two balls to go in this Test match.' But, on the field, all was confusion. Kline thought the scores were tied as he approached the crease but, with the scoreboard inert, most of the West Indians thought Australia two short of victory. So did Ian Meckiff. 'We'll run for anything,' he told his Victorian pal. 'Doesn't matter where the ball goes. Run even if it goes to the keeper.'

Hall walked back his thirty-four paces, tugging at the gold chain on his neck. 'Remember Wes,' Worrell called, 'if you bowl a no-ball you'll never be able to go back to Barbados!' There was a thought. As he approached the figure of umpire Egar, Hall was careful to land his feet legally. Kline turned the ball to leg between Solomon and Peter Lashley and, as he and Meckiff set off, Harburg called: 'Here's the single that wins the match for Australia…'

But it wasn't. Solomon sized the ball up, hissing to Lashley: 'Move! Move!' His throw, from fifteen yards, hit the stumps side-on. Eyes turned to umpire Col Hoy at square leg. 'God, it was easy,' he recalls. 'He was miles out. There was no-one there.'

A Tie?

No-one knew what had happened. The West Indians dashed from the field in a victorious ecstasy, heedless of Worrell's shouts: 'No, no, we haven't won!'

Norm O'Neill remembers: 'I was with Gerry Gomez and he picked me up and danced me round shouting: "We've won. We've won." And I said: "Wait a minute. I think we've won."' So preoccupied were they with reconciling their books that not even the scorers were sure. It was finally journalist Ray Robinson who realised. 'Ray always sat right next to us,' says Crouch. 'He was a gentleman, and he was first to realise that it was a tie. And he leapt to his feet and told everyone: "It's the first tie in Test history."'

Not that knowing the score prepared one for such an outcome. The ABC commentators were pushed beyond their lexicon. 'No-one could think of the words,' says Michael Charlton. 'No-one knew what to say. We knew it made no sense to say the match had been drawn, but the word "tie" wasn't one routinely used. Finally it was Johnnie Moyes who yelled out: "It's a tie!"' For Charlton's part he tried for a few words with the West Indian captain. A dazed Worrell averred: 'Michael, this is a game for cool fools.'

When Bradman visited Australia's dressing-room, the word 'tie' gradually gained currency. 'This was the greatest Test of all time,' he said. 'There were thrills every day. And what a finish today. You couldn't see anything better than that.' One of the last to find out was Meckiff, who at 6.30pm was still cradling his head in the belief that Australia had been defeated.

'What are you looking so upset about?' McDonald asked.

'Fancy losing like that,' Meckiff mourned.

'Losing?' said McDonald. 'It was a tie!'

In the heat of the moment, Benaud and Davidson were upset that their brave stand had come to nought. Davidson, whose unprecedented double of 11–222, 44 and 80 would have won any ordinary match, was particularly galled. Bradman consoled him: 'Don't be disappointed Alan. You've made history today. First tie ever.'

'That's some consolation I s'pose,' Davidson replied.

'By the way,' Bradman continued drily. 'You couldn't arrange to break your finger before every game, could you?'

A Tie

Not everyone was having a great time. Alan McGilvray and Keith Miller were approaching Sydney at 6pm when the hostess on their flight volunteered that the match had finished 'even'.

Home and Away: Shaking hands with his MCC rival Peter May, Richie Benaud (above left) faced a stern initiation in his first Ashes series as captain 1958–59. But he and Alan Davidson (above right, undergoing a fitness test under the scrutiny of selectors Sir Donald Bradman and Dudley Seddon) spurred Australia to a 4–0 victory with 57 wickets between them. The team then prevailed over Pakistan and India on a 1959–60 visit to the subcontinent, surviving illness and an alien environment. Top-scorer was NSW prodigy Norm O'Neill (below) who was wreathed in flowers after reaching three figures in the Second Test against Pakistan in Lahore.

Prime Minister and Patron: 'If I ever reach Valhalla,' said prime minister Robert Menzies, 'I hope to find cricketers seated on my left and right, because I feel I can be happy in their company.' The remark was based on a lifetime's experience of the society of cricketers, among whom Lindsay Hassett was a favoured companion. Above, they study Australia batting against Minor Counties at Stoke-on-Trent in May 1953. Menzies' Prime Minister's XI match, inaugurated in November 1951, became a fixture in the cricket calendar. Below, he sits between captains Trevor Goddard and Neil Harvey in the game against South Africa on 3 February 1964. Menzies' devotion to the game was always good sport for cartoonists (facing page). Note the pot: a reference to Menzies' elevation to Knight of the Thistle in 1963.

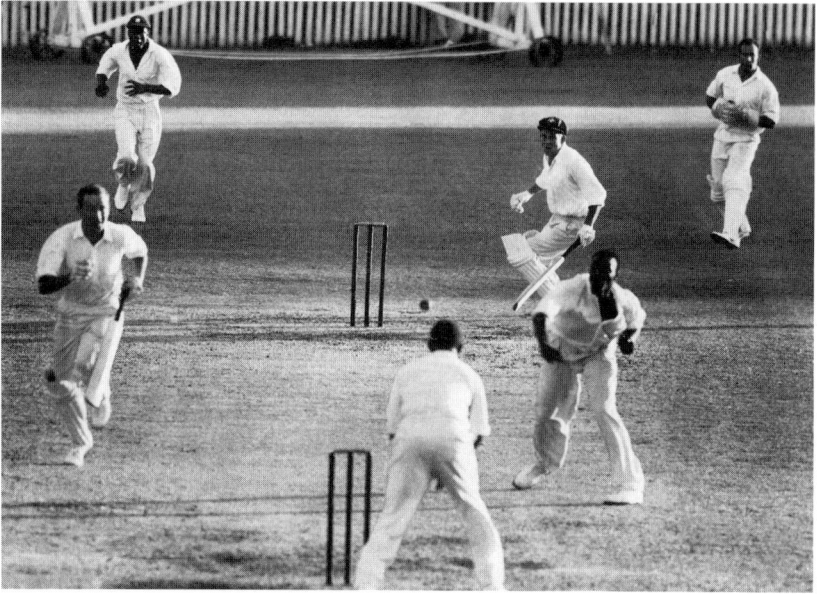

Photograph by Ron Lovitt

The Greatest Test of All: After five days of struggle and spectacle in the First Test at the Gabba, Australia and the West Indies ended perfectly square on 14 December 1960. The last over of the Tied Test was fraught with drama. Wes Hall failed to run out Ian Meckiff as he failed to respond to Grout's call for a bye (above), but Joe Solomon (at extreme left, below) did so with one ball remaining. His immortal throw was captured in an immortal picture by Ron Lovitt of the *Age*.

Photograph by Ron Lovitt

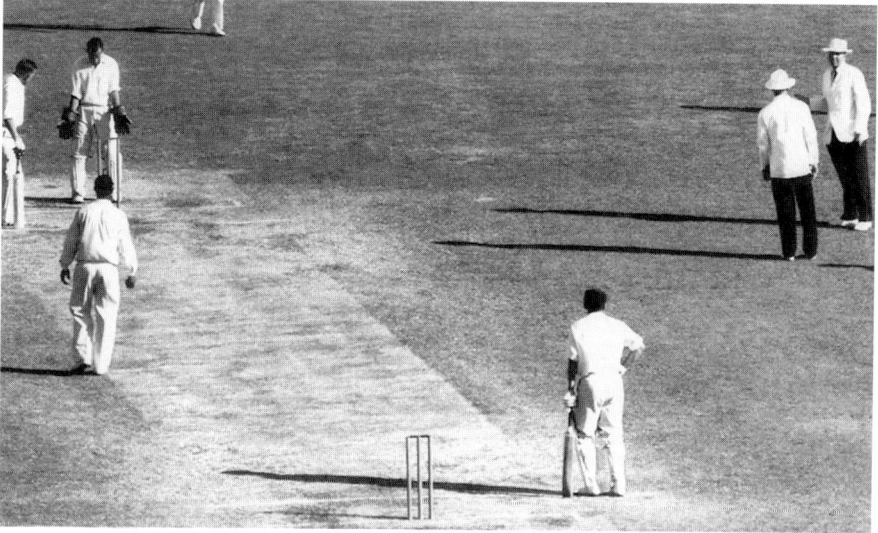

The Bail Tolls: After twenty-five days of twists and turns, the series concluded with heart-in-mouth drama in the Fifth Test at the MCG on 15 February 1961 as a bail fell from its slot behind Grout—apparently disturbed by a bottom edge—with Australia needing two runs to win. West Indies keeper Gerry Alexander pointed out the incriminating evidence (above), but umpires Col Egar and Col Hoy were unable to provide an explanation. Ken Mackay (below) saw the hosts home by two wickets with a bye, clinching the series 2–1.

'They Lost the Series—But They Won Australia': So read the front page headline for the *Daily Telegraph*'s report of the West Indies' motorcade send-off down Melbourne's Collins Street on 17 February 1961. Frank Worrell's team had illuminated the summer, so perhaps the photographer intended some symbolism in the prominence he granted the light pole.

Cricket Ahoy: Arriving at Tilbury aboard the *Himalaya* on 21 April 1961, Richie Benaud was greeted by MCC secretary Ronnie Aird. Australia's captain would shortly have problems with his martinet manager, Syd Webb, QC (above, left) and a shoulder injury that kept him from the Second Test at Lord's. But bold batting there from Bill Lawry and Peter Burge (below, hitting the winning runs) gained Australia a priceless series lead.

The Turning Point: Setting England 256 to win on the last day of the
Fourth Test at Old Trafford, Australia was threatened by the brilliant batting of
Ted Dexter. But, coming round the wicket, Benaud had Dexter caught at the
wicket: the first of four match-winning wickets for nine runs in 19 deliveries.
The Ashes were retained.

'You mean it was a draw?' Miller asked.

'No, it wasn't a draw,' she said.

'Then the West Indies won?' proposed Miller.

'No, nobody won it,' the hostess replied. 'I'll go back and find out.' By the time the tie was confirmed, McGilvray was inconsolable. 'I have spent nearly twenty-five years being furious with myself for leaving Brisbane that day,' he wrote in 1985.

Nor did the umpires have long to cherish their part in cricket history. Hoy had lent Egar some old football records for a speech he was giving in Brisbane but, when they got to their car, it had been robbed and their gear stolen. 'While everybody was celebrating that Test,' Hoy remembers, 'we were down the local police station.'

Arguments about the result continued for hours after stumps in the Cricketers' Club where Ken Archer, Bill Brown, Col McCool and Ray Lindwall congregated for a drink. Archer remembers:

> Inevitably this guy came up to Ray and asked: 'Was this the first tie in Test cricket?' Ray said that he didn't think so, that he thought it might have happened in India or Pakistan, and the bloke toddled off.
>
> Then Bill says: 'Ray, I saw the Don on the way round and he said it's the first tie ever.' So Ray got this guy and said: 'Sorry if you had a bet on, because I've given you a bum steer. Don Bradman says it's the first tie ever. And, even if I'm right, they'll change the records.'

Perhaps the most piquant tale of Test cricket's most famous encounter, however, concerns the scorebooks' fate. Shirley Crouch's returned to the Caribbean, but Vic Fisher's was apparently destroyed a few months later by the QCA. Barry Gibbs, who became association secretary in January 1961, tells the story:

> The system was that the scoresheets would be typed up and sent to the printers for the annual report. Then, after the proofs had been checked, they'd be destroyed. And one day in April 1962 I saw the secretary Jean Shaw doing the checking and, when she finished, ripping the scoresheets up and throwing them out. I said: 'What are you doing?' And she said: 'This is the way we've always done it.' Suddenly I thought: 'Oh no.' It wasn't her fault. She was just doing the job she'd done for years and years. But that was the end of the Tied Test scoresheet: torn up and put in the bin.

'GALLANT TO THE END—THAT'S SLASHER'

It would be a series in which nothing went to plan. The Australians felt that they restored order by winning the Second Test at the MCG a fortnight later, thanks to plucky batting from Mackay and Davidson's 8–114. Yet Worrell's team did not go quietly. As the Australians chased 70 on the final day, Hall bowled ten overs that recalled Larwood and Tyson at their slickest. Michael Charlton remembers:

> Wes bowled one that just flicked the peak of Colin McDonald's cap and spun it round so that the peak was jutting out sideways. I happened to be looking at Colin's face through the glasses at the time, and I could see the blood drain out quite palpably. And Johnnie Moyes, not a man to say such things idly, said: 'I think that is the fastest ball I have ever seen bowled.' And I said: 'If it isn't, I wouldn't like to see one faster.'

The tourists then achieved parity with a resounding 222-run victory in the Third Test at the SCG. Sobers' 168 in four and a half hours was spangled with 25 fours, and crowned with a six straight over Meckiff's head into the Sheridan Stand. Australia faced a fourth-innings chase of 464 after coolly calculated innings from Alexander and Worrell, and only Harvey and O'Neill detained off spinner Lance Gibbs long.

Under Worrell's serene stewardship, the lithe, long-fingered Gibbs quickly assumed match-winning proportions. His 5–66 at the SCG included three wickets in four deliveries, and he surpassed that with a startling hat-trick in the Fourth Test at Adelaide Oval: Mackay, lbw in crabbed defence; Grout, caught round the corner; and tailender Frank Misson, baffled and bowled. 'They crowded me,' Misson recalls. 'So I thought: "He'll try tossing an off spinner up to get me bat-pad". But, with that in my mind, he threw this quick yorker that was through me before I could think. Did me like a dinner: I hadn't even begun the downswing. I've seen Lance a few times since and he always slaps me on the back and says: "Thanks Frank."'

With Harvey, Davidson and Meckiff *hors de combat* in Adelaide, Australia looked distinctly underpowered. Twenty-five-year-old Rohan Kanhai, a strokemaker with an alchemist's zeal for experimentation, could not be contained, and his twin hundreds were amplified by Worrell and Alexander. Then, needing 460 to win, the home side dwindled to 3–31 by the close of the fourth day. Pundits foresaw the West Indies winning with about a session spare.

As it happened, Australia was still alive at tea on the fifth day, but ailing at 7–203. Practising in the nets behind the Giffen Stand to the bowling of Johnny Martin and Norm O'Neill, last man Lindsay Kline was dismissed eleven times in a quarter-hour. He heard a woman say: 'Well, it's a waste of time sending you in.'

Ten minutes after the adjournment, Kline was headed for the centre to join Ken Mackay with Australia 9–207. 'What would you like?' Kline asked Benaud. 'I'd like you to be there at 6pm,' said Benaud with an optimism he didn't feel. Watching Kline take guard in a flock of fielders, Mackay nourished few hopes. He might as well play a few shots to narrow the margin of defeat.

Yet every time he looked up over the next hour, the Queenslander saw Kline at the other end: silently stooped over his old Crockett bat, uncannily middling every ball, even taking a couple of fours. Their 50 partnership was raised in even time, and the only tremor came when Mackay propped at Worrell and squeezed a ball to Sobers eight yards away. The West Indians made to leave the field, but Mackay stood impassive and umpire Col Egar adjudged that the ball had bounced. Policemen shooed children from the field, and the stand resumed. At 4.55pm, Worrell took the second new ball after 800 deliveries with the old. Hall drew a few edges, but nothing more.

Each passing over now fanned Australian hopes. Every little while, Mackay would call his partner into a terse mid-pitch conference. 'How are you going Spinner?' he'd ask. Kline would mumble unintelligibly in reply and return to his end. As Kline had gone in, his teammates had begun packing their bags. Now, hope sprang eternal in Australia's dressing-room. As play entered the last hour, Benaud, a two-cigarette-a-day man, began chain-smoking. Wally Grout announced that he would have a beer at the end of every over, saying: 'I hope you have to carry me out.' Twelfth man Martin was ordered to drop his duties and watch with the rest of the team.

Beyond the ground and its crowd of 13,691, a listening audience estimated at 1.5 million was hanging on every word from Charlton and Moyes. All over Melbourne, people could be seen clustered round radios: on the steps of the GPO in Elizabeth Street, outside stores, clubs and hotels. The whole Kline family was tuned in. Lindsay's wife Stella, with three-year-old Elizabeth and eight-week-old Susan, was listening with Colin McDonald's wife Lois *chez* McDonald in Beaumaris. Brother Bruce stayed at work in Fitzroy rather than miss a ball. Kline's parents and grandfather were clustered round a wireless in Burwood, his mother trying to bake a batch of cakes while she eavesdropped on events. They heard Moyes remark on what he thought a West Indian tactical error: they were rushing their overs, cramming them in every two minutes, rather than bowling to a concerted plan.

In the last half-hour, time seemed to stand still. Mackay and Kline decided to stake out their ends: Mackay taking Gibbs and Valentine, who were turning the ball at one end into the breeze, Kline maintaining his vigil against Worrell. Runs were of no consequence, and they ran only two byes in the final ten overs. Seagulls grazed peacefully at mid on. Teammates, superstitiously keeping their seats, watched in silence. Grout ran out of beer, but was fearful of walking the six paces to fetch another. The antiquity of the Adelaide Oval clock exacerbated the tension: Norm O'Neill noticed that the minute hand took only twenty-three minutes on the way down, but thirty-seven minutes on the upward sweep.

Mackay was on strike when Hall began the last over at 5.58pm. He dug out a yorker, watched a couple pass, clipped one past point, then left another unmolested outside off stump. 'What's the matter, Wes? You're wasting them,' he thought. 'Hullo, something's cooking. Worrell's having a yarn to him. So he's going to bowl round the wicket. Trying a new angle, perhaps hoping for an lbw or to find something on the pitch. Well, it won't do any good.'

The next two, slanted in from wide of the return crease, were fast and straight, but Mackay dropped them lugubriously at his feet. 'One ball to go, Wes,' the Queenslander said to himself. 'This is your last chance. All right, let's get it over with.'

The Fourth Test, though, would not lie down. Running in for his final delivery, Hall missed his step, veered away and bounced the ball in annoyance. A tiny boy in a giant hat forded the fence and, to nervous gusty laughter from the commentators, held play up for a couple of minutes as he was retrieved by a policeman. Hall advised umpire Hoy that he would return to over the wicket and sauntered back towards the fence. Mackay leaned on his bat, chewing inscrutably.

When Hall tried again, he foot-faulted. But Hoy's cry went unheard. Australian players exulted prematurely, and hundreds of young fans swept toward the centre. 'And 20,000 children have rushed onto the Adelaide Oval,' said Charlton. 'And they've all got to get off again.' Policemen lumbered off in pursuit. Mackay stood in the centre waving: 'Get 'em off. Get 'em off.'

The last ball left a deep trace on Mackay's ribs, and an equally indelible mark on Australian cricket mythology. Rather than risk applying his bat, Mackay turned and allowed the ball to hit him on the body. 'I felt I had a knife in my ribs and staggered to the side of the wicket fighting to stop myself from going down,' Mackay recalled. 'They had not got me out and they were not going to knock me out.' The wirephoto in Melbourne's *Sun* was headlined: 'Gallant to the end—that's Slasher.'

Michael Charlton shouted: 'It's all over. It's a draw. It's a draw.' Mackay and Kline scrambled through a sea of spectators into a scrum of reporters, and it was an hour before Mackay could get to the shower and examine the soup plate bruise in his side, though it felt better when Benaud tapped him on the shoulder and said simply: 'Thanks.' The West Indians were equally gracious. Worrell would hear nothing of the disputed bump-ball catch: 'Any mistakes that may have been made are understandable when umpires have been standing so many hours in the sun.' He said of the result: 'I never took it for granted. I said to the boys when the last man came in: "Don't take it for granted—you can never tell with these Australians."' Gerry Alexander led his team into Australia's dressing-room and said: 'I think you chaps taught our young fellows a thing or two this afternoon. It should prove to them that no game is won or lost until the last ball is bowled.'

The attention almost overwhelmed Mackay. Teammates had to help him heft his gear back to the Glenelg Hotel. After he and roommate Des Hoare had spent the evening having dinner and watching TV in their room, the Queenslander spent a sleepless night replaying the innings in his mind. The next morning was more of the same: a photo shoot of Benaud serving Kline breakfast in bed, a press turn for Mackay at Mascot airport at which his now-celebrated bruise was photographed from every angle, plus the announcement by Brisbane's *Courier-Mail* of a 'Bob in for Slasher' fund, which would raise £800. 'Good on you Slasher,' read one note from an old lady. 'Your blood's worth bottling.'

THE FEEDING OF THE 90,000

As Benaud invited the West Indies to bat in the Fifth Test at the MCG on Friday, 10 February 1961, VCA secretary Jack Ledward took a telephone call from senior gateman Bill Ponsford. 'Waddya reckon about Saturday?' he asked. Ledward refrained from over-optimism: 'I think we'll be lucky to get 50,000.'

Approaching the ground the next morning to watch the West Indies resume at 8–252, Ledward's eyes bugged. Serpentine queues snaked all the way back to Richmond station: the kind one might expect for a VFL Grand Final, but not normally associated with the genteel entertainment of a Test match. When the turnstiles stopped ticking at a world record 90,800, Ponsford rang Ledward again and laughed: 'Great bloody judge you are.'

Spectators had actually been arriving well before the opening of the gates at 9am. Newspapers delighted in reporting symptoms of 'Test

Fever': the four schoolboys who, having been to the cinema on Friday evening, dossed in sleeping-bags outside the Olympic Stand; the bank department that ran a three-hour roster so that its employees could nip off to the cricket; the police radio channel D24 broadcasting regular scores.

All day long the crowd maintained a noisy vigil over local boy Colin McDonald, who was implacably pursuing his sixth Test century. Every forcing stroke detonated cheering and applause, every false shot set off roars of anguish. Out for 91, the batsman consoled himself by telling teammates: 'I guess I made one run for every thousand people here.' As Australia made stumps at 3–236, Ledward and Ponsford were left the task of storing the proceeds of Australian cricket's single biggest payday until banks opened on Monday. They ultimately secreted the £18,000 in sacks in the office of the Melbourne Cricket Club's assistant secretary. 'It's not as bad as it sounds,' says Ledward. 'The MCC was built like Fort Knox. They would have had to blow the place up with dynamite to get in.'

There was, in keeping with the series, a grandstand finish. Building on Simpson's foundation in the chase for 258, Peter Burge made a feisty 53 that saw the Australians to within 10 of their target. But, when he was seventh out, dragging Valentine on, the drama of the last half-hour emptied the MCG bars. As Grout bottom-edged a cut for two past the stumps with four needed, Alexander could be seen pointing at the wicket. 'Good God!' thought Hoy at square leg. 'The off bail's gone.' There seemed no explanation but that Grout had played on. Johnny Martin picked up his bat, ears full of advice from selectors Bradman, Seddon and Ryder seated in the dressing-room.

Neither umpire, though, had seen the bail topple. Hoy saw his colleague Egar walking towards him and said: 'Sorry mate. I didn't see a thing. It's up to you.' Egar returned to his position with a shake of the head. The crowd's uproar was prolonged when Grout sliced the next ball wildly to cover, and then when a slow-moving Hall failed to advance on Martin's mis-hit to mid on. The tension did not lift until the penultimate ball of Valentine's 22nd over skittered past Mackay and Alexander for a bye. Australia, home by two wickets, had won the series 2–1.

SO MANY GOODBYES

The statistics of the series make compelling reading. Where the five Tests of 1958–59 had oozed just 4140 runs at 35 per hundred deliveries, the five Tests of 1960–61 produced more than 6000 at almost 43. Where

May's Englishmen had been unable to project many more than 400 deliveries in a day during the Adelaide Test in January 1959, Worrell's West Indians hustled through nearly 900 on the last day of the corresponding match two years later.

But figures scarcely convey the sense of relief at such a *ritorno d'immagine* for Test cricket. As Fingleton put it: 'By taking the corpse of international cricket out of its winding sheet and infusing new life into it; by converting what used to be cricket wars of attrition into joyous events capable of attracting a crowd of over 90,000, Australia and West Indies have set an example which other cricketing countries will ignore only at the peril of their own cricketing status.'

Good fellowship between the teams had been transparent from the very beginning. Batsmen had walked, umpires had been heeded without question, catches on the bounce had been promptly disclaimed.* When Alf Valentine suffered problems with his spinning finger at the start of the trip, Benaud proffered his calomine boracic lotion. Despite bearing the brunt of Hall throughout the series, McDonald presented the paceman with his Australian sweater at its conclusion.

Praise was heaped upon Worrell's men. Johnnie Moyes wrote:

> They gave the genuine cricket lover a thrill he had not felt for a quarter of a century. They brought back to the grounds many who had left them in disgust at the mediocre fare served up to them. They proved what many of us had declared—that people would go to see cricket played as a game and an entertainment.

Worrell specially prized a letter he received from a blind cricket lover in Sydney, Len Hallett, who wrote: 'I have been blind for many years, Frank, but only once have I felt sorry about my disability and that was when I listened to Garfield Sobers play that unforgettable knock in Brisbane. Gee, if only I could have been granted my sight for the period he was batting, I would have been satisfied...So long Frank. Bring your lads back soon. Thanks to them, cricket is back in its rightful place—the world's number one sport.'

But for the West Indies, it had been far more than a cricket series. As C. L. R. James put it: 'Clearing their way with bat and ball, West Indians at that moment had a public entry into the comity of nations.' The team's

---

* Kanhai's cancellation of a catch in the state match at Adelaide Oval brought him a letter of gratitude from the South Australian Legislative Council. The lucky batsman was Barry Jarman.

deportment had often gone well beyond the call of duty. Opener Conrad Hunte, for example, even made a television appearance as one of three guest speakers responding to the Queen's Christmas message, and spoke lovingly of his allegiance to the Commonwealth:

> To me, the Commonwealth stands for orderliness, fellowship and freedom of movement. It seeks to encourage respect of one race for the other and of one nation for her sister nation. As an inhabitant of Barbados, now part of the Federation of the West Indies, and the oldest island member of the erstwhile British Empire, I am proud to be a citizen of the Commonwealth...It behoves every nation of the Commonwealth, at the head of which is Her Majesty the Queen, to renew their efforts in this great drive toward peace and goodwill among all men.

Indeed, it struck many as at least incongruous that Australia was so smitten with cricketers whom, because of its immigration policies, it could not accept as citizens. Dr Barton Babbage, Dean of Melbourne, sermonised during the Fifth Test: 'It is a sobering and humbling thought that the West Indians whom Australia welcomes as cricketers would not be welcome as citizens. Their skin is the wrong colour. They may play with us, but they may not stay with us.' He urged legislators to look to cricket's example in examining the inequities of Australia's international relations: 'It may be that the game of cricket will pave the way for more generous national policies. If only we could cultivate the spirit of cricket in all our dealings, one with the other. It is not far from the spirit of Christ.' The Melbourne-based Immigration Reform Group, dedicated to overthrowing the White Australia policy, was founded a year later.

Occasionally, in the rapturous acclaim accorded Worrell's side, the Australians felt rather hard done by. Benaud, they pointed out, had favoured attacking formations throughout the rubber, where Worrell had shown no compunction about setting run-saving fields. What of Davidson's 33 wickets from four Tests, O'Neill's 522 runs in 10 innings and Grout's 23 dismissals? Some demonstrations of public favour for the tourists also sat ill with the hosts. When Joe Solomon's burgundy cap slipped from his head to dislodge the bails in the second innings of the Second Test, for instance, his hit-wicket dismissal provoked howls of execration from the 65,000 spectators. Grout wrote: 'Maybe the Victorian crowd didn't realise we played this game for keeps, because they gave Richie the greatest blast I have ever heard handed a Test skipper, home-grown or foreign. And it lasted all day.'

Yet, half an hour after the Fifth Test finished on 15 February, all reservations were forgotten amid emotional scenes on the balcony of the MCG Members' stand. In a presentation ceremony orchestrated by Bradman and Michael Charlton, Worrell offered Benaud his cap, tie and blazer with the words: 'I give Richie my scalp, my neck and my body— the legs are not worth having.' Thousands below broke into a chorus of 'For He's a Jolly Good Fellow', affording Benaud time to craft an artful reply: 'Frank has given me, so to speak, his scalp, neck and body—but he is in every Australian's cricket heart for evermore.' Benaud also took into custody the handsome artefact that became known as the Frank Worrell Trophy—commissioned by Bradman, designed by former Test fast bowler Ernie McCormick and incorporating a ball from the Tied Test—which would become a perpetual trophy in future Australia–West Indies contests.

A couple of days later, at a ticker-tape send-off decreed by Melbourne's Lord Mayor Bernard Evans, Worrell's West Indians were ferried up Collins Street in ten open-topped saloons to the Town Hall before tens of thousands of well-wishers. Strebor Roberts, sports editor of Kingston's *Daily Gleaner*, wrote that female fans 'were so lavish with their kisses that, when the party arrived at the Town Hall for the Civic Reception, we had to spend some time wiping lipstick from our cheeks, lips and shirts.' Front page of Sydney's *Daily Telegraph* featured a picture of the motorcade the next day with the headline: 'They Lost the Series— But They Won Australia.'

The finale of the tour was a Prime Minister's XI match at Manuka Oval where, through shrewd contrivance, West Indies managed to tie with Robert Menzies' selection in a match of 576 runs from 56 overs. At a Canberra Hotel dinner, the prime minister toasted 'the Worrell–Benaud summer of cricket', saying: 'Cricket is like the government and politicians. It can occasionally defeat itself by defensive tactics and lose the public.' And in a far-sighted proposal of Worrell's health, Menzies said: 'The next time I meet you, I hope it will be as Sir Frank.' Worrell was knighted three years later.

'I Really Felt the Whole Team Was Behind Me'

AUSTRALIA V ENGLAND
1961

After the thrills and spills of their series against the West Indies, Benaud's Australians arrived at Tilbury aboard the *Himalaya* on 21 April with a heavy burden of expectation. Amid reports of financial distress at a number of counties, an MCC Committee of Inquiry into the state of cricket chaired by Colonel Rowan Rait-Kerr had published an interim memorandum that read like a clarion call:

> We have just seen the quite remarkable effect on the Australian cricket public of a Test series played in a thoroughly enterprising manner — producing as a culmination a world record attendance at Melbourne. The need for English County sides and Test teams to follow the lead set by the Australians and West Indies is strongly felt by both the Press and the public of this country. A failure to make full use of an opportunity which might not readily recur may well prove disastrous.

Benaud handled it coolly. Having worked for the *News of the World* in the 1960 English summer, he had the advantage of knowing most of the local journalists, and told the shipboard press conference that he intended risking defeat to press for victory in every tour match, and that he would encourage players to 'walk': an unheard-of statement of intent for an Australian captain. He was greeted by salaams. The *Evening News* introduced Benaud to the cricket public as the 'cricketer who has done most to restore life to the game'.

Only one aspect of the tour, at this preliminary stage, caused Benaud concern: his manager. Silver-haired sixty-year-old Syd Webb was an archetype of the Australian cricket administrator. Educated at Sydney High School and Sydney University's St Paul's College, he had all the right connections: he was a QC, a Mason, a member of the Australian Jockey Club and Sydney Turf Club. A past president of Sydney University Cricket Club, he'd joined the board on the death of Aubrey Oxlade in September 1955.

Webb could be a friendly and humorous man. He enjoyed and memorised a critic's comment about his cricket ability: 'I never saw a bowler sweat more for less turn than Syd Webb.' And in England, rushing about ineffectually in wonderment at all the finery and grandeur, he scarcely seemed a threat to the captain's authority. But Benaud had a disconcerting sense that Webb regarded the team as that of the Australian Board of Control, and therefore his to run. Perhaps it would sort itself out. Benaud kept the thought to himself.

THE SHOULDER

Benaud soon had a far greater problem on his mind. The tour opened in three-sweater weather at Worcester on 29 April 1961, rain having the final word in a low-scoring match. But, twisting his body to bowl a wrong 'un to Tom Graveney, Benaud felt something in his shoulder go. A few hours later at Droitwich's Raven Hotel, he could scarcely raise his arm without shooting pain.

Benaud bowled in the second innings, but in only one of the next half-dozen matches. Wearing a sling and shaving left-handed to ease the soreness, he began regular commutes to London for specialist treatment. Daily bulletins carried news of his injury's slow progress back to Australia. 9 May: 'I want to get back as quickly as possible to get a feel for things again.' 15 May: 'My shoulder is improving, but I shall have to see what the doctor says.' 22 May: 'I am looking forward to bowling against Gloucestershire.' After that trial spell: 'It's sore. I am disappointed with it. I thought it would have come up better than this.' Ray Robinson described Benaud's shoulder as 'the most-discussed since Venus de Milo's'.

There were reassuring omens elsewhere. Twenty-four-year-old Victorian left-hander Bill Lawry had struck a rich vein of form, O'Neill had taken up where he'd left off in Australia, and the policy of pressing for victory was bringing the best from the team. E. W. Swanton sang

Benaud's praises in London's *Daily Telegraph* when a bold declaration brought a 63-run victory against the MCC at Lord's: 'Benaud has no use for the process of insuring against defeat.'

Yet other problems were emerging and, in the process, hardening the senior players' attitude to their manager. The first was a curious run-in between Colin McDonald and Melbourne *Sun* cricket writer Kevin Hogan at The Oval. McDonald had been chatting to Percy Beames of the *Age* about batting in the second innings against Surrey: 'It was one of those situations which I never liked. Not many to get, plenty of chance to get out, nothing to gain, everything to lose. Percy, who was a fine journo, knew exactly what I meant.' McDonald was furious to discover Hogan had overheard the conversation and had in the *Courier-Mail* criticised his 'unsportsman-like' reluctance to bat. He told Webb that he wanted to sue. Webb blustered: 'For the good of the team, you will not.'

A week later at Cardiff, the Australians were reduced to ten by illness and injury. As Benaud had given the rest of his team the match off, a local sub was employed. Inevitably, Alwyn Harris took a catch.

Phil Tresidder of the *Daily Telegraph* recalls: 'I wrote a story that said how humiliating it was to see a bloke with a daffodil on his jersey catching one of his own players. And, unfortunately, it was sent to Syd and he got pretty angry.' The manager countermanded his captain's furlough policy, demanding that thirteen be present at each game. Again, it did not go down well.

Matters came to a head when O'Neill injured his knee in the last match before the First Test at Edgbaston. Webb and the three tour selectors—Benaud, Harvey and McDonald—found themselves in a Euston Station bar as the team changed trains for Birmingham. Reading from O'Neill's medical report, the manager announced with finality: 'Well, he won't be playing in the Test.' When Benaud pointed out that O'Neill hadn't undergone a fitness test, Webb said flatly: 'I'm saying he won't be playing.'

Benaud's gaze hardened: Webb was only the manager of the team, he said tersely, and his intercession in selection was unwelcome. If the selectors judged O'Neill fit, he would play. After a long confrontation, Webb finally backed down. But the manager would remember the slight.

THE DOC AND THE GAG

O'Neill did play at Edgbaston, making 82. And Benaud's Australians looked a fine ensemble, subduing England in 85 overs for 195, then building their best postwar total in England round a Harvey hundred. But, on the last day, *that* shoulder returned to prominence: Benaud could bowl only nine overs, and England escaped defeat in some style.

Following developments closely was Dr Brian Corrigan. An ebullient character who acted informally as NSWCA medical consultant, he'd followed the Australians to England and found a job at University College Hospital in Gower Street. Furthering his interest in sports injuries, he'd also been taken on by Bertie Mee's Arsenal Football Club. It was stimulating work: 'In general, the club doctor for a soccer team was a guy who sat up in the stands, was social with the ladies, treated the chairman's clap, and never went down to the rooms. Bertie Mee was the first manager who actually put his doctor down on the bench so that he could see the injuries as they came in.'

As word of Benaud's woes continued, Corrigan felt his sap rise. What a challenge! He contacted Webb, asking the nature of Benaud's treatment:

> When Syd Webb told me he'd sent Benaud to a mate of his, a radiotherapist, I screamed my head off. That was just witchcraft as far as I was concerned. I asked Syd if he'd mind me calling this guy and saying that I and [my colleague] Alan Bass wanted to take over Benaud's treatment, and he said he didn't, so I did. The guy went off his tree, but we got the job.
>
> It was a terrible tear, very extensive, very unusual. He'd torn the subscapularis right down to the capsule that contains the shoulder and, at the start, he couldn't lift his arm above the shoulder without crying out in pain. Alan and I put him on a series of exercises and stretches, slowly at first, to build up the strength and allow the tissue some time to heal. But Richie wasn't the easiest of patients. He was like a bear with a sore head. He was always saying he'd play tomorrow, but he was never right.

Shortly after, Benaud faced another problem. If Webb was content with his therapy, he was less happy with the attendant publicity. He bridled in particular at a hyperbolic report by Ern Christensen of the *Sydney Sun* of a telephone interview with Benaud, especially as the Fairfax tabloid was Benaud's employer. And, before the team headed to Canterbury to play Kent, Webb summoned Benaud and waved an air letter at him: it was, he said, from Bradman, empowering the manager to make all future press announcements. The captain would be limited to discussing on-field matters.

In retrospect, Benaud feels that he erred: 'The sensible thing for me to have done would have been to ask to see the message and from whom it had come. Instead, I said something to the effect that, if that was what the board wanted, then there was nothing I could do about it.'

On 18 June, the Australians were scheduled to visit the estate of the new governor-general, Lord De L'Isle. Benaud arrived late, having visited London for further treatment, and walked into the usual press posse. But when Tom Goodman of the *Sydney Morning Herald* inquired after his shoulder, Benaud replied blankly: 'I'm afraid you'll have to ask the manager about that.'

The journalists exchanged meaningful glances. When the team returned to the Abbot's Barton Hotel in the evening, Webb was closely interrogated. The manager insisted that the move had come at Benaud's request: 'Richie spoke to me about the great volume of work he was doing. He said that he preferred his press interviewing to be limited to on-the-field matters and asked that I do the rest. I agreed.'

The journalists returned to Benaud, asking if he was happy with the situation. 'If I answered that question I'd be commenting, wouldn't I?' he replied, deadpan.

Nobody was fooled. Percy Beames wrote in the *Age*: 'The Board of Control have never been keen on captains appearing in print and I am certain that in some way Benaud has been given an unofficial reprimand.' English pressmen delighted in the whiff of scandal. Beneath the headline 'Gag Slapped on Benaud', the *Evening News* featured a picture of Australia's captain with sticking plaster over his mouth. Brian Chapman commented in the *Daily Mirror*: 'The Australian manager, Mr Syd Webb, said the decision was made to lessen the burden of work on Benaud. My answer is…PHOOEY!'

'IT'S ALL YOURS'

As the Australians returned to the Waldorf on 21 June, however, their manager's intrigues were the least of their problems. Critics unanimously foresaw a five-day run-riot during the ensuing Second Test at Lord's. Keith Miller in the *Daily Express* was forecasting 'the biggest batting party since the War'. But the tourists looked like entering the match shorn of their two best bowlers. Corrigan and Bass had persuaded Benaud that he should not play. 'It broke Richie's heart, I reckon,' says Corrigan. 'But there was really no choice if he wanted to play for the rest of the tour.' And, after breaking down at Kent with a bad back, Davidson was equally doubtful. He spent the night being rubbed by Arthur James, climbing in and out of hot baths, hoping to restore some movement.

Harvey, at least, was indomitable. He'd largely given up on leading his country, yet here he was at Lord's taking the reins. 'I'll never forget

Richie telling me I was skipper,' he recalls. 'He just came up before the toss and said: "It's all yours." I asked him: "Is there anything you want me to do?" And he said: "Nope, it's your team." That was the way I wanted it.'

But it took some subtle psychological brinkmanship from Benaud to give Harvey the help he needed most. Knowing how difficult Davidson would find letting Harvey down, Benaud used his own absence as a spur. 'Alan, you just have to play,' he said. 'I'm out of the Test and Neil needs you badly.'

'It's all right for you,' Davidson protested. 'At least you can run.' Then he sighed and walked over to Harvey: 'I shouldn't be playing. I should be watching it with Richie. But I'll do it for you.' Davidson's back was lathered in half a tube of capsulin, and he accepted the new ball from Harvey at the Pavilion end. 'I hope I can pull out something special for you,' Davidson said.

He did. A shadow of himself all tour, Davidson suddenly found something in the surface to stir him. His grunt at release could be heard high in the Warner Stand. Raman Subba Row was beaten thrice in the first over, and his first run accrued from a ball that smacked the splice. Partner Geoff Pullar was hit in the shoulder and jabbed the pitch anxiously between overs. With the score on 14, Davidson made one rear at Pullar and it lobbed gently to point. Burge, astonishingly, fluffed the chance. 'Fair dinkum, my little four-year-old coulda caught it,' Davidson remembers. 'Normally I'd've sworn if a catch was dropped but, on that occasion, my mouth opened and nothing came out. Harv normally said nothing, but I heard him at mid on say: "I don't believe it."'

Finally, in his sixth over, Davidson struck. After running a series of deliveries away from Pullar, he made one straighten and bowled him. Burge came running from gully. 'There were 3000 Australians at Lord's that day and they'd been giving me a helluva time,' he says. 'I think I kissed him.' Pullar went on his way, staring ruefully at the pitch.

England's number three was Ted Dexter, a debonair twenty-six-year-old amateur fresh from 180 at Trent Bridge. Yet Davidson hit him twice in the chest, then Misson had him dropped at short leg. The home team almost struggled through but, with minutes left to lunch, Subba Row was lbw and Dexter caught at mid wicket. So much for the batting party.

In fact, all the pundits before the match had missed something: the pitch wasn't flat. 'It was really nasty into the Nursery end,' Harvey remembers. 'There was a ridge there about three yards in front of the batsman. If the ball pitched the bowler's side, you got one at the throat.

If it pitched your side, it came round your ankles.' Davidson resumed after lunch, and swept away May and Ken Barrington. Then the nineteen-year-old West Australian paceman Graham McKenzie, selected in Benaud's stead, brushed Cowdrey's gloves. England's ragged 205 ended at 5.23pm, Davidson crediting his 5–42 partly to the ridge, partly to the capsulin on his back: 'It was stuff they used to warm up an area of the body and, well, it really worked. When I started sweating, it started to slip down and burn the orifice. People said: "Christ, you got stuck into them." And I told them: "Well, if you'd had your backside on fire, you'd've done the same."'

THE BATTLE OF THE RIDGE

As he padded up that evening with Colin McDonald, Bill Lawry could reflect that he'd taken the long way to Lord's. Unlike the many fresh-faced Australian youths sent to England on the basis of a handful of first-class games, Lawry had been knocking round Sheffield Shield cricket for five years without attracting much attention, until an uncommon flush of form in the 1960–61 domestic summer. On the day of the touring squad's announcement, he'd gone to work as a plumber not expecting to be disturbed: 'When I didn't get picked in the last couple of Tests against the West Indies, I put it aside. It was a Friday, and I was on the thirteenth floor at the Royal Children's Hospital in Parkville when I saw two taxis pull up outside. I said to the apprentice with me: "Either someone's been killed, or I've been picked to go to England."' He and the twenty-seven-year-old NSW batsman Brian Booth had maintained a cheerful banter en route about which of them had been the last man picked.

A first net session at the Nursery on 22 April hadn't enhanced Lawry's confidence. Lawry diarised: 'My first bat on English soil at Lord's. I was shocking.' Yet, within a fortnight, it began coming together. There were three centuries in four matches leading up to the First Test, another on the eve of the Second. Lawry was an unprepossessing figure, built like a hat rack, with a sharp jaw and solid wedge of nose. But in England he quickly displayed a sharp scent for trouble outside off stump and a quiverful of attractive strokes.

In this Test, Lawry would need both. Brian Statham and Fred Trueman exploited the pitch as cruelly as Davidson. The former bowled McDonald at once, the latter slid one under Simpson's chin that steepled to gully. Lawry leant his angular frame behind everything, bat handle well forward and rigidly straight to quell the ball that bounced unexpectedly. Thirty-two overnight, he unveiled a hook on the second day so willing that its centrifugal force threatened his footing:

> Playing straight was the very first thing I learned because, when my Dad threw balls to me in the backyard at home, it was only seventeen feet wide. Then when I went to Northcote, [coach] Jack Baggott threw me hundreds of balls and got me hooking. I suspect I could hook because I'm actually right-handed in everything I do apart from bat, so my strength is in my top hand. Hooking and pulling was natural. I didn't cut so well, because it's basically a bottom-hand shot. I was in form that day and, when you're in form, you can make runs off anybody. I just batted normally. Whenever Trueman pitched short, I hooked. When he pitched up, I drove. I played and missed a lot but, because Col [McDonald] had drummed into me that cricket was a side-on game, I was less likely to nick 'em.

It was the innings Australia had needed and England had lacked. Trueman, Statham, even Dexter, peppered Lawry from short of a length, but he survived the physical interrogation with equanimity. Only after he was out did teammates appreciate the innings' toll. Says Davidson: 'When I'd been with Artie [James] before the Test, Bill had been there getting treatment, too, for shin splints. When the ball hit him on the shin in that innings, it musta hurt like hell. And when I went for physio on the second evening, Bill was there too: his right arm and his right side were a mass of black.'

AUSTRALIA TAKES COMMAND

Despite Lawry's 130 and a bold 44 from Burge, the tourists were only 32 to the good with eight down. If Cowdrey could expunge the last two wickets cheaply, England might yet loosen Australia's grip. But Cowdrey now made two tactical errors that permitted Mackay, McKenzie and Misson to tighten it. Mackay and McKenzie were allowed an hour of spin from Ray Illingworth and David Allen, in which they assembled an enterprising 50. Then, on the third morning, Cowdrey conceded Mackay singles in order to attack Misson: an invitation Mackay accepted, for Misson as last man was something of an imposter. Misson says:

> When I say I could bat a bit, I do mean a bit. But I'd opened for my club and I had a first-class 50. To start, Slasher tried sheltering me from the strike. Then he said: 'You look like you're hitting 'em all right. No need to protect you.' The other mistake Colin made was bowling Trueman and

Statham against me. I was probably more at home against pace than spin, and he should have tried to spin me out rather than knock me over.

The 102 added by Australia's last two wickets would prove decisive. England lost its top five clearing the arrears, every Harvey hunch paying dividends. He offered McKenzie the Pavilion end, and the strapping Perth paceman gathered 5–37. He whistled up Simpson to bowl against Illingworth, moved into leg slip for the wrong 'un, and caught him there for nought. He tossed Davidson the second new ball at the Nursery end and, in his second over, the left-hander bent one back to trap the tenacious Barrington.

Though Australia needed 69 on the fourth day, the ridge still had tricks to play. Trueman and Statham began their second sortie with a withering spell that reduced Australia to 4–19. Burge began uneasily, subduing his aggressive instincts, and took a physical and aural battering from Trueman. The Queenslander was dropped off a mishook at square leg, and Australia was still only halfway home at lunch.

Harvey had watched with mounting frustration and, over the salad plates, badgered Burge to attack: 'For Chrissake, Burgie. You're giving me the shits. Get out there and belt the thing.' The instructions were followed. Boundaries began volleying from Burge's bat, and partner Davidson watched him apply the finishing touches to the five-wicket victory: 'One ball from Statham got up and he pulled it, absolutely smashed it, for four. The next stayed down and—I still don't know how he did it—he brought his bat down from shoulder high and scythed it past me at the bowler's end.'

The Test that became known as the Battle of the Ridge was a triumph for Lawry, Davidson, Burge, McKenzie, Mackay and Misson, but above all for Harvey. 'I've never been in an Australian side that pulled so hard for its captain,' says Burge. 'Everyone respected Neil so much. They would have done anything for him.' Says Harvey: 'Yes, probably my proudest moment. We really got on the French champagne that afternoon. I knew it'd be my only Test match as captain and, being at Lord's, I decided to make the best of it. I did a pretty good job of myself I must admit. I was too crook to go anywhere that night.'

PITCH BATTLES

Within minutes of the end of the Lord's Test, surveyors commissioned by the MCC trooped onto the arena to study the pitch's topography.

Ground committee chairman Walter Robins announced solemnly that there *were* depressions in the surface—one notable undulation twenty-three feet from the Nursery end stumps—and that one end of the pitch was two inches higher than the other. The inquiry met a mocking reception, not least at Headingley, where northern officials planning the Third Test enjoyed the discomfiture of southern rivals. Yorkshire chairman Brian Sellers commented condescendingly: 'We know how to prepare *proper* wickets up here.'

Yet the Leeds pitch provoked just as much contention. Mackay concluded: 'A tennis net seemed more appropriate equipment here than two sets of stumps. The wicket was the colour and texture of a crumbling ant-bed tennis court.' He was out on the putting green of Harrogate's Hotel Majestic when Jim Laker walked past. 'Have you seen the wicket?' Laker asked. 'Think I'll make a comeback.' Ray Lindwall, writing a syndicated column for a news agency run by Englishman Reg Hayter, described the pitch as a 'disgrace to cricket'.

It was Fred Trueman, however, who eviscerated both Australian innings, with 5–16 in five overs in the first innings, 6–5 in eight overs in the second, sending up puffs of dust as his deliveries struck the surface. Harvey alone stayed long. For Benaud, back in the team thanks to the cumulative efforts of Brian Corrigan and Alan Bass, the match provided mixed blessings: a pair and two expensive wickets underlined his lack of match fitness.

For Benaud, it was a trying time. His injury demanded not only physical improvement, but the mental discipline to make a dispassionate assessment of his progress. Though Australia was desperately short of spin—neither Kline nor the Victorian left-armer Ian Quick had any form to recommend them—he could not afford to return prematurely and rub himself out of the rest of the trip.

There was also the protracted skirmish with his intransigent manager. But it was not a fight Webb was likely to win. With his journalist's nous and his public relations skill, Benaud was simply too poised. Subtly, Benaud and assistant manager Ray Steele, an intelligent and personable lawyer, were taking over the running of the tour. 'We were bloody lucky to have Ray,' says Colin McDonald. 'He carried the tour for Richie. Like us, he realised pretty early that we didn't have a manager. Syd simply didn't have a clue. He was a joke. And Benaud pushed his authority to the limit because, in a stand-up confrontation, he knew he'd win and Syd'd go to water.' Percy Beames recalls: 'Richie really played it for all it was worth. I'd ask him: "How's your shoulder Rich?" And he'd say: "Well, Perce, I'll just go and find out from Mr Webb." And he'd walk off for a bit, come back and say: "Mr Webb says that my shoulder is fine.'"

As the tour passed its halfway point, Benaud began feeling happier. A visit to Alan Bass after the Third Test was encouraging: Benaud's shoulder had responded well to its first serious workout. He rejoined the team at Northampton and bowled 35 overs. Fine again. Then, against Middlesex on the eve of the Fourth Test at Old Trafford, Benaud took 9–70 from 50 overs. 'I was still conscious of the shoulder,' he recalled, 'but this was by far the best it had felt since Worcester. I could not have felt happier.'

Memory of the Third Test was still raw. But, rather than consign it to memory, Benaud sought to exploit it. On the team noticeboard at Manchester he pinned one of the more damning Australian newspaper reports of Trueman's triumph, alleging that Benaud's team was in disarray and would squander the Ashes. It was a favourite Benaud ploy, and never failed to elicit a response. 'The reaction was good,' he remembered, 'though some of the language wasn't.'

'A MOST INGENIOUS PARADOX'

For the better part of four days, Benaud's motivational scribe could have felt pretty bullish. England forged a first-innings lead of 177 in the gloaming and, despite Lawry's sterling second-innings hundred, were firm favourites at the close of the fourth day: Australia, 154 in the black, had only four wickets in hand.

Yet, for the third consecutive Test, the pitch was becoming a factor. Strolling out to study the surface in the evening, Benaud noticed four distinct holes in a scarred and dusty quarter outside the right-hander's leg stump, apparently excavated by Trueman's trampling. He cast his mind back to an MCC–Australian XI match at the SCG in November 1958, where Trueman had left a similar trail of destruction, and recalled how effectively Tony Lock had used that rough in spinning his team to victory.

Such thoughts were still fresh in his mind as he ascended the stair to the Lancashire committee room for a drink, and bumped into Ray Lindwall. Benaud esteemed Lindwall's cricket wisdom and, after cornering him away from the crowd, posed him an interesting question: What would happen if Benaud bowled round the wicket and into the rough?

Lindwall ruminated. England had five left-handers and it would certainly cause them problems. But, against the right-handers, Benaud would want inch-perfect accuracy. Lindwall recalled: 'We talked the matter over and I said I thought it would be worth the risk providing he reverted to bowling over the wicket to the right-handers if England got ahead of the clock. In that way he could set a defensive field and slow them down again.' Benaud returned to the Midland Hotel that evening and, listening to his collection of Gilbert and Sullivan tapes in his room, experienced a 'sense of tingling excitement that refused to pass off'. Could he save a match by winning it? It was, as the librettist put it in *The Pirates of Penzance*, 'a paradox, a paradox, a most ingenious paradox'.

DAVO AND GARTH

Benaud's discussion with Lindwall appeared academic the next morning as England's off spinner David Allen claimed three wickets in 15 deliveries without conceding a run. Last man Graham McKenzie rose from the treatment table, hurriedly strapped on his pads, and joined Davidson with Australia only 157 in credit.

Only Lawry had outshone fast bowler McKenzie as the discovery of the tour: a handsome, husky physical education teacher from Perth's John Curtin Senior High School with a physique reminiscent of the comic strip hero 'Garth', and a laconic composure that never deserted him. Davidson saw it again as the young man took guard: 'I was the old seasoned pro and I was shaking like I had Parkinson's. And Garth comes in and he's in another world. He's whistling and talking and acting like he's going for a stroll with his dog on the beach.'

As Davidson tried to emulate McKenzie's sangfroid, home captain Peter May made a critical decision: he replaced Statham with the part-time spin of Yorkshireman Brian Close. Fifteen runs came in Close's two overs. They were the first balls that Davidson had middled in weeks and, suddenly confident, he turned his mind to the fetters that Allen had forged (25 maidens in 37 overs).

In Allen's 10th over of the day, Davidson went for broke: there was an off drive for six, cover-driven boundaries off front and back foot. As the ball was retrieved, thoughts rushed through his head about how Allen would respond: 'He was either going to bowl wide of me or, if he tried to bowl on line, it was going to be his straighty. When his action didn't signify that he was going to bowl wide, I decided to come at him. I picked it up on the half-volley and it hit the brick wall by the railway yards: the most incredible feeling I'd had in my life.'

When Trueman replaced Allen, Davidson's dander was up: 'Fred's first ball hit me on the toe and I thought: "Well, no matter where he pitches the next one, I'm after him.'" A square-drive for three and a slash for four raised Australia's 400. Not until the stand had swelled to 98 in 102 minutes, and Australia's lead to 255, were the pair separated. Tossing his bat in a corner, Davidson chirped: 'We'll do these jokers, Rich.'

It was a presumption that events did not, at first, bear out. At lunch, England's target was 236 in three and a half hours with all 10 wickets standing. And twenty minutes into the afternoon session, Pullar's dismissal brought to the crease Australia's sternest threat. Ted Dexter had been damned at his first Ashes appearance. An unsuccessful reserve for May's side in Australia in 1959, he had been labelled by Johnnie Moyes as 'one of the poorest batsmen to appear in a Test in Australia for 40 years'. His pedigree— Radley public school, Cambridge, amateur—and his manner—detached, off-hand, frivolous—completed the impression: a fop, a dilettante.

But Dexter's commanding 180 while warding off defeat at Trent Bridge had obliged the Australians to reconsider. What made Dexter so problematic, Davidson decided, was that he appeared ungoverned by the merit of bowling:

> They talk about players that worry you and Ted was always one who did. He was so unpredictable: one minute he'd be making a bad ball look like a good one, the next he'd be smashing your best ball to the boundary as though he was saying: 'I should have scored off the last one.' I don't think Ted ever realised what a good player he was because, when he was hot, there was no-one harder to stop.

This gloomy afternoon, Dexter looked hot. Davidson bowled him two perfectly respectable deliveries—one just short of a length, the next slightly fuller—and watched them vanish through mid off for fours. McKenzie replaced him, bowled two wides, and was promptly hit for two imperious boundaries. Benaud, beginning over the wicket, bowled tightly to Subba Row, but Dexter was batting, as Ron Roberts of London's *Daily Telegraph* put it, 'like a modern Ajax'.

Twelfth man Quick appeared at the gate with a refreshment tray: a quaint sight in chilly Manchester where there'd not been a drinks break for the whole match. But Benaud beckoned him on. Boos resonated round the field. Benaud must be trying to slow the game down, aiming for a draw. In fact, he was thinking about winning it. With England 1–128 after 117 minutes, Benaud was like the French marshal who observed: 'The enemy is behind me, to my left and right, and ahead. I will attack.' As he told Harvey: 'We've had it as far as saving this, Ninna. The only way we'll get out of it is to win.'

'Get into it then,' Harvey replied. 'I'm with you.' Benaud came round the wicket.

THE SWEETEST VICTORY

Left-handed Subba Row, as Lindwall had postulated, was immediately troubled by the new line. As the ball bit the rough, it was impossible to judge the degree of turn and bounce. Dexter was continuing in his own sweet way: he took 21 from four Simpson overs, pulled Mackay for four then drove him over long on for six to raise the hundred stand in an hour and twenty minutes. But then a single turned over the strike so that Dexter faced Benaud (0–40 from 17 overs).

It was the turning-point. Dexter dead-batted five deliveries, withdrew to flog the sixth through extra cover, and edged to Grout. Two balls later, out of the rough, May was bowled round his legs. 'There was that terrible fraction of a second as I waited for the ball to hit the leg stump,' wrote Benaud. 'And then an unrestrained yell of joy.'

England was still nominally well placed: 3–150, needing 106 in no better than even time. Yet Dexter's 76 in 84 minutes had created a rod for the home side's back. The chase had to be maintained, safety was not an option. The dilemma was embodied by Close, a fearless and resolute left-hander, but whose efforts to assault Benaud would be severely censured. He hit a superb six over long on, miscued three sweeps, and top-edged a fourth to O'Neill at square leg. Benaud was unstoppable. When he bowled the stubborn Subba Row off his pads in the last over before tea, he had taken 4–9 in 19 deliveries.

Australia won by 54 runs with twenty minutes spare when Davidson bowled Statham with a change of pace. 'I think it was the best Test I played in,' he says. 'We were never in it. It was Bill [Lawry] who gave us the chance. For his innings at Lord's I'd've given him the VC, but his 102 at Manchester was worth at least the Military Cross.' It was Benaud, though, who was the toast of a dressing-room that hugged itself in disbelief. O'Neill filled the bath and laughed: 'Go on, Rich, dive in. With your luck, you won't even get wet.'

The location made victory sweeter still. On the ground where Laker had prostrated them in 1956, the captain and Harvey sipped champagne on the players' balcony. The obligatory telegram from the prime minister arrived: 'Congratulations on the most brilliant fight back I can ever remember. My warmest greetings to you and the team.' But dignity was maintained. As celebrations continued over dinner at the Midland Hotel,

E. W. Swanton of the *Daily Telegraph* breezed past and asked: 'Would it be all right with you chaps if I had a photographer come and take your picture?'

'By all means,' Benaud replied. Then, as the snapper arrived, the skipper said solemnly: 'One moment. Bottles off the table, gentlemen.' Coffee cups were positioned, the picture taken, and retention of the Ashes savoured.

'THE FINEST TEAM I HAD ANYTHING TO DO WITH'

The captain's tangle with his manager notwithstanding, the 1961 Ashes tour was as contented a trip as most of the Australians could remember. Everyone got a chance. Where previous teams had often been dependent on two or three key bowlers, no fewer than eight exceeded 50 wickets. Supernumeraries played roles not much less important than the team's stars. Davidson remembers limping into lunch on the first day at Lord's and being smothered with attention: 'When I came in, I was so stiff I couldn't bend down to take off my shoes. But Barry Jarman was waiting for me with an iced towel and pulling up a chair for me. And there was one guy to take off one boot and another to take off the other one, and a fourth gave me a cold drink. Four blokes looking after me! The guys were tremendous. I really felt that the whole team was behind me.'

The team shared everything. Benaud had set the tone on the *Himalaya*: rather than stretch his £50 'captain's allowance' over twenty-eight weeks, he and Harvey had blown it in one go with a shipboard team party. The policy continued in England. 'Richie had a rule that if we were given anything, there had to be twenty-one of them,' recalls scorer Jack Cameron. 'For instance, Remington offered him an electric razor and a typewriter but he made sure that we all got them.' Past master of the appropriate gesture, Benaud presented Cameron with his cap, gloves and sweater after the drawn Fifth Test.

Expressive of the team's harmony were its pranks, of which Jarman, Lawry and Misson were the most avid perpetrators. One carefully choreographed routine was a stumble in The Oval dressing-room that splashed green ink over the shirt of journalist Ron Roberts. Misson recalls:

Ron always looked immaculate, like he'd stepped out of *Esquire*: starched white shirt, pin-striped suit. Barry had gotten this ink from a joke shop that turned clear after a few minutes and, when the plot developed, my role was to blunder across someone's path and send the ink flying. Poor old Ron, he was terribly upset, but the ink faded even as he was sounding off.

Syd Webb was often the butt of their fun, most famously when they planted spoons belonging to the Queen Mother in his pockets. Misson tells the story:

> Syd could be a bit pompous at times, and on royal occasions he could be very pompous. So Bill and I thought: 'How can we bring Syd down a peg or two?' Spider was always an untidy bugger: he'd have the flaps open and pockets out, so it was quite easy to slip a few spoons in them. We mentioned to the Queen Mother that we were playing a joke, and we asked her when we leaving to say: 'It's been a delight to have you and your team, but we'd appreciate it if you wouldn't take our silverware.'

The captain, though, wasn't immune either. During the team's final game at Dublin, Benaud slipped into his boots and remarked: 'Gee, I knew I was tired. But I don't seem to be able to lift my feet off the ground.' Lawry had nailed them to the floor. And such egalitarianism contrasted starkly with the anachronistic class distinctions that the Australians saw in the English game. Counties still maintained two dressing-rooms—one for amateurs, one for professionals—and often a separate antechamber for the captain.

For his part, Benaud remembered his squad as 'easily the finest team I had anything to do with' and the trip as 'by far the most enjoyable I have had from a team point of view'. On his return to Australia, the skipper was garlanded with praise and prizes. In December 1961, he edged out Lawry, Rod Laver, Margaret Smith and world 125cc motorbike champion Tom Phillis as ABC Sportsman of the Year. And in May 1962, NSW governor Sir Eric Woodward invested Benaud as an OBE. But as Davidson quickly reminded him, this stood for 'Other Bastards' Efforts'.

'The Myth of Australian Dynamism Exploded'

AUSTRALIA V ENGLAND AND SOUTH AFRICA
1962–64

Could cricket's new paradigm be sustained? The initial answer appeared to be yes. In the absence of a visiting international team, the 1961–62 Sheffield Shield was stacked with eventful, uninhibited cricket. Only three matches in twenty were drawn, two because of rain, and Benaud's NSW won the competition with riotous scoring and hyperkinetic over rates that wooed the best domestic cricket crowds for more than thirty years. The Saturday (6 January 1962) of the NSW–South Australia match at the SCG attracted almost 18,000, who witnessed 418 runs at almost six an over.

Not least exciting was the presence of three West Indians—Wes Hall in Queensland, Garry Sobers in South Australia and Rohan Kanhai in Western Australia—enticed by private sponsorship and feted as VIPs. Thousands of Brisbanites descended on Eagle Farm Airport to welcome Hall in October 1961, and 43 wickets at 20 amply repaid his backers at Atlantic Oil Company. Sobers stayed three seasons—sponsored by Prospect Cricket Club and the *Adelaide Advertiser*—and his handiwork inspired his state's first Shield in a decade.

Yet it did not last. The 1962–63 Ashes series would be the best attended since Bradman's last at home and, with almost £200,000 in gate receipts, the richest in history. But in providing only two results in five matches, it was among the most disappointing in Anglo-Australian annals.

Appointment of the glamorous Ted Dexter to lead the MCC promised much. Even Benaud thought him ideal: 'He is the man to weld the team together and to bring out the best in them by personal example on the field. Dexter as captain will mean the most successful MCC tour of Australia for thirty years, and a lively and tremendously hard-fought battle for the Ashes.' But Dexter proved a paradox: a batsman who knew no fear and a captain who knew every fear.

Dexter batted much as he had ever done, outscoring all previous MCC captains. But his infatuation with tactical fads quickly cost him his bowlers' confidence. Fred Trueman's disgusted comment was that his captain 'had more theory than Darwin'. And—despite the MCC's decision in 1962 to abolish the amateur–professional distinction—the side still appeared divided along class lines. Yorkshire off spinner Ray Illingworth recalled the inner circle of 'gentlemen'—Dexter, Colin Cowdrey, Alan Smith and blue-blood manager the Duke of Norfolk—keeping their distance from the 'players' throughout the trip. On one occasion while convalescing from illness, Illingworth was press-ganged into acting as twelfth man because Cowdrey was taking his wife to see *Mutiny on the Bounty*.

Yet not all blame could be heaped at Dexter's door. The unit that had helped Benaud restore Australian supremacy was reaching an autumnal stage. McDonald, Kline and Ian Craig had slipped quietly from the game in 1961–62, and were followed now by Harvey, Davidson and Mackay. The captain himself was in his final full series as leader, having announced he would not tour again, and disinclined to risk his unbeaten record.

Davidson and Harvey departed, suitably, in some splendour. Davidson raked English ranks one last time with a match-winning 9–79 in the Third Test at the SCG, while Harvey skated to 154 in five and a half hours in the Fourth Test at Adelaide Oval. But, as that match petered out, Keith Miller dubbed it 'The Battle of the Spineless Skippers'. And when England spent nine and a half hours making 321 in the Fifth Test at the SCG and Australia declined to chase 241 in even time in the fourth innings, John Clarke of the *Evening Standard* opined: 'The myth of Australian dynamism had been exploded. Cricket in both countries, not only one, needed to mend its ways.'

BENAUD SIGNS OFF

For all intents, this was Benaud's last hurrah as Test captain, and his sixth series without defeat. *Wisden* paid him glowing tribute: 'If one player, more than any other, has deserved well of cricket for lifting the game out of the doldrums, that man is Richard Benaud.'

Most of Benaud's distinction as a captain, in fact, was beyond the public gaze. No captain had so sedulously encouraged the doctrine of mutual support. No captain was so concerned to run a relaxed dressing-room. On the rare occasions he cracked the whip, it was to maintain that precious 'complete team spirit'. Brian Booth remembers a luncheon adjournment in the Australian dressing-room at Adelaide Oval when two batsmen who'd been involved in a run-out could be heard bickering about who had been at fault. Benaud let the argument run a while, then picked up his blazer and headed for the door. 'I don't know about you fellas, but I'm going to lunch,' he announced. 'And, when I get back, I don't want hear another word about that run-out.' The debate ended.

Benaud was a contriver by nature. Often, he gave the impression of planning his life down to the finest degree. Alan McGilvray recalled: 'Often he would buttonhole me after a day's play in England to suggest a restaurant worth a visit on our way to the next town. The fact that it would be 30–40 miles out of the way was of little concern to him. If the food was special, it was worth the trip, and he carried with him a gourmet's guide to England to point him in the right direction.' In an era not notable for it, his nimble mind was ever-alert to commercial opportunities: Benaud endorsed Gray-Nicolls bats from 1956 to 1964, designed their popular 'super short' bat and conceived another with a thin golf shaft filled with rubber in the handle (it proved too expensive for mass production). The Australian captaincy led to his advertising Milo, Mortein, Smoothex shaving foam, Victa mowers, Renault automobiles and Vaseline hair cream. 'I had no agent and I represented myself, with advertising agents coming to me to see if I would be prepared to advertise products,' he says. 'Remuneration was small, I'm afraid, but welcome.'

That same cool reserve and keen eye were evident in the middle. Watching Benaud deploy his men during the 1962–63 Ashes series, Alan Ross wrote:

> On the field Benaud is a source of endless fascination. He adjusts his players as if by references to some built-in electronic computer, assessing angles and distances. He appears calm, solicitous, involved; nothing happens that has not been foreseen, or that could alter the thoughtful, deliberate walk from gully to gully or back to his bowling mark. There has never been such a calculating cricketer.

Benaud's tactical intuition often beggared his players' belief. During the First Test at Edgbaston in June 1961, for instance, he greeted the arrival of Englishman Mike Smith by summoning Bill Lawry to a novel short gully position. 'Is that all right?' Benaud asked bowler Mackay. 'That's fine,' said Mackay, although he had no idea of Benaud's thinking.

Smith had been in stunning form—almost completing the elusive 1000 runs in May—but somehow his second ball flipped from pad to bat and straight into Lawry's hands.

But, despite Benaud's reputation for gambling, he was foremost a clinician. When he attacked, it was usually because either the circumstances were favourable or had eliminated any other option. As he said of his 1961 Old Trafford coup: 'At Manchester I am sure that England would have won with ten or twelve minutes to spare had we gone on the defensive…Defensively minded tactics would have increased England's chances and wiped out our own.'

The 1962–63 Ashes series, then, was not a departure from policy but an outcome of it. Once Benaud had decided that there was no prospect of victory in the Fifth Test, for instance, he emphatically instructed his batsmen not to get out. His response to criticism was to explain that, while chasing runs, one should 'either play wholeheartedly for a win or…play with equal determination for a draw'. As Alan Ross pointed out:

> What irked most people was simply Benaud's realism. They would have preferred at least some gesture towards a decision, remote though it might have proved. Benaud is not one for gestures of that kind: his reading of the possibilities may be questioned, but once accepting them his tactics were perfectly logical. No one took pleasure from the desultory playing out of the game, but that was the way the cards fell. You cannot rig the hands.

As Benaud began phasing himself out as a cricketer in 1963, he was phasing himself in as a commentator. He published his second book and, having wintered with the BBC and the *News of the World* in 1960, returned to England for a second stint as a television caller. He would lead Australia in only one more Test. It would be one of the most controversial in history.

CRICKET'S 'MOST COMPLEX QUESTION'

Not since Bodyline had cricket known an issue as divisive and destructive as throwing. As Sir Donald Bradman observed in July 1960: 'It is the most complex question I have known in cricket, because it is not a matter of fact but of opinion and interpretation. It is so involved that two men of equal goodwill and sincerity could take opposite views.'

For the preceding decade, in fact, the question had proved far too complex for authorities to even begin addressing by empowering umpires to act. English umpire Frank Chester was of a mind to call the South African Cuan McCarthy at Trent Bridge in June 1951, for instance, until Sir Pelham Warner told him he would receive no support from the MCC. Tony Lock *was* no-balled in a Test at Sabina Park in January 1954, but bowled on unchecked.

The result of this equivocation was that, by the late 1950s, there was a host of bowlers with actions of arguable purity: Lock (although he subsequently took steps to remodel his action), Harold Rhodes, Butch White, Derek Pearson, Keith Aldrige in England, Australians Meckiff, Rorke, Slater, Burke, Brian Quigley, Peter Trethewey and Alan Hitchcox, West Indians Charlie Griffith and Conrad Stayers, Springbok Geoff Griffin and New Zealander Gary Bartlett. Ian Craig, who faced most of his generation's speediest bowlers, describes a spell by Bartlett at Wellington as the most life-threatening he endured:

> There was a howling gale of the type behind him that you really only get at Basin Reserve and, when I went out to take strike, I looked behind me and I could barely see the keeper and slips they were standing back so far. I saw Bartlett let go of the ball, but the first I knew of where it had gone was the sound of it hitting the gloves yards behind me. I think it was the quickest bowling I faced.

As the 1958 English season commenced, the MCC Cricket Sub-Committee warned all umpires to be on the lookout for suspect actions. In the event, no bowler was called. What finally raised a flutter in the dovecote was Meckiff's deployment against May's Englishmen later that year. MCC manager Freddie Brown and deputy manager Desmond Eagar did not raise an official protest when they attended the Australian board's meeting during the Fourth Test in Adelaide, but did cast doubts on the wording of the existing Law 26 of the 1947 Code ('For a delivery to be fair the ball must be bowled, not thrown or jerked') and its Australian variant (which prohibited 'sudden straightening of the arm, whether partial or complete...at any time after the arm has risen above the level of the shoulder in the delivery swing').

Brown also gave an unflattering report on the actions of school cricketers he had seen. 'I have visited fifteen schools so far on this trip,' said Brown. 'And at practically every one there were around four or five boys of the first or second XIs who had suspicious actions.' His clear message was that the deviant strain would replicate itself until remedial action was taken.

Reaction in England was swift. In February 1959, the MCC Cricket Sub-Committee recommended that umpires begin preparing a list of bowlers with suspect actions. Three bowlers—including Lock—were called in the ensuing season. But in his Notes to *Wisden*, editor Norman Preston said that the problem was now greater than umpires could cope with: 'The danger of not stamping on offenders in the past has led to the problems which now confront the authorities. They have only themselves to blame for the spread of this menace to the game. Too much responsibility is left to the umpires, who, I feel, would take action if they knew they could rely on support from the officials above them.'

Notwithstanding its nebulous status and the imprecise extent of its powers, the Imperial Cricket Conference was clearly the only forum suitable for response. Gubby Allen, then England's chairman of selectors, raised the issue at its July 1959 annual meeting, with additional reference to the related question of 'dragging'. Law 26 was a model based on placement of the back foot: a no-ball could be called only if the umpire was 'not satisfied that at the instant of delivery, the bowler has at least some part of one foot behind the bowling crease and within the return crease'. For some bowlers, this was a distinct advantage. With a Brobdingnagian stride far beyond the front line, Gordon Rorke often appeared to release the ball from eighteen yards.

Objective benchmark for a fair delivery was elusive. One of Sir Donald Bradman's party pieces was screening film of a left-handed quick with a patently cocked elbow. When his audience unanimously agreed that the man was a thrower, Sir Donald would reveal that the image was of Harold Larwood—acme of fast bowling fairness—reversed.

Yet something had to be done. In June 1960, as the ICC prepared to convene again, Griffin was called for throwing eleven times in the Second Test at Lord's. The prospect of umpires proscribing Meckiff and Rorke when Australia toured England the following season suddenly seemed very real. Under the *Daily Mail* headline 'MCC Aim Fire at Meckiff—Courtesy Cannot Save Aussie Chuckers Now' Alex Bannister wrote: 'I say here and now that, as South Africa's Geoffrey Griffin failed to survive his first Test, Ian Meckiff has no chance at all of satisfying English umpires.'

The 14 July ICC meeting was the largest and most representative convened: fifteen emissaries from all the Test nations, including Pakistan's high commissioner Lieutenant-General Mohammed Yousuf. Two legislative changes were mooted. Law 26 was reworded, in an amalgamation of the English and Australian codes, to depict a throw more precisely: 'A ball shall be deemed to have been thrown if, in the opinion of either umpire, the bowling arm having been bent at the elbow, whether the wrist is backward of the elbow or not, is suddenly straightened immediately prior to the instant of delivery.' And, to combat 'dragging', it was recommended that ICC members adopt a policy of no-balling from the position of the front foot starting not before September 1962.

Bradman hailed the summit as a landmark: 'It is quite impossible to go on playing with different definitions of throwing. This was the great hurdle of the conference and it unanimously and amicably agreed on a uniform definition.' Further correspondence continued to minimise the likelihood of a Griffin incident on the 1961 Ashes tour. Having rejected several extreme suggestions—ranging from the postponement of the series to a season moratorium on throwing—Bradman and Dowling of the Australian board and Allen, Harry Altham, Ronnie Aird and Sir Hubert Ashton of the MCC agreed in November 1960 to a seven-week truce at the start of the trip: bowlers whose actions umpires felt doubtful would be reported to the MCC rather than called.

The stakes were high. 'If the doubtful bowling controversy goes unchecked, it could lead to an upheaval on the 1961 Australian tour of England,' Bradman commented. 'What a tragedy it would be if our tour was threatened. It could lead to the greatest controversy in cricket history.'

MAN IN THE MIDDLE

It was ironic that the most controversial cricketer of the age should have been one of its least controversial personalities. Ian Meckiff was a gentle and modest man with none of the histrionic belligerence associated with fast bowlers: son of a foreman at a grocery wholesaler, a salesman for the hardware firm of Roger Sellar and Myhall, who married a girl he met at a Mentone Town Hall dance and settled in Beaumaris.

It was impossible not to like him. But it was equally impossible to ignore his action. 'He is the most likeable individual and devoid of vice,' Springbok Roy McLean wrote of Meckiff in 1958. 'It is just that he has not been checked and naturally believes all is well. But someday somewhere the blare of publicity will flare round this young Victorian state bowler…'

It was a prescient comment. By year's end, Meckiff was a figure of such notoriety that teammates complemented his nickname of 'The

Count' with the additional pseudonym 'Sputnik'. The public knew him as 'Chucker', an epithet so adhesive that it even transferred to his son Wayne. Meckiff recalled:

> The frustrating part of it was that I had no way of fighting back. All I could do when I was asked if I did throw was shake my head and say no. I'd need an adding machine to work out how many times people asked me this question: people I didn't even know and often people who didn't even follow cricket…The whole thing built up to such an extent that, regardless of whether people believed I threw or not, they were calling me 'Chucker' Meckiff.

Meckiff's response was to alter his action. Before Benaud's team left for Pakistan in October 1959, Meckiff rehearsed a new approach holding his left arm rigid. Previously sceptical onlookers were impressed. Ron Roberts of London's *Daily Telegraph* accosted Meckiff at Lahore and said: 'I had my doubts about you, Ian, but your action now is 100 per cent OK as far as I'm concerned.' When Meckiff bowled against the West Indies a year later, Worrell and Kanhai also sought Meckiff out to offer their opinion that his action was fair.

Even as he was being pronounced fair, however, Meckiff was injured. He tore the tendons in his left ankle during the First Test, then hurt his back during the Third. After all the elaborate contingencies for their arrival in England in 1961, neither Meckiff nor Rorke made the trip.

Seventy-five wickets in the next two domestic seasons restored Meckiff's hopes of national selection. 'I knew Davo was close to retirement and I was about the only left-arm quick around,' he says. 'So I never felt that my career was finished. I always thought I was a chance to get back.' There were regular reassurances. When Victoria visited Adelaide Oval to play South Australia in January 1963, there was even one from umpire Col Egar. After the umpire had entertained him at the Adelaide Bowls Club, Egar told him: 'If your action hasn't changed in any radical way since I saw you last, you've no worries about being called.' Meckiff was delighted: Egar had no-balled Brian Quigley in November 1960 and Gordon Brooks in March 1962, and was known as one of the toughest and fairest umpires round.

Yet, with Egar at the bowler's end during that very match, Meckiff was called by square-leg umpire Jack Kierse. 'I was amazed,' says Meckiff. 'I think it was a shock to everyone. It wasn't as though it was my first over. I'd bowled quite a few that day and we'd come back. South Australia had been beating us badly and we were just starting to get on top of them.' For Meckiff and his bent-armed brotherhood, the end was nigh.

DINNER WITH THE DON

Richie Benaud's policy towards issues of bowling legality had always been to accept the umpire's decision, but it was beginning to shift. Ten days after Meckiff's no-balling, Benaud spelled Gordon Rorke simply on the suspicion that the fast bowler was bending his elbow in straining for pace. State and national selector Dudley Seddon later took his captain to task for it: obviously, in picking Rorke, the selectors had deemed his action fair.

Benaud was unimpressed: 'My reply was if I found in the NSW side in future any bowler I thought had in any way a suspect action then I wouldn't bowl him at all, but, to make my point, I would open the batting with him and they could do what they liked.'

During the Fourth Test of the 1962–63 series in Adelaide five days later, Benaud's Australians were guests at Sir Donald Bradman's Holden Street home. With four of the five Sheffield Shield captains present, Bradman screened a few of his fast-bowling films (again stumping everyone with the image of the cock-armed left-hand Larwood). At evening's end, Benaud made a resolution: 'I always had said I would take the umpire's decision on bowling actions but, at that meeting, I said I would not again bowl anyone called for throwing or whom I thought was throwing.' Benaud had no cause to do so for the rest of the season but, in Victoria's last Shield match of the summer, Meckiff was called again: by umpire Bill Priem at the Gabba.

Not only were umpires setting a higher hurdle for acceptability of bowling actions, but the front-foot no-ball rule—one Australia had acquiesced to only with reluctance—was about to arrive to curtail 'dragging'. As it happened, it wasn't only 'draggers' who suffered. Benaud and Graham McKenzie had a foretaste of the new ordinance in February 1963 while touring Rhodesia and South Africa with a Commonwealth XI mustered by Ron Roberts, and found it a painful experience. Benaud said:

> The front foot rule proved to be the bane of my life, so much so that after fifteen years bowling in first-class cricket, I was forced to develop a new run to the wicket, a new action and a new delivery stride to ensure my foot landed six inches behind the batting crease with every delivery...This threw my bowling into complete chaos...I bowled more full tosses in that three weeks of trying to conform to this new law than I have bowled in the past five years.

McKenzie also struggled to recalibrate his run and, as the 1963–64 home season began, took just five Shield wickets for 478 in the lead-up to the First Test against Trevor Goddard's South Africans. With Davidson's retirement, Australian pace bowling resources suddenly looked thin. Only one new-ball bowler was striking consistently: Ian Meckiff.

Despite Meckiff's form and recent record, there were no illusions about his prospects. From England—where Australia was to tour in seven months' time—came the usual denunciations. 'There is no room in cricket for throwers,' wrote Colin Ingleby-Mackenzie in the *News of the World*. 'Let us hope that Ian Meckiff and the Australian selectors realise this before next year, otherwise the throwing war will be waged in earnest.' Even in a home press generally wishing Meckiff well, Kevin Hogan of Melbourne's *Sun* warned: 'It would take only one no-ball call from either umpire to destroy all his hopes of a successful return to cricket.'

There was a genuine sense of foreboding in the prelude to the Test. At the Government House cocktail reception for the teams and selectors, Benaud noticed that Bradman, Ryder and Seddon seemed to be avoiding one another: 'In the room, as we sipped our drinks and nibbled our prawns and Moreton Bay bugs, it seemed to us players that the selectors were having a problem either in communication or navigation: if you had drawn a triangle, each of them would have been standing on one of the corners.' Every comment seemed loaded. Queenslander Tom Veivers, who was making his Test debut, remembers the greeting of umpire Lou Rowan: 'Congratulations on being selected. It's going to be a very interesting game Tommy.'

Some sensation of normality was restored on the evening before the Test at Lennon's Hotel. Benaud convened his usual Test match dinner. Scoring charts of the South Africans prepared by statistician Bob Spence were perused. When Meckiff went off for a drink with Benaud and Simpson, they were joined by the tennis star Frank Sedgman and Egar. 'How are ya, Chucker?' said Egar.

'Where's your seeing-eye dog?' Meckiff quipped back.

Egar had a gift for Meckiff: the trophy they'd won at the Adelaide Bowls Club back in January. Meckiff offered him two packets of cigarettes from the ration Australians were given before each Test. 'It's great to see you back,' said the umpire. 'Good luck.'

The First Test proceeded uneventfully. Brian Booth compiled a cultured 169 from 81 overs, and Australia reached 435 in 114. McKenzie took the new ball at the Stanley Street end as the South African innings began at 2pm—conceding 13 as he struggled for his footing—and Meckiff the second over from the Vulture Street end to Trevor Goddard. His initial loosener passed unmolested outside off stump. 'How's my front foot?' Meckiff asked Rowan as he walked back.

'It's OK,' said Rowan.

Meckiff's front foot was fine. It was his arm at issue. As he released his second delivery at Goddard, Egar's cry from square leg reverberated round the Gabba: 'No ball!'

Meckiff pulled up in his follow-through stunned. 'My God,' he thought. 'He's called me.'

THE LONGEST OVER

At first, no-one seemed to know what had happened. Brian Booth, standing near Egar, blamed himself. 'Gee, Richie'll kill me,' he thought. 'I must've just drifted behind Col, and Mecko's been no-balled for having three behind square leg.' Several players thought the crowd responsible, and Wally Grout cursed such tomfoolery: 'I snatched a look at Richie in the gully to see how he reacted to this type of barracking and his eyes were fairly popping. It was then I knew that the call came from square-leg umpire Col Egar.'

The 10,000 crowd, in fact, twigged quickly. QCA secretary Barry Gibbs and Springbok manager Ken Viljoen were standing near the Gabba Hill, and felt spectators igniting round them. Gibbs recalls: 'Just as the South Africans had started their innings, Ken popped his head in and asked if I could take him round to the scoreboard so that he could get some elevated shots of Meckiff using his 8mm camera. We'd just got round to square leg when Egar called the first no-ball. It was amazing. The feeling in the crowd got gradually more and more heated.'

When Meckiff's third delivery was also called, Benaud came from gully. 'We've got a bit of a problem,' Benaud said. 'Just concentrate on keeping your arm as straight as you can.'

'That's what I'm doing,' Meckiff said miserably. He ran in again holding his arm stiff and the ball passed muster. But Egar called the next—a full toss that Goddard hit for four—and Benaud came from gully again.

'I think you should either bowl as quick as you can, or just bowl it and get through the over,' he proposed. 'If you want to bowl underarm, that's OK.'

Griffin had bowled underarm at Lord's three and a half years earlier, but Meckiff was not so keen. 'No Rich,' he said. 'I really don't think I'm doing anything different.'

Egar condemned the over's second, third, fifth and ninth deliveries. 'I wasn't trying to bowl very quick,' Meckiff says. 'I was really just trying to get it up there and get it over with. But there's nowhere to hide on a cricket field. That was the hard part.' After the tenth delivery escaped attention, Meckiff asked Rowan: 'How many to go?'

'Two,' the umpire replied. 'If they're legitimate.'

Thankfully, they were. Rowan silently handed Meckiff his cap and sweater, and the bowler, head bowed, made for mid off as if in a dream. Grout tried to lighten the funereal atmosphere in slips at the end of the over by commenting that a horse the team was backing had failed to get up. Benaud snapped: 'I've got enough to worry about.'

Meckiff was cheered by spectators. 'They were all incensed,' the bowler recalls. 'They sensed that it was a set-up. I guess it's just that the Australian public love fair play and, when they see something they think isn't, they get upset.' Observers wondered whether Benaud would hazard him for a second over. When the captain turned instead to young Victorian Test debutant Alan Connolly, the response was predictably hostile.

'I was at mid off when Ian was bowling,' says Connolly. 'It was very, very unsettling. I took the ball to bowl my first over in Test cricket, and the crowd started booing. I know they weren't booing me but it felt like it.'

Normal service gradually resumed. The Springboks raised the 50 in even time, and Benaud came on at 0–67 to have Goddard caught at mid off for 51. The catcher was Meckiff. Benaud patted him on the back, and Meckiff gave a slight, sardonic smile. At tea, he slumped in a corner, lifting his head only to ask Grout about the team's horse. Hearing it had lost, he sighed: 'I've not only lost my money but I've lost everything else.'

Bradman came in and asked Grout if he could talk to Meckiff. He put an arm round the fast bowler's shoulders and said quietly: 'When all this has quietened down a bit, I'd like a word with you.'

THE LONGEST DAY

As it became clear that Benaud would not chance the fast bowler again, even at the opposite end, the crowd struck up a chant of: 'We want Meckiff.' When the day ended with the tourists 4–157, a group scooped the Victorian on their shoulders and freighted him to the pavilion gate—though they spoiled the effect by unceremoniously dumping him on the concrete. Umpires Egar and Rowan were hooted all the way in.

Remarkably, despite the day's sensations, there was no animosity between Meckiff and Egar. The umpire walked into the Australian dressing-room at the close and, after exchanging a few words with Norm O'Neill, made for Meckiff. 'I'm sticking round,' he said soberly. 'I'm not game to walk through the grandstand.'

'How do you think I feel, china?' replied Meckiff. 'The mob that chaired me off almost spilt my head open on the concrete path.'

Later in the evening at Lennon's, Meckiff and Egar found themselves together at the bar. Meckiff broke the silence by asking: 'Have you got a cigarette for me?'

'I've still got the two packets you gave me,' Egar replied. Then, softly, he made his first and last comment to the bowler on the affair: 'I'm sorry this had to happen. The second most upset person in the world is me.'

The following day, Sunday, was the rest day. But, for Meckiff, there was little relaxation. His first caller was Jack Ryder, who laid before his fellow Victorian an unappetising range of choices. Meckiff could either retire immediately, continue playing home Sheffield Shield games (with Victorian umpires arbitrating), or take a fortnight thinking it over.

When finally Meckiff met Bradman for two hours, it was obvious that the bowler's only option was a swift exit. 'It was more or less a straight-forward talk about what life's about,' says Meckiff. 'And it was probably the best man-to-man I've ever had. He asked me not to repeat what he told me, but the upshot basically was that I wouldn't be able to play Test cricket again.'

Bradman pencilled in for Meckiff a few details the bowler had always wondered about. Personally, Bradman had had a few doubts about Meckiff's action in 1958–59, but five years later thought him fair. His omission from the 1961 tour had been based on form, and nothing more. But the bottom line was straightforward. 'I think the best thing you can do, Mecky, is retire,' Bradman said.

Meckiff remained, of course, the hottest story round. There was much support for the bowler at home. Experts were found to dissent from Egar's ruling: Doug Ring, Ian Johnson, and the umpires Col Hoy and Les Townsend all told newspapers that they believed Meckiff's action fair. But there was less fellow-feeling in England, with comment ranging from told-you-so glee to sorry-but-it-had-to-happen sympathy. Ted Dexter wrote: 'The Meckiff controversy has been with us a long time and one might think that one courageous Australian umpire has brought it to a timely end. Much as I like Meckiff personally, I feel that this is the end of the road for him in big cricket.'

All that remained was for a word from Meckiff, and that was being organised. Bob Gray of Sydney's *Daily Mirror* had approached Meckiff with an offer following Saturday's play and, after discussing it with his friend Ian McDonald of the *Sporting Globe*, the cricketer agreed to a series of ghosted articles. He explains:

> I really felt I didn't have a lot of options. It wasn't a huge amount, but it was more money than I'd seen for a while, and I knew by that stage I wouldn't be playing again. Macca said: 'You'd be crazy if you didn't accept it. You won't get that amount from the Herald & Weekly Times. You might get more in an English paper but you won't know who'll be writing it for you, and at least you know Bob.'

In the series appearing under his name, Meckiff said that the calling had 'hit him like a dagger in the back', but that he felt Egar to be 'a fair and just man who acted according to his convictions' and that he was in all likelihood a thrower: 'In the cold hard light of everything, when it is looked at realistically, I must now concede I was a chucker.'

SINGLE BULLET THEORY

'It reminded me of an execution,' said the ABC broadcaster Victor Richardson in the aftermath of Meckiff's proscription. 'A very noisy execution.' Many shared his view, and parallels were freely drawn with the recent assassination of President John Kennedy. Egar and Rowan, indeed, were placed under armed guard during the Second Test at the MCG a week later when an anonymous caller told police that Egar would 'get the Kennedy treatment' when he came to Melbourne.

Like the Kennedy assassination, the Meckiff incident inspired any number of conspiracy theories. But none of the conjectures has been supported with evidence beyond hearsay, and the only man who really knows—Col Egar—declined to be interviewed for this book.

Among those who publicly proposed that the calling was premeditated was Dick Whitington, in his tour book *Bradman, Benaud and Goddard's Cinderellas*. He contended:

> I do believe Richie Benaud knew Meckiff would be called. And I believe that Meckiff strongly suspected he would be. Benaud bowled Meckiff to the end which would see Egar at square leg. Egar had travelled part of the way from Adelaide to Brisbane with Sir Donald Bradman. Benaud knew Bradman's views on Meckiff's action, Benaud as well as Bradman had watched the Geoff Griffin affair in England in 1960…Benaud had defended Griffin. But he must have realised that he would have no chance

to defend Meckiff, that Meckiff's inclusion in the 1964 tour of England would hardly assist Australia's chances of retaining the Ashes which he, Benaud, had defended through two series.

Bradman's presence in Australia's dressing-room at tea—there exists a widely published photograph of him talking to Benaud over a cuppa—has been advanced as further circumstantial evidence of a conspiracy.

Little of this, however, can be corroborated. Rowan has said that it was he who decided which end the umpires stationed. 'This is your ground, mate,' Egar told him as they came out. 'You pick it.' And Benaud's behaviour during the over was not that of one who knew in advance the course of events. Tom Veivers recalls:

> I was at leg gully and, after Mecko was called the first time, Benaud sent me down to the fine-leg fence. When he wasn't called Benaud called me back up. Then Mecko got called again and I was sent back. I said to Richie later: 'Did you realise that I was going back and forward like a shuttlecock. What was that all about?' And Richie: 'It's funny Tom, but I don't remember doing it.'

For his part, Benaud was and remains mystified by Meckiff's selection: 'Ian's selection, and the selectors at the cocktail party, are something I have never been able to solve since that day.' As for Bradman's appearance in the dressing-room and the famous photograph, he says: 'It was very rare in those days for Bradman not to come down at the tea break but I certainly don't recall anything out of the ordinary in our conversation, though I'd be quite happy to tell you if I could. It's not a much different photograph from the one in the same spot during the Tied Test when we were 6–108 and he asked me what the tactics would be after tea.' Of the idea that Meckiff was set up, Benaud comments: 'No, I certainly never had the feeling in any way that Egar's calling was premeditated, nor have I ever heard anything since to have me think so.'

One observation that Whitington made, however, was interesting. He pointed out that, in contrast to the English umpires who'd proscribed Griffin from a position forward of square leg, Egar addressed Meckiff from the conventional position, and seemed to pass judgment almost without reference to the actual delivery action. 'Egar clearly was merely calling Meckiff sufficiently to leave no doubts that he would continue calling him if Benaud persisted in bowling him,' said Whitington. This implies that—even if Rowan delegated Egar the square leg post—Egar was minded to call Meckiff before the over commenced.

No-one touched by the events of 7 December 1963 left them other than sorrowful, even those only peripherally involved. Lindsay Kline remembers vividly how he felt as news of the episode reached him:

Me and a few mates had gone up to Oakleigh to play and we'd been having a nice old time. Then, when we came off at tea, everyone was saying: 'Have you heard? Meckiff's been called.' It was a terrible feeling, one of the worst I've ever had. I said to the captain Val Holten: 'Look mate, I'm sorry, I feel sick. I don't want to bowl any more.'

'Tell Peter to Take Charge...'

AUSTRALIA V SOUTH AFRICA, ENGLAND, INDIA AND PAKISTAN
1964

When a broken finger ruled Benaud out of the Second Test against the Springboks on New Year's Day 1964, his successor was finally confirmed as Bob Simpson. There were broad similarities between Benaud and his heir: both were Sydney men who bowled leg spin, had trained as journalists, and succeeded to the post with little prior leadership experience. But comparison ended there. Australia's thirtieth captain was very much his own man.

Simpson had grown up in working-class Marrickville, at a time when its unpaved roads separated as many paddocks as houses. His first cricket pitch had been a disused tennis court. Father Jock was a former soccer player from Scotland's Stenhousmuir, his cricketing progeny an intriguing study in heredity. First son Bill was keen and determined, but never went further than first-grade for Western Suburbs. Second son Jack was a naturally blessed leg spinner who played for University, but wanted for application and eventually drifted from the game. Bobby combined Bill's tenacity with Jack's talent, and overlaid them with a confidence that effervesced even as a boy. He turned his hand to soccer, baseball, golf and cricket and excelled in each. Family circumstances were no handicap. Collecting lost balls at the local course for resale bought Simpson his first set of golf clubs.

Simpson was picked for his state eleven days before his seventeenth birthday with just a dozen first-grade games behind him. Phil Tresidder of the *Daily Telegraph* was sent to the Simpson home in Illawarra Road to talk to NSW's new prodigy: 'When we got there at 9pm, he was fast asleep and we had to get Jock to wake him up. I interviewed him in his pyjamas.' Arthur Morris looked Simpson up and down at their first meeting and said: 'Where are they then?' Where were what? Simpson wondered. 'Your bloody nappies,' said Morris. 'You're young enough...'

Great protectiveness was felt towards such a boy among men. Simpson made 44 in his first game against Victoria and was six not out in the second innings when the final ball of the match was bowled. Sam Loxton remembers:

> Bobby glanced one down to the fence at the Noble Stand and he came back quick smart for a second. I was standing by the square leg umpire, Hugh McKinnon, and Bobby was run out by ten yards. Anyway, Hugh says not out and I went absolutely mad and said: 'Would you like to reconsider your decision. He's not in *yet!*' And Hugh turns to me and says: 'Sam, it's the last ball of the game and his first match.'

But Simpson needed no cossetting. He was an uninhibited competitor. One day when Petersham-Marrickville was playing University, Bob appealed for lbw against Jack when everyone bar the umpire had heard the snick. In a January 1956 state match, Victorian John Shaw bent almost double to avoid a Pat Crawford bouncer and was hit in the head not far above the level of the stumps. As players rushed to Shaw's aid, Simpson was heard from gully hollering for lbw.

'I was a naturally ambitious person anyway and never had any doubts I could go further,' Simpson says. 'It sounds cocky but I always believed in my own talents.' His greatest obstacle in his junior years was persuading others to share that self-belief. The limelight in NSW was diffuse: senior players like Jim Burke, Sid Carroll, Keith Miller, Billy Watson, Richie Benaud, Ian Craig and Alan Davidson were augmented by youngsters of the calibre of Norm O'Neill, Brian Booth, Ray Flockton, Grahame Thomas and Neil Marks. Twenty-year-old Simpson took the unusual step of resigning his clerical job at Sydney Water Board and heading to unfashionable Western Australia, accepting a cadetship on the sports desk of Perth's *Daily News*, and living with Fremantle president Bob Ballantine. Within a season he'd earned national selection.

In South Africa in 1957–58, Neil Harvey made two recommendations to Simpson. Firstly, he should adopt a more side-on stance; secondly, he should consider opening the batting. Simpson accepted both and, though squeezed from the Test side against England at home, his Shield form the following summer was revelatory: his initial half-dozen innings of 98, 236 not out, 230 not out, 79, 98 and 161 not out amounted to 902 runs at an average of 300.66. He rejoined Colin McDonald at the top of the order in the next home Test series against Worrell's West Indians.

Simpson thought deeply about the theory of opening the innings. As he puts it: 'I spent two years turning myself into an overnight success.' Some of his youthful panache was sacrificed. The hook vanished from his repertoire, and against Wes Hall he became a disciple of the sway-away style against the bouncer. He also believed in the nostrum that the best way to play pace is from the other end. When he and Les Favell staged a partnership against Hall at his swiftest during the Second Test at the MCG, for instance, Simpson faced only four of 50 deliveries from the speedster.

Comment about Simpson's appointment as Australian captain was not universally favourable. Victoria's Bill Lawry had led his team to the 1962–63 Shield, and West Australian Barry Shepherd was attracting rave notices for his venturesome captaincy. Simpson could be abrasive, too, and had rubbed more than one cricketer the wrong way. During the Victoria–NSW Sheffield Shield match in Melbourne of December 1958, for instance, Lindsay Kline had invited for dinner those of the visitors who'd toured with him recently in South Africa. On arrival, Simpson commented ostentatiously: 'I'm only here for the free feed. I hate Victorians.'

There was also the fact that Simpson's Test record—1246 runs at 33 and 30 wickets at 32—was but loose translation of his talent. Simpson says:

> It was a ridiculous situation really, because I'd made so many big scores but hadn't cracked it in Tests and made a century. I'd become an opener and done well there, but I was up and down the order for Australia like a yo-yo. In the first three Tests in England in 1961, for instance, I batted everywhere from three to six…and, because Richie was having trouble with his shoulder, I was doing a lot of bowling.

But where an ordinary player might have professed some doubts about becoming Test captain after a 23-Test career barren of centuries, Simpson saw it as a challenge.

THE LAST AMATEUR

The side that Simpson led into the Second Test bore a decidedly green tinge: only the captain and Grout survived from the Tied Test team just three years earlier. Yet, after Simpson boldly inserted the South Africans, Australia prevailed convincingly by eight wickets. There were several propitious Australian performances, chief among them 97 on debut from twenty-three-year-old Victorian Ian Redpath.

One of four brothers from Geelong, Redpath had grown up in an auspicious patch of the town's Noble Street: the old Hassett home was five doors east; Hassett's nephew John Shaw lived four doors west. Like Hassett, too, Redpath was a Geelong Collegian.

But Redpath was not a schoolboy star, and it was only because a South Melbourne committeeman happened to see him make a few one day that he decided to tackle district cricket in the big smoke. 'I'd had four single-figure scores before this match at Melbourne Grammar, in which I got 50,' he recalls. 'And Bob Price asked if I'd like to come down for a hit during the holidays. Thinking back, if he'd seen me in any of the four previous matches, I might have ended up playing down here for Newtown-Chilwell.'

Redpath drifted round the seconds and thirds in his first district season: 'I wasn't a mature player. You get a guy like Doug Walters who was nineteen and playing Test matches like they were club games; I was nineteen and playing club matches like Tests.' But he persisted. There were a couple of other Geelong boys in the South Melbourne side at the time—left-arm spinner Ian Quick and paceman Alan Connolly—and the three shared driving duties to Melbourne. A year after his Sheffield Shield debut in December 1961, Redpath finally flowered with 261 against Queensland. His mother told him of his Test selection when he returned from an unsuccessful fishing expedition, and his father almost burst with pride. Redpath recalls: 'When I got my first blazer, Dad put it on and went for a walk down Noble Street. He said he just wanted to see that it fitted.'

Redpath and his father had an important decision to make as the Test approached. In winter, Redpath the cricketer became Redpath the footballer for Geelong Amateurs. The team's prohibition on payment of its players for any sport had been set in stone before the war when Bill Pearson—an all-rounder who played fourteen times for Victoria between 1936 and 1938—had been denied permission to play until he refunded all his cricket earnings. 'In those days, amateurs were whiter than white,' says Redpath. 'So I told the Board that I wouldn't accept the fee [£85 plus £15 expenses]. I didn't actually get any money for cricket until I went to England [in 1964]. I had to then, or I would have starved.'

It turned into a solid season for Australian batting. Booth played exquisitely, his 1180 runs including five centuries. But as the summer unfolded, Trevor Goddard's touring batsmen waxed. In the Fourth Test at Adelaide Oval at the end of January 1964, Springboks Eddie Barlow and Graeme Pollock mauled the home bowlers in a 341-run third-wicket stand at 80 an hour. When the ebullient Barlow followed his 201 with 3–6, Australia slid to its heaviest home defeat since the war. It was more through good luck than good management that Australia kept the series square in the Fifth Test at the SCG a week later: Booth's unbeaten 102 and 87 stood tall in two puny innings. London's *Daily Mail* announced: 'Australia is in a blue funk about her cricket.' And, although it was more a preliminary psychological jab than a considered observation, Australia's grip on the Ashes looked decidedly loose.

After his Second Test win, Simpson had proved a cautious and some-times dilatory leader. And when confirmed in the captaincy after the Fifth Test, he faced one of the most arduous assignments set a skipper: eight months, nine Tests and thirty other games. Nor did the selectors inspire much confidence among their picks. When the board held a farewell dinner for the team in Melbourne, Jack Ryder greeted South Australian leg-spinner Rex Sellers as Ray and Novacastrian medium-pacer Graeme Corling as nothing at all. 'I know someone who didn't vote for us,' thought Sellers.

THE FIRST MIGRANT

Jack Ryder may not have recognised him, but Sellers in 1964 was a pro-foundly significant cricketer: the first cricketing fruit of postwar Australian immigration. Born in the Indian town of Bulsar in August 1940, where his Anglo-Indian father was a bridge inspector for BB&CI Railways, he and elder brother Basil were raised in a home with eleven servants.

Indian independence in August 1947 uprooted them. 'The choice was between going back to England and coming out to Australia,' says Sellers. 'But my mother had read a lot about Australia in brochures, about the climate and the schools, and she decided to bring Basil and myself to Adelaide while my father stayed in India to earn some money.' They left on the *Strathaird*.

At first, Australia did not fulfil its utopian image. Thanks to the post-war housing shortage, the Sellers lived in a stifling boarding house attic. Mother, having relied on domestics most of her life, had abruptly to find work: she knocked on doors along Norwood Parade until she found a job sewing buttons at Australian Dry Cleaners. And the boys found discrimination at school, King's at Pembroke, at least until they proved themselves as cricketers. 'Basil and I were the only dark faces in the school, and our treatment we found quite hurtful at first,' Sellers recalls. 'But sport was the great breaker of barriers, the great leveller. When you made a few runs and took a few wickets, kids were that much more prepared to accept you.'

Sellers looked a good leg spinner in his youth, if not quite good enough. He was capped by his state in 1959–60, but dropped the following season, and decided to give the game away and buy a delicatessen in Goodwood's Road. But Kensington coach Howard Mutton implored him to stick with it, arranging one-on-one practices at 7am, and encouraging Sellers to develop a higher loop and greater overspin.

In October 1963, Sellers decided to give cricket another chance. Although planning to marry, he sold the deli and lived on casual work for Les Favell's *Adelaide Advertiser* coaching clinics. Then he had a stroke of fortune. South Australia's first-string spinner, David Sincock, missed the boat back from England, where he'd been playing as Lancashire League pro for Accrington. As stand-in, 'Sahb' Sellers impressed at once: his 46 wickets at 26 were fundamental to his state's Shield victory, and earned him a place in the Ashes squad.

Shortly before joining Simpson's team on the *Orcades*, he received an official envelope from Canberra: prime minister Menzies had expedited his Australian citizenship. Sellers was a full-fledged Australian on his way to being a full-fledged Australian cricketer.

'THE WEAKEST AUSTRALIAN TEAM EVER'

Even before it set sail, what was dubbed in England the 'weakest Australian team ever' was weakened further. It was the last party to play preliminary matches in Tasmania and Western Australia and illustrated some of their hazards. Alan Connolly's front foot slipped on a green pitch at Hobart on 28 March, and he sustained a back strain that would take months to heal. A week later in Perth, Bill Lawry wore a Laurie Mayne bouncer on the cheekbone:

> It was two days before we got on the ship and I had to have sixteen stitches. It closed my eye for about three weeks. I can remember Wally Grout getting really stuck into Laurie about it, how stupid he was to be bowling bouncers in a match just before the England tour, that sort of thing. The result was that, unlike in 1961, it took me a long time to get started in England that season. I didn't really find any form until the tour was half over.

It was no fairy-tale English visit for Sellers either. Before leaving, he'd noticed a swelling on his spinning finger. He thought it would improve with rest, but frigid English weather retarded its progress. Manager Ray Steele took him to Dr Alan Bass, who prescribed an operation to remove a cyst on the tendon and at least a fortnight's convalescence. Before the Tests had even begun, Simpson's team was under full strength.

Yet Australia's Benaud-inspired collegiate spirit remained intact. 'The manner in which the team swung four square behind Simmo was one of the strongest legacies of the Benaud endowment,' said Grout. 'To the printed comment from most critics that we were the worst side to come to England since the war, the worst attack yet etc., we merely gritted our teeth and said sotto voce: "We will thrash you."'

New personalities came to the fore. One was twenty-four-year-old Neil Hawke, a strapping South Australian medium-pacer with an unaesthetic, asymmetrical action, but a fine follow-through conducive to late movement, and stamina becoming of a first-rate Australian rules footballer. If his aura was that of a simple, sanguine man, Hawke had a scientific interest in his own art. Early on tour after taking 6–19 against Nottinghamshire, for instance, he recommended that the Australians switch cricket ball brands. He remembers: 'At Worcester we used a Twort, which had this huge seam but a lacquer finish. After it hit the bat a few times, the lacquer turned into a powder, and you'd have to rub it off to grip the ball. I couldn't get anything out of it. Later at Nottingham, we used a Duke, which had a narrow seam but a better finish.'

Tom Veivers' first scoring shot in England was a six. It was a characteristic introduction. Awaiting an innings, the hearty Queenslander would pace the dressing-room, bat in one hand, cigarette in the other. Laying the weed aside, he'd shadow-box a few strokes with a running commentary: 'That, gentlemen, is four.' That attitude remained with Veivers in the middle. 'Tom was amazing,' Hawke says. 'No matter what the situation, it was like he was playing in the park. He'd smack one away and give this little commentary as it went to the boundary: "That, gentlemen, is four."'

It was largely for his off spin, though, that Veivers was making the trip. And, like Hawke, he made an important early discovery. When Keith Miller learned that Veivers was troubled by a tender spinning finger, he introduced the Queenslander to Jim Laker. They arranged to have dinner at a pub called the Brown Bear, and the pre-eminent English off-spinner passed on the formula that he'd used to harden his digits: 10 per cent formalin, 85 per cent pure alcohol, 5 per cent surgical spirit. It would see Veivers through more than 750 first-class overs on tour: the most by an Australian slow bowler in England since the war.

Hawke and Veivers, however, would not an attack make. One bowler alone had the propulsion that hurried strokes and jarred bats. In the three years since his striking debut at Lord's in 1961, twenty-four-year-old West Australian Graham McKenzie had become by default his country's senior new-ball bowler.

'Garth' McKenzie was a gentle, even-tempered, thrifty man. So invariable was his rhythmic twelve-pace approach and body action that he never gave the impression of being flat out. Yet McKenzie was a superbly fit athlete. His winter training regime consisted of A1 hockey interspersed with long, lonely runs through the sandhills north of Swanbourne Beach. Watching him strip in the Australian dressing-room for the first time, Norm O'Neill remarked: 'If I had a physique like that, I'd sleep with the light on every night.'

McKenzie's rise was a point of West Australian pride. The state was granted full Sheffield Shield status in 1956 on iniquitous financial terms: it subsidised rivals' journeys from Adelaide, and had yet to be granted a Test. Yet McKenzie demonstrated almost daily that one of their own could cut it with the best of the eastern states. He hit the bat hard, not to mention the body, and not even Alan Davidson had moved the ball away so consistently and so late in favourable conditions.

Would this be enough? The Australians relied largely on rain to ward off Dexter's Englishmen in the first two Tests. Though McKenzie, Hawke and Veivers bowled pluckily, their batsmen could make little of Fred Trueman and the spin pair of Fred Titmus and Norman Gifford. Redpath spent the last three and a half hours at Lord's fretting and strutting over 36. John Clarke of the *Evening Standard* wrote: 'He was as helpless as a man in quicksand, whose every movement increases his peril.'

Selectors Simpson, Booth and Lawry, however, took an unchanged XII into the Third Test at Headingley beginning on 2 July. There was also the talismanic presence of Menzies, in England for the following week's Prime Ministers' Conference. The evening before the Test, Menzies hosted Simpson's squad at a dinner at Harrogate's Majestic Hotel. He took particular interest in Hawke and Booth, commending the former for his form, sympathising with the latter on his. 'You know, Brian,' he said. 'There's no reason why a good batsman like you shouldn't make runs.'

To O'Neill, who had withdrawn from the Test with a knee injury and was going to London for treatment, he offered a berth in his compartment on the train to the capital. The cricketer recalls:

I'd been looking for a way to get back to London to see the doctors, and Menzies said: 'Why don't you come with me, Norm?' So after a couple of days of the Test, I turned up at the station and I went down to London in his compartment, just him and me. Unbelievable, really: a prime minister giving a cricketer a lift. I mean, I idolised Menzies, and a lot of people did then, and I guess one of the reasons I liked him so much was that he loved his cricket.

By the time Menzies had gone, he had seen a Test of extravagant twists. On a pitch that looked full of runs, England had totalled only 268. The tourists reached 1–124 in reply, but a bad call from Redpath running out Lawry for 78 set the pack tumbling. The Ashes were well and truly in play.

The Man with the Bat and Ball Rattle

Peter Burge had long been the enigma of Australian cricket. Nobody in Sheffield Shield cricket hit the ball harder or further. Yet he had only two centuries to show for almost a decade at the top level, and had played only 32 of Australia's 54 Tests over that time.

Burge's cricket had always been burdened by expectations. His father Jack, a departmental manager at retailer D. & W. Murray, then state representative for textiler Nile Industries, had been a tireless QCA administrator and selector. Burge recalls:

> My dad was the best frustrated Test cricketer I ever knew. He always wanted to play, was involved in it for as long as I could remember. When I was born, my family reckoned that he gave me a rattle in the shape of a bat and ball. And from the time I picked up a cricket bat and showed some aptitude, he followed me everywhere. One day when I was nine, I made 223 for Baranda and retired because it was a really hot, and he got stuck right into me: 'Why'd you retire? Always make 'em get you out.' It was good advice. I never did it again.

Having a prominent Queensland cricketing father, however, had not been entirely advantageous. Although Burge senior resigned as a selector when Peter began ripening into a state player, Burge junior had to abide whispers of nepotism for many years. Matters were specially sensitive when the 1955 tour of the West Indies featured Burge *fils* as player and Burge *père* as manager. A team meeting was required to agree that the youngster could call his father 'Jack' rather than 'Dad'.

But even when illness after that tour confined Jack Burge to bed at his Queenslander in Eighth Avenue, Coorparoo, he was insistent that it not interfere with his son's cricket. He suffered cardiac problems while

Peter was playing in India in October 1956, but would not hear of his son returning early. Then, four months later, while Peter was batting in the McCabe–O'Reilly Testimonial at the SCG, Jack Burge suffered a fatal heart attack whilst talking to his friend and former Queensland player Ern Toovey. He was fifty-three.

Toovey telephoned QCA secretary Ted Williams, who in turn contacted NSWCA secretary Alan Barnes. And when Burge came in 43 not out at stumps, he was given the news. Burge recalls:

> Alan Barnes walked past and said something that I thought was: 'Well played.' So I said: 'Thanks, that's all right.'
> Alan said: 'You don't seem very upset.'
> And I replied: 'Why should I be upset?'
> So Alan says it again: 'I told you that your father is dead.'
> Well, I retired and they got me on a plane, and when I got back, Mum said: 'You'd better come and have a look at your Dad.' In those days it was the done thing. You viewed people. But, well, I wouldn't go within a bull's roar of him. Only row I ever had with my mother. But I said: 'The last time I saw him he was laughing. I'd like to remember him that way.'

A few weeks later, Peter Burge was off again to tour New Zealand with Ian Craig's team: 'Cricket had been so much a part of Dad's life that I think he would have wanted me to go.' But it wasn't until he came under Benaud's influence that Burge began to tap his talent effectively. Making yet another comeback in the Fourth Test at Adelaide in January 1961, he sought instructions before going into bat: 'I suppose you want me to stick around, Richie,' he said.

'Not at all, Peter,' Benaud replied. 'I want you to belt the hell out of it.'

Two hundred and fifteen runs in four innings secured Burge his second tour of England which, thanks to a generous piece of advice, culminated in a maiden Test century at The Oval. Burge recalls:

> Tony Lock had always given me a lot of trouble. He was very hard to get away. But just before that Fifth Test I watched Ken Barrington batting against Ian Quick, another left-arm spinner, and he seemed to sweep just about everything. So I asked him about it and he said that, if a spinner was just bowling out there to keep you quiet, the sweep was a good way to get runs. So I started to practise the sweep. And, at The Oval, I really got stuck into Lock and [David] Allen with it. Whenever I came in after that against England, Locky would say: 'Here's that bastard with his broom.'

But Burge then lost his place at home against England and, throughout the South African series, was afflicted by a grape-sized growth on his left foot diagnosed as a neuroma.

They used to say I was slow, that I couldn't run. They were wrong: I could hardly walk. By 3pm every day that season I was in agony. I saw the doctor and he said: 'I'm going to operate. If I do it now, you should be right for England.' He cut through the sole of my foot and the whole sole came away. When I turned up to the tour medical, I was on crutches with a bloody great bandage on my foot. Fortunately, they accepted the surgeon's advice that it would heal.

When the wound continued acting up in England, Burge found the going hard. Seventeen innings to the end of June yielded only three fifties and a host of galling dismissals. One at The Parks seemed to typify his luck: as the other Australians enjoyed a beanfeast, Burge was caught at point from a full-blooded cut that looked as good as four. He returned to his room at the Randolph Hotel, resigned to losing his Test spot again.

Fortunately, in his darkest hour, Alan McGilvray knocked at the door offering a sympathetic ear and a bottle of Scotch. They talked until 3am, the broadcaster advising him not to curb his attacking instincts. 'Whatever you do, Peter,' he said, 'you must keep playing your shots.'

At times, in fact, it seemed that others had more faith in Burge than he had in himself. Certainly, Simpson esteemed his panache and poise in a crisis, regarding him a 'big occasion player'. There would be no greater occasion than this Third Test at Headingley on 3 July 1964.

'HE WANTS YOU TO TAKE CHARGE'

Replacing Lawry, Burge searched interminably for his first run. He was still scoreless when Redpath fell to Norman Gifford, and still in single figures when Booth and Victorian left-hander Bob Cowper succumbed to Fred Trueman and Fred Titmus. Runs came at a crawl. Titmus grudged just 21 in his first 23 overs. When he did for Veivers and McKenzie in the third over after tea, six wickets had succumbed for 54, Australia was 90 in arrears, and Burge an almost covert 33.

Neil Hawke was next in. 'Tell Peter to take charge, to try and hit the bowlers off their length,' said Simpson. Then he added a psychological spur: 'You're always talking about your batting. Now's your chance.'

'Simmo says we're not doing any good this way,' Hawke advised his partner. 'He reckons you should take charge.' Burge agreed, but wondered how. The light was poor, the pitch was slow, and Titmus and Gifford were bowling mesmerically. Burge wondered, too, whether he should try to manipulate the strike, then decided against it. 'You can hold a bat,' he said to Hawke. 'I'm not gonna hog the strike. Just play sensibly.'

Hawke's arrival presented Dexter with a tactical dilemma. Though his spinners were harmonising exquisitely, a few volleys with the new ball from Trueman and Jack Flavell against the tail might be the ideal coup de grâce. He delayed as long as possible. But finally, in the 89th over, with Australia 7–187, Trueman was unmuzzled.

Burge and Hawke watched the handover from mid pitch. 'I'd been batting like an old fowl, scratching around at Gifford and Titmus,' recalls Burge. 'But I don't blame Dexter for taking the new ball: it was about 15 overs overdue and Hawkeye wasn't a batsman. Still, I was pleased to see it. When Trueman came on, I said: "I don't know why he's doing this, but I'm gonna make the most of it."'

It might have been Burge's relief after hours pecking at the spinners, it might have been Trueman's over-anxious desire to impress his home crowd, but the Australian pillaged 40 from half a dozen wantonly short overs with the second new ball. A fierce pull from Flavell raised the 200, a reproachful on-drive from Trueman Burge's 50, followed by a straight drive that defied the eye to follow it. Flavell changed ends to accommodate Dexter and, implored by his captain not to pitch short, offered two half-volleys that Burge cover-drove to the boundary. As Hawke pitched in with his rugged strokes, the 250 was reached after 15 overs of pace.

Titmus and Gifford were restored at 6pm, but their spell had been broken. Trueman resumed for the day's third last over, with Burge 89 and the light deteriorating fast. Hawke recalls: 'It was so dark that when someone lit a cigarette in the crowd you could see a face.' Burge pulled Trueman's first ball for four, then raised the 100 stand with two from an off drive. 'Get your hundred tonight, Burgie,' Hawke told him at the end of the over. 'You won't be sleeping on it.'

Second ball of the day's last over, Burge square cut for four to reach 99. And, from the penultimate delivery, Burge called for a single into the covers. Hawke responded, stretched for the line and scraped in.

Burge's jubilation was short-lived, however, for Hawke edged the day's final ball to slip. The Queenslander cursed his selfishness: he should never have taken that single and exposed Hawke so neglectfully. Not for half an hour after stumps would he willingly accept congratulations. But gradually Burge realised that they were in order. His 105-run stand with Hawke in ninety-five minutes had wrenched the match—and perhaps the Ashes—from England's grasp. And to Burge, a survivor of the Tyson and Laker ascendancies, it was the Ashes that mattered most: 'Test cricket to me *was* England. The first few years I'd been round, they'd trodden us into the dirt. So I didn't like the idea of England beating us again: we'd done a lot to win the Ashes back.'

Burge returned to his room at the Majestic for an early night. Had he gone out, he'd have discovered himself the talk of Leeds. After filing his report to the *Daily Telegraph* ('Burge: The Lion of Leeds'), Phil Tresidder did hit the town with Australian scorer Dave Sherwood and discovered the degree to which Burge had captivated the Yorkshire faithful.

There were no seats available when Tresidder and Sherwood bowled up to hear Sir John Barbirolli and the Halle Orchestra. Or at least there were none until Tresidder told the doorman: 'Actually, we're with the Australian cricket team.' Prime pews were obtained at once.

At the end of the concert, Tresidder was tapped on the shoulder by Sir John himself. 'Mr Burge?' said the great conductor. 'Sir John Barbirolli.'

'Actually,' said Tresidder, 'I'm not Peter Burge.'

'You're not?' replied Sir John. 'Even so, please come up to supper.'

Tresidder recalls: 'We went up and Barbirolli just talked and talked: he was a real cricket fanatic. There was the Mayor of Leeds and all these other dignitaries, but all he wanted to talk about was that day's play. It was my great moment of the tour: being mistaken for Peter Burge.'

ONE-UP

Burge and his new partner Grout were at Headingley early the next morning for nets, Burge hitting the ball confidently, Grout finding everything but the middle of the bat. But Grout had a healthy estimation of his batting ability that belied his average. He'd chided Brian Booth during the Sydney Test against South Africa six months earlier for hitting out as soon as he arrived at the wicket as last man. 'Hey Sam, I like a bat, too,' he said. 'Don't forget I used to open for Queensland.' And, this morning, he reminded Trueman of that residual talent, square cutting and hooking boundaries from his first two deliveries, then pulling a long hop for another four to register the 300.

Trueman tried raising the psychological stakes by approaching Grout between overs and looking dubiously at the pitch. 'I wouldn't like to be you fellas batting on this in the second innings,' the Yorkshireman remarked gravely.

'The way you've been bowling, Freddie, we won't have to,' chirped Grout.

Burge offered Gifford a red-hot return chance that went begging and celebrated with two unstoppable drives, then two delectable square cuts from Titmus. Not until Grout failed to offer at Titmus was their stand of 89 in ninety-seven minutes broken.

Burge's 160 in five and a quarter hours, with 98 in boundaries, had secured Australia a lead of 121, and himself a lasting renown. 'I think, after that innings, I finally felt accepted by the cricket aristocracy,' Burge remembers. 'Because when we got home for the next summer in Australia, I got an invitation to the Don's place. I knew I'd been accepted, because he thanked me for what I'd done. Don had this theory that, while you should always beat England in Australia, to really succeed you had to beat England in England.'

The beating was still to be done as England began its second innings, and Barrington and his Surrey comrade John Edrich built a patient stand in the afternoon that stymied the tourists. The home side was only 33 in arrears with nine wickets remaining at tea, and news that Margaret Smith had lost her Wimbledon crown seemed an ill omen for Australia.

But McKenzie had Edrich taken down the leg side with the first ball on resumption, and Veivers picked up a doleful Dexter and a defiant Barrington before the close. Wrote English journalist Denzil Batchelor: 'The more I analysed the day's play the more convinced I became that it was not in bowling superiority or batting supremacy that the Australians eclipsed us. It was in sheer intestinal fortitude, or to put it more briefly still: guts.' After Australia's six-wicket win on 6 July, Batchelor commented even more concisely: 'As for Burge, he *was* Australia.'

'IF THIS IS TEST CRICKET...'

To reclaim the Ashes, England now needed to win the last two Tests. Four new specialist bowlers were introduced around Titmus: Fred Rumsey, John Price, Tom Cartwright and John Mortimore. To retain the trophy, Australian needed simply to draw the Fourth Test. At their pre-match dinner at the Stanneylands Hotel, Simpson explained his policy simply: 'We'll win the toss and bat for two days.'

Simpson slapping his leg after the toss on Thursday morning, 23 July, indicated that the first part of the plan had been executed. And an exchange as Rex Sellers strapped on Simpson's pads suggested that the second part was taking shape in the captain's mind.

'Can I get you a drink?' asked Sellers.

'Yeah, I'll have a Coke,' Simpson replied. 'And I'll have one when I come in tonight, too.'

Simpson, without a Test century in 51 innings, made it evident from the opening overs that today was the day. Lawry hooked sixes from Price and Cartwright, but Simpson contented himself with nine in the first hour and did not acquire his first boundary until play had been under way an hour and a quarter. When Lawry raised his forthright 50 just after lunch, Simpson was a secretive 37. After Lawry swayed into a third six from Rumsey, the captain's half-century accrued in 156 minutes.

England's needle was still stuck in Australia's opening groove at tea. Lawry had 101 out of 183. And Lawry's dismissal after a drive from Mortimore showed just how dearly Simpson coveted his three-figure milestone. 'Simmo put his bat behind the crease, which was fair enough,' Lawry recalls. 'But it rebounded away from Mortimore and I called him for one. Well, Simmo stayed put, didn't move, and I ended up down his end, run out by the length of the pitch. He was pretty keen on that first hundred.'

Simpson proceeded gingerly through the 90s and finally, on the stroke of six, turned Price to leg for the decisive single. Australia's captain was 109 at the close in 2–253. His opening partner earned the day's plaudits—the *Manchester Evening News* wittily headlined its report 'Lawry, Lawry, Hallelujah'—but Simpson could reason that there was always the next day's edition.

Simpson recommenced his vigil with care on Friday. He added 46, 43 and 67 in the three sessions, immune to the poisonous reproaches of the English press, deaf to slow hand-clapping: Simpson's 200 was the slowest in Ashes history, containing only 11 fours. As Ray Robinson put it: 'Manchester University students could have reflected that the first medicinal user of chloroform was named Simpson, too.' Not until a return catch ended Booth's courtly 98 on Saturday morning did Simpson decide that the fourth new ball was more appetising than the preceding three. And, in the 253rd over, after 765 minutes, the captain finally snicked a slog at Price for 311. Sellers heard a Mancunian gripe: 'If that's fooking Test cricket, then you can stick it up your fooking arse.'

Australia finally declared at 8–656, leaving England to bat just over half the match to save it. Simpson was more than content. Jack Ledward recalls: 'On the Sunday of the Test I played a round at the Mere with Bobby against Denis Compton and Ken Barrington. He was a fit boy, Bobby.' A day-long holding action of 246 between Dexter (174) and Barrington (256) did the business.

Although McKenzie claimed 7–153 from 60 overs, principal interest by the final afternoon attended Veivers' longevity at the Warwick Road end. The public-address system announced that the Queenslander, in his 88th over, had passed the Australian record for overs in an innings, and that Sonny Ramadhin's Test record of 588 deliveries against England at Edgbaston in 1957 beckoned. A little collusion with the enemy was engineered. Last man Price agreed to leave anything wide, and umpire Syd Buller was advised that the Australians would not appeal for lbws.

Veivers, however, was so grooved in his action that he could not achieve the requisite width. Striving to throw the first ball of his 96th over wide, he released a full toss that bowled the startled Price. 'Well, you don't get many fullies in Test cricket,' he explained to Veivers apologetically. 'I thought it might be my one and only chance to hit a six.'

VICTORY AT SOME COSTS

Australia's retention of the Ashes had been a triumph of the Simpson will, for the captain's faith in his own ability throughout the tour had bordered on the messianic. At times, in fact, it was almost comical. A 'pair' is not normally the subject of hilarity but, when Simpson picked one up against David Brown of the President of MCC's XI, it sent Bill Lawry into paroxysms of laughter:

> I was the sort of guy who never went out with a plan. I'd just hope to get 50 by lunch, maybe 80 by tea and get a hundred before stumps. But Simmo was so confident that on the way out on the first day, he said: 'This Brown can't bowl. We'll knock him around a bit.' And, of course, Brown bowls him about second ball. Second innings comes around, Simmo and I are going out and he says: 'Come on Bill, we'll murder these guys.' And Brown cleans him up again, bowled third ball. I said to him later: 'We woulda been in a bit of trouble if that bloke Brown could bowl.'

But Simpson could afford to be cocky. If his was not a great team, it always seemed to have the answers. When the Australians hit trouble in that game, for instance, it was deputy stumper Barry Jarman who came to their rescue. He recalls:

> When Simmo got out in the second innings, I was the only guy with any pads on. Redders was next in but he was standing there in his jockstrap and his boots and I said to him: 'Awww shit, Redders, you're in.' In the end I just grabbed my bat and gloves and came out. I met Simmo coming in through the gate and he says: 'Where are you bloody well going?' I said: 'Sorry, but everyone's got their gear off.'

Jarman hit 105 out of 186 with Lawry in 165 minutes.

Simpson, Booth and Lawry all exceeded 1500 first-class runs, McKenzie, Hawke and Veivers shared 233 first-class wickets. And even for the supernumerary Sellers, the team spirit was palpable:

> Everyone supported everyone else. If you got a bit down, there was always plenty of company. I remember that I got a bit depressed about my form when we played Sussex and Tom Veivers, Ian Redpath and Barry Jarman took me out to keep me going. We had a real heavy night. In fact, all I can remember is the boys undressing me and pouring me into bed, and this voice saying: 'You wear red underpants, Sahb.'

Victory came, however, with some reservations. The Fourth Test had been as grim for watchers as it had been gripping for statisticians: in five days' perfect weather before 108,000 spectators, just 18 wickets fell. And when the Fifth Test at The Oval was also a stalemate, the series had to be considered a box-office flop. Profit of £30,000 was down 20 per cent on the 1961 tour, and less than a third of that repatriated in 1973.

It was wondered aloud whether the Ashes were stifling enterprising cricket. Denzil Batchelor's *The Test Matches of 1964* concluded:

> I hope that one result of this summer's campaign will be that no future rubber between England and Australia will be fought out to see who gains and retains the Ashes, a purely hypothetical gimmick invented by the press to stimulate a false interest in Tests, and a concept which leads to drawn games being accepted as achievements as good as victories by the side that happens to have won the previous series.

Not that Simpson cared for Fleet Street's strictures. 'I think the English critics' main problem was that they were suffering from an outsize guilt complex,' he wrote. 'They had opened their giant-sized mouths at the beginning of the tour and now they did not like it when their feet lobbed in them.' But the succession of grim Ashes series was, by degrees, having an effect on international cricket. And Simpson's Australians would have a sense of the changing landscape as they spent October in India and Pakistan.

SICK AND SORRY

After two weeks motoring on the continent, the Australians converged on Rome's Ciampano Airport for the flight to Bombay on 30 September 1964. And they were not long on the subcontinent before the usual grievances emerged. After the luxuries of English hotels, accommodation seemed squalid. After the gentility of English audiences, the combustible Indian crowds had to be treated with great care. At one practice before thousands of locals, Jarman referred to Redpath by his nickname of 'Gandhi'. Hundreds of heads swivelled: Redpath was 'Redders' for the rest of the trip.

In contrast to the uniform excellence of English umpiring, too, Indian arbiters seemed at best incompetent, at worst partisan. Even the committed Christian Brian Booth found it hard to bear when he was given out stumped for 74 off Bapu Nadkarni at Brabourne Stadium: 'I came down and missed it, and I was ready to keep walking. But the ball had jumped and it bounced off the keeper's chest back down the wicket, so I thought: "You beauty." Then, as I was walking back into my crease, the keeper whipped the bails off with his glove and appealed. Out.'

After a workmanlike 139-run victory in the First Test at Madras underpinned by McKenzie's 10–91, this Second Test at Bombay against the Nawab of Pataudi's side was a travail. As Simpson and Lawry were padding up to open on the first morning, Norm O'Neill keeled over clutching his midriff. No-one took much notice at first—O'Neill was known for his nervous vomiting before an innings—but eventually a doctor was fetched and O'Neill sent to hospital. The first the captain knew of this drama was when he saw Booth walking out at the fall of the first wicket. 'Where the hell's Normie?' he asked.

'He's in hospital,' Booth replied airily and continued on his way.

As the Test unfolded, it seemed like ten men were pitted against thirteen. One inexplicable decision followed another. One could only laugh. As they walked in to the Brabourne dressing-room at tea on the third day, Burge asked Booth: 'How do you think Pataudi batted today, Sam?' Booth replied: 'I thought his third innings was the best.'

As they sat in their room at Brabourne that evening, Booth recalls:

It had been one of those days. Incredibly hot, terrible umpiring, everyone had diarrhoea, Norm was crook, Johnny Martin had sunstroke, the cockroaches were running across the floor, the mattresses were a couple of inches thick and you couldn't sleep. And we just started laughing at the hopelessness of it, couldn't stop, laughed until we were almost sick.

Simpson and a few teammates went in seach of their comrade O'Neill, with only a doctor's address as a guide. When they knocked furtively at the appropriate door, it was opened by a short, swarthy man who looked nothing like a doctor and who issued the mysterious greeting: 'Would you like to see my pet?' When the doctor seemed very insistent about his animal companion, they finally agreed, and leapt back a few feet when he revealed a domesticated household python.

For all that, India was a far better side than that encountered four years before. Nadkarni and Bhagwat Chandrasekhar spun the Australian second innings from 3–246 to all out 274 and, when India prevailed by two wickets on 15 October, the tourists had to bear local jubilation philosophically. Officials at the airport advised: 'We're sorry, but we can't take you to the waiting area. You'd be trampled to death.' The Australians traipsed to a designated open area off the runway whose main feature was an abundance of aeroplane wreckage. Their Vickers Viscount twice aborted take-off before leaving for Calcutta.

Simpson and McKenzie saw their team through. In the Australians' whistle-stop Test at Karachi against Pakistan, the captain made 153 and 115 while his inexhaustible fast bowler claimed 8–131. Calendar 1964 brought them 1381 runs and 71 wickets respectively, and citations as *Wisden* cricketers of the year. Veivers, Hawke and Burge could also look back on the preceding eight months with satisfaction. But the unexpected resistance on the subcontinent portended greater changes to international cricket's balance of power. The next three years would be some of the most uncomfortable Australian cricket had endured.

'You Can Pack Your Bags'

TOURING LIFE IN THE
1950s AND 1960s

In an age where cricket trips are compressed into weeks rather than months, it's hard to imagine how huge an undertaking were the expeditionary tours of the 1950s and 1960s. Hassett's 1953 Australians were away more than seven months. Johnson's 1956 Australians were abroad eight and half. Bob Simpson's 1964 team played its first match in Hobart as March ended, and did not return until the start of November, having played in half a dozen countries (Australia, Ceylon, England, the Netherlands, India and Pakistan).

Being picked was a special privilege. Few Australians travelled overseas at the time. There were only 33,000 short-term departures (that is, for less than a year) from our shores in 1950 and, even a decade later, still only 78,000. Most of those, moreover, headed for England, Europe and New Zealand. Few visited the portions of the atlas to which Australia's cricket team was increasingly being despatched: South Africa, India, Pakistan, West Indies.

As the time for selection of a touring team neared, pulses quickened. On the eve of the announcement of the party to tour England in 1953, Alan Davidson was fielding in a Sheffield Shield match and heard a bellow from the bowels of the SCG's Sheridan Stand: 'Hey Davidson! You can pack your bags.'

Davidson's ears pricked. 'You beauty,' he thought. 'I've been picked.'

'Yep,' continued the anonymous orator. 'You can pack your bags for a boat trip!'

'Gee, he means it,' Davidson thought. 'I'm going to England.'

'Yeah, you can pack your bags for a boat trip,' the voice advised. 'To Manly!'

Two days later, however, the telephone rang at Davidson's Strathfield flat. It was his aunt from Epping: he'd been picked. There was silence at both ends of the line for a time, and Davidson replaced the receiver shaking. 'A dream come true,' he says.

For every dream come true was an ambition thwarted. When that Ashes team was read out in the Australian dressing-room after the Fifth Test against South Africa on 12 February 1953, teenager Ron Archer's pleasure at selection was muted by knowing that it had been at the expense of thirty-six-year-old Geff Noblet:

> Geff was a much more experienced player than me. A much better bowler, too. The sort of guy they said'd do well in England. I happened to be next to him when they announced the team: I was picked and he wasn't. I could tell he was really disappointed, because it was his last chance to go, but I can also remember how gracious he was congratulating me. It was a great lesson.

GETTING THERE

As did 95 per cent of Australian travellers during the 1950s, Australian cricket teams commuted by sea on the handsome P&O liners of the period. Ashes tours would begin with matches in Tasmania and Perth, before three weeks wending through Colombo, Aden, Port Said, Naples and Gibraltar on the way to Tilbury.

Many liked the sea journey. It was an opportunity to recharge before cricket recommenced, and to learn about new teammates. En route to England in 1956, for instance, Keith Miller was fascinated to discover that West Australian opener John Rutherford had science and mathematics degrees from the University of WA. Rutherford recalls:

> We were on the bridge one day and someone said: 'I wonder how far it is to the horizon.' So I pulled out my travellers' cheques, drew a triangle estimating that we were about 160 feet above sea level, and worked out that it was about eleven miles. Keith says: 'What! How did you work that out?' And I said: 'Well, I just used Pythagoras' Theorem.' From that day, I was Pythagoras.

Travelling first-class on a liner in the 1950s was a leisured life. Though team sheets and team photos had to be signed on the journey, official duties were otherwise simply to dress formally for dinner, participate in a few deck sports, and try not to eat too much: players often put on weight in transit.

But times were changing. Cricket authorities, if not cricketers, were becoming more interested in physical fitness. As the Australians sailed to England on the *Himalaya* in 1961, captain Richie Benaud deputised the physical education teachers Brian Booth and Graham McKenzie to run daily voluntary PT classes. Three years later on the *Orcades*, Bob Simpson made sessions run by Booth and Jack Potter compulsory. Manager Ray Steele even issued an official 5BX fitness chart: a daily exercise plan designed for the Canadian armed forces. Wally Grout recalled: 'I hadn't heard the "Call of the Wild" and one session of those exercises was enough for me. I can report that not once did Bill Lawry complete the full circuit on our daily jogs round the *Orcades* boat deck. He used to take a short cut between the funnel and the officers' quarters...The 7.15am reveille did nothing for my constitution or disposition and the resultant torture...spoilt my sea voyage.' Little did Grout know, this would be an Australian team's last taste of sea travel.

GETTING THERE (II)

Times had begun changing in the 1950s. Ian Johnson's XVI for the West Indies in February 1955 was the first Australian team to undertake its entire journey by air: a full ninety-six hours as it hopped from Canton Island, through Fiji, Honolulu, San Francisco, Vancouver, Calgary, New York and Nassau to Kingston. And air travel was quickly taking on a mystique: fast, expensive, exotic. Huge crowds headed to Mascot ten months later to watch the first landing of a jet airliner in Australia. The de Havilland Comet 3 in the livery of BOAC had to abort its first approach because hundreds stormed the runway. When it did touch down, the throng stood fifty deep to admire this feat of modern aeronautical engineering.

Non-stop journeys were still a couple of decades away. When Ian Craig's Australians took a Qantas Lockheed Electra to Johannesburg in October 1957, it was via Darwin, the Cocos Islands and Mauritius. And, even in a new-fangled Boeing 707 two years later, Richie Benaud's team proceeded to Dacca via Brisbane, Darwin, Singapore, Bangkok and Calcutta. But the world was taking wing. In 1960, there were fewer than

200,000 air arrivals and departures in Australia. A decade later, there were more than a million. Airliners were democratising international transport. The days of those gracious sea journeys were numbered.

For Australian cricketers, Simpson's 1964 team signalled the transition. It shipped to Bombay, then flew to Heathrow. Thereafter, players would need to accustom themselves to the cramped confines of jet interiors, and to keeping the stricter schedules of the airliner age.

Which, of course, some didn't. The morning of the departure for his first Ashes tour in April 1968, young South Australian batsman Ian Chappell omitted to set his alarm on the assumption that his two-week-old daughter Amanda would probably do the job. But Amanda slept, as it were, like a baby, and so did her father.

> The plane left Adelaide at 7am. And I woke up at 6.48am. I can still see the bloody clock in my mind: 6.48am! We lived pretty close to the airport, in Netley, and I still thought I was a chance, so I threw on my clothes, jumped in the car and drove like crazy. And I was actually there by 7am but the plane had stopped taking passengers.

Chappell was lucky: a later flight got him to Sydney in time to join the team. And, as the 1960s ended, cricketers were becoming as familiar with airport lounges at they were with dressing-rooms.

BEING THERE

Before cricket commenced on every tour, especially in England, there were numerous ceremonies and functions to attend, many with long histories. The captain sang for his supper: public-speaking was a care of office. Some, like Hassett and Johnson, were natural performers. Others were not. When Bob Simpson studied the itinerary for his team's 1964 tour, the thought of all that pomp and circumstance made him queasy. But who better to offer advice than a cricket-smitten PM?

Menzies' reply urged him to be himself, to speak his own mind and use his own language:

> There are some silly and snobbish Australians (very few, I am glad to say) who think that the right way to recommend themselves to their English hosts is to conceal or apologise for their own country. They defeat their own ends. In England there is a growing interest in Australia as a country quite different from England. Don't hesitate to tell them about your own country and background.

Various Menzies speeches were enclosed, and Simpson went to work. For a month before departure, he was a fixture on Sydney's luncheon and dinner speaking circuit: 'I accepted just about everything that came my way—which was twenty-five or thirty Lion's Clubs and Rotaries and the like—and once it became known that you were available you always had plenty to choose from.'

The day after the Australians' arrival, they were received at 10 Downing Street by PM Sir Alec Douglas-Home. Then there was the Cricket Writers' Dinner, with 150 guests at the Fishmongers' Hall, the Lord Mayor's Lunch at Mansion House, the MCC Dinner at Lord's, a Tribute Dinner for Frank Worrell at the Cafe Royal, and sundry others. Simpson counted twenty speeches in the first twenty days: a dozen official, eight extemporised.

It was not, of course, why he'd coveted the Australian captaincy. But Simpson learned to handle himself and, in a masochistic way, to enjoy the task: 'It took a long while to get used to, getting up on your feet after Lord Birkett and the Duke of Norfolk, but I did get to enjoy it. And Menzies' advice was so good, because that's exactly what they wanted: an Aussie.'

Tours were run by managers and, on Ashes sojourns, an assistant manager-cum-treasurer who balanced books, and collected pre-arranged portions of the outer gate. Players were paid in instalments. The £650 fee for the 1957–58 South African tour, for instance, was apportioned thus: £100 up front, £350 while away at not more than £75 a month, £100 'pocket money' at £5 a week, and £100 'good conduct' cash on return.

It was an inflexible system. When Grahame Thomas toured South Africa in October 1966, he asked board secretary Alan Barnes if half his tour fee could be retained and paid weekly to his wife. She was seven months pregnant and otherwise would have nothing to live on. Nothing was done. Thomas recalls: 'It was hopeless really. Something as simple as that, and they wouldn't do it. So I used to go to the Standard Bank, where there was an agent who'd help me wire the money home. Sometimes, of course, it got stuck, and it was more than a week before she got it.'

KEITH MILLER ON TOUR

Notwithstanding the modest remuneration and the odd paroxysm of discipline, touring in the 1950s and 1960s was fun. Schedules were busy but not yet hectic and, off the field, there was always plenty to amuse.

Nobody epitomised the clubbable touring cricketer more completely than Keith Miller. Having spent his war years in England, he seemed to have friends everywhere, from the highest to the humblest. John Rutherford remembers the day the 1956 Australians arrived in England: 'I looked in a paper when we got to London and saw that there was a performance of Beethoven's Ninth at Festival Hall, so I suggested to Keith that we go. And, as Keith walked in, all these people were coming up and saying: "Hello Keith, it's great to have you back." There must have been 50 or so, but Keith replied to them all by name.'

That tour was the peak of Miller's English celebrity. Teammates scarcely saw him off the field as, motoring about in a car provided by former Air Marshal Lord Tedder, he fulfilled a multitude of social engagements, from Royal Ascot to his Buckingham Palace investiture as an MBE. He even sponsored a migrant under the 'Bring out a Briton' scheme: the receptionist at the Australians' Hounslow hotel, twenty-year-old Patricia Ann Williams (Miller arranged a flat for her in Bondi when she arrived in Sydney on the *Strathnaver* a year later).

Only Bradman among Australian cricketers had been as recognisable and, where the Don's mailbags had been packed with letters of homage, Miller's usually bulged with correspondence from adoring women. As he told Donald Zec of the *Argus* in June 1956:

> I get all kinds of stuff. You know the sort of thing: 'Keith I adore you…Keith, I must see you…' all that sort of caper. Some of them send me photographs, others send trinkets, lucky charms, cuff links and things. It's a bit embarrassing at times, too. The other day my picture was published in a paper alongside an Australian girl. So I quickly called the missus in Sydney and asked her if she had seen the paper.
> 'Yes dear,' she said.
> 'With a girl?'
> 'Yes dear.'
> 'She was only an Australian model.'
> 'Yes dear. And if that's your story, dear, you stick to it, dear.'

Occasionally, the cricket seemed almost a backdrop to Miller's round of parties. After a break on Godfrey Evans' Thames houseboat, he took half the team to London for a Friday evening and failed to return on the morning of Australia's match against Hampshire. In a scenario club skippers would find gallingly familiar, his pal Ray Lindwall had only four others to begin the game.

'Don't worry,' Lindwall told his quartet. 'I've got a few ideas.' And when local captain Desmond Eagar sidled up to ask about the toss, Lindwall got in first: 'We can't toss, Desmond. The pitch is too wet.'

In fact, the pitch was quite dry, but precious minutes were wasted as the umpires inspected. 'You've got some problems now, Killer,' said Rutherford as he saw the officials returning, evidently satisfied with conditions.

'No, she'll be right,' Lindwall replied. 'All I've gotta do is win the toss. And that's easy.' As Rutherford watched, Eagar flipped, Lindwall grunted, then stooped over the coin. 'Yep, tails it is,' he said. 'We'll bat.' When Eagar had gone, he turned to Rutherford and Mackay: 'You boys can forget about runs today. Just don't get out.' When Miller's retinue breezed in half an hour before lunch, they were still there, though *Wisden* chided them for 'one of the dreariest batting displays of the tour'.

At the close, there was a knock on the Australian dressing-room door. It was Lord Louis Mountbatten, the former Viceroy now First Sea Lord, asking Miller to dinner at his country estate. 'No, I haven't got my dinner suit with me,' Miller replied. 'I wouldn't come out for the Queen tonight.'

'What about the Queen's sister?' Mountbatten asked.

'Princess Margaret?' said Miller. 'OK.'

Miller slipped into a grey lounge suit, and a black chauffeur-driven sedan arrived at 8pm to whisk him the six miles to Broadlands. He dined with the Mountbattens, their daughter, the Princess and her companion Billy Wallace. Postprandial entertainment was an Edward G. Robinson thriller, which Miller and the Princess watched from the same settee. He spent the rest of the match parrying pressmen's questions, aside from telling the *Argus*: 'It was an evening I'll never forget.'

'YOU BLOODY BEAUTY!'

Miller, with unshakeable belief in his own luck, was also a formidable punter. If there was a meeting anywhere in the vicinity of a venue at which Australia was playing, the dressing-room phone would run hot with calls from trainers, bookies and jockey pals like Billy Snaith and Scobie Breasley. Miller once described a 20 he made at Old Trafford in 1953 as the 'happiest runs of my life': his tip Matador had just won the Goodwood Stewards Cup.

Many of Miller's successors shared his interest. In 1961, Benaud, Norm O'Neill, Barry Jarman and Ray Steele leased a racehorse: Pall Mallan, trained by Sid Dale. When it won its fourth start during the match against Yorkshire, Jarman's cry echoed round Headingley: 'You bloody beauty!'

Jarman also invented one of the 1964 team's chief Sunday entertainments. Borrowing airmail copies of Adelaide's *Sunday Mail* being sent to West Torrens Football Club fan Rex Sellers, Jarman convened regular phantom race calls.

Gambling, however, was not an innocent outlet of high spirits for everyone. Wicketkeeper Wally Grout was a serious gambler and also, unfortunately, an unlucky one. As that 1964 tour commenced in Hobart, he had a devastating day at the Elwick races. A string of tips from a jockey friend, Ron Evans, failed to come home. A sizeable proportion of his £1000 tour fee ended up with bookie Ted Pickett.

The setback, however, did not curb Grout's punting propensities. When the Australians arrived in London, he began running up a sizeable tab with local bookie Sid Gordon. Little was known at the time about gambling addictions. Indeed, the Australian right to punt was thought as inalienable as the right to vote: it's estimated Australians in the 1960s spent three times as much on gambling as the nation did on defence. And captain Bob Simpson says that Grout made little fuss about his losing streak: 'Wally kept it to himself. He never broadcast it, and he certainly never let it affect his demeanour. He was always the perfect team man.'

Yet it seems obvious now that Grout had a pronounced gambling problem. He acknowledged in his autobiography the following year that dwelling on it compromised his form: 'My concentration had been lapsing and I knew why. I had been playing the horses fairly solidly and without much success. My attention at the wicket, therefore, was divided between the job at hand and the signals from the dressing-room telling me if my latest flutter had been successful or not. Like a cured dipsomaniac I can talk about it now.'

When Grout died prematurely three years later, the full toll of his gambling became known. Neil Hawke learned that, since that disastrous day at Elwick in March 1964, Grout had been sending Ted Pickett a monthly post-dated cheque to clear his arrears. Hawke organised an auction of Australian cricketana which raised $600 for Grout's widow Joyce, while Pickett and other bookmakers wrote off several thousand dollars in accrued debts.

MEETING PEOPLE

Functions were a feature—some felt an occupational hazard—of touring life. Some were fun, some were dull. A few were stiflingly pukka, a few teetered on the brink of anarchy. Bill Jacobs, whose salty turn of phrase made him a very popular manager of Bob Simpson's Australians in South Africa, recalls one of the latter, held by the Border Cricket Union at East London in December 1966:

> Everybody was drinking and it got a bit rowdy. The mayor of East London gave the welcoming speech, and he started speaking about Trumper in 1902–3, which nobody wanted to listen to. Well I did, but nobody else. And he went on and on. Finally it came to Simmo and then me, and it was really noisy. So, when I got up, I said: 'I know that I'm not making much sense to some of you but, if you don't wanna listen to me, piss off and go outside.' There was a deathly silence, so I was able to make my speech.

If the succession of functions could pall, players were often struck by the extraordinary people that cricket introduced them to. Transiting to the Caribbean in March 1955, Johnson's team was welcomed to Hawaii by Duke Kahanamoku, sheriff of Honolulu and progenitor of world surfing, who escorted them on a sight-seeing tour and hosted them at lunch at the Edgwater Hotel. In England in 1956, the team was entertained by the war heroes Douglas Bader and Leonard Cheshire: Lindsay Hassett and Ian Johnson performed a song called the 'The Kangaroo Hop' with Winifred Atwell for a Cheshire Homes function. At the Lord Mayor's reception in May 1961, Ken Mackay, Bill Lawry and Frank Misson were thrilled to encounter the horror icon Boris Karloff. 'Can I get you a drink?' asked the former Frankenstein. 'A pint of blood, perhaps.'

There were frequent gifts, ranging from semi-official perquisites (the 1953 team received a Roger David blazer, two pairs of Grip U cricket trousers, a bat and a Philips shelf radio) to anonymous jests (Keith Miller was always in receipt of hair nets to tame his flowing locks). An unknown admirer, in fact, apparently underwrote Norm O'Neill's only English Test hundred.

On the eve of the Fifth Test at The Oval in 1961, O'Neill received a 'lucky' coin whose owner hoped that its fortune would rub off. 'I don't put a lot of faith in superstition,' he recalls. 'But I didn't think it would do any harm so I just dropped it into my fob pocket.'

O'Neill felt for the coin instinctively when, at 19, he was dropped at second slip. The luck continued for another hundred runs. He recalls:

> Everything went right. The ball went where I wanted it to, my feet were moving. When I got out, I took off my batting trousers and watched the cricket for a while. Then I thought: 'Oh, reckon I'll go and get that coin.' I couldn't find it anywhere. And there was no address on the letter so I couldn't write back.

As tours meandered for months at a time, it was often possible to slip away for a restorative week or two. After the Fourth Test of the 1955 West Indies series, Ian Johnson allowed Ron Archer and Colin McDonald a ten-day sojourn stateside. They flew to New York and, staying at the Hotel Bevan in Larchmont, became minor key celebrities, players of a strange game of which few had heard. An interview with them in the *Daily Times* of Mamaroneck reads delightfully:

> There are only two innings to a cricket match but, because of the vagaries of this consummately British game, the match can go on for as long as five or six days and one batsman can score as high as 400 or more runs. According to these experts, a cricket match is played on an oval field in the center of which is the slot. Two batsman take their positions at either end of the slot and take cuts at offerings of the bowlers. The batsmen can knock the one seam ball to any part of the field, cracks known as fouls in baseball being perfectly legitimate. The fielders group themselves at various stations around the oval and make catches similar to baseball. A batsman is out when the ball is caught, when he is run down while exchanging positions with the other batsman at the other end of the slot, or if the bowler gets one past him and knocks down one of the three stumps in the wicket, directly behind the batsman.

The Australians absorbed New York sights as tourists. Guests in the Yankees' dug-out during a double header against the Washington Senators, they were introduced to the legendary Micky Mantle. 'Cricket?' he drawled. 'That's the game they play with the bat that's like an oar.' There was no high life on a £450 tour fee. But Barry Scott, a former Victorian paceman working on Madison Avenue, offered his expense account, while Archer's Shell employers provided accommodation in Washington, where the cricketers appeared on a TV sports program. And when their money ran out in Miami en route to Montego Bay, the pair snoozed in a park taking it in turns to stand guard. The rejuvenation must have worked: a week later, both scored centuries in the Fifth Test.

PRESSING ON

Players handled the swelling battalions of journalists warily: tour contracts restricted those who could be quoted during a tour to the captain and manager. Certain journalists could be trusted: old heads like Ray Robinson of the *Sun-Herald*, Tom Goodman of the *Sydney Morning Herald*, Percy Beames of the *Age*, Keith Butler of the *Adelaide Advertiser* and Phil Tresidder of the *Daily Telegraph*.

Others were treated cautiously, for the board's ordinances were strict and penalties steep. Miller and Lindwall were both docked portions of their £300 'good conduct' money for articles under their names while the Australians were away in 1956: Miller £100 for extracts from his book *Cricket Crossfire* in London's *Daily Express* in August, Lindwall £50 for a *Sun-Herald* series in October.

There were particular reservations about a group of sensation-seeking English journalists, in particular Lyn Wellings of the *Evening News*, Crawford White of the *News Chronicle* and *Daily Mail*, and Frank Rostron of the *Daily Express*. Novitiates were told to tread carefully in their company, lest they find one of their indiscreet mutterings in print the next day.

When Wellings, White and Rostron appeared in South Africa in 1957–58, for instance, the shutters went up. Ian Meckiff remembers: 'During the First Test, I was on the way down to breakfast when I started to talk to Frank Rostron, who was one of the terrible group. Just general things really, not about cricket as such. Then Richie [Benaud] beckoned me over and said: "Don't ever talk to that man. One day he'll write something quoting you saying something you haven't said."'

A team meeting spread the word, and Lindsay Kline recalls carrying out its instructions to the letter: 'A couple of days later in Durban, I got in the lift and one of them was in there and he said: "Good morning." He must've thought I was terribly rude, because I didn't say a word all the way to the ground floor.'

This was not mere player paranoia either. Although often a penetrating writer on matters of technique, Wellings became a kind of cricketing Hedda Hopper, his frequent reports of player misbehaviour often bearing only tenuous relation to fact. Most infamous was his claim after the Tied Test that West Indian players had run amok in Lennon's Hotel. 'Visiting tennis players here have previously earned an unenviable reputation for their behaviour,' Wellings reported. 'But they were eclipsed by this rock'n'roll troupe.'

The story was unanimously denied, Wellings banned from the West Indian dressing-room and furiously denounced by *Sydney Sun* sports editor Con Cimons: 'His vitriolic ways have for too long been a blot on cricket. I hear that he will be going home to England after the Third Test. It is a pity that the immigration department couldn't find some way to make it earlier.'

There was no red carpet for cricketers at customs when they returned from overseas. West Indian well-wishers plied Johnson's 1955 team with dozens of bottles of complementary rum as they traversed the islands, but the players discovered when it was forwarded on the SS *Wanganella* in August that a heavy duty was due. Manager Jack Burge took the issue up with the prime minister and a sympathetic Menzies passed the note to the Department of Trade and Customs, but minister Neil O'Sullivan insisted on full payment.

As each tour ended, cricketers would audit belongings and jettison surplus. Sometimes, at the very last moment. Gavin Stevens remembers the end of Australia's 1959–60 tour of the Indian subcontinent: 'Wally Grout had bought this pith helmet in Singapore and, wherever we'd gone in Pakistan or India he'd always turn up to the bus with it on. None of us could understand why. Eventually we were getting on the plane for home and Wally takes off his helmet, looks at it, and says: "What am I carrying this bloody thing for?" And throws it away.'

When Australia next toured the subcontinent, Neil Hawke and Rex Sellers came up with a more lucrative solution. Their room became 'The Hawk-Sparrow Trading Agency', a bazaar auctioning pads, bats, teamsheets, Test tickets and liquor brought from England. With Indian-born Sellers capable of a plausible Indian accent, he and Hawke raised and distributed more than £1000 in cash and kind.

POLITICAL CRICKET BALL

For all the conviviality of touring, the world was altering. As East and West bifurcated and the pink on world maps shrank, sport was politicising. Once evocative of a monolithic empire, cricket tours took on more ambiguous connotations in a fragmenting Commonwealth.

A foretaste was the 1955 Caribbean tour. Though conceived to strengthen Commonwealth ties, it was shaded by the activities of the United African National Council and the African Welfare League. When white all-rounder Denis Atkinson was nominated skipper for the Fourth and Fifth Tests, for instance, 1000 AWL supporters demonstrated in Kingston's King George VI Memorial Park, voting to cable both the selectors and Atkinson demanding the appointment of black Frank Worrell. Strident editorials in the *Barbados Advocate* condemned the rabblerousers as a communist front: 'West Indians will not be prepared to have a form of mob rule masquerading under a pretence of fighting prejudice.'

But mob rule did come to cricket in the 1960s. Seven Tests were disrupted over the course of the decade, one (an England–Pakistan Test at Karachi in March 1969) abandoned altogether. It was a rude shock. Although cricket had nothing to compare to the violent upheavals at soccer matches in South America, lovers of the game had always presumed it immune to extramural upheavals.* As Ray Robinson put it:

> The wish was to insulate cricket from the disturbing influences rampant in the surrounding world, to give it a separate existence, a dreaming detachment from an age of political cross-currents, racial and social spasms, civil war, anti-war agitation, disarmament marches, demonstrations of dissent and demands for reform…[But] It was idle to imagine that it could remain a solitary segment in the post-war pattern.

CRICKET UNDER APARTHEID

The scene of cricket's harshest encounter with politics, however, was a country where there were no crowd disruptions, virtually no protests, and a wholly artificial state of normality: South Africa. As the cancer of apartheid spread, nothing like the harmony of Australia's 1949–50 visit was seen again. By the time Craig's team toured eight years later, the nation's million coloureds had been disenfranchised and millions of Africans forcibly flushed from urban areas. Where Hassett's Australians had seen the British flag and heard 'God Save the Queen' everywhere, Craig's saw the South African Union flag and heard 'Die Stem Van Suid Afrika'.

Not that this interfered with the cricket. But, when they peered beyond the carefully sanitised version of South Africa prepared for them, Australian cricketers were made to feel distinctly unwelcome. One lay-day in Port Elizabeth, for example, Ray Robinson took Ian Meckiff, Barry Jarman, John Drennan and Lindsay Kline to a match played between two coloured sides. The Australians were stunned, first by the ground's rude conditions with its pavilion fashioned from two old tram-cars, second by the hospitality of their welcome. 'It was marvellous,' says Kline. 'These little black kids knew everything about the players. One

---

* The bloodiest was at Lima National Stadium in 1964: 318 were trampled after police overreacted to militants protesting a decision during a Peru–Argentina international. The most infamous, after two acrimonious World Cup elimination matches five years later, touched off a five-day war between Honduras and El Salvador.

said he was Harvey, one said he was Davo. We stayed all day. They were so enthusiastic.'

But next morning, after a local newspaper had published a story on the visit, the players were carpeted by manager Norton. 'Norton took the bat to us,' says Jarman. 'He'd had a complaint from the South African Cricket Assocation that we were fraternising with the natives. And he said that, if we did anything else like it, he'd send us home. Jeez, I was wild about it. I reckoned it was none of their business what I did with my time outside cricketing hours.'

Arranging it with Menzies' help, Jack Fingleton had a seventy-five-minute interview with the minister for native affairs Hendrik Verwoerd which snagged on the question of South African detention laws: 'In a most pleasant talk...I had the temerity to tell Dr Verwoerd that no democratic country could tolerate his detention laws. He claimed that desperate ills needed desperate remedies; that his government was certain that anybody "put inside" under the detention act was a communist, was a possible saboteur. That didn't wash.'

When Verwoerd succeeded the late Johannes Strijdom as prime minister in September 1958, matters worsened irrevocably. Two years later—amid international denunciation of South African segregationism that climaxed after the March 1960 Sharpeville massacre—South Africa voted itself out of the Commonwealth by deciding at a referendum to declare itself a republic.

This required South Africa to quit the Imperial Cricket Conference and it did so on 18 July 1961, technically denying its international encounters Test status. Non-whites represented by the dissident South African Sports Association welcomed the decision. Its secretary Dennis Brutus announced: 'South Africa should never have had Test status. The South African Cricket Association does not represent the whole country. It is a fact that the Association practised rigid apartheid long before the government required it and they show no desire to end it.'

But the SASA was to be disappointed. 'White' cricket nations continued playing South Africa without batting an eyelid. The New Zealand Cricket Council ignored petitions to cancel its 1961–62 tour of the republic, and the Australian Board and NZCC welcomed South Africa in 1963–64, conferring Test status on all international matches. In this, the Australian board had an enthusiastic supporter in Menzies, who clung to the popular ideal that sport and politics were separate. As he put it: 'The game comes first, and its promotion is not the prerogative of conservatives or socialists or any other political organisation...but it is the best means yet devised for increasing international understanding and mutual pleasure.' While the prime minister believed apartheid a doomed design, he advocated continuance of sporting relations on grounds that total isolation would deepen South African intransigence.

Holding this view became more problematic as the 1960s unfolded. The 'black' cricket nations steadfastly boycotted all Springbok players. Neil Adcock, Trevor Goddard and Roy McLean were denied permission to enter India and Pakistan as members of a Benaud/Lindwall-led International XI in March–April 1962. And, after South Africa's expulsion from the 1964 Olympics, invitations for the Pollocks and Colin Bland to join a Rest of the World XI playing Barbados in March 1966 were rescinded.

At the same time, however, Australian authorities were going to extraordinary lengths to ensure that its Test cricket ties to South Africa were maintained. And the case of the brilliant young New South Welshman Grahame Thomas led to some unappealing compromises.

THE GRAHAME THOMAS STORY

Grahame Thomas, one of seven children to a Maritime Services Board labourer, grew up desperate to play for Australia. He recalls:

> When I was eleven or twelve, I started going to watch Shield cricket on my own. I'd look at what guys did and how they did it: where they put their feet for a square cut, what you did with a ball on a certain length. I remember watching Hutton make 40-odd once when I was about thirteen, and not being able to imagine how you'd ever get him out. I preferred to go on my own so that there was no-one round me to distract me. Single-minded? I guess it was, but I wanted to be a success at cricket.

Within ten years, Thomas was: one of the hardest hitters of a cricket ball to wear an Australian cap. Yet, after a promising start to his Test career in April 1965, there was as much interest in Thomas's blood as in his batting. For his complexion was dark. Family lore had it that his maternal grandfather James Evans—who'd come to Australia 120 years earlier from Somerset, Kentucky—had been a Cherokee Indian. It was enough, with a tour of South Africa impending, for several members of the Australian board to be anxious about his reception there, especially when the mischief-making journalist Frank Rostron spread the story that he was of Aboriginal descent.

During the Fifth Test against England at the MCG in February 1966, in fact, Bradman invited Thomas to breakfast in his Windsor Hotel room and broached the topic: how would he feel if he didn't go? Thomas was adamant about his wish to play for his country: he told Bradman that he would be extremely upset if omitted. Bradman got the message and, as the conversation continued, began dropping phrases like 'when you go'. 'That pleased me no end,' Thomas recalls. 'Because it suggested I'd be in the team.'

Thomas's form couldn't be faulted: his last twenty first-class innings had yielded 1200 runs. But, before the team's announcement, one final check was made: Alan Barnes mentioned the board's concerns to Menzies, and the prime minister raised them in discussion with the South African ambassador. Menzies described the meeting to Fingleton:

> I remember showing him a few photographs of young Thomas and saying to him in a slightly facetious way that, though he was somewhat dark-complexioned, he was no darker than thousands of fully Caucasian types to be seen on the beaches of Sydney. I told him it was understood that Thomas had some Red Indian blood, though anybody who looked less like a hawk-faced Red Indian I could hardly imagine. The ambassador told me…that he thought that there would be no difficulty whatever, the objection on the part of his people being to people who presented what he called a 'negroid' appearance.

After Thomas was selected in the team in March 1966, manager Bill Jacobs himself visited the ambassador to discuss South Africa's political climate. In fact, it was clouding by the day. The Australians' first port-of-call, Rhodesia, was on the verge of quitting the Commonwealth after its UDI (Unilateral Declaration of Independence) in November 1965. And, just five weeks before the Australians left, Verwoerd was assassinated during a Pretoria parliamentary sitting. The tour proceeded in an atmosphere of some unease.

BUSINESS AS USUAL

When the tour commenced, of course, the Australians were carefully cocooned from the abnormalities of African society. They toured the game reserves, overflew Victoria Falls, went fishing on the Zambezi, had a ball with the South African women. (Neil Hawke took a girlfriend he met there, Bernie Nortier, to England with him at tour's end.)

Thomas' apprehensions gradually faded. Although there was one unpleasant incident in a bar at Cape Town, where a belligerent Afrikaner tried to have him evicted, he enjoyed the South Africa he saw, and suppressed concerns about what he knew he wasn't seeing: 'We knew what was happening. But it [apartheid] was the law of their land, and I think most of us felt that you didn't buck the system.'

Yet, if one looked, there were numerous unpleasant signs. Where Hassett's 1949–50 team had encountered so many fond affirmations of Commonwealth ties, there was now strong public antipathy for the Crown. When Australia played in Rhodesia at Bulawayo on 2–3 November, the match was attended by both government ministers and the last British governor, Sir Humphrey Gibbs. Neither would recognise the other: Gibbs watched from the VIP enclosure in the morning as patron of the Rhodesian Cricket Union, and left when the official party arrived. And, during the Rhodesian Sports Star of the Year Dinner at Meikle's Hotel, Prime Minister Ian Smith gave a bitter speech on the first anniversary of UDI concluding: 'I hope you Australians will tell the real truth about our country when you return home.'

Having come nine years earlier, captain Bob Simpson felt a changed atmosphere:

> It was a huge difference from 1957–58. First thing people had said to you then was: 'Welcome to our country. Would you like to come home for dinner?' By 1966–67, they weren't so keen. It was obvious that the whites were feeling a great deal more pressure. And things happened that would never have happened the first time I toured there: I remember when South Africa won the First Test, [Springbok captain] Peter van der Merwe gave an acceptance speech in Afrikaans. I had to say: 'I'm sure it was a nice speech, but I would have appreciated it more if I'd known how to respond to it.'

Tom Veivers was particularly depressed by the political climate. He heard the crowd boo when 'God Save the Queen' was played at Johannesburg. The segregated crowds shocked him: 'On the ground at East London they had this little isolated stand right away from the rest of the gound, where the coloureds were meant to watch the game from. I thought: "This can't be right."' He couldn't find much to like about the local whites, either: 'The Afrikaners were hard to deal with, especially in Orange Free State. I remember going to a barbecue in the Trekkerland, at Bloemfontein, and how, when the locals wanted to talk amongst themselves, they'd drop into Afrikaans. It was very awkward. They weren't very likeable people.'

Not everyone looked on South Africa with Veivers' gimlet eye, of course. Indeed, he was regarded as 'team worrier'. But the time was coming when cricketers in general would lose their political innocence. When an Australian team next toured the veldt, South Africa's excommunication was imminent.

'A General Very Much on His Own'

AUSTRALIA V WEST INDIES, ENGLAND AND SOUTH AFRICA
1965–67

Sometimes when going in to bat, especially when the going was hard, Brian Booth called to mind favourite, reassuring passages of Scripture. And as he wandered to the centre on 4 March 1965, the second day of Australia's First Test against the West Indies at Sabina Park, he found himself revisiting Philippians 4:13: 'I can do all things through Christ who strengthens me.'

Booth was ready for an ordeal. Far in the distance, he glimpsed the figure of the Barbadian Charlie Griffith. Booth knew him by reputation as the hastiest Test bowler since Tyson, and everything he'd seen that morning had confirmed it. Booth recalls: 'The first times I saw Griffith's name, it caught my eye that he'd bowled Ken Barrington a few times for over 50. I thought: "That's strange. You might bowl Kenny for six, but not for 60." That day, I'd started seeing why.' Then Booth looked round. The only fieldsman that West Indies' captain Garry Sobers had stationed in front of the wicket was at cover: he clearly wouldn't get much driving practice today. Booth thought again of Philippians 4:13, and leaned over his bat.

The first couple of deliveries took Booth by surprise. They were strictly medium pace, and pitched on an amiable length. Booth pushed the first suspiciously back, and nudged the second through mid on for a couple. 'Something's wrong,' he thought. 'Griffith must be holding himself back.'

Correct. Although Griffith chugged in for his next ball at the same disarming amble, Booth saw nothing after the arm's initial blur. All he felt was something graze his nose and touch the tip of his cap, followed by a roar from 30,000 Jamaican throats. Thoughts raced through Booth's mind: 'Gee, that was quick. What's next? Short backlift here. Get well in behind it. It could be a yorker. It could be another bumper.'

It was the former and, even with a truncated pick-up, Booth barely had time to raise his Stuart Surridge from the blockhole. Again he heard rather than saw the ball, though the clatter of timber was swiftly drowned by the ululation of the Kingston crowd. Some years later, West Indian keeper Jackie Hendriks told him enthusiastically: 'I'll never forget that ball, Brian. It started outside off stump and it hit your leg stump.'

Booth replied ruefully: 'Thanks Jackie. I'd always wondered. Can't say I saw it.'

He also told his fellow Christian Trevor Goddard how Griffith had made him think of Philippians 4:13. Goddard commented that Philippians 4:11 might have been more appropriate: 'Not that I complain of want; for I have learned in whatever state I am, to be content.'

PACE LIKE FIRE

The Australians were, as it happened, far from content. Like the Englishmen who'd faced Griffith in 1963, they saw him as a thrower, brutish and brazen. They waited for the umpires to intercede, then smouldered with indignation when they did not.

Griffith had the classic Caribbean cricket upbringing: one of eight children raised by parents from St Lucy at the northern end of Barbados and blessed with only a primary-school education, he'd hauled himself up in the world by his cricket bootlaces. But, with a menacing mien and bodybuilder's physique, Griffith had been a problem child of the international game since fracturing the skull of India's captain Nari Contractor at Kensington Park in March 1962, then being no-balled for throwing by his countryman Cortez Jordan in the same match.

Though Griffith had bowled unchecked through West Indies' 1963 tour of England, taking 119 wickets at 13, there were many private protests. The issue then became an eyesore in September 1964 when Ken Barrington declined to play against Griffith in three exhibition matches at Scarborough for the benefit of Sir Frank Worrell, and Australian umpire Cec Pepper informed the MCC that he would have called Griffith had the games been serious.

Protocol constrained Simpson and manager Bob Parish from pointing the finger at Griffith. 'We reported our concerns privately to the controlling authorities, but it wasn't in the best interests of the game to make a statement,' Simpson says. 'There was nothing we could do about it. It was up to the umpires. They were the only judges of fair play.' But no such diplomatic niceties inhibited reporters, and it was Richie Benaud, covering the tour for Sydney's *Sun*, who finally vented the feeling in Simpson's team.

Benaud had come to the Caribbean with the express objective of filming Griffith in action. Typically meticulous, he had taken instruction from the *Sydney Morning Herald*'s ace photographer Harry Martin, and invested in a Minolta SR7, 400mm Tamron lens, two tripods, a light meter and 100 rolls of film.

Examining photographs in his hotel room at Courtleigh Manor on the evening of 6 March—by which time Australia needed 353 to win with eight wickets in hand—Benaud discovered what he felt conclusive evidence: pictures of Griffith early in his action showed the arm bent, photos at and after release showed it straight. He filed, to the *Sun* and to Jamaica's *Daily Gleaner*, in the terse, direct tabloid English in which Noel Bailey had so adeptly instructed him: 'West Indian fast bowler Charlie Griffith throws. I am quite convinced of this having watched him in action in the First Test match of the series against Australia…He has not been called…though I implicitly believe that on many occasions he had contravened the section of Law 26 that relates to fair and unfair deliveries.'

The article provoked a storm. West Indian journalists, recalling how Lindwall and Miller had made them cower a decade earlier, pilloried Benaud for his accusation. They had 'taken their licks'. Why could the Australians now not take theirs? Even Benaud's sports editor at the *Gleaner*, Strebor Roberts, deplored the comments as endangering the 'friendly atmosphere' of the series.

But friendliness was fast evaporating. Counter-accusations were flung: Trinidadian journalist Charles Chichester branded Simpson's aggressive twenty-two-year-old West Australian paceman Laurie Mayne a thrower. And protestations of Griffith's innocence gained two notable adherents: Keith Miller, writing for London's *Daily Express* and the ABC's unimpeachable Alan McGilvray. Miller pronounced Griffith 'pure as the driven snow', while McGilvray proposed more guardedly that he was 'within the letter of the Law as it stood'.

For Simpson's side, it was rather bemusing. They believed unanimously that Griffith was transgressing. 'The West Indies worked on the

The Elbow of Fate: 'He is the most likeable individual and devoid of vice,' wrote Springbok Roy McLean of Ian Meckiff in 1958. 'But some day somewhere the blare of publicity will flare round this young Victorian state bowler...' It was a prescient comment. After bowling Australia to victory in the Second Test against England at the MCG in January 1959, he was branded a 'chucker'. The tag stuck.

The End: Meckiff's controversial career finished at the Gabba on 7 December 1963, during the First Test against South Africa, when umpire Col Egar no-balled him for throwing four times in his first over. Meckiff did not bowl again, standing at mid on, locked in his private thoughts (right).

Sir Donald Bradman's presence in Australia's dressing-room at tea was noted (left), but Richie Benaud cannot remember the Meckiff incident being discussed.

Simmo and Garth: Bob Simpson's Australians were widely disparaged when they arrived in England in 1964. But the captain made the Ashes safe by taking almost thirteen hours over 311 during the Fourth Test at Old Trafford (above, he drives John Mortimore straight for six). Inexhaustible paceman Graham McKenzie (right) took 50 wickets in nine Tests on the eight-month tour.

Trouble and Tranquillity: The hostility and unorthodoxy of West Indian fast bowler Charlie Griffith was decisive when Simpson's Australians toured the West Indies in March–May 1965 (above, he hits Bill Lawry in the cheekbone). Vice-captain Brian Booth (below) suffered more than most but, a committed Christian, he still had time to deliver the lesson at Trinidad's Tranquillity Church on 28 March.

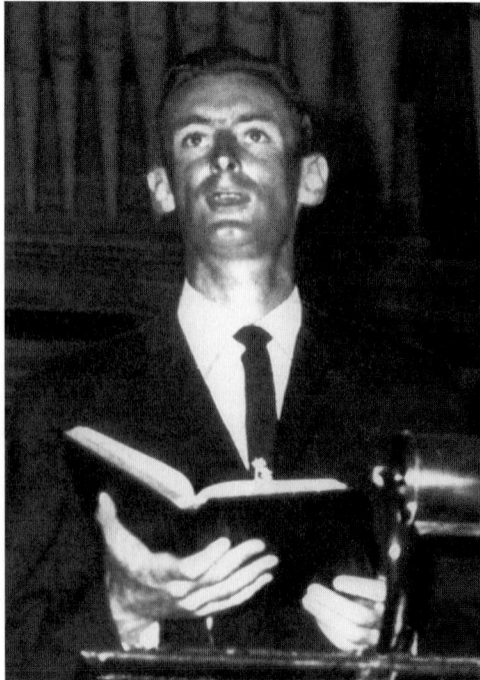

'Well Played...Sort of': A rueful Bob Simpson surrenders the Frank Worrell Trophy to West Indian captain Garry Sobers after the Fifth Test at Queen's Park on 17 May 1965. It had been an unhappy series. So evident was the 'bitterness' between the captains in their post-tour interviews that the ABC's Alan McGilvray decided not to put them to air.

New Kids on the Blockhole: When Bill Lawry succeeded Simpson as Australia's captain in January 1968, five fellow Victorians were crucial components in his side: Alan Connolly, Ian Redpath (above, left), Keith Stackpole, Bob Cowper (above right) and Paul Sheahan (below, left). Yet no star burned so bright as prolific New South Welshman Doug Walters (below right). Here he receives his Golden Peanut blazer as 'Cricketer of the Year' in April 1966 from Victorian governor Sir Rohan Delacombe. Note the fatigues: Walters had just begun his spell of national service.

Hard Times: Lawry's Australians defeated India 3–1 at the end of 1969, but the feature of the tour were the riots in Bombay and Calcutta. Brabourne Stadium burned at the end of the First Test (above), and Eden Gardens seethed at the end of the Third, where Lawry's skirmish with *Basumati* photographer Miren Adhikary (below) was one of a sequence of incidents that turned local fans against the tourists.

'They Won't Get Me the Way They Got Bill': Whitewashed in South Africa and trailing England at home, Bill Lawry became the first Australian captain to be dismissed during a series on 4 February 1971. His wife Joy and children greeted him when he arrived in Melbourne (above), and Lawry was remarkably philosophical about his retrenchment. But the decision incensed his successor Ian Chappell (left).

theory that Griffith was legal because his arm was straight at the point of delivery, but so is a baseball pitcher's,' Simpson says. 'It has to be to get rid of the ball. If you weren't straight you couldn't get any power out of it, and Charlie always got plenty of power.' But all they could do was read about it. As Norm O'Neill recalls: 'We'd get the back pages of the papers a couple of days after they appeared, and there was Richie saying that Charlie chucked, and there was Keith saying he didn't. I think Keith's attitude was that he wrote for a different paper so he had to say something different.'

When Australia breathed its last in the First Test on 8 March, the most successful West Indian bowler had been Wes Hall. Seven of his 9–105 were top-order batsmen, and it was he who sent O'Neill to hospital with a suspected broken hand. But the tourists nursed many more concerns about Griffith. 'Wes was quick, of course, but he was orthodox,' says Booth. 'Griffith was far harder to pick up, because the ball seemed to be coming from behind his head all the time. And Griffith always started wide of the crease so that it came back into the right-hander.' Grahame Thomas, Booth's twenty-six-year-old NSW colleague on his first tour, says: 'The main problem with Charlie was that he bowled three balls at 70mph, then one at 110mph and there was no way of telling from his run-up and action which was which.'

HARD TIMES

On a benign Queen's Park surface for the Second Test three weeks later, Simpson's men gave a far better account of themselves. Bob Cowper (143) and Brian Booth (117) grafted 228 for the third wicket, and Australia totalled 516 in reply to the home side's 429. On a ground without sightscreens, however, Griffith remained fiendishly difficult: Benaud counted seven direct hits, one sending O'Neill to hospital again for X-rays of a massively contused lump on his forearm.

In contrast to the tranquillity that Johnson's team had enjoyed in 1955, too, Simpson's team were finding the West Indies a prickly assignment. The fragile West Indies Federation had dissolved. Jamaica and Trinidad and Tobago had become independent nations within the Commonwealth in August 1962. Barbados and Guyana would become so in 1966. And, especially in Guyana, the Australians found disheartening poverty and burgeoning lawlessness. Even the mischief-making of crowds had a sinister edge. Batting on the last day of the tour match at Bourda on 10 April, Grahame Thomas was astonished to see a rock land a few yards away from him. Then another. Then another. They were evidently being catapulted from within the crowd. He turned to the local captain Basil Butcher and said: 'We're not staying out here if this sort of nonsense is going to happen.'

Butcher agreed, and had a message broadcast: 'Please will the public of Guyana show their sportsmanship and hospitality by not throwing stones at our visitors.' It was greeted by an ugly roar, and only timely police intervention prevented a nastier scene.

With the federal spirit gone, inter-island jealousies manifested themselves regularly. Before the Third Test at Bourda, the local umpires' association protested the appointment of an alien official, Barbadian Cortez Jordan. The wrangle was not resolved until Test selector Gerry Gomez agreed to stand.

Gomez had a tough match. His first duty was redrawing the pitch: Bourda's elderly groundsman, Badge Menzies, had painted the crease lines at an angle after mismeasuring the strip. And at stumps each evening, Gomez had to scurry off to the commentary box: bizarrely, in addition to his responsibilities as selector and umpire, he was providing expert summaries for local radio.

These curios aside, Australia's experiences were gruesome. They trailed by 176 on the first innings and, though Griffith found little encouragement in the soft surface, Lance Gibbs' 6–29 completed a 212-run rout. Benaud was among those who considered that Simpson's team had been psyched out. 'From where I sat watching the batting disaster the pitch never seemed difficult,' he wrote. 'Gibbs' bowling was superb, but it was aided by batting that was in a defensive mould and almost out of character as far as Australians are concerned.'

COMING BACK FOR MORE

A couple of days before the Fourth Test at Bridgetown, Neil Hawke suffered a back strain. He quietly informed his captain that he might not make it through the five days. 'Don't worry Ghoul,' Simpson said breezily. 'We're gonna win the toss and bat for two days.'

It seemed a remarkably buoyant forecast from one who'd made 87 in five Test innings. But, two days later, Australia *was* still batting, after a record opening partnership of 382 between the skipper and Lawry.

It rewarded some unflinching application. Griffith, peeved by the pitch's perfection, bowled a ceaseless succession of bouncers. After Lawry had taken one on the right cheekbone that opened an ugly gash under his eye, Simpson turned quizzically to umpire Cec Kippins and inquired after his definition of 'intimidatory bowling' under Law 46. Kippins demurred and, when eventually he did issue Griffith a warning, it seemed to Simpson more salutation than censure: 'It wasn't exactly a caution. Kippins merely put his arm round Charlie's shoulders and told him he'd better watch the way he was bowling. The warning made as much impression on Griffith as a mosquito buzzing round an angry lion. His next over to me he rocked down five bumpers out of six balls.'

Easier pickings ultimately arrived, and Simpson's 201 and Lawry's 210 were complemented by an attractive 102 from Cowper. But Australia's 6–650 was too much too late, and Simpson was obliged on the last day to close up the game in order to protect his declaration target. The draw delivered the West Indies the Worrell Trophy. As local newspapers exalted their team as 'World Champions', the Australians stewed.

PERCY

The Fifth Test at Queen's Park, beginning three days later, provided a consolation 10-wicket victory for Simpson's side. And not all was despondency in the Australian camp. Neil Hawke had bowled tirelessly throughout the trip, salvaging 10–115 amid the ruins of Georgetown. His twenty-four-year-old roommate Bob Cowper, an upright and elegant left-hander from Melbourne's Scotch College, had withstood Griffith with crisp and plucky strokes. Then there was the singular success story of a studious thirty-year-old English teacher nicknamed 'Percy'. Leg-spinner Peter Philpott's Indian summer climaxed one of Australian cricket's most intriguing careers.

Born in Manly in November 1934, Philpott was one of four brothers raised in the same Balgowlah street as Test batsman Jim Burke. At four years old, though, he suffered a severe bout of rheumatic fever that left him with a damaged aortic valve, from which he spent the better part of ten years convalescing.

As he recovered, Philpott read voraciously, especially of cricket and English history. And taking up the former as a teenager, he enjoyed such success that he topped the first grade averages for Manly in his sixteenth year (38 wickets at 12) and captained a First XI at North Sydney Boys' High that included Ian Craig. His health remained a constant concern. At eighteen, he was invalided out of National Service. At nineteen, he was refused life insurance on the grounds he was unlikely to live past forty. But his family doctor tendered advice that Philpott took, as it were, to heart: 'You can either rust out or wear out.'

'There may have been a feeling of temporariness, of urgency,' Philpott recalls. 'A feeling that I had to get on with it. By twenty, my intentions were fairly clear: I wanted to play cricket, teach and travel.' Once he'd made a successful debut for NSW, in February 1955, Philpott skipped off to England to play Lancashire League cricket for Ramsbottom. 'I knew all about it before I arrived,' he says. 'And to be there after all those years as a boy reading and romanticising about England meant more to me than I think it did to many others.'

On Philpott's return, he began teaching English and history at Shore under its inspirational head Basil 'Jika' Travers. But, after four further seasons, he decided to give first-class cricket away: with his constitution, it was simply too risky. He spent the years 1958 to 1960 abroad, playing in the leagues, making a short trip to South Africa with a Commonwealth XI, then staying to coach at East London's Selbourne College. He says: 'Basically, I was trying to stop playing first-class cricket…When eventually I came home from England at the end of the 1960 season, I took the long way. I crossed the US and boarded the *Iberia* at San Francisco, because it stopped in Japan and Hong Kong and all through Asia on the way back. I was sort of hoping I'd get back too late to start the season.'

As if to confirm his choice, Philpott met a girl who was to become his wife as the *Iberia* sailed underneath the Golden Gate Bridge. But it was no good. As the ship sailed down the Australian coast in December 1960, he was exhilarated by radio broadcasts of the Tied Test. Philpott was playing for Manly within a week of his return, made a hundred at Coogee Oval, and was promptly reinstated by NSW. 'I should've said no,' he says. 'I was terribly unfit, overweight and out of condition. I'd had three months in absolutely sinful luxury and no practice.' But once he scored a maiden shield hundred in his first match back against Victoria, Philpott recognised that his cricket addiction was hopeless.

Philpott did not immediately abandon his hemisphere-hopping lifestyle. He returned to England in 1962 for a season with East Lancashire, then spent a season coaching at the Wanderers Club in Johannesburg. And, despite a successful 1963–64 shield season, he felt that there were deeper priorities than an Australian cap. On missing selection for the 1964 Ashes tour and learning that his wife was pregnant, in fact, Philpott decided to retire: 'There was a little disappointment at missing the tour but also a feeling that I had to get around to the next stage of my life.'

It was 'Jika' Travers—a Rhodes scholar who'd won Blues at Oxford University for cricket and rugby just after World War II—who persuaded

Philpott to persist: having come so far, he would always regret not see-ing if he could cut it at Test level. On arriving in the Caribbean, Philpott at once made up for lost time: Conrad Hunte was caught at the wicket from his second Test delivery at Sabina Park, and he took 49 tour wick-ets. As a late starter, Philpott knew he wouldn't be round long in Test cricket. So he savoured every moment.

EXCHANGING UNPLEASANTRIES

The gloss that the Fifth Test applied to the overall Australian performance could not, however, disguise the team's inferiority. The guns of Simpson's team—the captain, Lawry, O'Neill and McKenzie—had been effectively spiked. As Alex Bannister put it in *Wisden*, 'Australia's finest hours were in the shadow of defeat.'

What was worse, it had been a rancorous tour. Relations between Sobers and Simpson had been particularly strained. Sobers thought the Australian pusillanimous: he lambasted him after the series, especially for his tactics at Bridgetown, both in batting so long, and in scattering eight men to the boundary in the game's closing stages. Simpson thought Sobers churlish and hypocritical: the West Indian skipper was not averse to slowing the game down for his purposes and, of course, condoned using an offensively illegal bowler. Alan McGilvray discovered the extent of the bad blood when he sought interviews with the captains at Port-of-Spain: 'Each agreed to an interview, but neither would do it until the other had gone first. For a time, it was an impasse. Eventually, Simpson relented. The interviews reflected the bitterness of the series, and the unhappy feeling between the two captains. That bitterness and feeling were so obvious, in fact, that I decided not to send the interviews back to Australia. Some things are better left unsaid.'

But the Australians would have their say. As he sat out the Fifth Test with a broken hand, Norm O'Neill agreed with Bob Gray of Sydney's *Daily Mirror* to produce a series of five full-page feature stories about the tour revealing the depth of Australian distaste for Griffith. 'I firmly believe that the West Indies were wrong to play Griffith against Australia,' O'Neill stated. 'He was such an obvious chucker that every West Indian selector and every Board of Control member must have known that he was throwing...If he is allowed to continue throwing he could kill some-one.' The articles were written, filed and despatched for publication when the batsman returned home: any earlier, and O'Neill would be in breach of his tour contract.

But it all went wrong. The *Mirror* syndicated the story to London's *Daily Mail*. The English paper, without troubling to inquire about a possible embargo, published immediately on 31 May, and the *Mirror* was forced to follow suit even as O'Neill was in transit to Sydney. 'When I got to Fiji, the papers were full of it,' he recalls. 'I knew there'd be some bother when I got home.'

At least initially, there didn't seem much problem. Although the West Indies Cricket Board of Control raised an official protest and O'Neill was summonsed to Cricket House to face a NSWCA committee shortly after his repatriation, the administrators did not seem overly perturbed. 'They were pretty understanding about it,' O'Neill says. 'When I came in, they said: "Don't worry. We know what happened. Come and have a drink."'

But O'Neill had raised the Australian board's ire a year earlier by failing to notify them of his autobiography *Ins and Outs*, and such refractory behaviour had not endeared him to authority. O'Neill, still only twenty-eight, did not add to his 45 Test caps or get the chance to enhance his average of 46.

If slipshod syndication was to blame, it was a ignominious end to a career that disappointed only in failing to realise over-inflated expectations. E. W. Swanton paid generous tribute when O'Neill announced his retirement two years later: 'The art of batting, he reminded us, was not dead, merely inexplicably dormant. A disappointment he was, perhaps, but his cricket will be recalled when those of lesser gifts are forgotten.'

THE ASHES AT HOME

With Dexter unavailable for business reasons, the MCC was led on its 1965–66 Australian tour by thirty-two-year-old Mike Smith of Warwickshire. If considerably Dexter's batting inferior, Smith was a far more personable individual and an adroit skipper. In the first half of the tour, at least, he brought a mix of cool understatement and genuine flair to his job. At the mayoral reception for the MCC in Perth on 25 October 1965, Smith mocked the Ashes tradition: 'I suppose we've come here to get back this miserable urn of dust.' He mandated his batsmen to play boldly, and matched them with deft declarations.

As the shortcomings of his bowling became more apparent, however, Smith showed more defensive instincts, and the series drifted into familiar terrain in the Fifth Test at the MCG: tortuously tall scoring by two sides stacked with batsmen on a bland pitch, with unambitious leadership on both sides. As *Wisden* summarised: 'Fear of losing frustrated the good intentions with which both sides doubtless entered this disappointing and quickly forgotten match.'

The rubber did touch some great heights. The peak was the Third Test at the SCG, where Smith's Warwickshire comrade Bob Barber and Yorkshireman Geoff Boycott compiled a coruscating 234 for the first wicket in the first two sessions. Barber, a carefree left-hander with a quiverful of unorthodox strokes, brought an affluence to English batting not seen since the war. Before a crowd of 40,000, he clubbed 185 from 225 deliveries in less than five hours. Even the manner of his departure reeked of extravagance, as bowler Neil Hawke recalls: 'I missed my run and almost tripped arse over tit delivering the ball, and Barber looked towards the Ladies' Stand and wound up. But the ball hit his inside edge, bounced onto his pad, rolled down his leg onto his boot, knocked against the stumps, and one bail fell off. And Bob goes: "Aww, fuck it." And that's the end of 185 of the best runs you'd ever see.'

Ultimately, though, the series was more notable for individual feats than overall result. After an epic opening stand of 244 between Simpson and Lawry, Australia won the Fourth Test inside four days. And ten days on in the Fifth Test, bowlers took only 18 wickets. Bob Cowper's 307 in more than twelve hours was as big in size as it was small in scope.

Simpson garlanded the season as 'the beginning of a new and exciting era for Anglo-Australian Tests' and 'forerunner of a new image for Australia–England Test series'. He lavished praise on his partner Lawry, whose 979 runs in 11 innings against the MCC had proved him 'a tremendous player—I think the finest opening batsmen in the world'. But he omitted to mention that Lawry's runs had consumed forty-one hours: a monumental feat of endurance, but hardly a transcendant feat of batsmanship. And, though the cricket had represented an improvement on the damp squib of 1962–63, crowds were down 22 per cent on that series: a disconcerting statistic.

EXEUNT OMNES

Just as 1962–63 had seen the exits of Neil Harvey, Alan Davidson and Ken Mackay, the 1965–66 Ashes series was the end of the road for three splendid Australian servicemen: Brian Booth, Peter Burge and Wally Grout. For the first, the fall was particularly steep: having led Australia in place of the injured Simpson in the First Test at Brisbane, and done so again when Simpson was stricken with chickenpox in the Third, he lost his place when the skipper returned.

Teammates sensed that Booth's sufferings in the West Indies had taken something out of him. He seemed over-anxious to attack, and squandered many starts. After scoring 49 runs in the first two Tests, Booth was looking forward to a long therapeutic net and a big innings to restore his form in the Third. But the sudden withdrawal of Simpson threw his thinking into disarray: 'I wasn't really mentally prepared. All of a sudden I was organising the practice rather than participating in it, dealing with the press, doing all the things that captains did in those days.' The first morning was a mess. After returning from losing the toss, Burge suddenly shouted from the window: 'Hey Sam! They're rolling the pitch again. Can they do that?'

'I don't know, Peter,' Booth replied. 'But by the time we find out, they will have done it anyway.' *

Booth also had only ten men: Philpott had been caught in a traffic jam at Taylor Square on the way from home, and did not arrive until the umpires were walking onto the field. Booth was still calming the frazzled spinner as the team came out and, when Barber and Boycott began their brilliant assault, could find no answer. Worse still, Booth failed twice to good deliveries.

A model of decorum to the end, Booth stood by the Englishmen's dressing-room door and shook each player's hand as they filed past. 'Congratulations, Mike,' he told Smith. 'You deserved to win. You played by far the better cricket.' When the Englishman looked forward to seeing him in the Fourth Test, Booth replied: 'I hope you're right, Mike, but I think this is it for me. There'll have to be changes and I'll be one of them.'

Back in his own dressing-room, Booth prayed for the strength to accept what was in store. A few weeks later, he and his wife Judith were picnicking at Terrigal when a radio bulletin confirmed his omission. One consolation was a letter from Bradman confirming the selectors' appreciation of 'the way you have always tried to do everything in your power to uphold the good name and prestige of Australia'.

The Fourth Test was the last of 42 for Peter Burge. Having declared himself unavailable for the forthcoming tour of South Africa, he also knew that the end was nigh, and accepted it with the pragmatism that had always characterised his cricket. When Simpson offered him a valedictory over as the game ended, Burge replied: 'I've gone 42 Tests

---

* Though such late rolling was highly unusual, it was permitted under Law 10 note 1 of the laws of cricket.

without a bowl. Why would I wanna start now?' He bowed out as twelfth man in the Fifth Test.

Burge's Queensland colleague Grout, within six weeks of his thirty-ninth birthday, gained his 51st and final cap in the same game. Only Godfrey Evans stood ahead of Grout's 187 dismissals on the Test keeping league table, and Evans' 219 had taken 91 Tests.

Like Evans, Grout had a flair for the inspirational dismissal. Many teammates cite one on the first day at Karachi in October 1964: Khalid Ibadulla caught off McKenzie for 166. It was the day's last ball, in the last match of an eight-month tour, but Grout skidded to his left to make the take. Booth recalls:

> We'd been out there all day in this incredible heat and dust. Most of us were thinking about how nice it would be to get off the field. And Wally goes yards down the leg side. Probably the best wicket-keeping catch I've ever seen. The only problem was that, whenever Wally did something like that and you complimented him, he'd say: 'Yeah, but you shoulda seen Don Tallon.'

But Grout's contribution to Australian success over eight years did not begin and end with his keeping. For one, there was his quick, droll wit. A collection of Groutiana would make a thick volume. When Ian Redpath returned from making 40 not out in four hours in that Karachi Test, for instance, Grout picked up his bat and examined it critically. 'Strewth Redders,' the keeper commented. 'I could put this bat straight back in the sports shop and sell it as new. It hasn't got a mark on it.'

For another, there was his gnomic cricket brain. One example was at Georgetown in April 1965. Grout noted how far West Indian Basil Butcher was moving across his stumps to counter Hawke's away swing, and passed the bowler a quiet word between overs. Hawke promptly slipped in a leg-stump yorker. Butcher, fresh from 117 at Port-of-Spain, was bowled for 18.

Nor did the public—and, indeed, most of his peers—appreciate the sacrifices Grout made to play cricket. Grout kept a closely guarded secret of a cardiac condition diagnosed after a mild heart attack he suffered midway through his career during preseason training for Queensland. QCA secretary Barry Gibbs, who took Grout to see the association's doctor, says that the keeper was well aware of the risks he was running in continuing to play after that warning:

> The prognosis was that, if Wally wanted to live to a ripe old age, he should stop playing immediately. He wouldn't, of course, because it meant so

much to him. But you could tell that Wally was suffering. He'd come in at the end of a day keeping for Queensland or Australia and he'd be grey in the face—puffing a cigarette, mind you—and he'd sit there motionless for three quarters of an hour before he could move.

The long, contented retirement that should have been Grout's was not. In November 1968, Neil Hawke caught up with his old teammate at the Hobart Royal Show. Hawke had come to play cricket for Tasmania, and Grout was in town to run a promotion for Rothman's. They were watching when a gust of wind swept a daredevil motor cyclist off his high wire and sent him plummeting to his death fifteen metres below. 'Poor bastard,' Grout commented. 'One minute you're here. Next moment, you're dead.'

A week later, Hawke was bowling in the nets at Launceston when a boy carrying a radio suddenly shouted: 'Wally Grout's dead.' He grabbed the boy and demanded how he knew. The boy said he'd heard it on the radio. Hawke wept. Grout was forty-one.

To the Cape

Booth, Burge and Grout were not the end of 1966's valedictees. When Bradman, Ryder and Seddon announced the Australian team to begin a twenty-three-match tour of South Africa later that year, it was simpler to name those absent than those present. Of the last team Simpson had led overseas, Philpott, South Australian spinner David Sincock and West Australian captain Barry Shepherd were also gone, while Grout's deputy Barry Jarman was unavailable and O'Neill apparently in internal exile. Also conspicuous by his absence was twenty-year-old Doug Walters, the hottest property in Australian cricket after two slick centuries against the Englishmen: his marble had come up for national service.

The squad that left Sydney by Lockheed Electra on Saturday 15 October was described as 'in the early stages of rebuilding', which was a euphemism for 'extremely inexperienced'. The junior half of the XVI mustered just a dozen Tests. Only the captain and Lawry could speak for more than 1500 Test runs. Only McKenzie had surpassed 100 Test wickets. Arriving at Johannesburg's Jan Smuts Airport, Simpson could point with some justification to the last bunch of untried Australians to visit South Africa: Ian Craig's team of nine years past had carried all before them despite their tender years. But there was a fundamental difference between this tour and that: where Clive van Ryneveld's 1957–58 Springboks had been a diffident XI, unsure of themselves even in positions of strength, most of those that Peter van der Merwe would marshal in the five forthcoming Tests already knew what it was like to beat Australia.

The tour began badly. After visits to Wankie Game Reserve and Victoria Falls, followed by a straightforward victory over Rhodesia, Simpson's side was overthrown first by Transvaal, then by a South African Invitation XI: the first first-class defeats inflicted on an Australian team in six tours to the Union. Several key players could find no form: Cowper and Thomas with the bat, Veivers and Hawke with the ball. Hawke, a yeoman servant in the West Indies and England, had come on the tour just a few months after dislocating his shoulder while playing football for West Torrens against South Adelaide and was patently below par. 'I'd been given encouraging reports about the shoulder,' he says. 'But in hindsight I shouldn't have gone. I tried very, very hard but I never did well.'

For Australian journalists covering the tour—Benaud, McGilvray, Bob Gray, Phil Tresidder and Dick Whitington—the key story very quickly became umpiring. Simpson developed strong reservations about the competence and character of forty-one-year-old Hayward Kidson, South Africa's most experienced official, much as Peter May had taken exception to Mel McInnes in Australia eight years earlier. But Kidson was not the only figure to push the series South Africa's way. And some of the others wore Australian caps.

DEFEAT FROM THE JAWS OF VICTORY

Kidson struck for the first time shortly after lunch on the second day of the First Test at Wanderers. Australia had played its way to a virtually unassailable position—1–204 in reply to the Springboks' 199—with Lawry on the brink of a valuable century. The Australian drove at a wide one from Trevor Goddard. He missed it. He was given out caught at the wicket. 'Actually, I wasn't sure what had happened,' Lawry recalls. 'And, in a way, Goddard did me. I'd got to 98 and he'd tied me down then thrown in the wide one that swung further away. So I didn't say anything at the time but, at the end of the day, one of the members came down and said: "Bill, you were this far away from it" [about eighteen inches].' It triggered a sickening collapse, and Australia was dismissed before stumps for 325.

The tourists were still well placed when Colin Bland was the fifth South African out at 268 with three quarters of an hour remaining on the third day. The Springboks led by only 142 on a pitch improving hourly, and one more breakthrough would suffice to shut them out.

What followed, though, was the stuff of nightmares. With Springbok keeper Denis Lindsay on 10, Jarman's replacement, New South Welshman Brian Taber, turfed an elementary chance off his state team-mate Dave Renneberg. Then, in the first hour of the fourth day, Kidson's colleague Les Baxter rejected a stentorian caught-behind appeal against van der Merwe (then 2) again off Renneberg. The Australians stood stupefied. Their piqued captain flung oaths from first slip.

Worse was to come. The very next ball flew from van der Merwe's edge at straightforward height to Simpson himself. It bounced out. Escaping to the other end, van der Merwe promptly edged McKenzie to second slip. It, too, escaped. In McKenzie's next over, van der Merwe feathered a glance. Taber failed to reach it. It was an incomprehensible sequence of cricket, and it cost Australia the match and perhaps the series: Lindsay added 172 after his reprieve, van der Merwe 74, and their 221-run stand took just 165 minutes. By 4.23pm on 28 December 1966, South Africa had beaten Australia before its own crowds for the first time, by 233 runs.

When the Second Test commenced at Newlands three days later, the cost of those catches became clearer. Australia won well, thanks to a masterly 153 from Simpson, a rumbustious 134 from the twenty-six-year-old Victorian Keith Stackpole, and McKenzie's 8–132 from 72 herculean overs, capped by a priceless and nerveless innings in the last hour from Tom Veivers.

But with victory came regrets. Had any of the chances offered by Lindsay and van der Merwe at Wanderers been taken, Australia might have had the series on a string. As it was, they had only achieved parity, and were still bickering about Kidson. The day after the Test, Simpson told manager Bill Jacobs that he wished to lodge a formal objection to the umpire: something an Ausralian captain had not done for thirteen years.

To Jacobs' mortification, the confidential objection lodged with South African Cricket Association president Boon Wallace quickly became public. 'It was all kept private,' Jacobs says. 'I certainly didn't tell anyone about it. But, virtually straight away, Mac [Alan McGilvray] comes up and asks to interview me about it all. In fact, my opinion didn't really matter. I had to be guided by the players, and Bobby didn't think he [Kidson] was up to it.'

Simpson was flayed by the press for the manoeuvre. 'Of course umpire Kidson has made mistakes,' wrote Denis Compton. 'But what umpire hasn't? None has been blatant and both sides have been affected…I hope Bobby Simpson's objection will be overruled by the South African Board and that the Aussies will get on with the game and take the rough with the smooth, as all cricketers have had to do in the past.' Dick Whitington's summary was tart: 'It did no good to Australia's name for sportsmanship and in the outcome achieved nothing.'

In fact, it did achieve something, but the precise opposite of what Simpson intended. Not only did the SACA appoint Kidson for the rest of the series, but the tall, bespectacled South African became an overnight sporting celebrity. The *Rand Daily Mail* even ran a profile of the umpire by his wife entitled 'My Life with Hayward', illustrated by a photograph of Kidson mowing his lawn. Winifred Kidson reported: 'Cricket enthusiasts have phoned and batches of telegrams have been received from all parts of the country urging my husband to be of good heart.' What had begun as a point of order had become a public relations calamity.

SIMPSON IN STRIFE

For Simpson, the tour was making the West Indies look like a picnic. At the end of the 1965–66 Ashes series, Simpson had put the finishing touches to an autobiography with *Daily Telegraph* crime reporter Ken Roberts. The most forceful chapter, entitled 'The Chuckers', was an eighteen-page excoriation of the 'cricket lawbreakers' and the 'insidious evil that is poisoning cricket at all levels'. As an opener facing bowlers from Meckiff to Griffith, Simpson had developed a deep sensitivity to thowers, and was quick to condemn anyone he thought was gaining an unfair advantage.

Simpson explains:

> I probably started to think about it when I began opening, and all of a sudden there were these blokes chucking it at me from eighteen yards. They seemed to be getting this huge advantage that wasn't within the Laws, and a thrower does get huge advantages: he doesn't have to disguise things much; he only has to straighten his arm to get change of pace; he gets more bounce; and it's not as physically demanding for him. I mean, I can't bowl an off spinner and make it turn. But when I chuck it, I can get it to do all sorts of things: I can make it swerve, I can make it drop...I didn't understand the sympathy that went out to chuckers: there seemed to be a great emotionalism about them. In my eyes, whether it was unwitting or not, they were cheating.

While Simpson was not alone in deploring infringement of Law 26, his blast in *Captain's Story* was in one respect unique: Simpson contended that Ian Meckiff and his ilk transgressed deliberately. 'I say the chucker *knows* he *throws*,' he contended. 'So let's not waste any sympathy on the bowler who literally throws himself out of cricket.' When the book was released in October 1966, the first response of many readers was to call Meckiff. One advised him to see Richmond Football Club chairman Ray Dunn, a prominent solicitor. 'Ray was a sports nut,' says Meckiff. 'He ran a legal practice, one very much in the sporting world. He was very strong about what he thought: Simmo had called me a "knowing cheat". I agreed with Ray that no-one should be allowed to write something like that and get away with it.'

Pressure was privately brought to bear on Meckiff not to sue:

> I was asked to go into the VCA offices for a private meeting. The official I met put it in such a way that they had things on me that they'd make public if I sued Simpson. I said: 'Well, I've got nothing to hide. You can't do any more to me than what's already been done, and there's nothing I've done on the field or off it that I'm ashamed of.'

A couple of days before the First Test at Wanderers, there was a knock on the door of Room 418 at the Langham Hotel occupied by manager Jacobs. 'I represent Ray Dunn,' said a visitor. 'I'd like to see Bob Simpson.' Jacobs rang Simpson's room and asked him to come up. 'You are Robert Baddeley Simpson?' the stranger inquired. Simpson confirmed that he was. The man handed him a bundle of papers: 'I hereby serve you with a writ of summons alleging defamation against our client Ian Meckiff.'

Jacobs was in an invidious position. He was an old friend of Meckiff's. They often made a point of pooling their birthdays: Jacobs' on 5 January, Meckiff's a day later. But his task as manager was to support the captain. 'Simmo wasn't terribly impressed at all,' he says. 'So I said: "Look, no-one knows about this, and I won't be telling anyone. If anyone asks you, just say: 'What did you think of the cricket?' Or: 'How's your golf?' Make no comment."'

Simpson did not. He retained a solicitor—Chick Lander, an old friend of Ray Steele's—and tried to get on with captaining Australia. 'It was a worrying time for me,' he says. 'It wasn't pleasant. Who wants legal action? But we had a Test series to play, and there wasn't the mass hysteria there might have been today. Fortunately, I was generally pretty good at putting others things out of my mind when I played cricket.' *

* The case was not resolved until 21 August 1971, when Simpson issued this apology: 'I, Robert Baddeley Simpson, being the author and writer of *Captain's Story*, hereby apologise for any reflection which may appear by any writings to have cast upon your character, reputation or integrity as a sportsman and a gentleman.' Costs were awarded against publisher Stanley Paul and

Simpson certainly added to his batting laurels on the trip. Although the South Africans bowled cunningly to him, bouncing the ball at his hip and policing his favourite source of leg-side singles, he compiled 1344 runs at 61. But it was a hard tour for Simpson the skipper. Where Ian Craig had been able to rely on the sagacity of Harvey, Benaud, McDonald, Davidson and Burke, Simpson had only Lawry and McKenzie of comparable experience. As former Springbok Jackie McGlew put it: 'Simpson was a general very much on his own.'

Several younger players on the trip also found the skipper stand-off-ish. They found it easier to seek counsel from Benaud and Bob Cowper, and the young Ian Chappell recalls many occasions where Benaud was a bigger participant in practices than the captain. Several older players, having felt the sharp edge of Simpson's tongue, also became disillusioned.

One was Hawke. He took particular exception to a comment from the captain at East London. After batting prodigy Barry Richards had charged Hawke twice in an over at East London, Simpson remarked acidly: 'Now you know how quick you're bowling.' Under the oaks at Newlands, Hawke told Dick Whitington: 'This is the happiest team I've been with so far as 15 members are concerned. It's one man we can't get through to...Bobby Simpson. We can't understand him.'

Tom Veivers, the third tour selector, was another who lost sympathy with Simpson. He knew that he was bowling indifferently and pined for a long spell, but the captain preferred to trust his own leg spin. To the end of the Second Test, Simpson had bowled 194 overs to Veivers' 165, and the Queenslander did not bowl at all in the Third and Fourth Tests.

But, for Veivers, it was more that Simpson could be thoughtless. When he returned from securing Australia's five-wicket victory on the last day at Newlands, Simpson slapped him on the back and said: 'You're batting well, Tommy, you little beauty.' Then he added deflatingly: 'Pity you're bowling so badly.' The spinner smarted. 'Simmo seemed a bit preoccupied on that trip,' he says. 'The Meckiff business got to him a bit, I think, and he was preoccupied with the umpiring. There was a lot of criticism of him there, and it wasn't a happy side. And Simmo's gotta wear a bit of that.'

---

the Hutchinson Printing Group. 'I got very, very little out of it,' says Meckiff. 'But that wasn't the point. What I wanted was an apology, which I got.' When *Captain's Story* was reprinted six years later, the offending chapter was excluded.

After victory at Newlands, Simpson forecast a 4–1 Australian victory. But in the last five weeks of the tour, the reverse almost came true. The Third and Fifth Tests were surrendered by eight and seven wickets respectively, and only a last-day deluge at Wanderers saved Australia from even heavier defeat in the Fourth Test. Denis Lindsay enjoyed a summer of unique all-round dominance—606 runs at 87 and 24 catches—while new cap Mike Procter and old head Trevor Goddard laid the tourists' batting waste. Of Australia's batsmen, only Simpson and the phlegmatic Redpath resisted. Of the bowlers, McKenzie was a solo performer.

With his imperious air and theatrical pedantries, Kidson continued to irritate the tourists in the Third Test. He gave Simpson out twice, caught behind for 6 and lbw for 94, with what looked suspiciously like enthusiasm. Simpson left the crease with a martyred air. Whitington commented in Melbourne's *Sun*: 'Simpson and some of his players are playing like angry men.'

Bill Jacobs had a neat idea at Pretoria a couple of days later, when Australian trade commissioner Ron Strange invited the players for an Australia Day barbecue and asked if there was anyone else the Australians wanted to bring. 'Why not ask Hayward Kidson and his wife?' Jacobs proposed.

'Kidson!' Strange exclaimed. 'I thought he'd be the last person you want to invite.'

'Well, I'm not sure he'll come,' Jacobs replied. 'But invite him and see what he does.'

Kidson accepted, attended and was cordially received. Jacobs was gratified. As the party broke up, he asked the umpire: 'Did you enjoy yourself, Hayward?'

'Thanks Bill, I did,' Kidson replied. 'I must say I got the shock of my life when I received your note.'

'I'm sure you did,' Jacobs responded. 'Nearly as big a shock as I got when you were appointed for the Third Test!'

Jacobs' stratagem may have worked, for Kidson was less conspicuous in the Fourth Test. He even upheld his first Australian lbw appeal. But the Fifth Test brought another decision that took the wind from Australian sails: Graeme Pollock, at 93, inside-edged Renneberg loudly to Taber. Despite having taken a couple of steps toward the pavilion, he was exonerated. Kidson was innocent this time; it was partner Gordon Draper. But that did not ease Australian irritation. Taber recalls: 'When Pollock reached his century, the PA announced: "It is Graeme Pollock's birthday today.". And a few of the boys said: "You'd better fucking believe it." The Australians left for home, gladly, nine days later.

AUSTRALIA V THE WORLD

Although the 15 Tests Australia played from April 1965 to February 1967 will never be remembered fondly by their participants, they are among the most significant in our cricket history.

Prior to the period, only England had inflicted a series defeat on Australia in almost ninety years of international cricket. After it, Australia's standing had slumped. For almost six hundred Tests, the cricket world had revolved on an Anglo-Australian axis. In less than two years, that polarity had been irrevocably altered.

Nor was this simply a factor of results. Australia's tour of South Africa, while a cricketing failure, had been an enormous financial success. Aggregate crowds of 577,700 exceeded those of the preceding Ashes series. Australia's profit share exceeded $66,000 from seventy-six days' cricket, compared to $60,000 from more than 100 days on its last tour of England. Where tours to countries other than England had been regarded hitherto as *pro bono* work, they were fast becoming attractive sources of revenue in their own right. A new cricket order was establishing itself. Never again would the Ashes be considered the only show in town.

'Sex, Religion, Politics'

THE PRIVATE LIVES OF AUSTRALIAN CRICKETERS
1949-71

A cricket pictorial staple of the 1950s and 1960s varied the old wartime theme: the dockside or airport snap of a player bidding farewell to adoring wife and uncomprehending children before disappearing for months to a foreign clime to defend national sporting honour. Hoary as these pictures are, they represent one of the few acknowledgments that cricketers actually had families and might suffer pangs in leaving them. Which they did: the length of tours during the period and the limitations of communications often placed relationships under intolerable strain.

GETTING TOGETHER

With the steady postwar drift towards younger marriages in Australia—by the early 1960s, the average age at first marriage was twenty-seven for men, twenty-four for women—most cricketers were either engaged or married by the time they took their first steps at Test level. It was cricket, indeed, that brought many couples together. A month after turning twenty-one in South Africa in 1949–50, Neil Harvey met a girl at a dance at Johannesburg's SA Party Club. It caused a minor scandal, for sixteen-year-old Iris Greenish had just left school to work at the local tramways office: her father told newspapers that he would not consent to their engagement until Iris was at least eighteen. They eventually married in Melbourne when Harvey came home on the *Strathaird* from the 1953 Ashes tour and, when his playing days ended a decade later, the pair went into partnership selling Tupperware as Har-V-Sales.

Returning with Harvey from England in 1953, his Victorian team-mate Colin McDonald met Lois Ahlston, a twenty-one-year-old *Argus* artist who'd just accompanied her father on a visit to the UK. They were engaged in August 1955 and married at the end of the 1956 tour at Chelsea's St Columba's Church, with Ron Archer as best man, and Ian Craig and Len Maddocks as ushers.

Ray Lindwall met model Peggy Robinson at a Slazenger party for Bobby Locke during a Gabba Sheffield Shield match in October 1950. They married nine months later. Craig met nursing sister Rosslyn Carroll on a blind date during an Adelaide Oval Sheffield Shield match in February 1961. They married early in 1962. And both Frank Misson and Ian Quick met their future wives while touring England in 1961: Misson met Carol Reben when the team were invited to Gray Nicolls to choose some equipment, Quick met Cora Beaumont at a dance at Northampton. Nor was romance confined to players. Bob Gray of Sydney's *Daily Mirror* met BWIA hostess Grace Shepherd in the West Indies in 1965, and married her in London during the Lord's Test three years later.

STAYING TOGETHER

Marriage for an Australian cricketer posed unusual problems. For one, the Australian Board of Control scarcely recognised wives' existence, and strictly prohibited contact with their husbands during home Tests and tours. When Richie Benaud and Marcia Lavender married in January 1952, for instance, they were not permitted to stay at the same hostelry during the subsequent Adelaide Oval Test. Richie lodged at the Ambassadors Hotel with the team, Marcia at the South Australian Hotel in Glenelg. At least, officially.

For another, partners had to accept that there might not be the home comforts that other couples enjoyed, and that family commitments would be accommodated only as and when cricket permitted. Typical was the case of Peter and Joan Burge. In February 1959, after seven months' married life, the partners at his small Brisbane accountancy firm summoned Peter to tell him that his future lay in accountancy and not in joining Australia's forthcoming tour of India and Pakistan.

Burge was inclined to agree. Joan was expecting their first child. He had few prospects and, on £4 a week, no savings. Then one partner commented gratuitously: 'Frankly, Peter, we don't think you're good enough to consolidate your place in the Australian side.'

Burge felt his dander rise. Family and financial pragmatism were one thing, not being up to snuff as a cricketer was another. He asked the partners for a fortnight to find a new employer and, after numerous rejections, found one: Harry Bolton of Rawlings Bolton & Co offered him a job at double the money, with as much time as he needed to play cricket.

Burge organised to meet his wife on the corner of Brisbane's Albert and Elizabeth Streets. 'It means I can go to India,' said Burge. 'But it also means that you'll be by yourself again.' Fortunately, Joan Burge was supportive: 'You have to take it. We'll be better off whatever happens.'

For Victorian all-rounder Keith Stackpole and his wife Pat, the situation was even tougher. Not long after they married in September 1963, Keith lost his job. Pat supported them by working part time at a Catholic school, and Keith's father gave them half the money for a deposit on their matrimonial home in Ivanhoe, but Stackpole was unemployed for four months. It wasn't until John Priestley of the *Herald* publicised his plight that Stackpole was offered a job selling office equipment. 'It was undoubtedly one of the toughest periods of my life,' says Stackpole. 'In those days, being unemployed was a real stigma. It certainly wasn't something you advertised, because people'd say: "Don't ya wanna work, ya lazy bugger?"'

THE ABSENTEE FATHER

The nomadic lifestyles that Australian cricketers accepted meant that absences from home were routine, and often long. Becoming a father was typically a secondhand experience. Many cricketers learned of their children through telegrams to the team hotel or by telephone calls, and memories of fatherhood are tied up with the cricket being played at the time. When Keith Miller's wife Peg bore him a second son while the Australian were playing Natal in February 1950, Miller decided, for want of inspiration, to name him Peter, after the town in which the Australians were staying, Pietermaritzburg. The third Miller boy arrived just after the 1950–51 Ashes series and was named Denis Charles in honour of Denis Compton. When fourth son Bobby arrived overnight during a November 1955 Sheffield Shield match at the SCG, his father, arriving late and dishevelled from celebration, claimed 7–12 in bowling South Australia out for 27.

Alan Davidson's first son was born while Australia was playing the Fourth Test of the 1953 series. He named it Neil, after his colleague Harvey. His second son was hatched while Australia was playing Jamaica in March 1955 just after Davidson had badly damaged an ankle and was inching round Courtleigh Manor on crutches. 'Congratulations on new son,' read the telegram from Davidson's bank colleagues. 'Sorry about the sympathy pains.'

Nat King Cole, who was a guest at the hotel, tried to ease his pangs of homesickness by playing 'Pretend You're Happy When You're Blue' followed by 'Dinner for One Please James', but it didn't work. 'Made me feel ten times worse, actually,' says Davidson.

Ray Lindwall also became a father in Jamaica, during the Fifth Test, receiving a celebratory bottle of whisky from WICBC chairman Sir Errol Dos Santos. Then Harvey's first son, Robert, was born as the team were sailing home on the SS *Rangitane*.

Waiting for news from home inevitably frayed players' nerves. In South Africa in January 1958, Richie Benaud, Ken Mackay and Lindsay Kline were all awaiting arrivals. Mackay observed: 'Waiting for a cable to come 7000 miles is infinitely worse than fidgeting in a hospital waiting room.' Marcia Benaud won the Stork Derby by two weeks from Jean Mackay, with Stella Kline delivering five days later. Her father marked the event by scoring a duck a few hours later.

Although global telecommunications improved over the next decade, Australians touring South Africa in 1966–67 found that they could only call home between the hours of 7pm and 9pm. With two expectant fathers in the side, Grahame Thomas and Brian Taber, manager Bill Jacobs arranged for news of their children's births to be communicated by ABC commentator Alan McGilvray. Thomas was particularly anxious, as his wife had miscarried the previous year, and learned of his baby's successful birth during Australia's match against Natal. Taber was informed of his new daughter after coming off the field on the first day of his first Test.

Radio also brought family news to South Australian all-rounder Eric Freeman at Kanpur in November 1969. When he answered the phone at his hotel one morning, Adelaide radio announcer Bob Francis explained in a barely audible tone between bursts of static that David Freeman had arrived. Freeman hurried to the ground and dialled home from the press box, but it was no better. 'The connection was so bad that I had to shout at the top of my voice,' he recalls. 'The boys on the ground reckoned they heard every word.'

Not that it was the fashion at the time for fathers to be present at childbirth. Most children of the period 1950–1970 were born in the hygienic conditions of a public hospital labour ward, while fathers stalked the waiting room. When Harvey's daughter Anne was due in September 1957, he whisked Iris into St Margaret's Hospital, then went home. 'I'm a coward, I admit it,' he says. 'It was a middle of the night job and I went in first thing in the morning.' Iris Harvey was still in hospital when Neil left for South Africa five days later.

Bill Lawry's first daughter was also born just before a tour of South Africa, nine years later, and, likewise, Joy Lawry went into hospital on her own. 'I wasn't very good at it,' says Lawry. 'Nowadays they hold their hands and all that, but I'm afraid I'd fail as a modern husband. I took my wife to the hospital door and dropped her off, and the nursing sister came and said: "Oh there's more to it than that Mr Lawry." I had to go to the registry and all that.'

Some players took remedial action. When Peggy Lindwall in Sydney became homesick for Brisbane because of Ray's frequent absences during the 1951–52 season, Lindwall moved them to live with Peggy's parents in Queensland while he commuted to Shield games. But, generally, wives had to accept sharing their husbands with the game. For the most laconic response to childbirth, it is hard to go past Joan Burge's during the First Test at Brisbane in December 1963. She and Peter were crossing the Storey Street Bridge on the way to her mother's house after a day's play at the Gabba when her waters broke. 'No, don't turn left here,' she said. 'Go straight ahead. That's the way to the hospital.'

THE ABSENTEE HUSBAND

Hardest for cricketers to endure while they were away was a mishap at home. No tour was complete without some anguished off-field drama. As Australia toured the West Indies in 1955, for example, Richie Benaud's wife Marcia and Arthur Morris's wife Valerie both fell seriously ill. Receiving a communique of his wife's hospitalisation, Richie Benaud found it impossible to concentrate. When his captain Ian Johnson joined him in the middle during the Fifth Test at Sabina Park, Benaud told him: 'Sorry Ian. I just can't seem to settle down.' Johnson told him to play his shots and not worry about getting out. All was well that ended well: Benaud scored a century in seventy-six minutes, the second fastest in Australian Test history, and Marcia recovered.

Arthur Morris, however, knew nothing of his wife's condition until he returned home. She explained that she hadn't wanted to worry him with the suspicion of her breast cancer, and waited until his return to seek treatment. Despite having a breast removed in October 1955, the cancer took hold, and Morris quit the game in order to be with her. 'I had to retire,' he says. 'I knew we wouldn't have long together, five years at the outside. The one thing I wanted was to take her to England one last time, which wasn't easy because we had no money, but I was a very lucky man.' One of Valerie's former impresarios sent a cheque for £500, while Lindsay Hassett sent another £500 with a note saying, 'Just pay me back when you can.' Morris repaid the money and took Valerie back to England one last time by accepting an offer to cover the 1956 Ashes tour for the *Daily Express*. Valerie died a year later.

There was then trouble on that 1956 tour for West Australian John Rutherford. At Nottingham in June, he received from his wife Bethanie a 'Dear John' letter. Though staying with her parents while John was away, she had just been relocated to a new and distant school and was so lonely that she wondered whether their marriage was salvageable.

Rutherford informed Johnson, spent three fruitless days trying to call home, and in the First Test found himself a very distracted substitute fielder for the injured Alan Davidson. Finally, at lunch on the third day of the game, the telephone rang in the Australian dressing-room. 'Pythagoras!' said a voice. 'It's your wife!'

The Australians were just about to resume, but Johnson said: 'John, I know what this means to you. You stay here and say what you have to.' So Rutherford stood there, pressing his ear to the receiver, trying to make out his wife's words, and, between the long pauses as the sound passed along the cable, initiate some of his own. It wasn't much good, but it was something.

When they'd finished speaking, Bethanie Rutherford returned to the wireless and heard a commentator reporting: 'And here comes Rutherford, back onto the field. He's obviously been indisposed.' Little did they know. Rutherford says: 'Touring for that long—we were away eight months—was very difficult. After a while you forgot what your wife sounded like, then what she looked like…When you saw one another again, it was a matter of picking up the pieces.'

When the going got tough for touring cricketers, it was often the manager who had to placate them. As the twenty-four-year-old Perth paceman Jim Hubble toured South Africa in 1966–67, he was expecting on his return to become engaged to his eighteen-year-old girlfriend

Cheryl Corbitt. He even bought a diamond at Kimberley for the occasion. But, just before the Fifth Test, Hubble received an anxious telegram from Cheryl expressing sudden ambivalence about their relationship.

Hubble sought Bill Jacobs' permission to go home, but the manager could not grant it: Hubble was contractually bound. The argument became heated. 'I'm sorry, Barney, but you can't just leave,' Jacobs said. 'You've signed to play for a certain amount of time here and that's that.'

'But I've got to go,' Hubble repeated.

'Well you can't,' Jacobs stated. 'And that's the bloody end of it.'

Hubble grabbed Jacobs' lapels and shook him, but the manager was firm: 'Barney, you can shake me until you bloody well get tired. You're not going home.'

The bowler eventually cooled down. 'It was just the time and the situation and the location,' he says now. 'It was a bit of a mess for a while.'

Both stories ended happily. The Rutherfords stayed together, Hubble wed Cheryl in 1969, and both couples remain married. But they were not the only relationships that long tours and long absences from home stretched to their tolerances, and beyond.

BREAKING UP

Marriage in the 1950s and 1960s was still a solemn estate. As many as nine in ten marriages were conducted in church with bride in white. Yet the incidence of divorce was also increasing. Where only four in every hundred marriages had ended in divorce at the turn of the century, by the mid-1960s almost one in eight was doing so.

Divorce claimed its share of cricketing marriages. Sometimes it was a case of the player meeting someone else on tour. Sam Loxton divorced his wife Hilda in February 1952 in order to marry Caryl Bond, whom he'd met in South Africa two years earlier. Richie Benaud divorced Marcia in March 1967 and married Daphne Surfleet, the thirty-year-old assistant of English cricket writer E. W. Swanton, four months later. Ian Redpath broke off his engagement to Geelong girl Patricia McAdam in order to marry BOAC air hostess Christine Koch, whom he'd met touring England in 1968, in February 1969.

Other times, it was the difficulty of adjusting to one another at the end of a tour. Neil Hawke married his schoolday sweetheart Merrilyn Huddleston in Alberton at the end of the 1956–57 season. When the couple settled in Seaton in 1960, Merrilyn bore a daughter, and Hawke picked up a good job at Coca-Cola Bottlers.

While Hawke was away touring England, India and Pakistan in 1964, however, Merrilyn spread her wings. She joined a singing group, the Del Rios, and they were an immediate success, gaining a string of television engagements. When CCB offered to fly Merrilyn to Sydney to meet her husband as he returned from the tour, she was reluctant to go because of musical commitments.

Hawke turned the other cheek. He could hardly begrudge his wife her chance to make a singing career as he had made his sporting one. When they did meet, however, he could sense something wrong. 'We felt like total strangers,' Hawke says. 'It wasn't exactly the reunion I'd hoped for.'

Hawke tried for reconciliation. When a Shield match in Sydney in January 1965 finished early, he decided to fly home and give his wife a surprise. He did, but not the way he'd intended. 'When I got there,' he recalls, 'Merrilyn was obviously not expecting me and got very flushed and embarrassed, couldn't look me in the eye. Well, I made some discreet inquiries, and I heard that Merrilyn had established a friendship with a prominent musical identity.' They decided to separate, and divorced later that year.

Despite it all, very few cricketers stood out of tours for personal reasons. Tom Veivers and Peter Burge did so in 1965, preferring to remain at home with young families rather than trek to the West Indies. 'My wife didn't put any obstacles in my path, and it was entirely my decision,' Burge says. 'But I had two young kids who didn't know me and, frankly, I was sick of being away.'

Barry Jarman withdrew from the 1966–67 South African tour eighteen months later when his wife was diagnosed as suffering a malignant melanoma on her ankle. 'I wasn't happy to leave her at home with three children to take care of while I was off playing cricket,' he says. 'I didn't think that was fair.' As it was, in his first fourteen years of marriage, Jarman spent just one New Year's Eve at home. And in general, cricketers and their wives took the chance that things would be the same when they were reunited.

THE PAT CRAWFORD STORY

The cruellest personal misfortunes to befall a cricketer during the 1950s and 1960s, however, are contained in the story of Pat Crawford. Rarely has a cricketer made such a striking first impression as this strapping young paceman from Dubbo, selected for his state in December 1954. Rarely, too, has one suffered such a hasty and undignified fall from grace.

Crawford was one of six children born to a railway ganger. By twenty, he was a striking athlete of 185 centimetres and 76 kilograms, with a dramatic action and a noticeable turn of speed. For two years, he did everything right. Taking 67 wickets in his first two seasons, he impressed writers as a natural successor to Ray Lindwall. Between times, he played with East Lancashire and married a Blackburn girl, Sheila Wormby, whom he brought back to Sydney.

When selected for the 1956 Ashes tour, however, Crawford was far from sure he wanted to make the trip. Sheila was pregnant, and Crawford had further offers to play county cricket in England. Finally he accepted, with the idea that Sheila would also come and stay with her parents while the tour was in progress. Both would travel on the *Himalaya*. Thinking it circumvented the prohibition on cricketers and wives travelling together, Sheila took a second-class cabin while Crawford travelled in first-class.

As they embarked in Sydney, however, Australian board secretary Alan Barnes observed them together and wired team manager Bill Dowling. When the boat stopped in Melbourne, Crawford was told that he was in breach of his contract: Sheila would have to travel on another vessel if he was to continue the tour. Dowling was apologetic, but firm. 'Look Pat, I'm sorry to do this,' he said. 'But the board has spoken.' Sheila was forced to wait a week in Melbourne until the *Strathaird* came through.

The craziest aspect of the scenario was played out in the Mediterranean. As Richie Benaud recalled: 'Our ship's captain announced the name of the vessel we could see in the distance sailing parallel to us, and it turned out to be the one on which Pat Crawford's wife was sailing. So there we were, two ships sailing the same direction, husband on one, wife on the other. The ludicrous aspect was that Crawford could have had a mistress on board but not his wife, and the board would have said nothing.'

Tour rules restricted contact between Crawford and his wife in England. They were permitted to see one another, but not to stay under the same roof. And when Crawford wanted to attend Sheila's birth at Blackburn Infirmary in September, the tour administration again opposed the request: it was Lindwall's turn for a match off, and he was planning to play golf at St Andrews. Crawford went anyway. 'Basically I walked out,' he recalls. 'I said: "I'm going. It's up to you whether I come back or not."' Eventually, Lindwall played.

Teammates sensed that the marriage might not be going well anyway. Crawford, an outgoing but ingenuous character, hadn't seemed terribly upset about the restrictions placed on his movement during the tour. And he wasn't all that surprised when, as he left England for Rome to join the Australian team's flight to Karachi, Sheila told him that she wanted to stay in Blackburn with their new son. Crawford could return to England, but she didn't like Australia.

Crawford, in fact, had an opportunity to return. Kent had sounded him out about playing in England in the 1957 season. But when he returned to Australia, he ran foul of an unnoticed clause in his contract: a prohibition on playing first-class cricket overseas within two years of playing for Australia.

By the time Crawford faced the board at Cricket House, he was unemployed. He had resigned from his job as a hospital X-ray technician to go on the tour of England, and been replaced. But the board was unsympathetic. Crawford recalls:

> I said that I'd got back to Australia and didn't have a job to go to. But the chairman said: 'That's your bad luck. If you didn't want to make the sacrifices, you shouldn't have played cricket.' When I said I was a professional cricketer, they said that, as far as they were concerned, there was no such thing. And that if I tried to play for Kent or anyone else they'd take me to court.

It didn't come to that. When the Suez crisis worsened in November 1956, Kent decided that it couldn't proceed with signing Crawford: he was only twenty-four, and might be conscripted if he came to England. A possible job with Cobb & Co then fell through when Treasurer Arthur Fadden placed an embargo on imported motors. Jobless, wifeless, living with a sister, Crawford played two matches for NSW in the next two seasons, but his fire was gone. 'I was worn out, bowling from memory,' Crawford says. 'Didn't want to play anymore. It wasn't the game I was sick of, but the politics. I'd never encountered anything like them before.'

Then Crawford disappeared from the face of cricket altogether. Nothing more was heard of the bowler anointed Ray Lindwall's successor. In fact, Crawford had run away: without the money to pay a taxation demand on his 1956 tour fee, he hit the road for country New South Wales. For seven years, he lived the life of an itinerant labourer, working for a windmiller, pulling beer in pubs, selling Bibles. 'I went off the rails a bit for a while,' he says. 'I was drinking pretty heavily. A couple of people tried talking me into playing again, but I wasn't interested.'

Finally, in 1963, while working as a cellarman in the Gymea Hotel, Crawford met a widow eight years his senior, Nona Hayes. Because

Crawford was Catholic and had not annulled his marriage, they began living as a de facto couple in Miranda. They still live there, keepers of a small but significant story in Australian cricket.

KEEPING THE FAITH

Australia still saw itself as a Christian country in the 1950s and 1960s, with 95 per cent of Australians professing a belief in God in 1949, and 87 per cent as late as 1969. Huge crowds attending the first Billy Graham crusade in 1959—130,000 at the Melbourne Cricket Ground alone—seemed to attest to the nation's spiritual hunger. But organised religion was in decline. A 1956 Gallup Poll concluded that fewer than a third of Australians were attending church regularly, and half the population was not going at all.

Cricketers were unexceptional as a cross-section of that community. Some had had strongly religious upbringings. Neil Harvey grew up in a household as devout in its Methodism as it was crazy about cricket. Even oiling a bat on Sunday was out of order. But there were few regular churchgoers in the Australian side. And the suspicions of sectarianism in the national team before the war—specifically the tensions between Mason Bradman and Roman Catholics O'Reilly and Fingleton—vanished soon after. Bob Simpson recalls a conversation with Bill Bowes, the Yorkshire fast bowler turned journalist who had played against Australia in the 1930s:

> We were talking one day when Bill asked: 'Have you still got that terrible problem in the Australian team?'
> I said: 'What problem's that?'
> Bill says: 'The Catholics and the Masons.' I had to admit that I didn't know anything about the beliefs of the guys in the Australian team.

The average first-class dressing-room in the 1950s and 1960s was ecumenical. One day at the SCG during the 1957–58 season when local captain Sid Carroll was using Jack O'Regan at one end and Norm O'Neill at the other, a lone voice hollered from the Hill: 'Hey, Carroll! Why don't you give the Protestants a go!' The fielding team convulsed with laughter: Carroll was Catholic, O'Regan was Anglican and O'Neill Methodist.

Yet Christian traditions—or at least their pretence—still wielded an influence in Australian cricket. Against the junior QCA and WACA, the NSWCA, VCA and SACA staunchly opposed the introduction of

Sunday play well into the 1960s (while agreeing at the September 1964 meeting of the Interstate Conference to allow Queensland and Western Australia to play Sundays in matches against one another). When the VCA allowed Sunday play during the Bushfire Test in April 1967, it kept bars closed: the *Herald* called it 'teetotal cricket'.

And if sport had also not reached the stage in the 1960s it has today, where every second athlete seems to be thanking God for something, Australian cricket did have a figure as well-known for his devout Christianity as he was synonymous with dignity and good sportsmanship: Brian Booth.

THE LIFE OF BRIAN

The divinities in Booth's upbringing at Perthville, near Bathurst, were cricketing. On the wall of his family's brick-and-fibro cottage hung pictures of Bradman and Stan McCabe. His market gardener father Snowy solemnly instructed his son: 'These are the two greatest living cricketers.'

When he came to Sydney to study at Sydney Teachers' College and play for St George a couple of years later, however, Booth was befriended by Roy Gray, an outstanding district batsman who had become a pastor in Hurstville. And one evening at a church supper, Gray suddenly asked Booth: 'Brian, do you know Jesus Christ in a personal way?' When Booth replied that he believed in God, Gray told him that this wasn't sufficient. 'You know the rules of cricket,' said Gray. 'If you're going for a run and you slide your bat in but it's on the line when the stumps are broken, what's the decision?'

'That's out,' Booth responded. 'The line's close, but not good enough.'

'Well, Brian, your life can be like that,' Gray said. 'You can lead a good life, but in God's sight that's not enough.'

On the spot, Booth decided to 'invite Christ into his life'. He joined Gray in prayer. 'Until that point, sport had really been my God,' says Booth. 'Now I sensed a greater purpose in living than success in cricket.'

Although Booth was anxious about how his beliefs might be received when picked for his state, captain Keith Miller soon assuaged his concerns. While Booth was acting as twelfth man in his first Sheffield Shield match at the Gabba, Miller asked if he wanted to enter a Melbourne Cup sweep that was being organised.

'Thanks,' Booth replied. 'But I'd prefer not to.'

A look of recognition crossed Miller's face. 'Hey boys!' he said. 'Give Brian the money to hold. It'll be safe with him: he's not a gambling man.'

Booth remembers: 'That was typical of Keith. That he was able to turn something that might have been a problem into something positive, giving me a responsibility, making me feel part of the team.'

FITTING IN

While there were a few Australian athletes prepared to acknowledge their beliefs—like Betty Cuthbert, Margaret Smith, rower Tom Tresidder and Wallaby Ian Mutray—Booth quickly became an exceptional figure.

At times during his 29-Test career, the press caricatured his Christianity for the purposes of headlines. After Booth compiled his maiden Test century at the Gabba against England in December 1962, reporters were interested in whether he had felt God was with him. 'Naturally enough, I said that I thought He had been,' Booth recalls. 'Next day there was this newspaper headline: "England can't win. God is on Brian Booth's side."' Reporting another match-saving century, Bob Gray referred to him as 'Australia's one-man Salvation Army'.

But while one who never smoked, drank, swore, bet or lost his temper seemed incongruous in the salty, sweaty confines of a dressing-room, Booth blended easily into the Australian side. 'The boys just accepted me for what I was,' he says. 'If they didn't share the strength of my convictions, they were quite happy for me to hold them.' Indeed, Booth enjoyed a high esteem among teammates for his self-deprecating sportsmanship. 'Brian had his beliefs, but he never imposed them on the rest of the team,' says Bob Simpson. 'I'm sure things happened occasionally that he didn't approve of, but you'd never have known it.'

As his cricket horizons widened, Booth also learned that he wasn't the only devout Christian in the game. There was England's Reverend David Sheppard, West Indian Conrad Hunte, New Zealanders Vic Pollard and Brian Yuile, Springbok Trevor Goddard and Indian Chandu Borde. When Sheppard toured Australia with the MCC in 1962–63, he and Booth spoke widely at churches and youth meetings. On the Sunday rest day of the MCC's match against the Australian XI in Hobart, Sheppard read the lesson at one church and Booth at another. 'So,' asked Fred Trueman next morning, 'which of you lads 'ad t' better gate last night?'

But religion was no laughing matter for Booth. His gravest dilemma was when Australia returned from England in 1964 through the Indian subcontinent, and several Tests featured Sunday play. Booth recalls:

That was a tough one for me. At the time we'd left, the itinerary for the matches in India and Pakistan had not been decided, and I got a bit of a shock when I read in England that there was going to be Sunday play. So I had a wrestle over that. I very nearly came home at end of the England tour. But I figured that I'd been with the boys for four months and, because I was vice-captain, I had a responsibility to them.

It was the end of cricket's sabbath observance that then persuaded Booth to retire. When the NSWCA finally consented to the first Sunday of first-class cricket at the SCG (17 November 1968) and the first Sunday of Test cricket at the Gabba (8 December 1968), Booth could see the writing on the wall. 'I didn't expect everyone to agree with me or follow me,' says Booth. 'But it was the way *I* felt.'

THINKING POLITICS

Cricketers seldom discussed politics in the 1950s and 1960s and, in this, they were far from unusual. A routine complaint of the time was that Australians were among the world's foremost political apathetes. 'Prosperity has deadened the interest of Australians in politics,' Craig McGregor griped after Menzies' retirement in January 1966. 'With no crises to face, no urgent pressure for reform, government has become a matter of complacent consolidation.'

If anything, most members of the cricket community were socially conservative and, as such, drawn to the Liberal ethos of free enterprise and moral decency. And, even if they weren't, Menzies could convert them. Umpire Col Hoy recalls visiting his father after a cricket trip to Melbourne at which, during a reception at the Windsor Hotel, the prime minister had handed round a box of hand-rolled Havana cigars.

Dad used to sit in this squatter's chair, with the long arms, and read the papers. When I gave him the cigar, he had a look at it, smelt it, bit the end off. Then he jumped up and poured himself some port—which we kept for medicinal purposes, you know—and got back into his chair and lit up.

'How much did these cost you?' he asked.

'Cost me nothing,' I said.

'Where'd you get them, then?'

'Robert Menzies gave them to me.'

Dad was a rabid Labor man, used to attend all the branch meetings and hated Menzies with a passion. I can still see his eyes crossing as he looked down at the cigar in his mouth, working out whether his love of the Labor Party should be allowed to interfere with his love of cigars. There was a pause I can only describe as pregnant. Then he kept puffing.

Prominent sportsmen, nonetheless, sometimes had the option of a political career either just before or after retirement. The master cyclist Hubert Opperman blazed the trail by entering federal parliament in the Menzies landslide of December 1949, and became first minister for transport and later for immigration. VFL players Don Chipp, Brian Dixon, Mac Holten, Darrel Baldock and Neil Tresize all reached varying political altitudes, while former Canterbury-Bankstown front-rower Francis Stewart became Labor MHR for Lang in 1953 and later federal minister for tourism and sport.

First cricketer to enter the fray was Sam Loxton who, at the instigation of state Liberal leader Henry Bolte, sought and won preselection for the seat of Prahran on 28 September 1954. 'You won't win,' said Bolte. 'But we'd like you to fly the flag.' Ever-bullish, Loxton replied that he didn't go into anything intending to lose.

Loxton played his cricketing hand for all it was worth. On 11 April 1955, he led Prahran into the final of the VCA district competition, took seven wickets, scored 129 and won the match amid scenes of local rapture. In the election that commenced Bolte's seventeen-year reign six weeks later, Loxton beat sitting Labor member Bob Pettiona by 14 votes with the help of DLP preferences. State teammates remember him attending assiduously to his electoral correspondence over the next couple of seasons, often while padded-up, waiting to go in. He became government whip in 1961 and stayed twenty-four years, surviving even a 1967 challenge from football legend Jack Dyer.

At the other end of the political continuum was Loxton's former teammate Gilbert Langley. He was an electrical contractor from the Adelaide industrial estate of Colonel Light Gardens and looked it on the field, inevitably trailing a long shirt tail and placing a stern strain on the seam of his trousers. When he retired in December 1956, John Priestley of Melbourne's *Herald* wrote that his teammates would miss 'one of the best team men who ever packed a cricket bag (with a sock hanging out)'. Langley ran successfully as Labor candidate for Unley six years later, became a whip himself in 1970 and later the Speaker of the House of Assembly.

TOM VEIVERS MP

While both Loxton and Langley were born into their ideological positions, Queenslander Tom Veivers' political consciousness flowed directly from his cricket travels. On the way through India in October 1964, he was astounded by its inequities: 'Coming from a pretty conservative background I was not exactly prepared for the shock of seeing the poverty and extremes of life in India. This caused me to think about political, economic, and social issues more than I had done.' One evening at the Australian Trade Commission in Bombay sticks in his mind: 'There were three aid guys there and they were talking about the famine. About how the wheat was there but just lying in the warehouses, and none of it was being distributed and the price was going through the roof.'

Veivers' next tour, to South Africa two years later, broadened his mind further. He recalls:

> Like most Australians at the time I subscribed to the view that sport and politics should not be mixed...It was nevertheless difficult not to form personal views, particularly in South Africa in 1966–67. Apartheid was then strongly entrenched. Even though we were isolated from the issue, one could feel the mounting pressures brought on by racial tensions. I came away concerned about what was happening. I'm sure there were a number of others who felt likewise, as did some of the South African players themselves...I think I was one of the few sportspeople at the time who supported the idea of sporting bans on South Africa as a means of getting some justice and merit back into the system.

When thoughts of going into politics dawned, Veivers was naturally drawn towards Labor and its hard line on South Africa. He became a federal MP at the second attempt: he missed out on McPherson in 1972, despite gaining a 6.5 per cent swing, but won Ashgrove in 1983. The Hawke years, though, were unkind on a politician motivated by principle. Dissatisfied with the party's direction, Veivers quit during a term as commissioner-general for the Australian section of the 1988 World Expo. As Aneurin Bevan put it: 'Politics is not the arena of morals. It is the arena of interests.'

'The Blind Leading the Blind, Really'

THE COMMERCIALISATION OF
AUSTRALIAN CRICKET
1960–70

The Prime Minister's XI match of 17 December 1965 was faithful to its half-dozen precursors. Teams led by the MCC's Mike Smith and Richie Benaud were welcomed at a cocktail party by British high commissioner Sir Charles Johnston, dined bibulously with Menzies, and batted with cheerful abandon to make 577 runs.

Yet, as with the entire summer, the crowd was disappointing. Where 11,000 had watched the MCC on their previous visit to Manuka Oval, this time only 4000 attended. Where previous matches had always gained front-page coverage, newspapers confined reporting of this occasion to their sporting sections. The game was destined to be the last of its kind. Five weeks later, Sir Robert announced his retirement after sixteen years as prime minister.

In every sense, it represented the end of an era. Menzies had presided over a period of untrammelled prosperity, in which average weekly earnings had grown by 250 per cent. At the end of his reign, unemployment was less than 2 per cent, inflation around 3 per cent, the nominal long-term interest rate stood at 5 per cent and net foreign debt was inconsequential: it was, in the judgment of London's *Financial Times*, the healthiest economy in the world. When Donald Horne's polemical *The Lucky Country* was published in 1964, many missed the name's intended irony: though Horne's proposition was that 'Australia is a lucky country run mainly by second-rate men who share its luck', its title was widely accepted at face value as confirming Australia's manifold blessings.

Disputing the Menzies legacy, contemporary critics discerned a fundamental contradiction. The prime minister had been, of course, the Commonwealth's greatest proponent and the monarchy's chiefest admirer. As he put it in his famous Smuts Memorial Lecture at Cambridge University on 16 May 1960, the royal family was 'a focal point, unmarred by political controversy, for our national tradition, consciousness and ambitions'.

Yet in his watch had occurred dramatic changes in Australia's cultural intonation: specifically the 'Americanisation' of Australian society, which during 1960 provoked architect and social critic Robin Boyd in *The Australian Ugliness* to satirically rename the country 'Austerica', with its 'hopeless yearning for the dazzling Hollywood night and the *Life* life', like 'the little boy mimicking his big brother's actions without fully understanding what he is doing'.

Much of this change was superficial. Britain was still by far the largest investor in Australia, controlling assets in 1966 worth more than $3 billion. Australia's machinery of public administration—parliament, the judiciary and the public service—still replicated British models. In higher education, private schools and the church, too, British policies and personnel remained pervasive.

But Boyd had a point. Deluged by American cinema and television, seduced by the self-conscious seediness of rock'n'roll, younger Australians saw the affectation of American mores as chic. As Craig McGregor put it in his *Profile of Australia* in 1966:

> Australians are more familiar with Dr Kildare, Disneyland and American westerns than with English or their own productions...the numerous commercial radio stations and their announcers follow the pattern of American broadcasting, with plenty of advertisements and glib patter jammed in between the endless hit parade records...Garages have begun to put their employees into American gas station uniforms, the police department have begun to plaster badges over their cars, American entertainers grace the more expensive nightclubs, Bar-B-Qs and drive-in steak bars line the highways, American-designed refrigerators, washing machines and cars dominate the production lines.

So many events seemed to embody this transition: public preference for the dollar over the 'royal' as Australia's new decimal currency; muted public response to the royal visit of February–March 1963, and the unction that oozed when US president Lyndon Johnson toured three and a half years later; Menzies' replacement by the self-consciously Australian Harold Holt, who eschewed the traditional entertainments of cricket and football for the individualistic pleasures of sun and surf.

The decade's watershed political event was, after reintroduction of national service in November 1964, Menzies' April 1965 announcement that Australia would despatch an infantry battalion to support the US in South Vietnam. A second was sent in February 1966, a third in October 1967. It resulted in another striking American import: the protest rally, derived from those of the US civil rights movement and the 'Students for a Democratic Society'. The banner-bearing march became a standard, almost formulaic, method of demonstrating dissent: from Brisbane's earnest 'Battle of Roma Street' in September 1967, where more than 100 protesting their right to rally were arrested, to the almost self-parodic November 1970 student strike at Melbourne's Mordialloc-Chelsea High School, over the issue of hair length.

When generations clashed, there was a profusion of (unintended) symbolism. One fleetingly famous incident was a rally outside the Bellevue Hill home of federal attorney-general Tom Hughes on 16 August 1970, at which forty protesters sought to present him with a list of young men defying the National Service Act. Hughes slammed the door in their faces, called the police, and emerged wielding his trusty cricket bat to augment their efforts dispersing the crowd. The *Age* depicted him on its front page, leaning on his bat like a man at the non-striker's end having just taken a single to complete his century. Menzies would have been proud of him.

SECOND THOUGHTS ON SPORT

On the face of it, this rejection of previous certitude had little impact on Australian sporting achievement. Tennis continued mass-producing heroes: Rod Laver, Roy Emerson, John Newcombe, Tony Roche and Margaret Smith. Dawn Fraser, John Konrads, John Devitt and Robert Rose ruled the pool, Herb Elliott, Ron Clarke, Ralph Doubell and Betty Cuthbert the track, and, unexpectedly as the decade ended, featherweight Johnny Famechon and bantamweight Lionel Rose the ring.

Yet it was newer, more fashionable pursuits that enjoyed greatest success. Within five years of Sydney's first public squash court opening, Ken Hiscoe, Geoff Hunt and Heather McKay were taking Australia to the top of the international game: McKay won the first of sixteen consecutive British championships in 1962 and was ABC Sportsman of the Year in

1967. Five years after an American film (*The Big Surf*) popularised the pastime, Midget Farrelly and Phyllis O'Donnell were winning surfing's inaugural world championships at Manly in May 1964. Having won the world Formula One crown in 1959 and 1960, Jack Brabham went a step better in 1966 by recapturing it in his own cars.

For traditional sports, the 1960s provided mixed blessings. Between 1962 and 1968, Victorian racing crowds declined by 10 per cent, average weekly attendances at Victorian Football League games by 20 per cent, those at NSW Rugby League matches by 15 per cent. Old followers maintained their allegiances, but younger people increasingly identified sport with outmoded social mores.

Various exogenous explanations were posited, but at least a few commentators sensed that old models of competitive sport risked archaism. A *Bulletin* article in September 1966 dubbing rugby league 'Australia's newest blood sport' concluded: 'Officials of the game would do well to reflect on the long-term results of the vicious trend of the game at present. The younger generation may have second thoughts about continuing in a game offering the prospects of serious injury and the public will be the eventual losers as prospective champions vanish into the limbo.'

As the most codified and ceremonial of games, cricket was intensely vulnerable to societal shift from established traditions. And, after the Benaud-led *risorgimento* from 1958 to 1963, the crowds for Australian home series dwindled. The 353,000 who attended Australia's five-match rubber with South Africa in 1963–64 represented a 10 per cent decline on crowds for the Springboks' previous visit, which itself had caused alarm. A one-off Test against Pakistan at the MCG in December 1964 drew 8300 a day, four Tests against India in 1967–68 a derisory 6400. Average daily attendances at Sheffield Shield matches, furthermore, fell from 5000 in 1961–62 to 3000 in 1967–68.

Even Ashes series were losing their lustre. Crowds for the 1965–66 rubber were the lowest for an Anglo-Australian series since 1928–29. Hopes that the 1968–69 West Indians would repeat the heart-warming successes of the 1960–61 team were unrealised: they attracted only 429,000, compared to 735,000 eight years earlier. Keith Miller's comment after Australia had reclaimed the Worrell Trophy 3–1 was typically astringent: 'What is the point of being world champions if nobody comes to see your team play? The Frank Worrell 1960–61 side…left Melbourne to a ticker-tape farewell from 92,000-odd people. Lawry received the trophy back before 200.'

The headline trend of declining cricket attendances at cricket, however, obscured a very complex story. If it didn't move as urgently as the world around it, cricket was undergoing profound changes prefiguring those of the sunnier 1970s. First and foremost came television.

'BITING OUR NAILS'

As Australia's 1956 Ashes tour concluded, the ABC's Michael Charlton received a message from his Sydney superiors. 'It wasn't an instruction so much as an encouragement,' he says. 'They thought it would be a good idea if I stayed on for a few weeks after the tour to do some training at the BBC in television. The BBC was looked on very much as the alma mater of broadcasting, and the ABC looked over its shoulder constantly because both were derivatives of the same idea.'

On his return, Charlton learned the reason. Seven years after Ben Chifley had committed to the new medium, television was about to commence. On 5 November 1956, Charlton compered the first evening of ABC TV with Menzies, postmaster-general Charles Davidson, Labor senator Nick McKenna and commission chairman Sir Richard Boyer.

It didn't go exactly according to plan: the first musical item, a gavotte by violinist Christian Ferras, came out silent; the first newsreel broke, and studio cameras cutting back to Charlton revealed him with a drink and a smoke. But television was on the road in Australia, and in the nick of time. The Melbourne Olympics were just weeks away. Michael's younger brother Tony, in fact, was part of a GTV-9 commentary panel there that featured Ian Johnson and Sam Loxton alongside Jack Kramer and Jesse Owens.

So began the long and occasionally rocky romance between sport and television in Australia. Television wanted sport. In the same week as Charlton inaugurated ABC television, the commission's federal sport supervisor Bernard Kerr was commenting in *ABC Weekly* that cricket, tennis and surf carnivals 'would provide much drama for the television camera'. He looked forward to seeing 'the look of anguish on the face of a batsman clean-bowled for a duck' and the 'agony of a tennis player holding set point who puts an easy smash into the net'.

Sport, however, returned television's embrace equivocally. The board was typically ambivalent. Knowing television would come sooner rather than later, secretary Jack Ledward had written to the MCC in September 1955 inquiring of their experiences with the medium. 'We wanted to know from them whether they'd noticed any effect on attendances from

TV and they wrote back they hadn't,' says Ledward. 'But that wasn't really any good from our point of view. They had such small grounds there.' When, a year later, the Interstate Conference came to negotiating television rights for selected 1956–57 Sheffield Shield matches with a consortium of ABC and commercial broadcasters, the administrators limited broadcasts to play after tea. Fees of £25 were paid to the VCA and the NSWCA, with a further £20 to the former for rights to the year's district final. The board minuted at its meeting of 8 September 1957: '[We are] watching the position most carefully—it being realised that unless TV is controlled, it could adversely affect attendances at matches.'

Haggling over television rights began in earnest for the 1958–59 MCC visit. The VCA—empowered to act also for the NSWCA—appointed a television subcommittee composed of Ledward, Bill Dowling, Leo Rush and Bob Parish, which began negotiations with the ABC-led consortium in January 1958. Neither side had much idea what it was doing. The broadcasters tried their familiar line that previous broadcasts had stimulated public interest in the game. The VCA subcommittee responded by demanding £32,000 for the rights to televise the last two hours of Tests and Sheffield Shield at the MCG and SCG. It seemed a figure plucked from nowhere, and it was. As Ledward puts it: 'When we were negotiating with the ABC, it was pretty much guesswork. Bob Parish and I would sit there biting our nails, wondering which way to jump next. They'd beat us down, we'd pump it up. It was the blind leading the blind really.'

The ABC and the two commercial stations in each city baulked. They offered £16,400: £9200 for the VCA, £7200 for the NSWCA. The subcommittee accepted. In fact, unbeknownst to them, the bidders had been prepared to pay up to £23,800. But the administrators were pleased. With the £5000 they had secured for radio rights, Australian cricket was £21,400 richer from a source undreamt-of a decade earlier. Perhaps there was something to be said for television after all.

THE TV GENIE

The early days of Australian sport's co-existence with television were tense. The Victorian Football League was particularly leery of the new device. Worried that the rival Victorian Football Association would cut a deal first, it had stampeded into an arrangement in 1957 under which the three Melbourne stations were allowed to cover final quarters live. But after 1958 attendances slumped by 150,000, then continued to ebb in the next two seasons, the VFL turned away from television altogether in 1961 and would consent only to replays from 1962.

Though buoyed by its handsome dividend for 1958–59, the cricket authorities also found television a fickle partner. While the ABC always presented for annual negotiations, the commercial stations were inconstant patrons. In June 1960, GTV-9 and HSV-7 withdrew from talks about covering the forthcoming Australia–West Indies series on grounds that the prices were too high. The former then scurried back in January 1961 seeking the right to telecast the decisive Fifth Test at the MCG, jazzing up the coverage with guest commentators like visiting American film star Fred Astaire. (Astaire's first question floored co-commentators Tony Charlton and Keith Miller: 'Why is the ball red?')

The pioneering Test telecasts, too, were primitive. Instead of seeing 'the look of anguish on the face of a batsman clean-bowled for a duck' fondly envisaged by Kerr, viewers had to settle for images seemingly shot through the wrong end of a telescope. And early broadcasts were confined to local environs. Not until the Fifth Test of 1960–61 were terrestrial relay stations used to transmit a full day's play interstate. Not until the Fourth Test of 1962–63 could eastern viewers watch live coverage of an Adelaide Oval Test. (A DC-3 leased by the ABC and GTV-9 circled over the Victoria–South Australia border, captured the signal from Mt Lofty and beamed it through Ararat and Ballarat receivers to Mt Dandenong.)

But television couldn't be ignored. By 1965, there were more than two million licence-holders. And as microwave and co-axial cable technology improved, viewers in Adelaide, Brisbane and Sydney could watch every ball of that summer's Melbourne Tests.

As gates continued to disappoint during the 1960s, the board *did* begin searching for reasons. In January 1963, it sought a royalty from the PMG's recorded telephone score service (instigated in 1958–59) on the grounds that the facility was costing money at the turnstiles. The PMG refused, contending that the service catered for those unable to attend matches and was therefore 'more likely to encourage attendance than to provide an attractive alternative form of entertainment'. The board tried again in October 1965, and was again disappointed.

Where television was concerned, however, the board seems to have accepted that the genie was out of the bottle. It sought simply to squeeze what it could from the arrangements. From six home Test summers between 1963 and 1971, it extracted about $250,000 in television and radio broadcast rights. Viewing figures may even have been a source of consolation for the authorities as they regarded their half-empty grounds. The ABC estimated that more than three million watched at least some of the first series carried nationwide: the 1970–71 Ashes clash between Bill Lawry's Australians and Ray Illingworth's Englishmen.

THE GOOSE THAT LAID THE GOLDEN PEANUT

Australia was not alone in the sorry state of its attendances in the 1960s. The buoyant English Test crowds that had followed the fortunes of Benaud's tourists in 1961 melted away in 1962 and, from their zenith of more than two million just after the war, county attendances hit 933,000. John Solan commented miserably in *Wisden*: 'As a game for the spectator on anything like the scale of 20 years ago, it seems to have had its day.'

In the 1963 season, however, two unrelated but parallel initiatives began that would revivify cricket. Having agreed to it in December 1961, the counties found their First-Class Counties Knock-out Competition an astonishingly successful formula. Underwritten by the Gillette Safety Razor Company and limited to 65-overs-a-side in its inaugural year, the final on 7 September 1963 played to a noisy packed house at Lord's. 'This may not have been cricket to the purists, but by golly it was just what the doctor ordered,' wrote columnist Peter Wilson. 'And I am sure that Dr W. G. Grace would have been one of the doctors concurring.'

Also under way that season were the International Cavaliers: a travelling troupe founded by Denis Compton and Godfrey Evans, later augmented by modern masters like Ted Dexter and Fred Titmus, who played a rota of strictly informal and highly entertaining Sunday afternoon games against counties and invitational XIs, splitting proceeds between authorities, ground administrators and nominated beneficiaries.

The games began modestly. But in 1965, with sponsorship from the tobacco giant Rothmans and BBC2 television coverage, the Cavaliers tour took off. Over the next three seasons, almost a quarter of a million spectators attended the matches and weekly viewing audiences exceeded a million. Enjoying the exposure, Rothmans began producing a cricket annual, sponsoring a knockout tournament for league clubs in the North and the Midlands, and underwriting the assembly of a Rest of the World team.*

---

* The teams for the original Rest of the World side—captained by New Zealander John Reid and including Sobers, Kanhai, Hall, Griffith, Gibbs, Grout, Barlow and Bland—were selected on the votes of readers of the *Radio Times* and viewers of BBC TV's *Sportsview*. A three-day match at

Commercial support for cricket had by this time also become a feature in Australia. In 1958–59, for instance, Frank Packer's Consolidated Press had endowed incentives for fast scoring, ranging from £500 for a century in a session to £5 for a six. Phil Tresidder recalls: 'Arthur Mailey frightened Sir Frank by saying: "The players'll gang up on you. They'll make sure someone gets the hundred and split the prizemoney." When Sir Frank asked me, I said: "No-one would do that. Not Australia versus England."' Tresidder was right. Cons Press executives were hangdog when they had to fork out £500 to Peter May for a hasty hundred against the Australian XI but, in the event, had to come up with £5 more for a Fred Trueman six.

Tobacco companies had followed. Since the arrival of Rothmans and Philip Morris in 1953 to tackle British Tobacco's WD & HO Wills, they had been especially persistent in efforts to identify their brands with sport and sportsmen. In 1959, it was announced that Wills would set aside £10,000 for awards to teams and individuals during Australia's next four series. During the 1960–61 series, for instance, each side stood to win £300 per Test, and £130 was offered in each of the following categories: best batting average, best bowling average, highest score, best innings bowling, best batting and bowling aggregates, fastest scoring rate, and most catches by a fielder. Leading money winner was Alan Davidson with £485/16/8.

Another emerging form of quasi-sponsorship was employing sportsmen. From the late fifties, tobacco companies hired a host as advertising and sales representatives: the Rothmans payroll came to include Norm O'Neill, Wally Grout, Barry Shepherd, Doug Walters, Keith Stackpole and Brian Taber, while Wills in due course employed Bob Simpson, Ian Chappell, Peter Allan and Des Bull. As players were allowed unlimited paid leave for cricket, they regarded tobacco companies as ideal employers. Simpson commented in 1966: 'Companies like British Tobacco are doing a great service to sport. Without them, semi-amateur sports like cricket would find it very hard to survive.'

Australian authorities, however, had traditionally scorned the corporate dollar. And even the English were reluctant to take sponsorship too far. When Ted Dexter commented rather intemperately in February 1963

Scarborough was drawn, while the World won a rain-interrupted Lord's sequel shortened to a 70-overs-a-side match. Rothmans sponsored similar matches in the next four seasons, until Guinness backed the Rest of the World tour of 1970.

that the Ashes were a nuisance and that there would be more results if cash was the victory incentive, his statement was deplored. Alan Ross of the *Observer* commented: 'I trust he did not fully understand the implications of what he said: if he did, then he had forfeited every right to go on being England's captain.'

But, gradually, watching the good works of Gillette and Rothmans in England, Australian administrators began to soften. There was big money around, being backed by big names. In March 1964, Rothmans set up its National Sports Foundation under the chairmanship of Sir Dallas Brooks, pledging to support all forms of sport to the extent of £100,000 annually. And a few low-key, officially sanctioned sponsorships began. In 1963–64, Wills offered £200 prize money to the winner of the VCA district competition, while Rothmans bankrolled the new NSWCA coaching manual and two WACA weekend training camps at Point Peron. A 'Cricketer of the Year' prize was also instituted: the so-called Golden Peanut Award, sponsored by the Peanut Marketing Board. Inaugural winner of trophy, blazer and bat was Brian Booth.

Imitating clinics run by the *Adelaide Advertiser* since 1958, the Rothmans NSF began large-scale coaching tours, enlisting players like O'Neill, Shepherd, Ken Archer, Ray Flockton, Jack Walsh and the English emigrés Tony Lock and Peter Loader. Ray Lindwall instructed more than 1000 young players on a tour of the Northern Territory. A series of coaching films was produced. By 1967, tobacco companies were staking club knock-out competitions in Victoria, New South Wales and South Australia. And columnist Graham Eccles of Melbourne's *Herald* was commenting knowingly: 'I know that several high-ranking Australian administrators are now enthusiastic about outside investment and promotion for their game.'

A TIME OF EXPERIMENT

The success of the Gillette Cup and the International Cavaliers also seemed to indicate that crowds could be wooed by variants on the conventional cricket spectacles of Tests and tours. And the board did nurture one very ambitious plan: at its December 1963 meeting, Sir Donald Bradman mooted a tri-cornered Test championship involving England and the West Indies in a dozen Tests for the 1965–66 season. Nothing similar had been attempted since England's unsuccessful 1912 Triangular Tournament, but the board believed that such a cricket feast would 'generate great interest' as well as allowing 'the early return of the West Indies' (not then scheduled to tour for another five years). The plan was stifled at birth, however, when the MCC expressed outright opposition. And, with Bradman vacating the chair for the colourless Ewart Macmillan of NSW, board meetings regressed to their usual reactionary tone.

It wasn't until Victorian Bob Parish, a thoughtful fifty-one-year-old timber company executive, succeeded to the chairmanship in September 1967 that the board again entertained anything out of the ordinary. Even then, it was a submission from outside the administrative elite: a proposal from theatrical impresario Jack Neary for a double-wicket competition involving sixteen top internationals to be staged round Australia. The players would play off in pairs in stretches of eight six-ball overs, accumulating points on the basis of runs made and wickets taken.

Neary had a successful track record as a promoter of overseas acts from Jack Benny to Winifred Atwell. With Kenn Brodziak, he had enticed the Beatles to Australia. With Michael Edgley, he had lured out the Moscow Circus. And he had concluded that sport would be the 'next big thing'. He says:

> I was a cricket lover from way back and, far as I was concerned, they were entertainers like Jack Benny or the Beatles. People wanted the big stars, the personalities. I could remember as a boy going to see Bradman bat at the SCG. The newspapers would put up a poster saying 'He's In' and 30,000 people would show up. The other thing I thought they wanted was a result. I loved Test cricket—still do—but I could see that there were people who wanted to go home having seen someone beat someone else.

Parish's board approved the World Cricket (Doubles) Competition at its meeting in December 1967 on condition that it receive 10 per cent of takings. And Neary gathered a veritable galaxy of talent: Simpson, McKenzie, Walters and Lawry from Australia; Basil D'Oliveira, Fred Trueman, Colin Milburn and Ken Barrington from England; the West Indians Sobers, Hall, Kanhai and Griffith; and the Pollocks, Denis Lindsay and Trevor Goddard from South Africa. He promoted it in the same way he would have any attraction: flashy print, radio and TV ads designed by his aide Betty Stewart.

Neary struck a snag when his sponsors withdrew at the eleventh hour, but he put up the $20,000 prize money and paid the players' $1500 appearance fees himself, and this peculiar cricket caravan rolled through each of the mainland capitals on three consecutive weekends in October 1968. Notwithstanding the novelty of the variation on the standard cricket format—when either team fielded it was complemented by a contingent of Sheffield Shield players—the matches drew more than 70,000 people and were watched by many more on television. Sobers and Hall won the $6000 first prize, and Neary made a profit of $5000. As plans were laid for a sequel, Simpson wrote: 'Whilst not suggesting that this type of cricket could ever supersede the more conventional form of the game, there is hope that it will attract more people to the game. If this is the result, the promotion will have been more than worthwhile.'

The same meeting that had endorsed the World Cricket (Doubles) proposal also approved in principle an official domestic one-day competition, and empowered Bob Parish to seek a sponsor. It was hardly trail-blazing—England's Gillette Cup had been thriving for five seasons—but it did constitute the first time that the board had deliberately solicited financial support.

Parish found the backers in England while managing the 1968 Ashes tour. London-based Vehicle and General Insurance were staking the Tests of that series to the tune of £5000 and being described in *Cricketer* as 'the really big noise of Test sponsorship'. Parish liked the sound of that and, at the first board meeting on his return, announced that the insurer had agreed to support the V & G Knockout Competition between the Australian states and New Zealand for five years from 1969–70 to the tune of $100,000.

But, by the end of the decade, the attitude of English and Australian administrators towards 'private promoters' had hardened. Having seen the Cavaliers demonstrate the viability of Sunday cricket packaged for television, the counties in February 1968 approved their own limited-overs Sunday League: sponsorship from tobacco group John Player & Son was sealed in October, while the BBC threw in its lot with the authorities in December. And when Ian Chappell in January 1969 sought board approval to play with the Cavaliers, he was refused. The board minuted 'its concern about the growth of private cricket promoters and their contractual agreements with first-class players'.

Ted Dexter mourned the counties' 'ungrateful backhander' and the Australian board's 'nonsensical and indefensible restriction'. But it was the beginning of the end for the Cavaliers: after a few years on off-piste grounds under the waning gaze of independent broadcasters, they wound up.

At the same meeting that kiboshed Chappell's winter plans the board sent Neary packing. He had returned to the authorities with an even more ambitious suggestion: an eleven-a-side pre-season one-day competition featuring invitation sides from Australia, England, the West Indies and South Africa. The idea was rejected. Neary recalls:

Sir Donald Bradman was very interested and very co-operative. But I think the cricket associations were still run by people then who liked to go to the cricket and have a bit of a drink, and they didn't like the idea of someone taking their game away from them. Now, I was the last person who would have done that: I loved Test cricket. But their attitude was that they didn't want private promoters involved.

It could be said that, by dealing so off-handedly with two such inoffensive and polite promoters as the Cavaliers and Jack Neary in 1969, the authorities condemned themselves to confronting a rather more ruthless entrepreneur in Kerry Packer eight years later.

GETTING OUT

For all the board's commercial dabblings, nothing altered its attitude to players. Cricketers were to be seen and not heard, and certainly not to be paid. Average weekly wages more than doubled from £80 in 1954–55 to $190 in 1968–69, but the base Test fee increased just 19 per cent. The Australians flattened by Tyson and Statham received more than four times the average weekly wage for each game. The Australians who beat Hall and Griffith received about twice.* And those who kept the Ashes from England's grasp between 1959 and 1971 received less than 3 per cent of the total gate and broadcasting revenues accruing to the board in those series.

The upshot was a staggering attrition among experienced cricketers in the mid-1960s. Grahame Thomas was typical. A compositor with printers Waite and Ball, he retired after the 1966–67 South African tour. 'It was simply a question of money,' Thomas says. 'Playing cricket was fruitless. At the end it was actually costing me money to play Shield cricket, because my wages were greater than my pay in cricket. The guys on the gates were being paid more than we were.' He was twenty-eight.

If one had the prospect of a career, cricket was even harder to justify. Shortly after losing his Test place, Ian Craig became a production manager at Boots Pure Drug Company. He decided that 1960–61 would be his last Australian season and to miss the 1961 Ashes tour. 'The company were saying that it was time for me to make a decision,' he says. 'And I thought that was fair enough.' It took a little longer than Craig expected to work the cricket bug from his system. He batted so well that season that he changed his mind about the 1961 tour—just missing out to Bill Lawry—and didn't actually play his last match until February 1962. But

* English Test cricketers, by comparison, were far better paid. They received £120 sterling for 1969 home Tests, increased to £150 by 1971.

he was still only twenty-six when he quit. He went on to become Boots' Australian managing director.

As Craig was exiting cricket, another very exciting young Australian batsman was emerging in Adelaide. Ian McLachlan was a St Peter's College prodigy and a Cambridge University blue who hit 188 not out on his Sheffield Shield debut in December 1960, and three hundreds in four games the following season. Awesomely powerful off the back foot and through the covers, he was twelfth man in the Adelaide Test of January 1963.

The following season, however, form eluded McLachlan. 'I had an eye infection,' he recalls. 'I took all sorts of antibiotics, but I couldn't get rid of it. I also made a few changes to my batting and almost lost my place in the side.' So it was decision time. 'I'd had a helluva good time playing cricket, but enough was enough. I'd just got married, and there was no money in it.' He was twenty-seven.

McLachlan bought a property near Mt Gambier and turned to farming. In 1990, after four years as president of the National Farmers Federation, he stood successfully for Liberal preselection in Barker. In 1996 he became minister for defence.

One of McLachlan's most promising colleagues was teenage left-arm wrist spinner David Sincock, who took 9–195 on his Sheffield Shield debut against NSW. If his accuracy fluctuated, no-one since the war had spun the ball so far so often. Sincock graduated to Test cricket in December 1964, and bowled Garry Sobers at Port-of-Spain five months later with a wicked delivery pitching outside leg and hitting off. 'What happened?' Sobers asked. 'Evil Dick's done it again!' replied Wally Grout.

Yet cricket quickly palled for Sincock, a thoughtful young man who doubted the logic of playing cricket day-in day-out. Within a year, he was gone, having moved to Sydney to marry and to accept a sales job at 3M. He explains:

> I never really reflected on exactly what I wanted to do. I'm still not sure really. I would *like* to have performed better than I did at Test level, and I would *like* to have been a permanent member of the Australian team. But I knew I definitely didn't want to be a professional sportsman. I was probably bowling better at the start of my career when things were fresh and new than towards the end. Once I'd got a guy out I couldn't really see the point in getting him out again next week.

Sincock was twenty-four. He moved on to executive positions at the Sara Lee Corporation, South Pacific Hotels, TNT and Telstra.

Perhaps Australian cricket's most grievous early loss was Victorian left-hander Bob Cowper. In 1963, Ted Dexter singled Cowper out as Australia's most promising batsman. A couple of years later, after some doughty innings in the Caribbean, Jack Fingleton nominated him a future national captain.

Cowper appeared, in fact, to have it all: he was handsome, charming, naturally gifted and smart. The young Ian Chappell revered him: 'I learned more about cricket standing next to Cowps at slip than I did from just about anybody in the Australian side.' But Cowper lacked one thing: the confidence of administrators. He was felt a little too clever, a little uppity. The board overlooked him as third selector for the 1966–67 South African tour, preferring Tom Veivers. The VCA overlooked him as a replacement for retiring vice-captain Jack Potter, preferring Ian Redpath.

A further source of disenchantment for Cowper was that—as a rising stockbroker at Guest & Bell—cricket cost him heavily in wages forgone. When Guest & Bell posted him to Perth for twelve months in October 1968—to open an office as its frontline for the nickel boom—Cowper turned his back on Test cricket at the age of twenty-seven. 'There's no easy way to make a dollar,' he explained. 'You've gotta work for it. No-one's putting any pressure on me to quit big cricket. The time has simply come…when I must put my career first.'

It was little wonder cricketers settled for financial security ahead of sporting distinction. Cricket was a fragile pursuit. West Australian John Rutherford could testify to the frailty of the sporting life. One minute he was captaining his state against Worrell's West Indians at the WACA Ground in October 1960, the next he was in hospital. He recalls: 'Frank was batting on the last afternoon and I chased one to the boundary, threw it in and jogged back to my position. Then my entire right side froze. I couldn't move. I couldn't feel anything. Frank and I were great friends—we'd played together in England while I'd been there in 1959 and 1960—and he said: "John, are you all right?" I tried to answer him but I found I couldn't speak, so Frank said: "This man is ill. He should leave the field."'

When Rutherford awoke in hospital, he was told that he'd suffered a stroke. He was also informed that the Education Department would not pay his medical expenses, because he'd not been back teaching for six months. Rutherford's wife Bethanie then developed cancer of the eye and was herself hospitalised. Within six weeks, Rutherford had to return to teaching in Merredin in order to support them. There was no more cricket for John Rutherford.

The statistics are quite alarming. Between 1964 and 1967, for example, an entire Australian XI was lost to the game when it still had good cricket left: the aforementioned Burge, O'Neill, Thomas, Craig, McLachlan and Sincock, plus Veivers (thirty), Philpott (thirty-one), Des Hoare (thirty-one), Ron Gaunt (twenty-nine), Barry Shepherd (twenty-nine), Jack Potter (twenty-nine) and, not least, Simpson (thirty-one).

And this was more than simply a pity. Towards the end of the 1960s, Australian teams experienced a serious dearth of senior players. Look at a team photograph from the early 1950s with its many older players, then one from the late 1960s with its younger, fresher faces, and what you see is a semi-amateur cricket economy in action.

NOT TO REASON WHY

Yet money did not grate nearly so much as administrators' high-handedness. The prohibition on cricket wives accompanying their husbands remained absolute. The player–writer rule continued to hamper. After the O'Neill fiasco in May 1965, both Johnny Martin and Ian Chappell were reprimanded for granting interviews immediately after the South African tour. The board even entertained prolonging the three-month embargo on post-tour comment to two years.

Where players and administrators met at all, it was usually in situations of chill formality. Neil Hawke paints a vivid picture of lunches with the SACA gerontocracy during home Sheffield Shield matches:

> The committee'd be sitting there, always in suits even though it might be a hundred degrees. And on the table there'd be plates with a few slices of chicken, about five bits of cucumber, some shredded lettuce and tomato. There'd also be a slab of sultana cake which was so hard that no-one could ever cut it; in fact, the boys reckoned that it travelled with us from match to match. And on the tray with the cordials there'd always be one bottle of beer. But it got cobwebs on it because nobody was game to touch it in front of the committee.

A minor classic of board ineptitude was the selection of the team for the Third Test against India at the Gabba on 19 January 1968. Simpson had scored 55, 103 and 109 in the first two Tests, whilst Graham McKenzie had just bagged 10–151 at the MCG. Yet, without warning, when the Third Test team was announced, neither was included.

If the philosophy was comprehensible—the desire to trial more players ahead of the forthcoming Ashes tour—execution was lamentable.

Both players were stunned. Bill Lawry, Simpson's replacement, kept his peace, even when the Test went to the wire by 38 runs. 'When you think about it, it wasn't a great selection,' he says. 'But the only time I said anything was when Bradman said to me later: "You ran it a bit close in Brisbane didn't you?" And I said: "Well, you did take our two best players out."'

Equally bizarre a year later was the sacking of Simpson's successor in the NSW captaincy: the brilliant colt Doug Walters. After just six games as skipper, Walters was invited to Cricket House, where secretary Alan Barnes put him on a telephone line to selector Ron James. James explained that the selectors wanted his resignation: they felt his batting had deteriorated since the appointment. This rather nonplussed the twenty-three-year-old—that season he made 700 runs in four Tests against the West Indies—but he agreed that it would be less embarrassing if he announced the decision as being of his own volition.

It was only after helping Barnes draft a press release that Walters realised that he had done the association's dirty work for it:

> I walked out of Cricket House and got into my car and I was driving home when, for the first time, it hit me that perhaps the embarrassment wasn't necessarily going to be all on my side…I felt—for probably the only time in my life—a tremendous surge of anger and I had to stop the car and pull into the side the road and have a rest for a few minutes whilst I thought of the implications of what had happened to me that night.

Reminiscent of Arthur Morris's retrenchment seventeen years earlier, Doug Walters' demotion indicated how little had altered in the cloister of Australian cricket administration. But, unfortunately for the authorities, the world was changing.

'We Did What We Came to Do'

AUSTRALIA V INDIA, ENGLAND AND WEST INDIES

1967–69

One evening during the Fifth Test of the 1964 Ashes series, Jack Fingleton and Neville Cardus were returning from dinner in Soho when their cab became marooned in a theatre crowd. A young dandy rapped impatiently on their vehicle with the handle of his umbrella. As the writers watched in astonishment, their driver leapt out and flattened the fop with a quick one-two. When Fingleton summoned the courage to commend him, the driver replied: 'I've been watching that Lawry all day down at The Oval. I'm in no mood to put up with any more bloody nonsense.'

Watching Bill Lawry bat could have that effect. In the six years between his Test debut and his nomination as Australian captain, he had steadily stripped his game to the essentials. He was an international synonym for stubbornness, a butt of barrackers' humour. 'What's the matter, Lawry?' a Sydney Hillite hollered one day during a particularly strokeless stretch. 'Have you taken the Pill?'

Not that such comments bothered Lawry. He was conservative by disposition: a non-smoking, non-drinking, hard-working man who, long after giving up plumbing to sell whitegoods for Osco Hot Water and Malleys, retained his membership of the Plumbers' Union, just in case. He was never happier than when tending the loft at the rear of his Reservoir home, which housed eighty racing pigeons.

279

Nor did Lawry's bad press concern teammates. They knew him as the most insatiable cricketer of his day. He'd set out to conquer English conditions in 1961, and wasn't satisfied even when he had. One day late in the tour, he was forced to sit a match out. Colleagues discovered him watching solitarily from the stands. 'You never know when you might learn something,' he explained. When the *Himalaya* docked in Fremantle on its return, most players lolled about on deck. Not Lawry. He and Frank Misson were hailing a cab and driving to the WACA nets for a few hours' practice.

Lawry's rigid exoskeleton of defence was founded on physical courage. He batted against Griffith and Hall at Port-of-Spain with a broken hand. He batted against Peter Pollock and Mike Procter at Durban with a bandage round a head wound inflicted by Pollock. No-one left the crease less willingly. If there was only one stump standing behind him, bowlers griped, Lawry still needed persuasion to go. Ask Lawry today about a few of the umpiring controversies he was involved in, and you get a coy smile followed by a laugh.

Did he touch that seventh ball of the Brisbane Test in December 1965 from David Brown, the day he made 166? 'Weeell, it was a very good appeal, that's all I'll say. I'd've gone if he'd put his finger up. I probably got a little touch. But only [Jim] Parks went up, Brown followed him and [Col] Egar gave the only decision he could have given.' What about the hit-wicket for Victoria against England a few weeks later? 'Errr, well, that was out, because I could feel the stump as I pulled it. I ran down the other end rather sheepishly and, to my relief, the umpire gave me not out. I wasn't one for offering my dismissal as you know. Colin [Cowdrey] was very good about it. He just said: "Well, what about that?"'

Take Lawry off a cricket field and he was a friendly man, an incorrigible prankster, a gifted mimic. Nature had endowed him with a sardonic sense of humour. Fingleton once found Lawry by the pool in the West Indies reading an article about himself in *Wisden*. 'Don't think much of that,' Lawry commented. 'It's a bit too close to the truth.'

It was simply that, where cricket was concerned, Lawry bordered on fanaticism. As skipper of his state from December 1961, he became renowned for his intensity. Teammate Alan Connolly recalls: 'You'd room with Bill and he'd be up at 6am saying: "Jeez, we've gotta win the toss today." And I'd go: "Aww, go back to sleep Bill."' Lawry had little time for display. Playing his first Shield match, keeper Ray Jordon tried a little trick he'd developed in imitation of Godfrey Evans: flicking the ball sideways after taking it. The first hit slipsman Bob Cowper on the arm.

Lawry looked Jordon up and down and sniffed: 'You better save your circus tricks for Wirth's.'

The Australian captaincy further stiffened Lawry's spine, and sharpened the paradox of his nature. When the Indians were playing in Melbourne, he struck up a friendship with their vice-captain Chandu Borde, and invited him home for dinner. Yet a few weeks later, leading Australia in the Fourth Test at the SCG, Lawry refused Borde a runner. 'I knew he'd been hurt in Melbourne and that he'd gone into the game with the injury,' Lawry recalls. 'Those are the rules.'

THE MYSTERY MAN

Unlike Simpson, Lawry was unfortunate in the timing of his inheritance. The host of talented cricketers squeezed from the game in the two preceding years had left chasmal gaps in the Australian XI. Yet he could afford at least a little optimism. After all, what other country could unearth a cricketer of the singularity of spinner John Gleeson?

Gleeson seemed to step straight from a storybook: specifically the October 1950 edition of *Sporting Life*. For it was that issue that contained Dick Whitington's intriguing tale of the artifices of Jack Iverson. Gleeson, twelve-year-old son of a railway worker in the hamlet of Wiangaree, was hypnotised by the magic eye sequence of Iverson's mighty middle finger imparting its double-dealing tweak, and began experimenting with a tennis ball against a jacaranda tree.

Nothing came of Gleeson's speculation for years. When he flirted with Sydney grade cricket for Western Suburbs six years later, it was as a third and fourth grade keeper-batsman. And it was in the same capacity that, after moving to Tamworth a couple of years later, he reached the heights of touring New Zealand, Malaysia, Singapore and Canada with the Emu Club: an itinerant team comprising the cream of northern NSW players.

But one day in a game against Vancouver, Gleeson's captain trusted him to bowl his cryptic spin for the last over before lunch. He took a wicket, followed by another three, and finished the trip a bowler. After taking 4–80 for Gunnedah against one of Jack Chegwyn's missionary XIs in 1965–66, the wires began to buzz about this inscrutable country character who bowled leg breaks that looked like off breaks. Richie Benaud encouraged Gleeson to try his luck with Balmain and, despite having to undertake the 1000km trek from Tamworth to Sydney every weekend, he was swiftly recognised by state selectors as a unique talent. Twenty-three wickets in half a dozen Sheffield Shield matches earned him a berth on the auxiliary Australian tour of New Zealand in March 1967, where he was leading wicket-taker.

Gleeson did not spin the ball as sharply as Iverson, and was more effective with the wind on faster surfaces which compensated for his lack of pace off the pitch. Yet he was just as difficult to decode and, with his rustic roots and a straightforward job as a technician at West Tamworth Telephone Exchange, a far hardier character. As he mooched about the outfield in flannels of a decidedly autumnal shade, it was hard to believe he was a cricketer at all. *Daily Mail* columnist Ian Wooldridge decided that he resembled a man looking for his horse.

And somehow this slouching nonchalance added to Gleeson's aura. Although the after-effects of a bad case of mumps handicapped him against India, the number of times he beat the bat enlarged his myth. Even the soberest journalists classified him evocatively as 'mystery spinner John Gleeson'. And Gleeson was not about to disabuse them.

NEW KIDS ON THE BLOCKHOLE

As Australia bested India in all four Tests of 1967–68, supporters also looked hopefully on two local batting talents who seemed to have the world at their feet.

Like Gleeson, Dungog-born Doug Walters had first been spotted by Jack Chegwyn, and enticed to Sydney as a sixteen-year-old to play NSW Colts. He was an unprepossessing figure: wiry, flat-footed, unburdened by too many theories on batting. Yet even then, Alan McGilvray had felt a presence about him: 'The way he strode to the wicket…established him as something special. He had the same country roughness that Bradman had when he first came to the city.'

The Bradman tag stuck. From the moment Walters entered Test cricket as a nineteen-year-old against England at the Gabba in December 1965, he batted with the same unflustered intent of a man mowing his lawn. The Don was regularly invoked as he proceeded coolly to 155. The headline in Rupert Murdoch's new daily, the *Australian*, screamed: 'Toast of the Test'. Which he was: when Wally Grout ran a book on how many telegrams the youngster would receive by lunch the following day, Queenslander Peter Allan won with a bet of close to a hundred. Slazenger signed Walters at once on a £1000 annual contract.

Walters made 25 and 115 in the Second Test and, by the Third in front of his home crowd, was firmly installed as a national favourite. Coming out as nightwatchman at the SCG, David Sincock had an intimation of

Walters' new popularity: 'I remember I got a standing ovation and I couldn't understand why. Then I looked up at the board and saw Doug's name in the slot. I thought: "I can relate to that. I wish it *was* Doug out here."'

Quickly as he arose, though, Walters was gone again. His marble came up in the national service lottery and, though he suspected he might flunk the medical, the elderly examining doctor sagely observed: 'I've seen every game at the SCG since 1901. You're fit enough for me.' For the next two years, Private Walters of First Battalion at Holsworthy, 1 RAR, was free to play only a handful of times when on leave.

Not that it concerned Walters overmuch. He had come to cricket young and figured that, if he accumulated enough leave, could be back playing at least some Sheffield Shield cricket by 1967–68. In fact, he played the Third and Fourth Tests against India and reached the nineties in each before running short of partners.

There, Walters coupled with Australia's other great batting hope: Paul Sheahan, polished and presentable, every mother's idea of the young man they hoped their daughters would bring home.

Jack Sheahan, a North Melbourne cricket stalwart, desperately wanted his sons to succeed at the game. And when his older boy showed no aptitude, all paternal aspirations fell on Paul. The lad wore the burden lightly. He was a transparently talented all-round sportsman. At Geelong College, he excelled at cricket, baseball and Australian rules football. His feats even reached the ears of the prime minister. When Menzies came to open the school's new science block during Sheahan's 1964 tenure as school captain, he said: 'I've heard a bit about you, Paul. I understand that you're a handy cricketer. Why don't you come and play one of my matches?'

The following year, when Sheahan was studying at Melbourne University to become a teacher, an official-looking envelope arrived for him at Ormond College: an invitation to play in the Prime Minister's XI match against the MCC on 17 December. Dinner at the Lodge took the impressionable Sheahan somewhat by surprise: 'I was nineteen and stricken with a fairly Protestant attitude, so the banter and the chiacking of the prime minister took me aback a bit. As did the sight of Neil Harvey at the ground the next morning barely able to stand up.' He made an eye-catching 79, nonetheless, and was capped by his state a few weeks later.

Sheahan was hardly a versatile player. Though he drove thrillingly off the front foot, his back-foot technique was rudimentary. Yet during

Victoria's 1966–67 Sheffield Shield victory and an end-of-season trip to New Zealand with Australia's second-string side, that scarcely seemed to matter. A Test cap eight months later came almost as a birthright. The day of its receipt, Sheahan wore his baggy green to bed.

Against India, Sheahan assuredly looked the goods, averaging 45 from eight innings. And, as he and Walters combined at the SCG, it was possible to believe that Australia had lucked onto a newbred Bradman and a miniature McCabe. When they were named to tour England, Benaud joined the promoters. 'Paul Sheahan and Doug Walters arrive with a reputation that will take some living up to,' he wrote in England's *Cricketer*. 'I believe that by the end of the tour, they will have confirmed their rating as two of Australia's finest young players to travel overseas since the end of the War.'

A CHIP OFF THE OLD BLOCK

Gleeson, Walters and Sheahan notwithstanding, the Australian party selected to tour England in 1968 by Bradman, Ryder and Neil Harvey (who had replaced the retired Dud Seddon in September 1967) looked decidedly moderate.

The glut of premature retirements since 1965 had taken measurable toll. Only three of those from whom Lawry and his co-selectors Barry Jarman and Graham McKenzie would choose had previous experience on English soil. And some seemed exceedingly fortunate to be there at all.

One such was twenty-four-year-old South Australian Ian Chappell, ostensibly an all-rounder, though he averaged less than 24 with the bat and almost 100 with the ball from a dozen Tests. Young Australians have been picked for England on flimsier reputations, but not many.

Yet something about the infant Chappell recommended him. Perhaps it was his solid cricketing stock. His maternal grandfather was Victor Richardson, a buccaneering batsman and peerless all-round fieldsman who'd won four of his five Tests as Australian captain in South Africa in 1935–36, and father Martin was a first-grade player legendary for his abrasiveness. Perhaps it was Chappell's unquenchable self-confidence. He had approached first-class cricket with an assertiveness that older colleagues struggled to bridle. 'Young Chappell?' says Jarman. 'He was pretty brash, an expert on everything.' To keep Chappell quiet on one occasion, Jarman had to push him in a half-nelson into the wall of the Adelaide Oval dressing-room and warn: 'Shut up and speak when you're spoken to, son.'

It did little good. Chappell was ever the young man in a hurry, savouring the freedoms of a more permissive age. He drank, he swore, he patronised pubs and nightclubs. Much of Chappell's outspokenness he attributes to his Prince Alfred College education:

> There was freedom to think. You didn't necessarily get the shit belted out of you for asking questions, even disputing things. Certainly I never felt restricted about expressing my opinion, and I can remember saying at cadets a few times that what they were saying was bullshit. As a result, I was never any good at accepting things without question. It was also an era where younger people were starting to question older people. It's often said about cricket, and I'm sure it's true, that cricket reflects the society of the time. And I think that's what started to happen.

As Chappell was initiated into first-class cricket, his mentor was Les Favell. Since playing his last Test in 1961, Favell had become a tenacious and competitive Sheffield Shield leader famous for his freedom of expression. Sometimes while batting, he'd strike up a running commentary describing his mastery of the bowlers spiced with exhortations of his partner. On one occasion batting with Chappell against WA, he greeted the arrival of leggie Terry Jenner by smashing his first ball down the ground, then advised his protege: 'Don't think you're gonna see too much of this bowling, young 'un.'

Although Chappell was principally employed as a bowler on his first tour, to South Africa in 1966–67, he wasn't displeased when Favell told him on his return: 'You might be doing a lot of bowling for Australia, son, but you won't be bowling longer than four fucking overs for South Australia. Your job is to break a few partnerships and get a bloody lot of runs at number three.' For Chappell's deportment was somewhat deceptive. As a batsman, he was almost Lawry's equal in intensity: standing four-square at the crease, he bared his teeth at the bowler as though he wanted to take a bite from the ball.

Chappell was also deeply self-critical and, considering his initial Test performances, right to be so:

> I took a while to adjust to the standard. And I took a while to adjust to the idea of batting in different places. It was partly immaturity. And it also had something to do with playing on the Adelaide Oval, which was such a good pitch. It wasn't like I expected every pitch to be like Adelaide. It's just that I hoped they would be and I'd be a bit disappointed when they weren't.

Even after his first Test century at the MCG against India in January 1968, Chappell was dissatisfied. He was dropped three times—at 16, 52 and 82—and played many loose strokes. 'Once I got to 50 I started playing all sorts of shots,' he remembers. 'I was hitting balls in the air all over the place, which wasn't my game at all. Dunno what was going on in my head. I got away with it, but it wasn't a great innings. Once again I hadn't adjusted to the level.'

The turning point for Chappell was the last shield match of the season, not because of a breakthrough innings, but because of an embarrassing epilogue to his dismissal. Run out for 79, Chappell stalked up the steps in the old Members' Stand and discovered that he had been locked out. He had to sit outside and stew with his pads on, waiting for the twelfth man to come with the keys. 'You fucking idiot!' he thought. 'You've probably just cost yourself a trip to England.' Then, Chappell made a resolution to himself: 'If I do get picked, that's it. I'm gonna have a good time. It might be my last tour, so I might as well enjoy myself and not get uptight about cricket all the time.'

The Australians' Anzac Day departure date seemed somehow fitting. The XVII had an average age of twenty-four, little comprehension of their destination and faced overwhelming odds. Colin Cowdrey's team had just won brilliantly in the Caribbean, and London bookmakers rated their chances of regaining the Ashes at 5–4. Even worse, forty-nine of the Australians' first sixty playing hours were lost to rain, and they beat only one county in the first six weeks of the trip.

THE BIG STEAL

'Absolute bandits,' says Paul Sheahan of the 1968 Australians, and it is hard to disagree. By all benchmarks, it was the worst performed in nine decades of Australian Ashes tours: two batsmen only exceeded 1000 runs, two bowlers 50 wickets (compared to seven achieving each benchmark in 1948). And, for the first time since the award's inauguration in 1889, not one touring Australian featured in *Wisden's* select Five Cricketers of the Year. Yet the Ashes were retained. The Australians coalesced at Old Trafford and Lawry never surrendered that slender advantage.

It was the captain who made the two decisive gestures of that decisive opening Test. First, he won the toss on 6 June. Second, after shepherding his partners through the morning session, he seized the initiative from spinners Pat Pocock and Bob Barber with an unusually vivacious 81. 'I always felt that if you made 300 on the first day of a Test you were a good chance of winning,' says Lawry. 'So that was our plan. Pocock was a good bowler with a big reputation, and he would have done a bit of damage if he'd got among some of our younger players. But I played English spin pretty well, so I got after him.'

Walters (81), Sheahan (88) and Chappell (73) emulated Lawry so successfully that the tourists tallied 357 on a surface that promised to deteriorate and did so. Gleeson's prestidigitation and Cowper's niggardly offies rounded England up twice by the fifth morning, leaving Lawry to accept bouquets as architect of the 159-run victory.

There were still plenty of bumps on the route to retaining the Ashes—for the Second and Third Tests were drawn with the hosts in overwhelming command—and not all reflected well on the skipper. He lacked the public poise of the journalists Benaud and Simpson, and some found him autocratic. The gregarious Neil Hawke, for instance, found himself banished to the outfield after issuing a greeting as Cowdrey came in: 'Bill felt that to be fraternising with the enemy. And that was the way it was the whole tour. There was no consultation about fields. You were kept in the dark. I'd been used to captains like Favell and Benaud who involved you, whatever they were doing. With Lawry, you were just a pawn. As a bloke, Bill is a great fellow. As a captain, I thought he was hopeless.'

Ian Chappell was impressed with Lawry's tactical nous:

Bill was a far better captain than Simpson. He was very good putting pressure on batsmen. I always knew that the hardest runs I'd get every year would be against Victoria. You get a bit of a clue about a captain when you come out to bat: with Bill, you'd look around and there'd be someone in every position where you like to get off the mark. He didn't just place a field. He placed a field with you in mind.

But Chappell's faith was damaged on the last morning of the Fourth Test at Headingley on 30 July when Australia—starting the day 296 to the good—declined to declare and allow its bowlers a full day to bowl England out. Jarman was leading Australia in the match, for Lawry had broken a finger at Edgbaston. But the philosophy—for the draw meant that the Ashes were safe—seemed indisputably his.

Chappell came into the dressing-room at the close and tossed his cap loudly into his metal locker. 'If that's Test cricket you can stick it up your fucking arse,' he said.

Lawry tapped him on the shoulder. 'What's the trouble?' he asked.

'We didn't ever try to win that,' Chappell protested.

'We did what we came to do,' Lawry answered.

'What was that?' asked Chappell.

'We came to win the Ashes,' replied the captain. And that, for Lawry, was that.

'THAT PERKY LITTLE COOT'

Chappell, nonetheless, thrived under Lawry's leadership. He made runs: 1261 including a double hundred at Edgbaston. He relaxed: he even took to napping before innings. While it was Walters and Sheahan who had come to England with the handsome reputations, it was Chappell who truly excelled while they marked time: he topped the tour averages and impressed in every match, especially after Lawry promoted him to number four at Edgbaston. Going in with the score at 10 on that occasion, his 71 was an epiphany. 'Batting in that position, making those runs, gave me the confidence to go on,' he says. 'I'd made the mental adjustment back that day at the MCG, and the runs in that innings convinced me I had the ability to play at the top level.'

But it wasn't just his runs that set Chappell apart from his fellows. Increasingly, he stood out as a personality. Paul Sheahan says:

> Ian had inherited a lot of Vic Richardson's characteristics. He was a tremendously ebullient character, had an almost messianic belief in his own capacity, and was an exceedingly good partner. He was such a perky little coot that he'd drive the bowlers mad. If you weren't under control as an opposing bowler, he'd get you in. You'd start trying to knock his block off. Once he got in, you had to blast him out. He just set like concrete.

One incident especially impressed Sheahan, when the pair were involved in a run out at Manchester. Sheahan was palpably to blame and, in agitation, got out shortly after. What struck Sheahan was that Chappell never mentioned the mishap, not even in jest. 'He could easily have let loose on me, but he didn't,' says Sheahan. 'I was very upset, because I knew how terrible it felt to be run out in any circumstances. But to his credit, Ian never said a word.'

The steady transformation of Chappell's cricket on that tour had another far-reaching effect. The more assured he became of his own game, the more inclined he was to notice events around him. And two incidents towards the end of the tour left deep impressions.

One at Canterbury, when Australia played Kent, involved the team's manager, Australian board chairman Bob Parish. Chappell recalls: 'Bob was in the bar with us, which was very unusual for him, because he was usually off having a gin and tonic with the officials. In fact, we used to call him Bob the Snob. And we were drinking and telling stories and carrying on and, out of the blue, Bob says: "Ian, you'll have to curb your swearing if you're going to be captain of Australia."'

Chappell was startled, not only by mention of his name in the same breath as 'captain of Australia', but by the implication that language might be a criterion for election to that office. He replied deliberately: 'Bob, I've been swearing since I was about nine. My dad took me into dressing-rooms as soon as I was old enough to walk and he always said that, considering what I'd heard, it's a wonder I didn't start earlier. And why would I curb my swearing anyway? There's no way in the wide world I'll captain Australia.'

The other episode involved Bob Cowper. Chappell admired the Victorian, and revered his cricket brain. He also knew that stockbroker Cowper was fast losing interest in the game: touring on less than $100 a week was costing him heavily. Yet Cowper's performance at the end-of-tour dinner at the Waldorf stunned him. Chappell remembers:

> Cowps had been down to the City [London's financial centre] that day, and I think he'd been to lunch because, when he got back, he'd obviously had a few drinks. We were in the Waldorf bar from 5.30pm and Cowps said: 'Right, this fucking speaking tonight. I'm first cab off the rank. None of you fuckers jump up ahead of me. I'm having first say.'
>
> That was funny coming from Cowps. He wasn't that sort of guy. But before anybody could speak at the dinner, Cowps was on his feet and paid out on the board something terrible: payment, conditions, the lot. It had a big effect on me, because Cowps had always had a strong influence on my cricket thinking. I guess I started thinking about some of the things he said that night myself.

THE WORRELL TROPHY RETURNS

Despite a 226-run defeat on a quagmire in the Fifth Test at The Oval on 27 August, Lawry left England sanguine. 'Coming home, I really thought that we'd be a super side,' he says. 'Chappell had batted really well. Redpath was coming good. Sheahan and Walters were good players. We were probably just one fast bowler short.'

The home summer—a 3–1 usurpation of Garry Sobers' West Indians—continued the regeneration. The tourists were a team on the wane: Hall and Griffith were past their best, Sobers and Kanhai were feeling the strain of a decade's constant cricket. But they still required beating, and Lawry sunk all his efforts into the task. His 667 runs towered over the series. Keith Dunstan of Melbourne's *Sun* described him as 'delivering centuries with the reliability of a milkman delivering the daily bottle'. Phil Tresidder of the *Daily Telegraph* likened him even more momentously to Ayers Rock.

The Second Test at the MCG was a particular triumph. Sending the visitors in on a chilly Boxing Day morning, Lawry saw them bowled out for 200. He then spent almost seven and a half hours over 205. Retired prime minister Menzies poked his head into Australia's dressing-room and commented: 'Lawry! I believe that you're the only captain who's ever sent the opposition in, then made more than them on his own when he batted.'

What satisfied Lawry most, though, was the way that responsibility for victory was shared. Benefiting from some twenty-eight missed chances, Chappell made hundreds in the First and Second Tests, Walters hundreds in the Third, Fourth and Fifth (where he accomplished the unprecedented double of 242 and 103). And, though McKenzie remained the beating heart of Australia's attack with 30 wickets at 25, a further 60 were shared by the less lauded trio of John Gleeson, Alan Connolly and Eric Freeman. Gleeson, in particular, was intermittently mesmeric.

Australia made changes, all of them progressive. Redpath went down the list and compiled his maiden Test century. Barry Jarman was succeeded by the agile Brian Taber as keeper and the assertive Chappell as vice-captain. Perhaps Lawry was right. Perhaps this would be a super side.

A COUPLE OF VICS

For two Victorian cricketers long on the fringe of the Australian side, the West Indies series was particularly gratifying. And what was most remarkable about the rises of Alan Connolly and Keith Stackpole was that they did so in specialist roles to which they'd only latterly converted.

Connolly, educated at Geelong High School and trained as a plumber, had begun his Test career in Ian Meckiff's last Test at Brisbane in November 1963 as a tearaway paceman with a marathon approach. But a lingering back injury on the 1964 Ashes tour seemed to quash his career as soon as it began, for he missed Australia's next two journeys abroad.

Reflecting on his disappointments, however, altered Connolly's attitude to the game. He was a relaxed, self-sufficient sort, quietly confident he could handle Test cricket. What he required, Connolly decided, was a reputation for utmost reliability. He says: 'The worst thing about the injury [in 1964] was that everyone thought I was swinging the lead. After that I made a promise that never again would I leave the field in a first-class match, even if I was injured. I didn't want anyone to say I wasn't pulling my weight.' In the winter of 1967, Connolly reinvented himself: he slashed his run from twenty-one steps to eleven and bowled medium pace with a variety of grips, including a 'knuckle ball' from his days as a state baseballer.

Not everyone approved. 'It was criticised quite openly,' Connolly says. 'The comment was that I'd had it because I'd dropped my pace. But I went with it because people were now playing eight balls an over rather than three.' The upshot was a trip to England in 1968, where he took 26 Test wickets, and a regular spot against the West Indies at home, where he claimed a further 20.

As Connolly had been fading back into Test cricket, Stackpole had been fading out. A chunky, cheerful leg-spinning all-rounder, he had been capped against England and South Africa, fallen by the wayside in 1967–68 then missed the subsequent Ashes tour. It was a crushing blow.

Much had been expected of Stackpole. His father had been a pillar of the Collingwood Cricket Club and played 119 games of VFL football. In August 1963, on Bill Lawry's recommendation, no less than the prime minister had paid for Stackpole junior's leg-spin tuition under the great Clarrie Grimmett.

Stackpole recalls:

> I paid the air fare to Adelaide myself—which wasn't easy for a young man in my position—and arranged to stay for a week in the cheapest hotel I could find. Then I met Clarrie at Adelaide Oval. It was footy season so there were no nets and I remember pacing out twenty-two yards and setting up this rough net with him.
>
> Clarrie said: 'Listen. The most important thing for a leg spinner is to be able to have one ball that you can pitch on one spot again and again. Variation comes later.' He'd cut out this piece of cardboard, about ten inches by ten, which he stuck on a perfect length. Then he put on a blindfold and—I couldn't believe my eyes—he actually hit it with his first ball. 'That's what you've gotta do,' he said.

Menzies repaid Stackpole's £200 investment when the twenty-three-year-old returned home, and later attended his Test debut at Adelaide Oval in January 1966. But, over the next few years, Stackpole couldn't help feeling that he was letting people down. He seemed neither penetrative enough as a bowler nor consistent enough as a middle-order batsman, and his omission from the 1968 side brought a personal reassessment. He recalls:

That [1967–68] season was a real setback. I was so obsessed about getting to England that I let it get to me a bit. I started thinking about how other guys were getting on. I can remember listening to Alan McGilvray reading out the team and hearing the names John Inverarity and Les Joslin and knowing I hadn't been picked. I followed the tour from home in Melbourne, and it was a rotten feeling. Every time you heard a score on the radio, it hurt. I thought: 'I'm as good as those guys. I've gotta do something about it.'

When the West Indies visited Melbourne for their tour match on 15 November 1968, Stackpole saw it as make or break. He took his chance, making a stoical 110 in sticky heat, taking four wickets and four catches. But the transmogrification was incomplete. As the Australians were leaving the field in the Third Test at the SCG at 12.42pm on the second day, having dismissed the West Indies for 264, Lawry suddenly turned to Stackpole and said: 'I want you to put the pads on.'

Stackpole says: 'I'd been thinking: "You beauty. I can put my feet up for the rest of the day." Then Bill tells me to get ready to go in. I couldn't figure out what he was on about. I thought maybe he wanted a lunch watchman or something. But no, he wanted me to open.' Lawry's intuition was promptly rewarded: Stackpole passed 50 in his first three innings at the top of the order without curbing his natural belligerence, and steadily put behind him his unpleasant winter memories.

THAT MAN CHARLIE

Press watchers at the start of the 1968–69 series had made capital of the rematch between Australia and Charlie Griffith, their 1965 Caribbean bête noire. And the big Barbadian did touch off one of the rubber's few days of genuine drama at Adelaide Oval on 29 January 1969. Australia was 2–215 chasing 360 on the final afternoon when Griffith stalled in his action and demolished the non-striker's stumps, marooning Redpath by a yard. Though Griffith had issued no warning, umpire Lou Rowan was obliged to raise his finger.

There was a pregnant pause as Redpath started for the gate. He recalls: 'I just looked at him, said, "Well played," and walked off. It was a bit hard for me to argue with big Charlie, 'cos he was built like the trunk of a tree. But there was a bit of an atmosphere, and a few heads hanging down among the West Indies fielders as I went.'

Every subsequent Griffith delivery was accompanied by a chorus of boos, and scandalised occupants of the Giffen Stand showered him with abuse as he came in for tea. But Griffith continued to menace the Australians after the break. At one point he jostled Sheahan as the batsman hastened for a single. The youngster turned angrily, bat upraised, then thought better of it: 'I was big and brave in those days and when I turned around I was shaping up to whack him. Then I saw how big he was and beat a hasty retreat.'

The Australian chase eventually dissolved into a comedy of running errors. Sheahan was implicated in three run-outs—Walters, Jarman and Eric Freeman—which obliged him in the last twenty-five minutes to hold the fort with tailender Connolly. Again, Australia ended an Adelaide Test against the West Indies with its last pair anxiously fending off defeat. When Sheahan dead-batted the last ball from Griffith, he bolted from the ground for the sanctuary of the dressing-room. 'When I got there, I broke down in tears,' he recalls. 'I just couldn't handle it. I mean, we'd been cruising, and we'd ended up scratching an entirely dishonourable draw for which I felt to blame. No-one said anything in the rooms. No-one needed to. I could read their minds pretty well.'

The last word on Griffith, however, belonged to Lawry. When Sobers sent the Australians in on a soporific morning in the Fifth Test at the SCG, Griffith really hit his straps. But Lawry stood firm. Stackpole recalls:

> It was overcast and a really tricky pitch with a fair bit of moisture, and the ball was cutting and bouncing. Charlie had been bowling within himself most of the season, but this morning he really bent the elbow and started letting 'em go. In the first few hours, Bill was amazing. There were no chest pads in those days and thigh pads were light and small, but Bill kept taking them on the body, turning and copping them in the side and back. Probably the most courageous innings I've ever seen. When he came in at the end of the day and took off his shirt, his side was red raw, like he'd been in a boxing match rather than a cricket match.

Lawry batted eight hours twenty minutes for 151, Australia made 619 and won by 382 runs. A fortnight later Griffith was dropped, never to return.

PROS AND CONS

On \$190 a Test, none of the Australians who beat the West Indies so convincingly made themselves wealthy. But at the end of the series, two cricketers were about to take the largely untravelled route of making their game their profession: having signed three-year contracts during the

1968 Ashes tour, Graham McKenzie was set to play for Leicestershire, and Alan Connolly for Middlesex.

Their recruitments had been expedited by the counties' endorsement, for the 1968 season, of the Immediate Registration Rule (which obviated the need for overseas players to serve a period of residence in the counties they wished to represent). A dozen counties had immediately augmented their ranks with foreign stars—including Somerset, for whom Ian Chappell's twenty-year-old brother Greg made 1163 runs—and the move had been judged a great success. *Wisden* editor Norman Preston commented: 'The overseas players by their enterprise and natural approach brought a breath of life into the three-day match.'

What McKenzie and Connolly were undertaking was unique. Though Australian cricketers had long plied their trade in the leagues, those who'd tackled the English first-class game (like Colin McCool, Alan Walker and Bill Alley) had long left their Australian cricketing days behind. Here were two current Australian cricketers—and pacemen at that—about to undertake the routine of cricket for twelve months of the year. There was some wary local newspaper comment about the risks of the regimen, but nobody really knew what to expect, and no-one focused on the move's implication: that Australian cricketers had no choice but to play overseas if they wished to earn more than a subsistence income.

Both McKenzie and Connolly prospered in their initial seasons, each taking 74 wickets. Both earned far more than they had for Australia the previous season: McKenzie about £3000 and Connolly £1750 versus $2150 in 1968. They then flew to Madras with West Australian Laurie Mayne (who'd been playing in Scotland) to join the Australian team commencing its tour of India. So far so good.

By the time McKenzie and Connolly saddled up for their second English seasons in April 1970, however, they'd been playing almost continuously since October 1967. Soldiering on, McKenzie took 76 wickets. But, after starting well, Connolly broke down. He remembers:

> There'd been some criticism in 1969, because neither Graham nor myself had taken 100 wickets, and I was determined I would. I was going along nicely, with 17 after three games, when the hamstring blew up at Taunton. I missed ten games and really struggled for the rest of the season because there was never the opportunity to rest. What they injected it with in England was unbelievable as well: my hamstring calcified and curled into a knot in the back of my leg. I had to have an operation when I came home.

When it came to the home series against England in 1970–71, both bowlers were labouring. McKenzie played the first two Tests and achieved little, while Connolly sat them out. Both were picked for the Third Test at the MCG, abandoned due to rain. Finally, in the Fourth at the SCG, McKenzie took 1–139, Connolly 1–81. Both appeared jaded. Both had played their last Tests. Trying to earn a living in a semi-amateur cricket economy, they had bowled themselves into the ground.

While McKenzie continued in the Sheffield Shield until February 1974 and county cricket until September 1975, Connolly decided to finish with cricket before it finished with him: 'I'd really had a gutful of cricket at all levels, even the beach. I remember walking back during that [Fourth] Test, and I said to Stacky at mid-off: "I've lost it. My heart's not in it. It's time to give it away."'

'I Don't Think They Understood How Shattered We Were'

AUSTRALIA V INDIA AND SOUTH AFRICA
1969-70

In revisiting Australia's twin tours of India and South Africa in 1969–70, it pays to recall the series that Lindsay Hassett's team undertook against the Springboks twenty years earlier.

Those were cricket's days of grace. The journey began with a long sea voyage. The hospitality was lavish, the crowds polite, the games pleasant, the team harmonious. No-one was paid terribly much, but the spirit of the game was paramount. Guests and hosts, too, shared a strong kinship, as members of the Commonwealth who had recently fought a world war as allies. And if the inequities of South African society were intermittently visible, that was no concern of cricketers.

Bill Lawry's 1969–70 tourists travelled by air. The conditions they encountered in India were rarely less than appalling, the crowds often incendiary. The games in South Africa were rugged and ruthless, the Australian team there increasingly disunited. The players were paid even less in real terms than Hassett's had been, and the parsimony of the authorities was a cause of growing restlessness.

Nor could Australian cricketers assume any longer that they shared much with countries they were touring. India had been a republic since January 1950, and in recent years an unruly one, racked by frontier wars and internal strife. South Africa had become a republic in May 1961 and, over the course of the decade, an international pariah.

Cricket had been slow to comprehend the increasing fractiousness of its member nations. The few changes to its organisation had been cosmetic, like the July 1965 decision to change the name of the Imperial Cricket Conference to International Cricket Conference. But the stage was approaching where cricket could no longer count itself a secular state.

GOODBYE DOLLY

From its inception, the 1969–70 tour was shaded by politics. It had been conceived as a journey to the subcontinent, retracing the steps of Benaud's 1959–60 team. But the Pakistan Board of Control rescinded its invitation on 27 October 1968, citing strict exchange controls just introduced by the new military government of General Yahya Khan.

The South African Cricket Association immediately offered to fill the breach. The country had not played Test cricket since defeating Bob Simpson's Australians and was longing for sporting contact of any kind. The Australian Board of Control accepted. In retrospect, the decision is staggering. For, at that very moment, South Africa's government was obliterating the country's last vestige of credibility as a cricket destination: the so-called 'D'Oliveira Affair'.

A talented Cape Coloured all-rounder, Basil D'Oliveira was the outstanding 'non-white' South African cricketer of his generation. Arriving in England to play for Middleton in the Central Lancashire League in 1960, he decided to qualify for Worcestershire in 1964, and played for his adopted country within two years.

Though his presence in the England team dramatised the plight of other 'non-whites' in his native country, D'Oliveira did not become a cause célèbre until his inclusion two years later in the Fifth Test against Australia at The Oval as a late replacement for the unavailable Roger Prideaux. On 23 August 1968, sensationally, D'Oliveira made 158. Five days later, even more sensationally, his name was missing from the MCC party to tour South Africa in 1968–69.

The possibility that MCC selection policies had been influenced by political expediency scandalised many in England's cricket community. Nineteen MCC members resigned in protest. A chorus of calls for the tour's cancellation was orchestrated by the prominent cricketing cleric Rev David Sheppard.

In a bizarre twist three weeks later, however, the tour effectively cancelled itself: D'Oliveira was nominated as a replacement for the injured

Tom Cartwright. At a Nationalist convention in Bloemfontein on 17 September, South Africa's prime minister John Vorster deplored the decision: 'It's the team of the anti-Apartheid movement. We are not prepared to accept a team thrust upon us—it is a team of people who don't care about sports relations at all.' When the team's unacceptability was officially confirmed a week later by South African cricket officials, the tour was officially called off.

Yet so ardently did the majority of Australians hold to the maxim that sports and politics should not mix, that the board's decision to tour passed with scarcely a murmur. The cricketers, indeed, were preceded in August 1969 by an Australian rugby union tour. Even so, sportsmen visiting South Africa as the 1960s ended were on borrowed time.

TWO TOUGH GUYS

A dozen of the fifteen-man squad assembled at the Sydney Regent on 14 October 1969, where they were met by Alan Barnes and manager Fred Bennett, a mild-mannered ABC personnel officer. Also in attendance was Dr Brian Corrigan, who lectured on staying healthy in India and issued tablets. 'There were white ones and brown ones,' remembers Keith Stackpole. 'The brown ones we were supposed to take every day, the white ones occasionally, and we did religiously. I don't know what they were. They could have been steroids for all I know.'

A few players, in fact, weren't especially well already. Redpath had barely recovered from a bout of glandular fever. Taber was taking six cortisone tablets a day to combat asthma he had developed after the 1968 Ashes trip. But a tour was a tour, and there were some hardy men round them to take up any slack.

One was the barrel-chested South Australian all-rounder Eric Freeman. The son of a coxswain with the Department of Marine and Harbours, he still alternated summers of cricket and winters of football for Port Adelaide. He had topped his state's goalkicking in 1966 and, after arriving home from the Ashes tour on the day of the 1968 first semi-final, had played in the preliminary and grand finals. Accordingly, Freeman's cricket made up in gusto what it lacked in grace: his first Test scoring shot had been a six from India's Erapalli Prasanna in January 1968, his maiden first-class hundred four months later had taken an hour and a half.

Freeman's value to the Australian side was in his long spells of medium pace and fearless short-leg fielding. Lawry told him in England: 'Eric, you'll either go back to Australia a hero or a corpse.' And he almost finished up the latter during the Second Test against the West Indies at the MCG in December 1968, when Seymour Nurse pulled Gleeson straight into the back of Freeman's head. As Freeman crumpled, he heard Jarman shouting: 'He's out! He's out!' Freeman wondered: 'Is he talking about me?'

He wasn't: Stackpole had caught the rebound thirty metres away. In typical fashion, Freeman stayed on the field until Australia had won, only afterwards complaining of a headache.

Perhaps the side's most remarkable member of the side, however, was thirty-three-year-old deputy keeper Ray Jordon of Victoria. His way to Test honours had been barred for years by the likes of Grout, Jarman and Taber, but he had never given up hope of Australian selection: born the same day as Jarman, he had enhanced his eligibility by sawing a year off his age.

Jordon was known universally as 'Slug', not a comment on his indolence but testament to his apparent indestructibility. For, just before his nineteenth birthday while on National Service in the RAAF at Laverton, Jordon had been shot point-blank by another sporting soldier, Geelong full-back Harry Herbert, whose rifle had mistakenly been loaded with live ammunition.

Jordon recalls:

We were on manoeuvres, Blue Army versus Red Army, and to signify that you'd captured another soldier you were meant to fire a blank. I ran into Harry and fired my gun into the ground, and this dirt flew up in our faces. We must've been a bit slow because we didn't realise straight away that the armourer had actually given us live ammo. But Harry says: 'Oh I'll get you, ya cunt.' And he fires his gun at me from about ten feet away. When I saw him raise his gun I turned round, and this bullet hit me in the back, ran round my ribs and lodged in my guts. No-one really knew what had happened. In fact they all ran to see if Harry was OK, because he fainted when he saw my blood. Eventually they realised I'd been shot and took me to Laverton Hospital.

An official inquiry demoted Jordon's sergeant, and the armourer deserted. But Jordon achieved a certain celebrity when the services newspaper published a story about 'the man who walks round with a slug inside him'. And eight weeks later, he was back playing football for Coburg (he played ninety-nine games there as rover).

A loud, cheeky and partisan Victorian, Jordon played state cricket with similar flintiness. When a Laurie Mayne bouncer shattered his jaw at the WACA in November 1965, Jordon missed only one Shield match. There

was also about Jordon an appealing homespun naivety. When finally a
Qantas official arrived at the team meeting to explain travel arrange-
ments and collect passports, Jordon muttered ingenuously to his
Stackpole: 'Eh Stacky? What's a passport?'

Stackpole laughed. Jordon was such a humourist. Then he saw that
Jordon wasn't joking. Stackpole took his sheepish mate to see Barnes.
The secretary turned luminously purple.

A Passage to India

The Australians' first impressions of India echoed those of Benaud's team
ten years before: dirty, poor and slightly scary. As a coach took them from
Madras Airport to the Connemarra Hotel, Stackpole studied the reactions of teammates and his own:

> You could see the mouths of the blokes drop. You could see them think-
> ing: 'What's happening here?' It was close to midnight, there was hardly any
> light, and it was pelting with rain. Yet I could see people sleeping in the
> street. 'Hey, look at that bloke.' We got to this old-style, high-ceilinged
> place, a little bit cold, and suddenly we realised we were in a country
> where, even at the hotel, everyone was coloured. We were virtually fright-
> ened to leave our mates and go to our rooms.

After a warm-up match against West Zone at Poona, thousands greeted
the Australians' arrival for the First Test in Bombay. Thousands more
watched the Australians practise. The players thought the local habit of
garlanding them with jasmine and marigolds rather charming, until they
realised that they also invited a penumbra of flies and mosquitos. They
also thought the idea of staying in the digs at Brabourne Stadium pretty
nifty, until they studied the dormitory. The beds were three-inch kapok
mattresses on wooden bases, the air-conditioning almost unusable. 'You
couldn't sleep with it on because it was as noisy as a diesel truck,' says
Paul Sheahan. 'Then you couldn't sleep because it was so damned hot.'

The clincher was the food. They'd listened to Corrigan's warnings
with mounting alarm, but now found that he'd understated the situation.
Chappell recalls:

> One evening, some of the players were looking for toasted sandwiches at
> the stadium. They were told that the cook had gone but that there was
> some bread in the kitchen. Brian Taber went downstairs and came back
> with a loaf under his arm. 'If you want to eat another meal in this place,
> don't go down and look at the kitchen,' he said. Being curious, a couple of
> us went to investigate and we found cats in the refrigerator, cats running

over the uncovered food, green slime on the floor, barred windows with no glass, and a rubbish tip with an unbelievable stench outside the window.

Test cricket in India, the team also discovered, could be excrutiating. Outfields for the First Test were shorn to a stubble, the pitch was of reddish soil laid on bricks, and the hard Indian cricket balls hit the bat like armour-piercing bullets. India's pawky off-spinner Prasanna frequently employed seven leg-side fielders, and batting any length of time was like walking through Death Valley in the noonday sun.

Replying to India's laborious 271 in half as many overs, Stackpole spent almost five hours over a hundred gripped by cramps and dehydration. Redpath felt the after-effects of his glandular fever as he made 77: 'The first few runs I took in India almost killed me. I was panting and puffing even when I was running singles. I thought I'd never see out the tour.' Walters, who helped him add 118 in three hours, found the mirrors that the crowd flashed in his eyes a sore distraction: 'The mirrors worried us a bit, especially when we were batting, but we soon found that the best idea wasn't to complain, because if we made complaints to the umpire it only incited the crowd to do it more.'

But the Australians sensed their grip on the match tighten as they secured a 74-run first innings lead on the fourth morning. They clustered round the bat, appealing insistently, and hastened through their overs. When umpires Shambu Pan and Gopalakrishnan denied him another over before lunch, Lawry remonstrated by throwing his cap to the ground.

After the break, the Indian innings began to expire. Connolly bowled economically, Gleeson enigmatically and twenty-four-year-old off spinner Ashley Mallett savoured his first taste of Indian conditions. Born in Sydney and raised in Perth, he had forged a path to Test cricket by heading for Adelaide in the winter of 1967 with his leg-spinning pal Terry Jenner to take a job in the local hospitals department and take advantage of counsel from the sapient Clarrie Grimmett. The effect had been immediate: a tour berth to England in 1968, a cap in the Fifth Test at The Oval, and Colin Cowdrey's wicket with his fifth delivery.

A tall, myopic figure, more reminiscent of a book-keeper than a bowler, Mallett was known for long silences and an occasionally spectacular lack of co-ordination. At the Poona Turf Club the week before, for instance, he had started a frame of billiards, taken careful aim with his cue…and torn an agonising zigzag straight through the felt. Yet, with his height, he used the breeze like a weathervane, and now bowled maiden after teasing maiden as India declined rapidly to 7–89.

The Australians finally struck resistance when left-hander Ajit Wadekar was joined by tailender Srinivasaraghavan Venkataraghavan. The crowd, which had been incensed by the fragility of India's batting, settled for fifty minutes to encourage them. But at 114 Venkat executed a rude cut at Connolly that travelled through to the keeper missing the bat by a foot. To the bemusement of Taber and first slip Chappell, Stackpole hollered an appeal from gully. To their further bemusement, umpire Pan raised his finger. Taber laughed to Chappell: 'Bit of a roughie, eh!'

'HELL, WE NEED A WICKET'

Venkat, a little disconcerted, went on his way. In the Australians' celebratory huddle, Taber cheerfully chided Stackpole: 'You only appealed 'cos you're a Victorian.'

'I thought I heard something,' said Stackpole

'Well, it wasn't his bat,' Taber replied. 'He missed it by a foot.'

What they weren't to know, however, was that the spectators' disappointment was being turned to disenchantment. Ears pressed to their transistors round Brabourne, listeners heard the judgment of commentator Devraj Puri that the bat had not even neighboured the ball. As the Australians returned to their positions, bottles began to litter the outfield. Outfielders Walters and McKenzie moved in to stay out of range.

As Connolly continued to Prasanna, the demonstration worsened: hessian round the tennis courts behind Brabourne's East Stand was ignited. Smashed chairs and awning covers were incinerated in the North and Bombay Cricket Association Stands. Smoke began blowing across the arena. Lawry told umpires Pan and Gopalakrishnan he wanted to go on, for his side was close to a handsome victory. Connolly agreed. 'I reckon I can clean up the tail with this smoke,' he said. 'They won't be able to see the ball.' Others were less keen. From the press box at square leg traipsed the septuagenarian scorer Jehangir Irani and *Indian Express* reporter Ghulam Menon, who protested that they could no longer see the game through the haze. The umpires and Lawry turned them back.

But there were shortly other intruders to worry about. Mallett pointed out a mob hurling their collective weight against a mesh barrier in front of the smoking East Stand. Lawry ignored them. As riot police attended to the displaced spectators huddled round the sightscreen, he again insisted that play continue. Even when his deputy Chappell suggested that the dressing-room might be a safer vantage, all the captain would say was: 'Hell, we need a wicket badly.'

Five minutes before stumps, he got one: Mallett bowled Prasanna to leave India 9–125. But, after another over, stumps were drawn: by the Australians rather than the umpires just in case their withdrawal was impeded. Walters, arriving late, secured a bail. 'I'll try and poke someone's eye out with it,' he explained drily.

The local police chief advised the Australians to remain on the ground while insurgents in the Members' Stand were removed, and it wasn't for another twenty minutes that riot police began escorting them through a hail of missiles to their Brabourne quarters. Gleeson was hit a stunning blow on the back of the head by a flying bottle, while Lawry was narrowly missed by a wicker chair. The mob's most persistent members then laid siege to the dressing-room and broke every window, encouraging further retreat to the toilet block. Finally—having given all interlopers five minutes to leave the ground—the police chief ordered a lathi charge across the arena to evict the last troublemakers. The official casualty list numbered fifty injured.

The Australians were advised not to leave Brabourne that evening, not that anyone was planning a night on the town. An eight-wicket victory was completed next morning. No-one felt much like celebrating.

LOSING THE PLOT

Following riots during Tests at Calcutta in January 1967 and Hyderabad just a month before, the insurrection at Brabourne caused deep local self-examination. K. N. Prabhu of the *Times of India* lamented: 'It is a novel and sad state of affairs that the violence latent in our public life should spring to the surface on our cricket fields.' Henceforward, the Australians would be chaperoned everywhere by a contingent of police and armoured cars.

The threat of violence, however, was not nearly so confronting as the quotidian experiences of touring life. Lawry bemoaned the absence of Australian journalists to tell his side of the story: remarkably, not one Australian media organisation had sent a correspondent. Although the drawn Second Test at Modi Stadium passed without incident, tempers frayed again as the team went to the Kanpur Terminus to catch the 8pm train to Jullundur for their game against North Zone.

There seemed to be thousands of people there, both well-wishers and itinerants looking for shelter, and the Australians had to cart their cricket cases and luggage over four tracks and through hundreds of beggars in order to reach the platform. Lawry and Bennett had requested a hot meal for the team on the train but, when porters freighted the platters aboard, they revealed only cold chicken and cold vegetables: neither of which the Australians could eat. Lawry grabbed the local liaison officer, seething: 'We can't eat this food! Take it away!'

Ian Chappell kept a level head. Leading Australia for the first time at North Zone, he belted 164 in three hours including 24 in an over from Ashok Gandotra. And four days later he stood tall amid a jerry-built Australian total of 296 in the Third Test at Delhi's Feroz Shah Kotla, making 138 in four and a half hours.

But it wasn't enough to stem the tide of Prasanna and Bishen Bedi. Before a increasingly frenzied crowd, they spun Australia to a seven-wicket defeat. The not-out pair of Wadekar and Gundappa Viswanath performed a lap of honour with their captain, the Nawab of Pataudi, while the Australians traipsed from the field with the sound of firecrackers ringing in their ears.

THE SEEDS OF REBELLION

It was the Australians' lowest ebb. They slunk away to Gauhati for a game against East Zone, where they were picked up from the airport by a truck for the thirty-mile drive to another festering hotel. Half a dozen players were ill to varying degrees. Stackpole woke at 6am on the morning of the match feeling queasy and, crawling to the toilet, vomited violently all over the bathroom floor. His roommate, Sheahan, had Bennett fetch a doctor, but hotel staff didn't clean the mess for another twelve hours. Fred Bennett gave a speech to the local dignitaries oozing diplomatic unction: 'And may I say that Australia genuinely looks forward to playing a Test match in Gauhati.' Fifteen cricketers quietly but audibly chorused: 'Bullshit!'

The Australians' next stop, Calcutta, was in social and political turmoil. Hundreds of thousands of refugees had poured into East Bengal after floods in East Pakistan, exacerbating its usual overcrowding, while the city had been wracked by the indiscriminate violence of Maoist extremists called the Naxalites.

The Australians soon learned, in fact, why Calcutta was known as 'the city of dreadful night'. At 6.30pm on the day of their arrival, the Great Eastern Hotel was ringed by 3000 demonstrators, with placards protesting the presence of former National Serviceman Doug Walters: they believed, mistakenly, that he had served in Vietnam. Every window in the hostelry was systematically smashed. Practice at Eden Gardens then proved impossible. The team was virtually overrun by a crowd of 20,000, whom not even the baton-wielding paramilitaries of the Eastern Frontier Rifles could repel.

Yet it wasn't India at whom the players directed their discontent. Touring such a country, in fact, could be fascinating, and not without its humour. Connolly, McKenzie and Stackpole once boarded a cab which lurched away, evidently on the power of only one cylinder. 'Jeez mate,' said Connolly. 'What's wrong with your car?'

The taxi driver responded philosophically: 'Mister, there is nothing wrong with my car except that it was made in India.'

The Australians' real beef was with their board. It was hard not to believe that the authorities had deliberately stinted on costs. Several players who would align with Kerry Packer's breakaway World Series Cricket eight years later—Chappell, Walters, Mallett, McKenzie, Stackpole and Lawry—look back on the trip as a watershed. Stackpole says:

> India was a fabulous place to tour. Everyone was really friendly and mad about their cricket. But I reckon the seeds were sown then of the WSC revolution. The conditions we toured under were appalling. Some of the hotels were so pathetic you wouldn't have had a pig in them. And we all started to wonder: was it the board trying to save money?

Such recalcitrant thoughts were checked by the beginning of the Fourth Test, where the Australians moved inexorably into a winning position over the first three days. Complemented by Mallett, McKenzie bowled skilfully in the heavy, misty air. Then Chappell, adding a cubit to his stature with every innings, batted four and a half hours for a poised 99. Finally, last man Connolly hoisted four sixes in a quarter of an hour, using a bat he'd bought in Bombay from former Test spinner Bapu Nadkarni. With a 123-run first innings lead, Lawry scented victory. But in India, nothing was so straightforward.

DEATH IN THE MORNING

The strife of Tuesday 16 December began as the Australians were poking gingerly at their breakfasts. With only 8000 tickets available, queues of 20,000 outside Eden Gardens quickly became a stampede. Police waded in with lathis and tear gas, leaving six dead and 100 injured. The tourists were stunned. Lawry and Bennett drew up a message of sympathy. But the tone had been set for an unruly day. There was a palpable tension in the ground when play began and, as Connolly and an inexhaustible

Eric Freeman barged through the Indian middle order, the atmosphere grew uglier.

The butt of the spectators' anger became Pataudi, who continued a wretched run with the bat by pulling injudiciously at Mallett. His exit was followed by a volley of missiles from the Ranji Stand and, after four deliveries had been bowled in Australia's second innings chase of 39, all hell broke loose. Spectators from the stand, discomforted by bottles and rocks thrown from above, spilled onto the field. Two thousand police were unable to contain the bombardment, and play ceased. Lawry and Stackpole stood guard over the stumps.

As the Ranji Stand's refugees were steered across the ground to a less populated quarter, a dozen photographers rushed to the centre of the ground. One, Miren Adhikary of the Bengali daily *Basumati*, advanced on the Australian openers shouting: 'Riot! Riot! Photos!'

'Get off the wicket!' Lawry shouted back. 'Go on, get off it.' He chased Adhikary off the pitch and gave him a shove to indicate he wanted no-one on the ground. The photographer went down like a decked prizefighter. Adhikary's colleagues delightedly captured the tableau, which did not flatter Australia's captain.

Order was restored after twenty minutes and, with the complicity of an apprehensive Pataudi, the arrears was cleared in another half-hour. With the scores tied, Lawry advised Stackpole quietly: 'Pat's just told [Subroto] Guha to bowl you a full toss. Just push it away for one.'

'Gee,' thought Stackpole. 'That's the first time anyone's ever told me he's going to bowl a full toss. I'll have a go at it.' With some relish, Stackpole pulled it for four.

'You bastard!' Lawry laughed as they made for the dressing-room.

'Bill,' Stackpole replied, 'you woulda done exactly the same thing!'

'Hang on Stacky,' said Lawry as they neared the pavilion. 'This could get ugly. We'd better protect Pat.' He called to Pataudi: 'Hey Pat! Follow us!' They flanked the Indian captain as he walked through a hail of abuse, spit and wicker chairs on the way to the dressing-room.

But it wasn't over yet. Back at the Great Eastern Hotel, Lawry and Bennett decided to throw a small team celebration. To their amazement, twenty Indian journalists turned up in expectation of joining in. A harassed Bennett had to explain that the function was private. Under protest, the reporters repaired to the hotel's Permit Room (where guests and visitors equipped with a permit could buy liquor).

Dinner broke up around 9pm, and a few players went out: Lawry and Bennett went to the movies; Connolly and Jordon to see Geoff Lewis, a

British jockey racing in India for the English winter. Most, though, retired to their rooms. And later in the evening a whole posse of reporters huddled outside the door to the room occupied by Freeman and Mallett.

Freeman recalls:

> A few of us were sitting around having a few drinks with not much on, when there was this knock at the door. It's this photographer wanting to take our pictures. Well, I told him to piss off. Then he starts knocking again, so I tell him to go away a second time. Third time, he just opens the door, goes flash bang, and runs off down the stairs. Well, that was it. We'd really had enough. I set off after him, and I ran down three flights of stairs. When I caught up, I grabbed his shirt, but it just came off in my hand, so he got away.

By the time Connolly and Jordon returned at midnight, the hotel was in uproar. 'We had a helluva job getting back into the hotel,' Connolly says. 'It was all boarded up and we spent ages trying to convince these guards that we were Australian cricketers.'

Having won a Test, the Australians had inadvertently lost a public. The next day's newspapers were full of Lawry apparently coshing Adhikary, and the story that 'McKenzie and Redpath' had set upon other innocent members of the photographic profession calling them 'bloody Indian dogs'. Calcutta's English-language daily the *Statesman* belied its masthead in a report of Adhikary's 'disgraceful' treatment: 'Lawry…could not keep his temper in check and knocked over the poor photographer and struck him with his bat. It was a horrible sight, and one was led to wonder what Lawry thought himself to be. Would he have done the same in England or South Africa?' Bennett, meanwhile, was wearily drafting a statement explaining the true circumstances of the hotel fracas.

It was futile. As the Australians set off to Dum-Dum Airport for their flight to Bangalore, their bus ran a 200-metre gauntlet of stone-throwing demonstrators while it ascended a hill just outside the city centre. Lawry was stunned:

> Before we had time to collect ourselves, rocks the size of half house bricks were smashing into both sides of the bus, shattering nearly all the windows…The driver tried to accelerate up the hill while all members of the team flung themselves on the floor wondering whether they would be dragged out and stoned to death if the bus stalled.

One rock flying through an open window just missed Freeman's head. 'I felt it as it went past,' he says. 'If it had hit me I would have been history.'

With unusual presence of mind, he collected the projectile as a souvenir, joking that he would give to Sir Donald Bradman as a Christmas present.

The tour was becoming farcical. As the Australians prepared to play South Zone, they heard that the Press Photographers' Association secretary Shyamal Bose was threatening a strike. In the event, photographers covered the match wearing black armbands. Lawry was wondering what he could do wrong next and found out on the last day when, as he and Gleeson saved the game, he tried to waste some time by claiming that a woman in a bright sari by the sightscreen was distracting him.

Repercussions followed when the Australians left the next day:

> On the flight from Bangalore to Madras I asked the beautifully gowned Indian air hostess for a cup of tea. She replied politely, but with a trace of feeling, that she wasn't sure whether I would be getting a cup of tea. When I asked why, she produced a newspaper which suggested that, when I had objected to the woman in the sari standing in front of the sightscreen at Bangalore, I had insulted India's national dress and Indian woman-hood...Denied my cup of tea, I should have realised by then that this was not going to be my tour.

A HELLUVA TOUR

From a cricketing perspective, the tour was a triumph for Lawry. When Australia won the Fifth Test in Madras by 77 runs over Christmas 1969, thanks to a hundred from Walters and 10–144 from Mallett, it completed a notable 3–1 victory. Australia had not won an away series so conclusively for a decade.

Yet the trip had been a public relations disaster. Where the approachable and animated Benaud had commanded a rapt Indian following in 1959–60, the remote and ruthless Lawry had been followed everywhere by catcalls and jeering. Some spectators at Madras had even dangled him in effigy from a noose. Detractors looked back on Lawry's attitude at Bombay as having set the tone of the whole series. The Indian Wadekar wrote: 'With a little graciousness, the unfortunate episode at the Brabourne Stadium could have been avoided. We had only one wicket left and there was a whole day to go. Yet, with a pall of smoke blowing across the field and the umpires unable to communicate with the scorers, Lawry insisted on continuing the game. The riotous incidents of the last half-hour left their mark on the rest of the series.'

In hindsight, Lawry agrees:

I think any criticism I got in India was probably right. Normally I take those sort of things in my stride, but I think I had an attitude that had been ingrained in me by Peter Burge and Col McDonald, who'd told me about their tours there. So I was a bit outspoken when I shouldn't have been, because I was really on edge to make sure that the food was adequate and the hygiene was all right. Which it wasn't. It was disgraceful really and I think we were badly let down. It was probably all right if you were a drinker on that tour because at least you could write yourself off. But the Redpaths and Lawrys and Stackpoles and Sheahans, who weren't big drinkers, who were just trying to be dedicated sportsmen, found it hard. Relaxing was nearly impossible.

Nor was there scope to relax now. Though the Australians cheered lustily as they left Bombay for Nairobi on New Year's Eve, they still had another dozen first-class matches including four Tests against South Africa ahead, and did not realise how depleted conditions in India had left them. All the team were underweight, sick or both: Graham McKenzie had shed six kilograms and felt woefully lethargic; Alan Connolly had come down with bronchial pneumonia after ill-advisedly choosing fish at the team's Christmas dinner. The ABC's Alan McGilvray was shocked when he met the team's BOAC VC-10 at Johannesburg's Jan Smuts Airport on 2 January 1970: 'They looked haggard. Their eyes seemed to be standing out of their heads and some of them looked positively yellow.'

Lawry indulged in some old-fashioned boosterism on his arrival. 'You will find a tremendous improvement in the batting of Ian Chappell,' he told the local press. 'In my opinion he is equal to any batsman in the world on all types of wickets.' But there were more worrying signs than he was prepared to admit. When McGilvray walked past the Australian enclosure at Pretoria's Berea Park four days later, he was surprised to find most of the team asleep on benches out the front just half an hour after the start of play.

The contrast between guests and hosts could hardly have been more acute. South Africa had not played a Test for three years, and their hopes of completing a scheduled tour to England in May 1970 were dwindling. Protestors mobilised by the dissident South African Non-Racial Olympic Committee had given a foretaste of opposition to come by disrupting a seven-match private tour of the UK organised by cricket philanthropist Wilf Isaacs in July 1969 with sit-ins and vandalism. And a newly formed ginger group challengingly titled Stop the Seventy Tour was in the process of hounding Dawie de Villiers' Springbok rugby tourists the length of the British Isles. Local journalist Eric Litchfield overheard a senior cricket official in the welcoming party for the tourists muttering: 'I wonder if we are not welcoming the last cricket touring team to South Africa for a long, long time.'

If this *was* it, South Africans would make the most of the situation. The cricket would be a national advertisement. The South African Cricket Association even issued an edict that its first-class cricketers should eschew long 'hippie-style' haircuts. 'We regard cricket as a game for gentlemen,' the association said. 'The players should look and be dressed like gentlemen.' And, studying their heavy advance bookings, the SACA's Jack Cheetham sought out Bennett during the Australians' second match against Griqualand West on 13 January 1970 to propose a Fifth Test at Johannesburg. Bennett forwarded the proposal to the board, and its 29 January meeting consented on condition that all fifteen tourists accepted an offer of $200 on top of their $2800 tour fee. The offer would come close to derailing the whole tour.

'WE'VE GOT THE BASTARDS'

By the time the board had sanctioned a Fifth Test, Australia had lost the First by 170 runs. As with the Kidson kerfuffle three years before, there'd been cause to doubt the competence of the umpiring. But the wealth of talent at Springbok skipper Ali Bacher's disposal—the Pollocks, Barlow, Procter, Goddard plus two new caps in Barry Richards and Lee Irvine—was as obvious as the Australians' weary haplessness.

The tourists were hardly in the mood for the meeting to which they were summoned in the lounge of Johannesburg's Casa Mia Hotel on the morning of 1 February (the rest day of their match against Transvaal). Bennett and Lawry explained the SACA proposal: the final two first-class matches against Western Province and Orange Free State would be scrapped and the tour extended by two days to accommodate an additional Wanderers Test.

The players were ambivalent. Paul Sheahan says: 'I thought it was astonishing. Again, I think it was indicative of the board's desire to make as much money as they could, to milk the situation. I don't think they had any understanding of just how shattered most of us were by that stage.' At the same time, though, one did not routinely gainsay the board. If it decreed a further Test, what power did the players have to stop them?

At least some, thought vice-captain Ian Chappell: prolongation of the tour would entail extension of the Australians' contracts. In fact, he believed, this was a chance to show the board exactly what the players thought of being dictated to, and of the dismal fleapits they'd just encountered on their tour of India. 'For once,' he thought, 'we've got the bastards.'

'Two hundred dollars?' he said. 'That's bullshit. The board can get fucked. If they want us to play, we should get at least $500.'

'There's no chance the board will agree with that,' said Bennett.

Lawry intervened: 'It's all-in or all-out. Even if only one of us is against the Test, it can't go ahead.'

As the meeting broke up, Chappell learned that he wasn't alone. Walters, Gleeson and McKenzie privately informed Chappell that they were also opposed to playing an additional Test for so derisory a sum. Brian Taber didn't want to stick his neck out—he'd just been appointed to head a national coaching program under the auspices of the Rothmans National Sports Foundation—but he also assured Chappell he was against the proposal. When the Australians arrived at Durban's Eden Roc Hotel a couple of days later for the Second Test, Bennett announced that the Fifth Test proposal had been shelved.

Keith Miller, for one, applauded the conscientious objectors: 'The Australians lost the First Test, but won their greatest victory in years here today. They thumbed their noses at the Australian Board of Control by deciding against playing a Fifth Test…The days of playing for the honour and glory of your country have long passed…Hats off to Bill Lawry and his tired bunch of boys.' But the fight wasn't over yet.

A TEAM DIVIDED

What had been a landslide at Cape Town quickly became an avalanche at Durban on Thursday, 5 February. Only Lawry's subtle subterfuges prevented twenty-four-year-old Richards, a handsome blond athlete from Durban High School, achieving a hundred from scratch before lunch. And there was nothing Lawry could do, once Freeman had bowled Richards for a chanceless three-hour 140, about Graeme Pollock.

Paul Sheahan recalls:

When Pollock came to the wicket, it felt like he said: 'Well you've seen the apprentice. Now have a look at the master.' Richards did bat beautifully, but Pollock smashed us all over the shop. It was amazing really. You could understand how a bloke like Sobers hit so hard, because his backlift was this enormous arc. But Pollock never seemed to lift his bat up and hardly followed through. At one stage, Garth McKenzie was bowling with four in the covers and Pollock was still beating them. The only good thing about it was that you didn't have to run far, because the ball would career back off the fence.

The twenty-five-year-old left-hander reached 50 inside an hour. McKenzie was exhausted, the ball leaving his hand with the force of a meringue. Lawry set Freeman a 7–2 off-side field and still Pollock penetrated it. At one stage near stumps, the scoreboard jammed: it seemed that not even the statisticians could keep up. At the close it registered 160 not out in four hours.

Almost 16,000 watched the carnival resume on Friday. At only one stage, when Connolly bowled a frugal spell at Pollock in the 190s, was the batsman delayed. Connolly recalls:

> I had two short legs and I bowled round the wicket to him so the only shot he could really play was to mid wicket which we had blocked. I bowled about five maidens on the trot and he was on 196 and looking a little nervous. Then finally I overpitched one. Soon as I released it, I said: 'Oh shit!' And he smashed it back past me at 2500 kilometres an hour, and a split-second later it hit the sightscreen.

After batting just shy of seven hours for 274 with 172 in boundaries, Pollock finally belted his 401st ball back to Stackpole. And, when Australia replied to South Africa's 9–622, Barlow knocked them bow-legged with three wickets in 15 deliveries, and had them following on 465 in arrears early on Saturday afternoon. After further maladroit umpiring from Carl Coetzee and Gordon Draper—though it affected the margin rather than the result—the Australians succumbed by an innings and 129 runs at 5.18pm on Monday.

By now, however, the tour was proving as difficult off the field as on. The Australians were aggrieved by the umpiring but, when they sought to have Coetzee replaced, the SACA appointed him for the final two Tests. They felt they were getting a raw deal from the press, but no-one seemed to be listening. Stackpole and Sheahan were downstairs at the Eden Roc Hotel one evening during the Australians' game against Natal when Keith Miller came in and asked: 'So, how'd you boys get on today?'

'We did pretty well, thanks,' Sheahan replied. 'Didn't you go?'

'No,' said Miller. 'I went to the races.'

'Did you write a story?' Stackpole asked.

'Course I did,' Miller answered. Then, studying the players' stunned expressions, he added: 'You boys don't bother paying any attention to that stuff, do you?'

Worst of all, however, was that clear differences were emerging in the team between Lawry's roundhead Victorians and the more cavalier clique from NSW and South Australia. The former thought the latter lacked dedication and were too inclined to play up. The latter considered the former aloof and antisocial. 'It's really the only time I ever felt that an Australian team I played in was divided,' says Stackpole.

Of particular dispute were the differing attitudes to after-hours fraternisation with the Springboks. As Sheahan recalls:

Bill had come out of the school of hard knocks, where the only remedy for failure was working harder. And most us Victorians felt empathy with Bill and tended to fall in line. But the young turks felt quite differently. They reckoned that cricket started when you arrived at the ground in the morning and ended at close of play, and you could do what you liked in between times. The NSW boys had long had a reputation as a bit of a party group, and Ian [Chappell] fitted in well with them. Myself, I felt that nobody should have been surprised when Bill decided that he wouldn't go in for a drink with the opposition. He'd never done it. It was unfortunate that he couldn't do it in some ways, but social graces to him didn't mean a great deal. It was bad enough getting beaten on that tour. But the divisions in the team made it really miserable.

A few selection decisions didn't help. Having taken 28 Test wickets in India, Mallett was omitted from the Second Test. He blamed Lawry:

Bill preferred bowlers who kept it tight like Alan Connolly and John Gleeson, and he didn't really understand spin bowling…When the South Africans put together a good pace barrage in this series, we decided to stack the side with medium pacers. It wasn't great thinking. In fact, I thought it was ridiculous that we were fighting fire with fire when we didn't really have any firepower.

In the opposite camp, Ray Jordon had begun thinking he was a great chance to break into the Test side. Terribly handicapped by asthma, Taber had been keeping poorly. Making two quicksilver leg-side stumpings against Border on 13 February, Jordon felt at the peak of his form. But, when the team for the Third Test was read out five days later, Jordon wasn't in it. He told Bennett: 'Do you mind if I don't come to the team meeting? I reckon I might say something I'll regret.' Jordon went to the pictures by himself instead: seething through the blockbuster *Battle of Britain*.

When the subject of a Fifth Test was raised again a few days later, it became a messy business. The affluent Wanderers Club had made it known that they were prepared to make up the difference between Chappell's $500 *ballon d'essai* and the Australian board's $200 offer. Chappell wouldn't hear of it: 'It's got nothing to do with them. It's between us and our board. And if we don't stand up for our rights here, we deserve to be pushed around for the rest of our lives.'

West Australian Laurie Mayne interjected: there were enough players to field an XI in a Fifth Test even if the others didn't want to play, so why shouldn't they just go ahead? Chappell exploded, pulling a chequebook from his back pocket. 'If $200 means so much, I'll give it to you now,' he said. 'Listen, we've got a chance to stand up to the bastards. We should do it.'

Lawry interceded to calm the meeting down: 'I said at the start this had to be unanimous. It's all-in or all-out.' When McKenzie and Gleeson confirmed their opposition, the Fifth Test was finally scotched. Its ramifications would be lasting.

VANQUISHED

The South Africans made the best of their four Tests, running roughshod over their guests at New Wanderers by 307 runs and in the Fourth Test at Port Elizabeth's St George's Park by 329. The 4–0 margin was the worst Australian defeat in more than ninety years of Test cricket. Redpath (283 runs at 47) and Connolly (20 wickets at 26) alone had acquitted themselves with credit. The performances of Chappell (92 runs in eight innings) and McKenzie (one wicket for 333) had shrunk unrecognisably. And the Australians' fielding—uniformly excellent for the last couple of years—had disintegrated. Twenty chances had been turfed in the Tests alone.

As their last four wickets fell in twenty minutes at Port Elizabeth on Tuesday 10 March, Australia's dressing-room was quiet. The superiority of their rivals, South African schadenfreude, tension in their own ranks, all made the spectacle hard to bear. The close of the series was tinged with unpleasantness. Umpire Coetzee entered with a gift for Lawry—a souvenir plaque made from lion hide—but the Australian captain refused it. He thought Coetzee a rank bad umpire, and that was that. 'I can't take it off you,' Lawry said. 'I'm not a hypocrite.'

There was then bitterness at the end of tour dinner at the Marine Hotel in the evening. The Victorians who had assembled punctually were needled when the NSW clique arrived late, making some pointed comments about their quick exit from the ground and refusal to join the

Springboks in a drink. Stackpole was furious: 'We got to the team dinner on time and the others arrived a bit late, a bit inebriated, and they started having a go at us for being anti-social. And I got a bit angry and stood up and said: "Look, I'm not putting up with this. I'm going." But Redders tugged my sleeve and pulled me down in my seat and calmed me down a bit.'

When tempers cooled, Lawry made a creative proposal. Since Jullundur in India, he had been considering a letter to the board spelling out a series of grievances. Now he circulated one that left no doubt about where the players stood: he recommended in particular that there be no further double-tours, and that future visits to the subcontinent only take place in the event of cast-iron assurances about the standards of accommodation and security. It was a detailed and, in its tone, unprecedented testament of player discontent. Much as they agreed with it, some players felt it dangerous. As the contents were perused, Redpath said: 'I think we should all sign this.'

'No,' Lawry said firmly. 'I'm captain. It's my responsibility.'

'WITH GREAT REGRET...'

So ended five of the most convulsive months in Australian cricket. In a broadcast message to India before the First Test at Bombay, Sir Donald Bradman had echoed the old Menzies line: 'We fervently believe that cricket is unrivalled in its ability to harmonise people of two countries on a common level.' Five rancorous Test matches had proved him wrong, demonstrating that a cricket tour could be as much a crucible of cultural strife as a superior form of diplomacy. Other countries had second thoughts about visiting the subcontinent: as the lessons of Bombay and Calcutta were digested, the MCC cancelled its scheduled 1971–72 tour.

At the beginning of the tour's South African leg, both Lawry and Bennett had assured their hosts that there was no possibility that politics would interfere in cricket relations between Australia and South Africa. Lawry had said that there was 'no chance' that the Springboks' scheduled 1971–72 trip to Australia would be cancelled: according to Eric Litchfield, 'a good stiff upper lip counter to the would-be troublemakers'. The players, well-shielded from apartheid, didn't trouble themselves about its implications. 'We just got on with playing the game,' says Eric Freeman. 'You knew the situation because you could see at the grounds the separate stands for the whites and blacks. But we were just out there to entertain.'

They, too, were misguided. An outspoken alliance of British MPs, church organisations and trade unions maintained their rage until South Africa's 1970 tour was no more. After petitions from Home Secretary James Callaghan to Cricket Council chairman Maurice Allom and secretary Billy Griffith, the cancellation was announced on 22 May 1970.*

Attention switched to Australia. The sight of demonstrations against South African tennis player Brenda Kirk at White City in January 1971, and a series of violent protests against the Springbok rugby union tourists in June and July, finally lowered the boom on South African cricket at international level. At a press conference on 8 September 1971, Sir Donald Bradman finally announced: 'The board decided to advise the South African Cricket Association, with great regret, that in the present atmosphere the invitation to tour must be withdrawn.' The *Bulletin* editorialised: 'It was a sad sight, Sir Donald Bradman conceding defeat with nary a ball bowled. If ever there was a pathetic victim of politics being inextricably interwoven with sport, it is Sir Donald.' **

For Australian cricketers, the 1969–70 tour was also a watershed. Ian Chappell's resistance to a Fifth Test and Bill Lawry's scathing tour report marked a turning point in player–administrator relations.

Nothing changed overnight. Indeed, both vice-captain and captain acknowledged they had gone out on a limb. Chappell heard from Alan McGilvray that a senior board official had told him: 'Ian Chappell will never captain Australia.' And at the board's September 1970 annual meeting, manager Bennett failed to support Lawry's report: he submitted that the tour was 'neither too long, nor imposed undue strain'.

But the players had served notice that the pay and conditions under which Australian cricket teams had played in the 1950s and 1960s would be unsuitable for the 1970s. They suspected that the board had made a packet from the 1969–70 tour, and rightly: although earnings had been reduced by the Indian government's limitations on the export of hard currency, the $93,000 profit had been the greatest for fourteen years. Yet

---

* The Cricket Council was an authority established in 1969 overarching the Test and County Cricket Board, the National Cricket Association and MCC: its role in the 1970 tour controversy pushed it into prominence.
** As had the Cricket Council, the Australian Board harnessed a Rest of the World XI for five unofficial 'Tests' in the Springboks' stead. Ironically, the side led by Garry Sobers and managed by Bill Jacobs and Jack Ledward, included four South Africans: both Pollocks, Hylton Ackerman and all-rounder Tony Greig (who was then qualifying to play Tests for England).

the board had penned them up in squalid Indian hotels, then offered them just $200 each to play a Fifth Test in South Africa. 'We were all pretty disillusioned by the time we got home in 1970,' says Sheahan. 'Not only about the tour, but because the administrators seemed to be taking no notice of us at all.'

In hindsight, a full seven years before the World Series *sans-culottes* gave full vent to those feelings, the board and its players seemed set on a collision course. One change of personnel made it inevitable.

ENVOI

Bill Lawry rose early in the Australian team's Adelaide hotel on 4 February 1971. The Melbourne flight for the Victorians who'd just played in the Sixth Test against England didn't depart until 10.50am, so the Australian captain had planned an early morning visit to the residence of Bert Minards, a local with whom he shared his zeal of pigeon fancying. In Adelaide Tests gone by, the non-drinking, non-smoking Lawry had preferred Minards' company to the traditional rest-day sojourn at Wyndham Hill-Smith's winery. 'A lovely man with a lovely home,' Lawry recalls. 'We'd sit there by his grapevines and talk pigeons for the day.'

Honours in the Sixth Test the previous day had been shared with Ray Illingworth's Englishmen and the series remained open. And, though Australia trailed, not much blame for its Fourth Test defeat at the SCG could be laid at Lawry's door: while Englishman John Snow had been extracting 7–40, Lawry had been carrying his bat for 60 of a miserable 116.

All the same, there were daggers drawn for Lawry, and he knew it. The series had introduced some handy young players: Ian Chappell's upright brother Greg, brawny wicket-keeper Rod Marsh and a rangy paceman Dennis Lillee. But, with neither Lawry nor his obdurate Yorkshire rival prepared to concede an inch, the series had come dangerously close to gridlock. Keith Miller's front page peroration in the *Australian* that morning was headlined 'To Hell with the Ashes', and called for the banishment of Lawry, Illingworth *and* the sacred urn: 'Dump them. Get rid of them…The public just cannot tolerate the play-safe cricket we have so often seen this series.'

So, before heading out, Lawry went to see Sam Loxton, who'd joined Australia's selection panel on Ryder's retirement in September 1970, and in whose company he'd spent most of the previous day watching the draw's last rites. But Loxton, he was told, had taken the early flight out.

'That's strange,' he thought. 'Why would Sam take the 5.06am or whatever out? That's unlike him. Oh, well. Better get moving.'

Just over an hour later, the telephone rang in the room occupied by Lawry's fellow Victorians Stackpole and Redpath. It was cricket writer Alan Shiell, a former state player known to all as 'Sheffield'. 'Is Bill round?' Shiell asked.

'No, Sheff, he's not,' said Stackpole. 'Why?'

'Well, there are quite a few changes to the Test side,' Shiell began, then dropped his bombshell. 'Bill's been dropped and Chappell's been made captain.'

When Stackpole put the phone down, he turned to Redpath. 'Bill's been dropped,' he said. 'Jeez, how are we gonna tell him?'

As if on cue, Lawry knocked at the door and walked in with a breezy: 'G'day boys!'

Stackpole tried to be as sensitive as possible: 'Err, Bill, you'd better sit down.'

'Why?' Lawry replied. 'Have I been dropped?'

Stackpole was amazed. Lawry hadn't broken stride. When Stackpole confirmed that he had been omitted from the side for the Seventh Test in nine days' time, Lawry said merely: 'Well, I thought I might have been. The selectors usually come over for a word after the Test and last night they didn't.'

It wasn't a front, either. Lawry genuinely didn't feel it was the end of the world. He was an uncompromising cricketer, to be sure, but he had been brought up to believe that, if one suffered a check, one got on with it. On reflection, Lawry came to believe that it was his terse captain's report on the 1969–70 tour that marked his card. But no matter there either. He says:

> I've no anger at all about being dropped. I hadn't been playing well that series, and I had no compassion when I was dropping players as a selector. I was disappointed that I'd been with the selectors [Loxton, Neil Harvey and Bradman] in the dressing-room most of the previous day. But I should probably have woken up when Sam hadn't been in his room next morning…In our day, everyone was dignified. It was the way we'd been brought up by Jack Ryder, Neil Harvey, Len Maddocks, Colin McDonald, to take the good with the bad.

That Lawry should speak of his 'day' is significant. For the ascension of Ian Chappell very clearly marked the dawn of a new one. Brought up in the 1940s, a young adult in the 1950s, Lawry had been of the age that accepted Australia's growing wealth as a blessing after the rigours of war and placed unstinting faith in its institutions. Raised in the 1950s and maturing in the 1960s, Chappell was of a generation free to take prosperity and freedom for granted, one that enjoyed the latitude of answering back. In Lawry's era, leaders had made plans, given orders and been able to expect their completion. In Chappell's, they would invest more in charisma, instinct and consensus.

Paul Sheahan puts it well:

> I don't think the board acted very meritoriously. The fact that no-one had the courage to tell him that he was to lose his job as Australian captain was disgraceful. Someone who'd done as much for his country as Bill. At the same time, Bill was not the sort of captain who stood alongside you and drew the best out of you. He was a bit of an autocrat. And there were a lot of social forces in Australia at the time encouraging people to be agin the government—the Vietnam war, an increasing liberalism in the community, the beginning of the 'Me Generation'—and that style of leadership, I think, was disappearing. And I don't think there's any doubt that Ian Chappell was a forceful personality of the new age and became its focal point.

So where *was* Lawry's heir? That morning, Chappell had returned to work at Wills' Adelaide office in Mile End, then strolled down Hindley Street for a counter lunch at the Overway Hotel, just off North Terrace. Strangely, as he paid for his schnitzel and a couple of schooners, he came upon a crumpled piece of paper in his wallet and unfolded it. It read: 'Captain Australia.'

Chappell understood its provenance at once. Many years before, he'd played in an under-sixteen competition in Adelaide. Coach Geff Noblet had told his charges: 'Boys, I want you to write down your ambition on a bit of paper, then put it in your wallet.'

Chappell folded it again and replaced it. Not much chance of that ambition coming true. He remembered Bob Parish's words in 1968: 'Ian, you'll have to curb your swearing if you're going to be captain of Australia.' He recalled McGilvray's intelligence that at least one board member was stating: 'Ian Chappell will never captain Australia.' 'Captain Australia'? Not in this lifetime.

As he was dining, however, the telephone rang in the Overway and Chappell was called over. It was Alan Shiell. 'G'day Sheff,' said Chappell. 'What's up?'

'Congratulations,' Shiell replied.

'What for?' asked Chappell.

'Don't you know?' said Shiell. 'You're captain of Australia.'

'Shit,' said Chappell.

There was a long silence before Chappell could think of anything to add. 'It's unbelievable,' he said finally. 'I am completely surprised. I feel sorry for Bill. He's been a good captain.'

The rest of the day was a blur. Photographers descended on the family home at Netley to take pictures of the twenty-seven-year-old Chappell frolicking on the living-room floor with his three-year-old daughter Amanda. They decorated front pages the next morning alongside photos of a harried-looking Lawry dead-batting questions at Essendon Airport. Chappell's quotes already carried a ring of youthful zest: 'The selectors have obviously chosen an attacking team by the inclusion of two fast bowlers and two leg spinners. This means all-out attack from the start. In its present position of one-down, Australia might as well lose two-nil as one-nil.'

Once they had gone, however, Chappell's thoughts clarified. Everything he knew suggested that he was captain under sufferance. And if the selectors could get rid of Lawry so easily, they could do the same to him. Well, he wouldn't give them the satisfaction. 'The bastards won't get me the way they got Bill,' he told his wife. And they never did.

'He's Merely Our Worthy Prime Minister'

During his dinner for Lindsay Hassett's Australian team at the Savoy Hotel on the evening of 27 June 1953, Robert Menzies delivered the following long poem devoting itself to the merit of the team's individuals.

Some folk think civil servants 'not the thing'!
But ah! They do not know our Douglas Ring.
Those who expect the ball to dip or break
Find out, too late, from Jack, their Great mistake.

Bedser can scarce succeed his game to ruffle
When Arthur falls into that damned shuffle.

When the Australian Board of Cricket Control
(With Sid's approval) opened up its soul
And made George manager of seventeen stars
It also loaned him six third-rate cigars.

When the wise men raise a reproving finger
At Colin Mac for edging the outswinger
Mac glares at them, and thinks, for all I know,
He's back among the Campbells at Glencoe.

In team work, you'll agree the art
Is that the whole is greater than the part
In cricket you'll agree the same
Is true when Graeme Hole is on his game.

When Langley keeps, it's as if a ship
Had moved, stern first, from its reluctant slip.

Lindsay's a wit, Lindsay has feet like lightning
But all the critics thought his form was frightening
But Lindsay knows, there comes another day
When those who came to mock remain to pray.

If Ronald Archer were no good at all
Instead of adept with both bat and ball
I still would cheer him both louder and faster
For Queensland lately saved me from disaster.

Oh, for a word of rare Cardusean fire
Oh, for a song upon the poet's lyre
Oh, that the bells should ring a noble peal
To hymn the glories of our sinister Neil.

I care not whether Keith gets runs or not
(That statement is, of course, the purest rot)
But what I swear is that his off-drive yet
Is worth a lengthy paragraph in Debrett.

The clutching Tallon oft the Umpire hails
Before he's actually removed the bails
(I know that this is libellous, but stay
I could not get a rhyme another way)

Morris the calm, the nerveless, the genteel
Still has some lovely wonders to reveal

The infant Craig reclining in the shade
Takes comfort from the history of McCabe.

This is a very solemn night my friends
Though it may cheer up yet, before it ends
Here at this miserable board there sit
Men without skill or eagerness or wit.

The gloomy Hassett sulking in his tent
Saying that shot was not quite what I meant.

The ancient Miller, too old now to bristle
Nursing his something something something muscle.

Lindwall with versatility inhuman
Bowling his slows faster than Fred Trueman.

Benaud the bold, Benaud the giant killer
Bowls like Doug Ring but gestures like Keith Miller.

The infant David took a rounded stone,
And smote Goliath through both skin and bone
With equal art, but much less lethal fun
Similar things are done by Davidson.

Some people study kangaroos or fish
The duck-billed platypus, or other birds
Some practise late cuts as their dearest wish
But Jim de Courcy concentrates on words.

Bill Johnston, smiling darling of society
Bowler of lengths and widths a fine variety
But Tallon always wishes he could know
Whether Bill's going to bowl it fast or slow.

A few notes of explication may be useful. Doug Ring was a public servant and worked for Menzies' elder brother Les in Victoria's Department of Primary Industries. 'Jack' was Jack Hill, third spinner on the tour (known for his accuracy but not his turn), 'George' George Davies, the manager of the tour, from Victoria.

There is evidence of Menzies' keen eye for cricketing character in the allusion to Richie Benaud's subtle imitations of Keith Miller. There's also a hint of his profound knowledge of cricket history in that he consoles teenager Ian Craig on his poor form by drawing attention to the fact that the teenager Stan McCabe did not score a century on his first tour of England in 1930, yet went on to be one of Australia's greatest batsmen.

There is one piquant reference to politics in the suggestion that the Queensland of Ron Archer has 'lately saved me from disaster'. In the recent half-Senate election of 9 May, only in Queensland had the coalition won more seats than Labor.

Hassett replied thus:

With his iron grey hair and his pugnacious air
His appearance tends to the sinister
But there's no need to fear for he'll quaff down his beer
And he's merely our worthy Prime Minister.

When they play on the swards of the Oval or Lord's
Though the state of Australia's distressing
His time he'll employ at a pub called Savoy
For external affairs are more pressing.

But we'll hide our hate of this terrible state
Though the blot on our conscience will stay
We've eaten and drunk and can now do a bunk
But he's got to bloody well pay.

Australian Test Matches

1949–1971

SOUTH AFRICA v AUSTRALIA 1949–50

FIRST TEST

Ellis Park, Johannesburg, 24 to 28 December 1949

AUSTRALIA 413 (Hassett 112, Loxton 101, Johnson 66)
defeated SOUTH AFRICA 137 (E. Rowan 60, Miller 5–40) and 191 (Johnston 6–44) by
an innings and 85 runs.

SECOND TEST

Newlands, Cape Town, 31 December 1949 to 4 January 1950

AUSTRALIA 7–526 declared (Moroney 87, Miller 58, Hassett 57, Harvey 178,
Mann 4–105) and 2–87
defeated SOUTH AFRICA 278 (E. Rowan 67, Nourse 65, McCool 5–41) and 333
(Nourse 114, Tayfield 75, Lindwall 5–32) by eight wickets.

THIRD TEST

Kingsmead, Durban, 20 to 24 January 1950

SOUTH AFRICA 311 (E. Rowan 143, Nourse 66, Johnston 4–75) and 99 (Johnson 5–34,
Johnston 4–39)
lost to AUSTRALIA 75 (Tayfield 7–23) and 5–336 (Harvey 151 not out, Loxton 54)
by five wickets.

Australia's first innings was its lowest total against South Africa.

FOURTH TEST

Ellis Park, Johannesburg, 10 to 14 February 1950

AUSTRALIA 8–465 declared (Morris 111, Moroney 118, Miller 84, Hassett 53,
Harvey 56 not out, Melle 5–113) and 2–259 (Moroney 101 not out, Harvey 100)
drew with SOUTH AFRICA 352 (E. Rowan 55, Fullerton 88, Mann 52).

FIFTH TEST

St George's Park, Port Elizabeth, 3 to 6 March 1950

AUSTRALIA 7–549 declared (Morris 157, Harvey 116, Hassett 167)
defeated SOUTH AFRICA 158 (Miller 4–42) and 132 (Nourse 55) by an innings
and 259 runs.

AUSTRALIA v ENGLAND 1950–51

FIRST TEST

Woolloongabba, Brisbane, 1 to 5 December 1950

AUSTRALIA 228 (Harvey 74, Bedser 4–45) and 7–32 declared (Bailey 4–22)
defeated ENGLAND 7–68 declared (Johnston 5–35) and 122 (Hutton 62 not out,
Iverson 4–43) by 70 runs.

SECOND TEST

Melbourne Cricket Ground, 22 to 27 December 1950

AUSTRALIA 194 (Hassett 52, Bedser 4–37, Bailey 4–40) and 181 (F. Brown 4–26)
defeated ENGLAND 197 (F. Brown 62, Iverson 4–37) and 150 (Johnston 4–26)
by 28 runs.

THIRD TEST
Sydney Cricket Ground, 5 to 9 January 1951
ENGLAND 290 (Hutton 62, F. Brown 79, Miller 4–37) and 123 (Iverson 6–27)
lost to AUSTRALIA 426 (Hassett 70, Miller 145 not out, Johnson 77, Bedser 4–107,
F. Brown 4–153) by an innings and 13 runs.

FOURTH TEST
Adelaide Oval, 2 to 8 February 1951
AUSTRALIA 371 (Morris 206, Wright 4–99) and 8–403 declared (Harvey 68, Miller 99,
Burke 101 not out)
defeated ENGLAND 272 (Hutton 156 not out) and 228 (Simpson 61, Johnston 4–73)
by 274 runs.
*Burke scored a century on his Test debut at twenty but played only two further Tests
in the next four years.*

FIFTH TEST
Melbourne Cricket Ground, 23 to 28 February 1951
AUSTRALIA 217 (Hassett 92, Morris 50, Bedser 5–46, F. Brown 5–49) and 197
(Harvey 52, Hole 63, Bedser 5–59)
lost to ENGLAND 320 (Simpson 156 not out, Hutton 79, Miller 4–76) and 2–95
(Hutton 60 not out) by eight wickets.
Bedser achieved 30 wickets in the series at 16.

AUSTRALIA v WEST INDIES 1951–52

FIRST TEST
Woolloongabba, Brisbane, 9 to 13 November 1951
WEST INDIES 216 (Lindwall 4–62) and 245 (Weekes 70, Gomez 55, Ring 6–80)
lost to AUSTRALIA 226 (Lindwall 61, Valentine 5–99) and 7–236 (Ramadhin 5–90) by
three wickets.
Valentine and Ramadhin bowled 86 in every 100 balls during Australia's innings.

SECOND TEST
Sydney Cricket Ground, 30 November to 5 December 1951
WEST INDIES 362 (Worrell 64, Walcott 60, Christiani 76, Gomez 54, Lindwall 4–66)
and 290 (Weekes 56, Goddard 57 not out)
lost to AUSTRALIA 517 (Hassett 132, Miller 129, Ring 65, Valentine 4–111) and 3–137
by seven wickets.

THIRD TEST
Adelaide Oval, 22 to 25 December 1951
AUSTRALIA 82 (Worrell 6–38) and 255 (Ring 67, Valentine 6–102)
lost to WEST INDIES 105 (Johnston 6–62) and 4–223 by six wickets.
Morris led Australia in the absence of Hassett (pulled hip muscle).

FOURTH TEST
Melbourne Cricket Ground, 31 December 1951 to 3 January 1952
WEST INDIES 272 (Worrell 108, Miller 5–60) and 203 (Stollmeyer 54, Gomez 52)
lost to AUSTRALIA 216 (Harvey 83, Trim 5–34) and 9–260 (Hassett 102, Valentine 5–88)
by one wicket.

FIFTH TEST
Sydney Cricket Ground, 25 to 29 January 1952
AUSTRALIA 116 (Gomez 7–55) and 377 (McDonald 62, Hassett 64, Miller 69, Hole 62,
Worrell 4–95)

defeated WEST INDIES 78 (Miller 5–26) and 213 (Stollmeyer 104, Lindwall 5–52)
by 202 runs.
*West Indies' first innings remains its lowest in Australia. Test debuts for Richie Benaud and
Colin McDonald.*

AUSTRALIA v SOUTH AFRICA 1952–53

FIRST TEST
Woolloongabba, Brisbane, 5 to 10 December 1952
AUSTRALIA 280 (Harvey 109, Hassett 55, Melle 6–71, Watkins 4–41) and 277
(Morris 58, Harvey 52, Tayfield 4–116)
defeated SOUTH AFRICA 221 (Ring 6–72) and 240 (McGlew 69, Funston 65,
Lindwall 5–60) by 96 runs.

SECOND TEST
Melbourne Cricket Ground, 24 to 30 December 1952
SOUTH AFRICA 227 (Murray 51, Miller 4–62) and 388 (Waite 62, Endean 162 not out)
defeated AUSTRALIA 243 (McDonald 82, Miller 52, Tayfield 6–84) and 290
(Harvey 60, Ring 53, Tayfield 7–81) by 82 runs.
*Tayfield's 13–165 is unsurpassed by a South African. It was South Africa's first win against
Australia in nearly forty-two years.*

THIRD TEST
Sydney Cricket Ground, 9 to 13 January 1953
SOUTH AFRICA 173 (Funston 53, Lindwall 4–40) and 232 (Endean 71,
McLean 65, Lindwall 4–72)
lost to AUSTRALIA 443 (McDonald 67, Harvey 190, Miller 55, Ring 58, Murray 4–169)
by an innings and 38 runs.
Harvey completed 1000 runs against South Africa in only eight Tests.

FOURTH TEST
Adelaide Oval, 24 to 29 January 1953
AUSTRALIA 530 (McDonald 154, Hassett 163, Harvey 84, Hole 59, Tayfield 4–142)
and 3–223 declared (Morris 77, Harvey 116)
drew with SOUTH AFRICA 387 (Endean 56, Funston 92, Watkins 76, Johnston 5–110,
Benaud 4–118) and 6–177 (McGlew 54).

FIFTH TEST
Melbourne Cricket Ground, 6 to 12 February 1953
AUSTRALIA 520 (Morris 99, Harvey 205, Craig 53) and 209 (Fuller 5–66)
lost to SOUTH AFRICA 435 (Waite 64, Watkins 92, McLean 81, Cheetham 66, Mansell
52, Johnston 6–152) and 4–297 (Endean 70, Watkins 50, McLean 76 not out) by six
wickets.
As the series was still open, the match was played to a completion.

ENGLAND v AUSTRALIA 1953

FIRST TEST
Trent Bridge, Nottingham, 11 to 16 June 1953
AUSTRALIA 249 (Morris 67, Hassett 115, Miller 55, Bedser 7–55) and 123
(Morris 60, Bedser 7–44)
drew with ENGLAND 144 (Lindwall 5–57) and 1–120 (Hutton 60 not out).
Rain stymied England's chase for 307.

SECOND TEST
Lord's, London, 25 to 30 June 1953
AUSTRALIA 346 (Hassett 104, Harvey 59, Davidson 76, Bedser 5–105, Wardle 4–77)
and 368 (Morris 89, Miller 109, Lindwall 50, F. Brown 4–82)
drew with ENGLAND 372 (Hutton 145, Graveney 78, Compton 57, Lindwall 5–66)
and 7–282 (Watson 109, Bailey 71).

THIRD TEST
Old Trafford, Manchester, 9 to 14 July 1953
AUSTRALIA 318 (Harvey 122, Hole 66, Bedser 5–115) and 8–35 (Wardle 4–7)
drew with ENGLAND 276 (Hutton 66).
Rain restricted play to less than fourteen hours.

FOURTH TEST
Headingley, Leeds, 23 to 28 July 1953
ENGLAND 167 (Graveney 55, Lindwall 5–54) and 275 (W. Edrich 64, Compton 61)
drew with AUSTRALIA 266 (Harvey 71, Hole 53, Bedser 6–95) and 4–147.

FIFTH TEST
The Oval, London, 15 to 19 August 1953
AUSTRALIA 275 (Hassett 53, Lindwall 62, Trueman 4–86) and 162
(Lock 5–45, Laker 4–75)
lost to ENGLAND 306 (Hutton 82, Bailey 64, Lindwall 4–70) and 2–132
(W. Edrich 55 not out) by eight wickets.

AUSTRALIA v ENGLAND 1954–55

FIRST TEST
Woolloongabba, Brisbane, 26 November to 1 December 1954
AUSTRALIA 8–601 declared (Morris 153, Harvey 162, Hole 57, Lindwall 64 not out)
defeated ENGLAND 190 (Bailey 88) and 257 (Edrich 88) by an innings and 154 runs.

SECOND TEST
Sydney Cricket Ground, 17 to 22 December 1954
ENGLAND 154 and 296 (May 104, Cowdrey 54)
defeated AUSTRALIA 228 (Bailey 4–59, Tyson 4–45) and 184
(Harvey 92 not out, Tyson 6–85) by 38 runs.
Morris led Australia in the absence of Johnson and Miller (both injured).

THIRD TEST
Melbourne Cricket Ground, 31 December 1954 to 5 January 1955
ENGLAND 191 (Cowdrey 102, Archer 4–33) and 279 (May 91, Johnston 5–85)
defeated AUSTRALIA 231 (Statham 5–60) and 111 (Tyson 7–27) by 128 runs.

FOURTH TEST
Adelaide Oval, 28 January to 2 February 1955
AUSTRALIA 323 (Maddocks 69 not out) and 111
lost to ENGLAND 341 (Hutton 80, Cowdrey 79) and 5–97 by five wickets.
England completed a successful Ashes defence at 5.22pm.

FIFTH TEST
Sydney Cricket Ground, 25 February to 3 March 1955
ENGLAND 7–371 declared (Graveney 111, May 79, Compton 84, Bailey 72)
drew with AUSTRALIA 221 (McDonald 72, Wardle 5–79) and 6–118.
Rain delayed play for three and a half days. In the shortened time allowed,
England forced Australia to follow-on.

WEST INDIES v AUSTRALIA 1954–55

FIRST TEST
Sabina Park, Kingston, 26 to 31 March 1955
AUSTRALIA 9–515 declared (McDonald 50, Morris 65, Harvey 133, Miller 147)
and 1–20
defeated WEST INDIES 259 (Walcott 108, Lindwall 4–61) and 275
(Holt 60, Smith 104) by nine wickets.

SECOND TEST
Queen's Park, Port-of-Spain, 11 to 16 April 1955
WEST INDIES 382 (Walcott 126, Weekes 139, Lindwall 6–95) and 4–273
(Walcott 110, Weekes 87 not out)
drew with AUSTRALIA 9–600 declared (McDonald 110, Morris 111, Harvey 133,
Archer 84, Johnson 66).

THIRD TEST
Bourda, Georgetown, 26 to 29 April 1955
WEST INDIES 182 (Weekes 81, Benaud 4–15) and 207 (Walcott 73, Worrell 56,
Johnson 7–44)
lost to AUSTRALIA 257 (McDonald 68, Benaud 61) and 2–133 by eight wickets.

FOURTH TEST
Kensington Oval, Bridgetown, 14 to 20 May 1955
AUSTRALIA 668 (Favell 72, Harvey 74, Miller 137, Archer 98, Lindwall 118,
Langley 53, Dewdney 4–125) and 249 (Favell 53, Johnson 57, Atkinson 5–56)
drew with WEST INDIES 510 (Atkinson 219, Depeiza 122) and 6–234 (Walcott 83).
*Denis Atkinson and Clairmonte Depeiza held Australia at bay an entire day, adding an
unequalled 348 for the seventh wicket.*

FIFTH TEST
Sabina Park, Kingston, 11 to 17 June 1955
WEST INDIES 357 (Walcott 155, Weekes 56, Worrell 61, Miller 6–107) and 319
(Walcott 110, Sobers 64)
lost to AUSTRALIA 8–758 declared (McDonald 127, Harvey 204, Miller 109,
Archer 128, Benaud 121) by an innings and 82 runs.
*Australia's total remains its highest in Test history. Last Tests for Arthur Morris and
Bill Johnston.*

ENGLAND v AUSTRALIA 1956

FIRST TEST
Trent Bridge, Nottingham, 7 to 12 June 1956
ENGLAND 8–217 declared (Richardson 81, May 73, Miller 4–69) and 3–188
declared (Richardson 73, Cowdrey 81)
drew with AUSTRALIA 148 (Harvey 64, Laker 4–58) and 3–120 (Burke 58 not out).
Davidson chipped an ankle bone in his tenth over and played no further part in the game.

SECOND TEST
Lord's, London, 21 to 26 June 1956
AUSTRALIA 285 (McDonald 78, Burke 65) and 257 (Benaud 97, Trueman 5–90,
Bailey 4–64)
defeated ENGLAND 171 (May 63, Miller 5–72) and 186 (May 53,
Miller 5–80, Archer 4–71) by 185 runs.
Langley set a Test record with eight catches and a stumping that stood for thirty-four years.

THIRD TEST
Headingley, Leeds, 12 to 17 July 1956
ENGLAND 325 (May 101, Washbrook 98)
defeated AUSTRALIA 143 (Laker 5–58, Lock 4–41) and 140 (Harvey 69, Laker 6–55)
by an innings and 42 runs.

FOURTH TEST
Old Trafford, Manchester, 26 to 31 July 1956
ENGLAND 459 (Richardson 104, Cowdrey 80, Sheppard 113, Johnson 4–151)
defeated AUSTRALIA 84 (Laker 9–37) and 205 (McDonald 89, Laker 10–53)
by an innings and 170 runs.
Laker's unprecedented match figures were 68–27–90–19.

FIFTH TEST
The Oval, London, 23 to 28 August 1956
ENGLAND 247 (May 83 not out, Compton 94, Miller 4–91, Archer 5–53) and 3–182
declared (Sheppard 62)
drew with AUSTRALIA 202 (Miller 61, Laker 4–80) and 5–27.
Laker's 46 wickets for the series cost 9.60 each. The best in an Ashes series.

PAKISTAN v AUSTRALIA 1956–57

ONLY TEST
National Stadium, Karachi, 11 to 17 October 1956
AUSTRALIA 80 (Fazal Mahmood 6–34, Khan Mohammed 4–43) and 187
(Benaud 56, Fazal Mahmood 7–80)
lost to PAKISTAN 199 (Wazir Mohammed 67, Abdul Kardar 69, Johnson 4–50)
and 1–69 by nine wickets.
*Australia lost its first Test in Pakistan, played on matting. The first day was the slowest in
Test history—95 runs and 12 wickets—and Ian Craig's 'duck' took fifty minutes.
Keith Miller's last Test.*

INDIA v AUSTRALIA 1956–57

FIRST TEST
Corporation Stadium, Madras, 19 to 23 October 1956
INDIA 161 (Benaud 7–72) and 153 (Lindwall 7–43)
lost to AUSTRALIA 319 (Johnson 73, Mankad 4–90) by an innings and five runs.

SECOND TEST
Brabourne Stadium, Bombay, 26 to 31 October 1956
INDIA 251 (Ramchand 109) and 5–250 (Roy 79, Umrigar 78)
drew with AUSTRALIA 7–523 declared (Burke 161, Harvey 140, Burge 83).
Lindwall led Australia in the absence of the injured Johnson and Miller.

THIRD TEST
Eden Gardens, Calcutta, 2 to 6 November 1956
AUSTRALIA 177 (Burge 58, Ghulam Ahmed 7–49) and 9–189 declared
(Harvey 69, Mankad 4–49)
defeated INDIA (Benaud 6–52) and 136 (Benaud 5–53, Burke 4–37) by 94 runs.
Ian Johnson's last Test.

SOUTH AFRICA v AUSTRALIA 1957–58

FIRST TEST
New Wanderers, Johannesburg, 23 to 28 December 1957
SOUTH AFRICA 9–470 declared (McGlew 108, Goddard 90, Waite 115, Endean 50,
McLean 50, Meckiff 5–125) and 201 (Waite 59, Endean 77, Davidson 6–34)
drew with AUSTRALIA 368 (McDonald 75, Simpson 60, Benaud 122, Heine 6–58)
and 3–162 (Mackay 65 not out).
Bob Simpson's first Test.

SECOND TEST
Newlands, Cape Town, 31 December 1957 to 3 January 1958
AUSTRALIA 449 (McDonald 99, Burke 189, Mackay 63, Tayfield 5–120)
defeated SOUTH AFRICA 209 (Benaud 4–95) and 99 (Goddard 56 not out,
Benaud 5–49).
Kline's second innings 3–18 included the hat-trick with his last three deliveries.

THIRD TEST
Kingsmead, Durban, 24 to 28 January 1958
AUSTRALIA 163 (Craig 52, Adcock 6–43) and 7–292 (Burke 83, Harvey 68,
Mackay 52 not out)
drew with SOUTH AFRICA 384 (McGlew 105, Waite 134, Benaud 5–114).
McGlew's century took just over nine hours and was the slowest in Test history for twenty years.

FOURTH TEST
New Wanderers, Johannesburg, 7 to 12 February 1958
AUSTRALIA 401 (Burke 81, Benaud 100, Mackay 83 not out, Davidson 62,
Heine 6–96) and 0–1
defeated SOUTH AFRICA 203 (Funston 70, Benaud 4–70) and 198
(McGlew 70, Funston 64, Benaud 5–84) by ten wickets.

FIFTH TEST
St George's Park, Port Elizabeth, 28 February to 4 March 1958
SOUTH AFRICA 214 (Tayfield 66, Davidson 4–44, Kline 4–33) and 144
(Davidson 5–38, Benaud 5–82)
lost to AUSTRALIA 291 (McDonald 58, Mackay 77 not out) and 2–68 by eight wickets.

AUSTRALIA v ENGLAND 1958–59

FIRST TEST
Woolloongabba, Brisbane, 5 to 10 December 1958
ENGLAND 134 and 198 (Bailey 68)
lost to AUSTRALIA 186 (Loader 4–56) and 2–147 (O'Neill 71 not out)
by eight wickets.
Batsmen on both sides managed just 632 runs from 2422 legitimate deliveries.

SECOND TEST
Melbourne Cricket Ground, 31 December 1958 to 5 January 1959
ENGLAND 259 (May 113, Davidson 6–64) and 87 (Meckiff 6–38)
lost to AUSTRALIA 308 (Harvey 167, Statham 7–57) and 2–42 by eight wickets.

THIRD TEST
Sydney Cricket Ground, 9 to 15 January 1959
ENGLAND 219 (Benaud 5–83) and 7–287 declared (May 92, Cowdrey 100 not out,
Benaud 4–94)
drew with AUSTRALIA 357 (O'Neill 77, Favell 54, Mackay 57, Davidson 71, Lock
4–130, Laker 5–107) and 2–54.

FOURTH TEST
Adelaide Oval, 30 January to 5 February 1959
AUSTRALIA 476 (McDonald 170, Burke 66, O'Neill 56, Trueman 4–90) and 0–36
defeated ENGLAND 240 (Cowdrey 84, Benaud 5–91) and 270 (May 59, Graveney 53
not out, Benaud 4–82) by six wickets.
McDonald was the fiftieth Australian to score a century against England.

FIFTH TEST
Melbourne Cricket Ground, 13 to 18 February 1959
ENGLAND 205 (Richardson 68, Benaud 4–43) and 214 (Graveney 54)
lost to AUSTRALIA 351 (McDonald 133, Benaud 64, Grout 74, Trueman 4–92,
Laker 4–93) and 1–69 (McDonald 51 not out) by nine wickets.
*Benaud sent England in. His series record was 31 wickets at 18.8. In his last Ashes Test,
Lindwall surpassed Clarrie Grimmett as Australia's highest Test wicket-taker (216).*

PAKISTAN v AUSTRALIA 1959–60

FIRST TEST
Dacca Stadium, 13 to 18 November 1959
PAKISTAN 200 (Hanif Mohammed 66, Sharpe 56 not out, Davidson 4–42, Benaud
4–69) and 134 (Benaud 4–42, Mackay 6–42)
lost to AUSTRALIA 225 (Harvey 96, Fazal Mahmood 5–71) and 2–112 by eight wickets.
Benaud sent Pakistan in, and led Australia to its first win against Pakistan.

SECOND TEST
Lahore Stadium, 21 to 26 November 1959
PAKISTAN 146 (Davidson 4–48) and 366 (Imtiaz Ahmed 54, Saeed Ahmed 166,
Kline 7–75)
lost to AUSTRALIA 7–391 declared (O'Neill 134) and 3–123 by seven wickets.
Australia won its first and last series in Pakistan with twelve minutes to spare.

THIRD TEST
National Stadium, Karachi, 4 to 9 December 1959
PAKISTAN 287 (Hanif Mohammed 51, Saeed Ahmed 91, Ijaz Butt 58, Benaud 5–93)
and 8–194 declared (Hanif Mohammed 101 not out)
drew with AUSTRALIA 257 (Harvey 54, Fazal Mahmood 5–74) and 2–83.
Intikhab Alam's first ball in Test cricket bowled Colin McDonald.

INDIA v AUSTRALIA 1959–60

FIRST TEST
Feroz Shah Kotla, Delhi, 12 to 16 December 1959
INDIA 135 and 206 (Roy 99, Kline 4–42, Benaud 5–76)
lost to AUSTRALIA 468 (Harvey 114, Mackay 78, Umrigar 4–49) by an innings
and 127 runs.

SECOND TEST
Green Park, Kanpur, 19 to 24 December 1959
INDIA 152 (Davidson 5–31, Benaud 4–63) and 291 (Contractor 74, Kenny 51,
Davidson 7–93)
defeated AUSTRALIA 219 (McDonald 53, Harvey 51, Patel 9–69) and 105
(Patel 5–55) by 119 runs.
*Australia batted a man short in the second innings (Rorke, ill). McDonald was first in and last
out for 34. Two bowlers dominated: Alan Davidson 77.4–30–124–12 and Jasu Patel
61.3–23–124–14.*

THIRD TEST
Brabourne Stadium, Bombay, 1 to 6 January 1960
INDIA 289 (Contractor 108, Baig 50, Davidson 4–62, Meckiff 4–79)
and 5–226 declared
drew with AUSTRALIA 8–387 declared (Harvey 102, O'Neill 163, Nadkarni 6–105).

FOURTH TEST
Corporation Stadium, Madras, 13 to 17 January 1960
AUSTRALIA 342 (Favell 101, Mackay 89, Desai 4–93)
defeated INDIA 149 (Kunderan 71, Benaud 5–43) and 138 by an innings and 55 runs.
Les Favell's only Test century and Ken Mackay's highest Test score.

FIFTH TEST
Eden Gardens, Calcutta, 23 to 28 January 1960
INDIA 194 and 339 (Jaisimha 74, Nadkarni 62, Benaud 4–103)
drew with AUSTRALIA 331 (Grout 50, O'Neill 113, Burge 60, Desai 4–111)
and 2–121 (Favell 62 not out).
Ray Lindwall's last Test.

AUSTRALIA v WEST INDIES 1960–61

FIRST TEST
Woolloongabba, Brisbane, 9 to 14 December 1960
WEST INDIES 453 (Sobers 132, Worrell 65, Solomon 65, Alexander 60, Hall 50,
Davidson 5–135) and 284 (Kanhai 54, Worrell 65, Davidson 6–87)
tied with AUSTRALIA 505 (McDonald 57, Simpson 92, O'Neill 181, Hall 4–140)
and 232 (Davidson 80, Benaud 52, Hall 5–63).
Test cricket's first tie in the 500th fixture since March 1877.

SECOND TEST
Melbourne Cricket Ground, 30 December 1960 to 3 January 1961
AUSTRALIA 348 (Favell 51, Mackay 74, Martin 55, Hall 4–51) and 3–70
defeated WEST INDIES 181 (Nurse 70, Kanhai 84, Davidson 6–53) and 233
(Hunte 110, Alexander 72).
*In West Indies' second innings, Johnny Martin took the wickets of Kanhai, Sobers and
Worrell in four deliveries.*

THIRD TEST
Sydney Cricket Ground, 13 to 18 January 1961
WEST INDIES 339 (Sobers 168, Davidson 5–80, Benaud 4–86) and 326 (Smith 55,
Worrell 82, Alexander 108)
defeated AUSTRALIA 202 (O'Neill 71, Valentine 4–67) and 241 (Harvey 85, O'Neill 70,
Gibbs 5–66, Valentine 4–86) by 222 runs.
In Australia's first innings, Lance Gibbs dismissed Mackay, Martin and Grout in four deliveries.

FOURTH TEST
Adelaide Oval, 27 January to 1 February 1961

WEST INDIES 393 (Kanhai 117, Worrell 71, Alexander 63 not out, Benaud 5–96) and 6–432 declared (Hunte 79, Kanhai 115, Worrell 53, Alexander 87 not out)
drew with AUSTRALIA 366 (McDonald 71, Simpson 85, Benaud 77, Gibbs 5–97) and 9–273 (O'Neill 65, Mackay 62 not out).

Gibbs' first innings hat-trick consisted of Mackay, Grout and Misson.

FIFTH TEST
Melbourne Cricket Ground, 10 to 15 February 1961

WEST INDIES 292 (Sobers 64, Misson 4–58) and 321 (Hunte 52, Alexander 73, Davidson 5–84)
lost to AUSTRALIA 356 (Simpson 75, McDonald 91, Burge 68, Sobers 5–120, Gibbs 4–74) and 8–258 (Simpson 92, Burge 53) by two wickets.

Benaud sent West Indies in.

ENGLAND v AUSTRALIA 1961

FIRST TEST
Edgbaston, Birmingham, 8 to 12 June 1961

ENGLAND 195 (Subba Row 59, Mackay 4–57) and 4–401 (Subba Row 112, Dexter 180)
drew with AUSTRALIA 9–516 declared (Lawry 57, Harvey 114, O'Neill 82, Simpson 76, Mackay 64).

Bill Lawry's first Test.

SECOND TEST
Lord's, London, 22 to 26 June 1961

ENGLAND 206 (Davidson 5–42) and 202 (Barrington 66, McKenzie 5–37)
lost to AUSTRALIA 340 (Lawry 130, Mackay 54, Trueman 4–118) and 5–71 by five wickets.

Harvey captained Australia in the absence of the injured Benaud. Graham McKenzie earned his first Test cap and took 5–37 on his twentieth birthday.

THIRD TEST
Headingley, Leeds, 6 to 8 July 1961

AUSTRALIA 237 (McDonald 54, Harvey 73, Trueman 5–58) and 120 (Harvey 53, Trueman 6–30)
lost to ENGLAND 299 (Pullar 53, Cowdrey 93, Davidson 5–63) and 2–62 by eight wickets.

Australia lost 8–21 in its second innings. Colin McDonald's last Test. Benaud's 'pair' as Test captain is an indignity subsequently shared by both Allan Border and Mark Taylor.

FOURTH TEST
Old Trafford, Manchester, 27 July to 1 August 1961

AUSTRALIA 190 (Lawry 74, Statham 5–53) and 432 (Lawry 102, Simpson 51, O'Neill 67, Davidson 77 not out, Allen 4–58)
defeated ENGLAND 367 (Pullar 63, May 95, Barrington 78, Simpson 4–23) and 201 (Dexter 76, Benaud 6–70) by 54 runs.

Brian Booth's first Test.

FIFTH TEST
The Oval, London, 17 to 22 August 1961
ENGLAND 256 (May 71, Barrington 53, Davidson 4–83) and 8–370
(Subba Row 137, Barrington 83, Mackay 5–121)
drew with AUSTRALIA 494 (O'Neill 117, Burge 181, Booth 71, Allen 4–133).
Mackay's match figures 107–35–196–7.

AUSTRALIA v ENGLAND 1962–63

FIRST TEST
Woolloongabba, Brisbane, 30 November to 5 December 1962
AUSTRALIA 404 (Simpson 50, Booth 112, Mackay 86 not out, Benaud 51) and 4–362
declared (Lawry 98, Simpson 71, O'Neill 56, Harvey 57)
drew with ENGLAND 389 (Dexter 70, Barrington 78, Parfitt 80, Benaud 6–115) and
6–278 (Pullar 56, Sheppard 53, Dexter 99).
Fourteen fifties equalled the previous Ashes record.

SECOND TEST
Melbourne Cricket Ground, 29 December 1962 to 3 January 1963
AUSTRALIA 316 (Lawry 62, Titmus 4–43) and 248 (Lawry 57, Booth 103,
Trueman 5–62)
lost to ENGLAND 331 (Dexter 93, Cowdrey 113, Davidson 6–75) and 3–227
(Sheppard 113, Dexter 52, Cowdrey 58 not out) by seven wickets.

THIRD TEST
Sydney Cricket Ground, 11 to 15 January 1963
ENGLAND 279 (Pullar 53, Cowdrey 85, Davidson 4–54) and 104 (Davidson 5–25)
lost to AUSTRALIA 319 (Simpson 91, Harvey 64, Shepherd 71 not out) and 2–67 by
eight wickets.
Benaud's twelfth and last win as Test captain.

FOURTH TEST
Adelaide Oval, 25 to 30 January 1963
AUSTRALIA 393 (Harvey 154, O'Neill 100) and 293 (Simpson 71, Booth 77,
Trueman 4–60)
drew with ENGLAND 331 (Barrington 63, Dexter 61, Titmus 59 not out,
McKenzie 5–89) and 4–223 (Barrington 132 not out).
Ken Mackay's last Test, Harvey's twenty-first and final Test hundred.

FIFTH TEST
Sydney Cricket Ground, 15 to 20 February 1963
ENGLAND 321 (Barrington 101) and 8–268 declared (Sheppard 68, Barrington 94)
drew with AUSTRALIA 349 (O'Neill 73, Burge 103 not out, Benaud 57, Titmus 5–103)
and 4–152 (Burge 52 not out).
First Test for Neil Hawke, last for Alan Davidson and Neil Harvey.

AUSTRALIA v SOUTH AFRICA 1963–64

FIRST TEST
Woolloongabba, Brisbane, 6 to 11 December 1963
AUSTRALIA 435 (O'Neill 82, Booth 169, P. Pollock 6–95) and 1–144 declared
(Lawry 87 not out)
drew with SOUTH AFRICA 346 (Goddard 52, Barlow 114, Waite 66, Benaud 5–68)
and 1–13.
Benaud's twenty-eighth and last Test as captain.

SECOND TEST
Melbourne Cricket Ground, 1 to 6 January 1964
SOUTH AFRICA 274 (Barlow 109, Bland 50, McKenzie 4–82) and 306 (Barlow 54,
A. Pithey 76, Waite 77)
lost to AUSTRALIA 447 (Lawry 157, Redpath 97, Shepherd 96, Partridge 4–108) and
2–136 (Simpson 55 not out) by eight wickets.
Simpson, sending South Africa in, won his first Test as captain.

THIRD TEST
Sydney Cricket Ground, 10 to 15 January 1964
AUSTRALIA 260 (Simpson 58, Booth 75, P. Pollock 5–83, Partridge 4–88) and 9–450
declared (Lawry 89, O'Neill 88, Benaud 90, McKenzie 76, Partridge 5–123)
drew with SOUTH AFRICA 302 (Goddard 80, G. Pollock 122, Bland 51) and 5–326
(Goddard 84, Bland 85, A. Pithey 53 not out).

FOURTH TEST
Adelaide Oval, 24 to 29 January 1964
AUSTRALIA 345 (Simpson 78, Burge 91, Booth 58, Shepherd 70, Goddard 5–60)
and 331 (O'Neill 66, Shepherd 78)
lost to SOUTH AFRICA 595 (Barlow 201, G, Pollock 175, Hawke 6–139) and 0–82
by ten wickets.
South Africa's then-highest total against Australia.

FIFTH TEST
Sydney Cricket Ground, 7 to 12 February 1964
AUSTRALIA 311 (Burge 56, O'Neill 102 not out, Partridge 7–91) and 270 (Booth 87)
drew with SOUTH AFRICA 411 (Goddard 93, Bland 126, Lindsay 65, Benaud 4–118)
and 0–76.
Benaud's last Test.

ENGLAND v AUSTRALIA 1964

FIRST TEST
Trent Bridge, Nottingham, 4 to 9 June 1964
ENGLAND 8–216 declared and 9–193 declared (Dexter 68, McKenzie 5–53)
drew with AUSTRALIA 168 (Simpson 50) and 2–40.
More than half the match was lost to rain.

SECOND TEST
Lord's, London, 18 to 23 June 1964
AUSTRALIA 176 (Veivers 54, Trueman 5–48) and 4–168 (Burge 59)
drew with ENGLAND 246 (J. Edrich 120, Corling 4–60).
Over half the match was lost to rain.

THIRD TEST
Headingley, Leeds, 2 to 6 July 1964
ENGLAND 268 (Dexter 66, Parks 68, McKenzie 4–74, Hawke 5–75)
and 229 (Barrington 85)
lost to AUSTRALIA 389 (Lawry 78, Burge 160, Titmus 4–69) and 3–111
(Redpath 58 not out) by seven wickets.

FOURTH TEST
Old Trafford, Manchester, 23 to 28 July 1964
AUSTRALIA 8–656 declared (Lawry 106, Simpson 311, Booth 98) and 0–4
drew with ENGLAND 611 (Boycott 58, Dexter 174, Barrington 256, McKenzie 7–153).
*Simpson's first Test century is the highest score by an Australian captain. Veivers bowled an
Australian record 571 deliveries to take 3–153.*

FIFTH TEST
The Oval, London, 13 to 18 August 1964
ENGLAND 182 (Hawke 6–47) and 4–381 (Boycott 113, Titmus 56, Cowdrey 93 not
out, Barrington 54 not out)
drew with AUSTRALIA 379 (Lawry 94, Booth 74, Veivers 67 not out, Trueman 4–87).

INDIA v AUSTRALIA 1964–65

FIRST TEST
Corporation Stadium, Madras, 2 to 7 October 1964
AUSTRALIA 211 (Lawry 62, Nadkarni 5–31) and 397 (Simpson 77, Burge 60,
Veivers 74, Nadkarni 6–91)
defeated INDIA 276 (Nawab of Pataudi jnr 128 not out, McKenzie 6–58) and 193
(Hanumant Singh 94, McKenzie 4–33) by 139 runs.

SECOND TEST
Brabourne Stadium, Bombay, 10 to 15 October 1964
AUSTRALIA 320 (Burge 80, Veivers 67, Jarman 78, Chandrasekhar 4–50) and 274
(Lawry 68, Booth 74, Cowper 81, Chandrasekhar 4–73, Nadkarni 4–33)
lost to INDIA 341 (Jaisimha 66, Nawab of Pataudi jnr 86, Veivers 4–68) and 8–256
(Sardesai 56, Nawab of Pataudi jnr 53) by two wickets.
Australia batted with ten in both innings, owing to the illness of O'Neill.

THIRD TEST
Eden Gardens, Calcutta, 17 to 22 October 1964
AUSTRALIA 174 (Lawry 50, Simpson 67, Durani 6–73) and 1–143 (Simpson 71)
drew with INDIA 235 (Jaisimha 57, Borde 68 not out, Simpson 4–45)
Nawab of Pataudi jnr sent Australia in. Rain washed out the last two days.

PAKISTAN v AUSTRALIA 1964–65

ONLY TEST
National Stadium, Karachi, 24 to 29 October 1964
PAKISTAN 414 (Khalid Ibadulla 166, Abdul Kadir 95, Intikhab Alam 53, McKenzie
6–69) and 8–279 declared (Javed Burki 62)
drew with AUSTRALIA 352 (Simpson 153, Burge 54) and 2–227 (Simpson 115).
In addition to his twin centuries, Simpson bowled 50 overs in the match.

AUSTRALIA v PAKISTAN 1964–65

ONLY TEST
Melbourne Cricket Ground, 4 to 8 December 1964
PAKISTAN 287 (Saeed Ahmed 80, Hanif Mohammed 104) and 326 (Hanif Mohammed
93, Intikhab Alam 61, McKenzie 4–74, Hawke 4–72)
drew with AUSTRALIA 448 (Shepherd 55, Booth 57, Cowper 83, Veivers 88,
Arif Butt 6–89) and 2–88.
Pakistan's first Test in Australia was played over only four days. Ian Chappell's Test debut.

WEST INDIES v AUSTRALIA 1964–65

FIRST TEST
Sabina Park, Kingston, 3 to 8 March 1965
WEST INDIES 239 (White 57, Mayne 4–43) and 373 (Hunte 81, Butcher 71,
Solomon 76, Mayne 4–56, Philpott 4–109)
defeated AUSTRALIA 217 (Hall 5–60) and 216 (Booth 56, Hall 4–45) by 179 runs.

SECOND TEST
Queen's Park, Port-of-Spain, 26 March to 1 April 1965
WEST INDIES 429 (Hunte 69, Davis 54, Butcher 117, Sobers 69, O'Neill 4–41)
and 386 (Hunte 53, Davis 58, Kanhai 53, Simpson 4–83)
drew with AUSTRALIA 516 (Cowper 143, Booth 117, Thomas 61).
Simpson sent West Indies in.

THIRD TEST
Bourda, Georgetown, 14 to 20 April 1965
WEST INDIES 355 (Kanhai 89, Hawke 6–72) and 180 (Hawke 4–43, Philpott 4–49)
defeated AUSTRALIA 179 and 144 (Gibbs 6–29) by 212 runs.

FOURTH TEST
Kensington Oval, Bridgetown, 5 to 11 May 1965
AUSTRALIA 8–650 declared (Lawry 210, Simpson 201, Cowper 102, O'Neill 51) and
4–175 declared (Lawry 58 retired hurt, O'Neill 74 not out)
drew with WEST INDIES 573 (Hunte 75, Kanhai 129, Nurse 201, Sobers 55, Griffith 54,
McKenzie 4–114) and 5–242 (Davis 68).
*Though they failed to achieve a victory target of 253 in 270 minutes, West Indies gained custody
of the Worrell Trophy for the first time. O'Neill's last Test.*

FIFTH TEST
Queen's Park, Port-of-Spain, 14 to 17 May 1965
WEST INDIES 224 (Kanhai 121) and 131 (Hunte 60 not out, McKenzie 5–33)
lost to AUSTRALIA 294 (Simpson 72, Cowper 69, Griffith 6–46) and 0–63
by ten wickets.
*McKenzie ended West Indies' second innings with the wickets of Hall, Griffith and
Gibbs in four deliveries.*

AUSTRALIA v ENGLAND 1965–66

FIRST TEST
Woolloongabba, Brisbane, 10 to 15 December 1965
AUSTRALIA 6–443 declared (Lawry 166, Walters 155, Veivers 56 not out)
drew with ENGLAND 280 (Barrington 53, Parks 52, Titmus 60, Philpott 5–90) and
3–186 (Boycott 63 not out).
*With Simpson suffering a broken wrist, Booth captained Australia. Doug Walters was the third
youngest Australian to begin his Test career with a century.*

SECOND TEST
Melbourne Cricket Ground, 30 December 1965 to 4 January 1966
AUSTRALIA 358 (Simpson 59, Lawry 88, Cowper 99, Knight 4–84) and 426
(Simpson 67, Lawry 78, Burge 120, Walters 115)
drew with ENGLAND 558 (Boycott 51, J. Edrich 109, Barrington 63, Cowdrey 104,
Parks 71, Titmus 56 not out, McKenzie 5–134) and 0–5.

THIRD TEST
Sydney Cricket Ground, 7 to 11 January 1966
ENGLAND 488 (Boycott 84, Barber 185, J. Edrich 103, Allen 50 not out, Hawke 7–105)
defeated AUSTRALIA 221 (Thomas 51, Cowper 60, D. Brown 5–63) and 174
(Allen 4–47) by an innings and 93 runs.
Booth led Australia in his last Test, Simpson suffering chickenpox.

FOURTH TEST
Adelaide Oval, 28 January to 1 February 1966
ENGLAND 241 (Barrington 60, McKenzie 6–48) and 266 (Barrington 102,
Titmus 53, Hawke 5–54)
lost to AUSTRALIA 516 (Simpson 225, Lawry 119, Thomas 52, Jones 6–118) by an
innings and nine runs.
Keith Stackpole's first Test.

FIFTH TEST
Melbourne Cricket Ground, 11 to 16 February 1966
ENGLAND 485 (J. Edrich 85, Barrington 115, Cowdrey 79, Parks 89, Walters 4–53)
and 3–69
drew with AUSTRALIA 8–543 declared (Lawry 108, Cowper 307, Walters 60).
Cowper's remains the highest score by an Australian in a home Test.

SOUTH AFRICA v AUSTRALIA 1966–67

FIRST TEST
New Wanderers, Johannesburg, 23 to 28 December 1966
SOUTH AFRICA 199 (Lindsay 69, McKenzie 5–46) and 620 (Barlow 50, Bacher 63,
G. Pollock 90, Lance 70, Lindsay 182, van der Merwe 76)
defeated AUSTRALIA 325 (Lawry 98, Simpson 65) and 261 (Veivers 55, Goddard 6–53)
by 233 runs.
Brian Taber made eight dismissals in his first Test.

SECOND TEST
Newlands, Cape Town, 31 December 1966 to 5 January 1967
AUSTRALIA 542 (Simpson 153, Redpath 54, Stackpole 134, Watson 50, Barlow 5–85)
and 4–180 (Redpath 69 not out)
defeated SOUTH AFRICA 353 (G. Pollock 209, van der Merwe 50, McKenzie 5–65)
and 367 (Lance 53, Lindsay 81, D. Pithey 55, P. Pollock 75) by six wickets.

THIRD TEST
Kingsmead, Durban, 20 to 25 January 1967
SOUTH AFRICA 300 (Lindsay 137) and 2–185 (Bacher 60 not out,
G. Pollock 67 not out)
defeated AUSTRALIA 147 and 334 (Simpson 94, Redpath 80, Procter 4–71)
by eight wickets.
*Simpson sent South Africa in. Eddie Barlow was caught and bowled by McKenzie from the first
ball of the match.*

FOURTH TEST
New Wanderers, Johannesburg, 3 to 8 February 1967
AUSTRALIA 143 (Procter 4–32) and 8–148
drew with SOUTH AFRICA 9–332 declared (Lindsay 131, Renneberg 5–97).
A thunderstorm after tea on the last day saved Australia from defeat.

FIFTH TEST
St George's Park, Port Elizabeth, 24 to 28 February 1967
AUSTRALIA 173 (Cowper 60) and 278 (Cowper 54)
lost to SOUTH AFRICA 276 (Goddard 74, G. Pollock 105, McKenzie 5–65)
and 3–179 (Goddard 59) by seven wickets.
Lawry was run out without facing a ball returning from a third to deep fine leg in the first
innings. McKenzie finished the series with 24 wickets at 26.

AUSTRALIA v INDIA 1967–68

FIRST TEST
Adelaide Oval, 23 to 28 December 1967
AUSTRALIA 335 (Simpson 55, Sheahan 81, Cowper 92, Abid Ali 6–55) and 369
(Simpson 103, Cowper 108, Surti 5–74)
defeated INDIA 307 (Engineer 89, Borde 69, Surti 70, Connolly 4–54) and 251
(Surti 53, Subramanya 75, Renneberg 5–39) by 146 runs.

SECOND TEST
Melbourne Cricket Ground, 30 December 1967 to 3 January 1968
INDIA 173 (Nawab of Pataudi jnr 75, McKenzie 7–66) and 352 (Wadekar 99,
Nawab of Pataudi jnr 85)
lost to AUSTRALIA 529 (Simpson 109, Lawry 100, Chappell 151, Jarman 65,
Prasanna 6–141) by an innings and four runs.
Simpson led Australia for the twenty-ninth and last time. Chappell scored his first Test century in
his sixteenth innings.

THIRD TEST
Woolloongabba, Brisbane, 19 to 24 January 1968
AUSTRALIA 379 (Lawry 64, Cowper 51, Sheahan 58, Walters 93) and 294
(Redpath 79, Walters 62 not out, Prasanna 6–104)
defeated INDIA 279 (Surti 52, Nawab of Pataudi jnr 74, Jaisimha 74) and 355
(Surti 64, Jaisimha 101, Borde 63, Cowper 4–104) by 39 runs.
Lawry's first Test as captain. Nawab of Pataudi jnr sent Australia in.

FOURTH TEST
Sydney Cricket Ground, 26 to 31 January 1968
AUSTRALIA 317 (Lawry 66, Sheahan 72, Walters 94 not out) and 292
(Lawry 52, Cowper 165, Prasanna 4–96)
defeated INDIA 268 (Abid Ali 78, Nawab of Pataudi jnr 51, Freeman 4–86) and 197
(Abid Ali 81, Cowper 4–49, Simpson 5–59).
Simpson achieved his best Test figures in his last Test for ten years.

ENGLAND v AUSTRALIA 1968

FIRST TEST
Old Trafford, Manchester, 6 to 11 June 1968
AUSTRALIA 357 (Lawry 81, Walters 81, Sheahan 88, Chappell 73, Snow 4–97) and 220
(Walters 86, Pocock 6–79)
defeated ENGLAND 165 (Cowper 4–48) and 253 (D'Oliveira 87 not out) by 159 runs.

SECOND TEST
Lord's, London, 20 to 25 June 1968
ENGLAND 7–351 declared (Milburn 83, Barrington 75)
drew with AUSTRALIA 78 (D. Brown 5–42) and 4–127 (Redpath 53).
Australia's second lowest total since the war. Half the match was lost to rain.

THIRD TEST
Edgbaston, Birmingham, 11 to 16 July 1968
ENGLAND 409 (J. Edrich 88, Cowdrey 104, Graveney 96, Freeman 4–78)
and 3–142 declared (J. Edrich 64)
drew with AUSTRALIA 222 (Cowper 57, Chappell 71) and 1–68.

FOURTH TEST
Headingley, Leeds, 25 to 30 July 1968
AUSTRALIA 315 (Redpath 92, Chappell 65, Underwood 4–41) and 312
(Walters 56, Chappell 81, Illingworth 6–87)
drew with ENGLAND 302 (J. Edrich 62, Prideaux 64, Connolly 5–72) and 4–230
(J. Edrich 65).
*With the injured Lawry and Cowdrey absent, Barry Jarman and Tom Graveney captained their
countries for the only occasions in Test cricket.*

FIFTH TEST
ENGLAND 494 (J. Edrich 164, Graveney 63, D'Oliveira 158) and 181 (Connolly 4–65)
defeated AUSTRALIA 324 (Lawry 135, Redpath 67) and 125 (Inverarity 56, Underwood
7–50) by 226 runs.
*England won with five minutes to spare after rain had threatened to thwart them. John Inverarity
was first in and last out.*

AUSTRALIA v WEST INDIES 1968–69

FIRST TEST
Woolloongabba, Brisbane, 6 to 10 December 1968
WEST INDIES 296 (Carew 83, Kanhai 94, Connolly 4–60) and 353 (Carew 71,
Lloyd 129, Gleeson 5–122)
defeated AUSTRALIA 284 (Lawry 105, Chappell 117, Gibbs 5–88) and 240
(Chappell 50, Sobers 6–73) by 125 runs.
Clive Lloyd's first 100 against Australia fell on the first Sunday of Test play here.

SECOND TEST
Melbourne Cricket Ground, 26 to 30 December 1968
WEST INDIES 200 (Fredericks 76, McKenzie 8–71) and 280 (Nurse 74, Sobers 67,
Gleeson 5–61)
lost to AUSTRALIA 510 (Lawry 205, Chappell 165, Walters 76, Sobers 4–97)
by an innings and 30 runs.
Lawry sent West Indies in. McKenzie achieved his best Test figures.

THIRD TEST
Sydney Cricket Ground, 3 to 8 January 1969
WEST INDIES 264 (Lloyd 50, McKenzie 4–85) and 324 (Kanhai 69, Butcher 101,
Gleeson 4–91)
lost to AUSTRALIA 547 (Stackpole 58, Redpath 80, Walters 118, Freeman 76)
and 0–42 by ten wickets.

FOURTH TEST
Adelaide Oval, 24 to 29 January 1969
WEST INDIES 276 (Butcher 52, Sobers 110, Freeman 4–52) and 616 (Carew 90, Kanhai
80, Butcher 118, Sobers 52, Holford 80, Connolly 5–122)
drew with AUSTRALIA 533 (Lawry 62, Stackpole 62, Chappell 76, Walters 110,
Sheahan 51, McKenzie 59, Gibbs 4–145) and 9–339 (Lawry 89, Stackpole 50,
Chappell 96, Walters 50).

The highest-scoring Test match in Australia. Sheahan and Connolly survived the last twenty-six deliveries to ensure a draw.

FIFTH TEST
Sydney Cricket Ground, 14 to 20 February 1969
AUSTRALIA 619 (Lawry 151, Walters 242, Freeman 56) and 8–394 declared
(Redpath 132, Walters 103)
defeated WEST INDIES 279 (Carew 64, Lloyd 53, Connolly 4–61) and 352
(Sobers 113, Nurse 137) by 382 runs.

Sobers sent Australia in. Lawry set West Indies 735 to win in the fourth innings. Walters was the first man to score 200 and 100 in the same Test. Redpath's maiden Test century was in his forty-ninth innings.

INDIA v AUSTRALIA 1969–70

FIRST TEST
Brabourne Stadium, Bombay, 4 to 9 November 1969
INDIA 271 (A. Mankad 74, Nawab of Pataudi jnr 95, McKenzie 5–69) and 137
(Gleeson 4–56)
lost to AUSTRALIA 345 (Stackpole 103, Redpath 77, Prasanna 5–121) and 2–67
by eight wickets.

Batsmen scored 781 runs from 2535 deliveries.

SECOND TEST
Green Park, Kanpur, 15 to 20 November 1969
INDIA 320 (Engineer 77, A. Mankad 64, Connolly 4–91) and 7–312 declared
(A. Mankad 68, Viswanath 137)
drew with AUSTRALIA 348 (Walters 53, Redpath 70, Sheahan 114) and 0–95.

Viswanath scored a century in his first Test match.

THIRD TEST
Feroz Shah Kotla, Delhi, 28 November to 2 December 1969
AUSTRALIA 296 (Stackpole 61, Chappell 138, Bedi 4–71, Prasanna 4–111)
and 107 (Bedi 5–37, Prasanna 5–42)
lost to INDIA 223 (A. Mankad 97, Mallett 6–64) and 3–181 (Wadekar 91 not out)
by seven wickets.

Lawry carried his bat in Australia's second innings for 49 in 195 minutes.

FOURTH TEST
Eden Gardens, Calcutta, 12 to 16 December 1969
INDIA 212 (Viswanath 54, McKenzie 6–67) and 161
(Wadekar 62, Freeman 4–54, Connolly 4–31)
lost to AUSTRALIA 335 (Chappell 99, Walters 56, Bedi 7–98) and 0–42 by ten wickets.

FIFTH TEST
Chepauk, Madras, 24 to 28 December 1969
AUSTRALIA 258 (Walters 102, Prasanna 4–100, Venkataraghavan 4–71)
and 153 (Redpath 63, Prasanna 6–74)
defeated INDIA 163 (Nawab of Pataudi jnr 59, Mallett 5–91) and 171
(Wadekar 55, Viswanath 59, Mallett 5–53) by 77 runs.

SOUTH AFRICA v AUSTRALIA 1969–70

FIRST TEST
Newlands, Cape Town, 22 to 27 January 1970
SOUTH AFRICA 382 (Bacher 57, Barlow 127, Mallett 5–126) and 232
(G. Pollock 50, Connolly 5–47, Gleeson 4–70)
defeated AUSTRALIA 164 (Walters 73, P. Pollock 4–20) and 280
(Lawry 83, Procter 4–47) by 170 runs.

SECOND TEST
Kingsmead, Durban, 5 to 9 February 1970
SOUTH AFRICA 9–622 declared (Richards 140, G. Pollock 274, Lance 61)
defeated AUSTRALIA 157 (Sheahan 62) and 336 (Stackpole 71, Walters 74,
Redpath 74 not out) by an innings and 129 runs.

THIRD TEST
New Wanderers, Johannesburg, 19 to 24 February 1970
SOUTH AFRICA 279 (Richards 65, G. Pollock 52, Irvine 79) and 408
(G. Pollock 87, Barlow 110, Irvine 73, Gleeson 5–125)
defeated AUSTRALIA 202 (Walters 64, P. Pollock 5–39) and 178 (Redpath 66)
by 307 runs.

FOURTH TEST
St George's Park, Port Elizabeth, 5 to 10 March 1970
SOUTH AFRICA 311 (Richards 81, Barlow 73, Connolly 6–47) and 8–470 declared
(Richards 126, Bacher 73, Irvine 102, Lindsay 60)
defeated AUSTRALIA 212 (Redpath 55, Sheahan 67) and 246 (Procter 6–73).
*In dismissing Connolly, Pat Trimborn bowled South Africa's last ball in Test cricket for
twenty-two years.*

AUSTRALIA v ENGLAND 1970–71

FIRST TEST
Woolloongabba, Brisbane, 27 November to 2 December 1970
AUSTRALIA 433 (Stackpole 207, Chappell 59, Walters 112, Snow 6–114)
and 214 (Lawry 84, Shuttleworth 5–47)
drew with ENGLAND 464 (Luckhurst 74, Knott 73, Edrich 79, D'Oliveira 57)
and 1–39.
Rod Marsh's first Test.

SECOND TEST
WACA Ground, Perth, 11 to 16 December 1970
ENGLAND 397 (Boycott 70, Luckhurst 131, McKenzie 4–66) and 6–287 declared
(Boycott 50, Edrich 115 not out)
drew with AUSTRALIA 440 (I. Chappell 50, Redpath 171, G. Chappell 108,
Snow 4–143) and 3–100.
*Greg Chappell's first Test. He was the sixth Australian to score a hundred on debut. The WACA
Ground became the sixth venue to host a Test in Australia.*

THIRD TEST
Melbourne Cricket Ground, 31 December 1970 to 5 January 1971
Abandoned without a ball bowled.

FOURTH TEST
Sydney Cricket Ground, 9 to 14 January 1971
ENGLAND 332 (Boycott 77, Edrich 55, Gleeson 4–83) and 5–319 declared
(Boycott 142 not out, D'Oliveira 56, Illingworth 53)
defeated AUSTRALIA 236 (Redpath 64, Walters 55, Underwood 4–66) and 116 (Lawry
60 not out, Snow 7–40).
Lawry carried his bat.

FIFTH TEST
Melbourne Cricket Ground, 21 to 26 January 1971
AUSTRALIA 9–493 declared (Lawry 56, I. Chappell 111, Redpath 72, Walters 55,
Marsh 92 not out) and 4–169 declared
drew with ENGLAND 392 (Luckhurst 109, D'Oliveira 117) and 0–161
(Boycott 76 not out, Edrich 74 not out).

SIXTH TEST
Adelaide Oval, 29 January to 3 February 1971
ENGLAND 470 (Boycott 58, Edrich 130, Fletcher 80, Hampshire 55, Lillee 5–84) and
4–233 declared (Boycott 119 not out)
drew with AUSTRALIA 235 (Stackpole 87, Lever 4–49) and 3–328
(Stackpole 136, I. Chappell 104).
*Dennis Lillee's first Test. Bill Lawry's last. Ray Illingworth did not enforce the follow-on, and set
Australia 469 to win in 500 minutes.*

SEVENTH TEST
Sydney Cricket Ground, 12 to 17 February 1971
ENGLAND 184 and 302 (Edrich 57, Luckhurst 59)
defeated AUSTRALIA 264 (Redpath 59, G. Chappell 65) and 160
(Stackpole 67) by 62 runs.
*In his first Test as captain, Ian Chappell sent England in. Crowd disturbances caused Illingworth
to lead his team from the field late on the second day. England recaptured the Ashes after twelve
years at 12.36pm on the fifth of six scheduled days.*

Bibliography

GENERAL HISTORY

Alexander, Fred, *Australia Since Federation,* Thomas Nelson, Melbourne, 1976

Bolton, Geoffrey, *The Oxford History of Australia, Volume 5, 1942–1988,* Oxford University Press, Melbourne, 1988

Booker, Christopher, *The Neophiliacs: A Study of the Revolution in English Life in the Fifties and Sixties,* Fontana/Collins, London, 1970

Boyd, Robin, *The Australian Ugliness,* Cheshire, Melbourne, 1960

Bunting, John, *R. G. Menzies: A Portrait,* Allen & Unwin, Sydney, 1988

Chaudhuri, Nirad, *Thy Hand, Great Anarch!,* Chatto & Windus, London, 1987

Crisp, L. F., *Ben Chifley: A Political Biography,* Angus & Robertson, Sydney, 1977

Crockett, Peter, *Evatt: A Life,* Oxford University Press, Melbourne, 1993

Crowley, Frank, *Modern Australia in Documents 1939–1970,* Wren Publishing, Melbourne, 1973

Dutton, Geoffrey et al, *Australia in the 1960s,* Rigby, Sydney, 1980

Gerster, Robin and Bassett, Jan, *Seizures of Youth: 'The Sixties' and Australia,* Hyland House, Melbourne, 1991

Gunn, John, *High Corridors: Qantas 1954–1970,* UQP, St Lucia, 1988

Henderson, Gerard, *Menzies' Child: The Liberal Party of Australia 1944–1994,* Allen & Unwin, Sydney, 1994

Horne, Donald, *The Lucky Country,* Angus & Robertson, Sydney, 1964

Horsfall, Jack, *The Liberal Era: A Political and Economic Analysis,* Sun Books, Melbourne, 1974

Inglis, Ken, *This Is the ABC: The Australian Broadcasting Commission 1932–1983* Melbourne University Press, Melbourne, 1983

James, Lawrence, *The Rise and Fall of the British Empire,* Little Brown, London, 1994

Lighton, Conrad, *Sisters of the South,* Hodder & Stoughton, London, 1951

McGregor, Craig, *Profile of Australia,* Penguin, Sydney, 1966

Marshall, Alan, *The Gay Provider: The Myer Story,* F. W. Cheshire, Melbourne, 1961

Martin, Allan, *Robert Menzies: A Life, Volume 1, 1894–1943,* Melbourne University Press, Melbourne, 1993

Menzies, Sir Robert, *Afternoon Light,* Penguin, Melbourne, 1969

Menzies, Sir Robert, *The Measure of the Years,* Coronet, London, 1972

Sparkes, Alister, *Tomorrow Is Another Country: The Inside Story of South Africa,* Hill & Wang, New York, 1995

Stephens, Ian, *Pakistan: Old Country/New Country,* Pelican, London, 1964

Tennant, Kylie, *Evatt: Politics and Justice,* Angus & Robertson, Sydney, 1970

HISTORIES AND LITERATURE

Arlott, John, *Concerning Cricket,* Longman Green & Co, London, 1949

Barker, Ralph, *Innings of a Lifetime,* Collins, London, 1982

Beckles, Hilary and Stoddart, Brian (eds.), *Liberation Cricket: West Indies Cricket Culture,* Manchester University Press, 1995

Benaud, Richie, *Way of Cricket,* Hodder & Stoughton, London, 1961

Benaud, Richie, *Benaud on Reflection,* Collins Willow, London, 1984

Bose, Mihir, *A History of Indian Cricket,* Andre Deutsch, London, 1990

Butler, Keith, *Howzat!,* William Collins, Sydney, 1979

Cashman, Richard and others (eds.), *The Oxford Companion to Australian Sport,* Oxford University Press, Melbourne, 1994

Cashman, Richard and others (eds.), *The Oxford Companion to Australian Cricket,* Oxford University Press, Melbourne, 1996

Cashman, Richard, *Ave a Go Yer Mug! Australian Cricket Crowds from Larrikin to Ocker,* Collins, Sydney, 1984

Chappell, Ian, *The Cutting Edge,* Swan Publishing, Sydney, 1992

Christen, Richard, *Some Grounds for Appeal: Australian Venues for First-Class Cricket,* self-published, Parramatta, 1994

Coleman, Robert, *Seasons in the Sun: The Story of the Victorian Cricket Association,* Hargreen Publishing, Melbourne, 1993

Derriman, Phil, *True to the Blue: A History of the New South Wales Cricket Association,* Sydney, Richard Smart, 1985

Down, Michael, *Is It Cricket? Power, Money and Politics in Cricket since 1945,* Queen Anne, London, 1985

Dunstan, Keith, *The Paddock That Grew,* Cassell Australia, Melbourne, 1975

Fingleton, Jack, *Masters of Cricket,* London, Pavilion Books, London, 1990

Fingleton, Jack, *Fingleton on Cricket,* Collins, London, 1972

Harte, Chris, *A History of Australian Cricket,* Andre Deutsch, London, 1993

Harte, Chris, *The History of the South Australian Cricket Association,* Sports Marketing (Australia), Adelaide, 1990

Hopman, Harry, *Aces and Places,* Cassell, London, 1957

James, C. L. R., *Beyond a Boundary,* Stanley Paul, London, 1963

Lemmon, David, *Cricket Mercenaries,* Michael Joseph, London, 1987

Linnell, Garry, *Football Ltd,* Pan Macmillan, Sydney, 1993

McGilvray, Alan and Tasker, Norm, *The Game Is Not the Same,* ABC Books, Sydney, 1985

McGilvray, Alan and Tasker, Norm, *The Game Goes on...,* ABC Books, Sydney, 1987

McGilvray, Alan and Tasker, Norm, *Captains of the Game,* ABC Books, Sydney, 1992

Manley, Michael, *A History of West Indies Cricket,* Andre Deutsch, London, 1988

O'Hara, John, *A Mug's Game: A History of Gambling and Betting in Australia,* NSW University Press, Sydney, 1988

Philpott, Peter, *Spinner's Yarn,* ABC Books, Sydney, 1990

Pollard, Jack, *Australian Cricket: The Game and the Players,* Angus & Robertson, Sydney, 1988

Pollard, Jack, *From Bradman to Border, Australian Cricket 1948 to 1989,* Angus & Robertson, Sydney, 1989

Reyburn, Wallace, *There Was Also Some Rugby: The Sixth Springboks in England,* Cassell, London, 1970

Robinson, Ray, *Between Wickets,* Fontana Books, London, 1958

Robinson, Ray, *From the Boundary,* Collins, London, 1951

Robinson, Ray, *Green Sprigs,* Collins, Sydney, 1954

Robinson, Ray, *On Top Down Under,* Cassell Australia, Sydney, 1975

Robinson, Ray, *The Wildest Tests,* Cassell Australia, Sydney, 1979

Selth, Don, *The Prime Minister's XI,* Woden Printers, Canberra, 1990

Sissons, Ric, *The Players: A Social History of the Professional Cricketer,* Pluto Press, Sydney, 1988

Stewart, Bob, 'The Commercial and Cultural Development of Australian First-Class

Cricket 1946–1985', PhD thesis, Bob Stewart, La Trobe University Faculty of Arts, Melbourne, 1995

Stoddart, Brian, *Saturday Afternoon Fever: Sport in Australian Culture,* Angus & Robertson, Sydney, 1986

Swanton, E. W., *As I Said at the Time,* Collins, London, 1983

Whimpress, Bernard and Hart, Nigel, *Test Eleven: Great Ashes Battles,* Wakefield Press, Adelaide, 1994

Wooldridge, Ian (ed.), *The International Cavaliers Cricket Book,* Purnell, London, 1969

Wynne-Thomas, Peter, *Cricket Tours at Home and Abroad,* Guild Publishing, London, 1989

TOUR BOOKS

Arlott, John, *Test Match Diary 1953,* James Barrie, London, 1953

Batchelor, Denzil, *The Test Matches of 1964,* Epworth Press, London, 1964

Benaud, Richie, *Tale of Two Tests,* Hodder & Stoughton, London, 1962

Benaud, Richie, *Spin Me a Spinner,* Hodder & Stoughton, London, 1963

Benaud, Richie, *The New Champions: Australia in the West Indies 1965,* Sportsman's Book Club, London, 1966

Bowes, Bill, *Aussies and Ashes,* Stanley Paul, London, 1961

Cheetham, Jack, *Caught by the Springboks,* Hodder & Stoughton, London, 1953

Clarke, John, *Challenge Renewed: MCC Australian Tour 1962–63,* Stanley Paul, London, 1963

Clarke, John, *The Australians in England 1964,* Stanley Paul, London, 1964

Clarke, John, *With England in Australia: The MCC Tour 1965–66,* Stanley Paul, London, 1966

Fingleton, Jack, *Brown & Company,* Collins, London, 1951

Fingleton, Jack, *The Ashes Crown the Year,* Collins, Sydney, 1954

Fingleton, Jack, *Four Chukkas to Australia,* Collins, London, 1959

Fingleton, Jack, *The Greatest Test of All,* Collins, London, 1961

Harris, Bruce, *Ashes Triumphant,* (Australia v England 1954–55), Hutchinson, London, 1955

Hughes, Margaret, *The Long Hop,* Stanley Paul, London, 1955

Landsberg, Pat, *The Kangaroo Conquers: West Indies v Australia 1955,* Museum Press, London, 1955

Lindwall, Ray, *The Challenging Tests,* Pelham, London, 1961

Litchfield, Eric, *Cricket Grand-Slam,* Reed Books, Sydney, 1970

McGlew, Jackie, *Six for Glory,* Howard Timmins, Cape Town, 1967

Mackay, Ken, *Quest for the Ashes,* Pelham, London, 1966

McLean, Roy, *Sackcloth Without Ashes,* Hodder & Stoughton, London, 1958

Miller, Keith and Whitington, R. S., *Catch!,* Latimer House, London, 1951

Miller, Keith and Whitington, R. S., *Straight Hit!,* Latimer House, London, 1952

Miller, Keith and Whitington, R. S., *Cricket Typhoon,* MacDonald and Co, London, 1955

Miller, Keith, *Cricket from the Grandstand,* Oldbourne, London, 1959

Morris, Arthur and Landsberg, Pat, *Operation Ashes,* Robert Hale, London, 1956

Moyes, Johnnie, *With the West Indies in Australia 1951–2: A Critical Story of the Tour,* Angus & Robertson, Sydney, 1952

Moyes, Johnnie, *The Fight for the Ashes 1954–55,* Angus & Robertson, Sydney, 1955

Moyes, Johnnie, *The West Indies in Australia 1960–61,* Angus & Robertson, Sydney, 1961

O'Reilly, Bill, *Cricket Task Force,* Werner Laurie, London, 1951

Peebles, Ian, *The Fight for the Ashes 1958–59,* Angus & Robertson, Sydney, 1959

Roberts, L. D., *Cricket's Brightest Summer,* Bailey Bros and Swinfen, London, 1961

Roberts, Ron, *The Fight for the Ashes 1961,* Angus & Robertson, Sydney, 1961

Ross, Alan, *Cape Summer* and *The Australians in England,* Hamish Hamilton, London, 1957

Ross, Alan, *Australia 63,* London, Pavilion Books, 1991

Simpson, Bob, *The Australians in England 1968,* Stanley Paul, London, 1968

Swanton, E. W, *Elusive Victory: With F. R. Brown's MCC Team 1950–51,* London, Hodder & Stoughton, London, 1951

Swanton, E. W., *The Test Matches of 1953,* The Daily Telegraph, London, 1953

Tresidder, Phil, *Captains on a See-Saw,* Souvenir, London, 1969

West, Peter, *The Fight for the Ashes 1953,* Australasian Publishing Company and George G. Harrap, Sydney/London, 1953

Whitington, R. S., *Bradman, Benaud and Goddard's Cinderellas,* Bailey Bros and Swinfen, London, 1964

Whitington, R. S., *Simpson's Safari: South African Test Series 1966–7,* Heinemann, Melbourne, 1967

Whitington, R. S., *Fours Galore,* Cassell Australia, Sydney, 1969

BIOGRAPHIES AND AUTOBIOGRAPHIES

Allen, David Rayvern, *Arlott: The Authorised Biography,* Harper Collins, London, 1994

Alley, Bill, *My Incredible Innings,* Pelham, London, 1969

Barnes, Sid, *It's Not Cricket,* Collins, London, 1953

Benaud, Richie, *Willow Patterns,* Hodder & Stoughton, London, 1968

Booth, Brian, *Booth to Bat,* Anzea Publishers, Homebush West, 1983

Bose, Mihir, *Keith Miller,* Allen & Unwin, Sydney, 1979

Brown, Freddie, *Cricket Musketeer,* Nicholas Kaye, London, 1954

Chappell, Ian, *Chappelli,* Hutchinson, Sydney, 1976

Davidson, Alan, *Fifteen Paces,* Souvenir, London, 1963

Evans, Godfrey, *The Gloves Are Off,* Hodder & Stoughton, London, 1960

Eytle, Ernest, *Frank Worrell: The Career of a Great Cricketer,* Hodder & Stoughton, London, 1963

Favell, Les, *By Hook or by Cut,* Investigator Press, Adelaide, 1970

Ferguson, Bill, *Mr Cricket,* Nicholas Kaye, London, 1957

Fingleton, Jack, *Batting from Memory,* Collins, Sydney, 1981

Gover, Alfred, *The Long Run: An Autobiography,* Pelham, London, 1991

Green, Michael, *Sporting Campaigner,* Stanley Paul, London, 1956

Griffith, Charlie, *Chucked Around,* Pelham, London, 1970

Grout, Wally, *My Country's Keeper,* Pelham, London, 1965

Hall, Wes, *Pace Like Fire,* Pelham, London, 1965

Harvey, Neil, *My World of Cricket,* Hodder & Stoughton, London, 1963

Hawke, Neil, *Bowled Over,* Rigby, Sydney, 1982

Howat, Gerald, *Len Hutton: The Biography,* Mandarin, London, 1990

Hutton, Len and Bannister, Alex, *Fifty Years in Cricket,* Stanley Paul, London, 1984

Illingworth, Ray, *Yorkshire and Back,* Queen Anne Press, London, 1980

Jaggard, Ed, *Garth: The Story of Graham McKenzie,* Fremantle Arts Centre Press, Perth, 1993

Johnson, Ian, *Cricket at the Crossroads,* Cassell, London, 1957

Lawry, Bill, *Run-Digger,* Souvenir, London, 1966

Lee, Alan, *Lord Ted: The Dexter Enigma,* Gollancz/Witherby, London, 1995

Lindwall, Ray, *Flying Stumps,* Arrow Books, London, 1957

McHarg, Jack, *Arthur Morris: An Elegant Genius,* ABC Books, Sydney, 1995

Mackay, Ken, *Slasher Opens Up,* Pelham, London, 1964

Mallett, Ashley, *Rowdy,* Lynton, Blackwood, 1973

May, Peter, *A Game Enjoyed,* Stanley Paul, London, 1985

Meckiff, Ian and McDonald, Ian, *Thrown Out,* Stanley Paul, London, 1961

Miller, Keith, *Cricket Crossfire,* Oldbourne, London, 1957

Mosey, Don, *Laker: Portrait of a Legend,* Queen Anne Press, London, 1989

Moyes, Johnnie, *Benaud,* Angus & Robertson, Sydney, 1962

O'Neill, Norm, *Ins and Outs,* Pelham, London, 1964

Peel, Mark, *England Expects: The Life of Ken Barrington,* Kingswood, London, 1992

Redpath, Ian, *Always Reddy,* Garry Sparke & Associates, Melbourne, 1976

Ringwood, John, *Ray Lindwall: Cricketing Legend,* Kangaroo Press, Sydney, 1995

Rowan, Lou, *The Umpire's Story,* Jack Pollard, Sydney, 1972

Simpson, Bob, *Captain's Story,* Stanley Paul, London, 1966

Simpson, Bob, *The Reasons Why,* Harper Sports, Sydney, 1996

Sobers, Sir Garfield and Scovell, Brian, *Twenty Years at the Top,* Pan, London, 1989

Stackpole, Keith, and Trengrove, Alan, *Not Just for Openers,* Stockwell Press, Abbotsford, 1974

Stollmeyer, Jeff, *Everything under the Sun: My Life in West Indies Cricket,* Stanley Paul, London, 1983

Walcott, Clyde, *Island Cricketers,* Hodder & Stoughton, London, 1958

Walters, Doug, *Looking for Runs,* Pelham, London, 1971

Walters, Doug and Laws, Ken, *The Doug Walters Story,* Rigby, Sydney, 1981

Whitington, R. S., *Keith Miller: The Golden Nugget,* Rigby, Sydney, 1981

Whitington, R. S., *The Quiet Australian: The Lindsay Hassett Story,* Heinemann, Melbourne, 1969

PERIODICALS AND ANNUALS

ABC Weekly, Age, Australian, Australian Cricket, Barbados Advocate, Brisbane Courier-Mail, Bulletin, Cricketer (UK), Daily Express, Daily Gleaner, Daily Telegraph (UK), Daily Telegraph (Sydney), Daily Mirror (UK), Daily Mirror (Sydney), Evening News, Evening Standard, Guardian, Herald (Melbourne), Kingston Star, NSWCA Yearbook, News of the World, Natal Sunday Post, Rand Daily Mail, Sporting Life, Sporting Traditions, Sunday Express (South Africa), Sun (Melbourne), Sun (Sydney), Sydney Morning Herald, Sunday Times (UK), The Times of India, VCA Yearbook, Who's Who, Wisden Cricketers' Almanack

Index